THE LEGO

The LEGO® BOOST Activity Book

a beginner's guide to robotics

daniele benedettelli

Printed in USA

Second Printing

22 21 20 19 18   2 3 4 5 6 7 8 9

ISBN-10: 1-59327-932-9
ISBN-13: 978-1-59327-932-5

Publisher: **William Pollock**
Production Editor: **Meg Sneeringer**
Cover Design: **Mimi Heft**
Interior Design: **Mimi Heft and Kim Scott, Bumpy Design**
Developmental Editor: **Annie Choi**
Copyeditor: **Paula L. Fleming**
Proofreader: **Emelie Burnette**
Indexer: **Susan Brown, S.L.A.M. Resource**
Compositor: **Kim Scott, Bumpy Design**

For information on distribution, translations, or bulk sales, please contact No Starch Press, Inc. directly:
No Starch Press, Inc.
245 8th Street, San Francisco, CA 94103
phone: 415.863.9900; info@nostarch.com
www.nostarch.com

Library of Congress Cataloging-in-Publication Data:
Names: Benedettelli, Daniele, 1984- author.
Title: The LEGO BOOST activity book : a beginner's guide to robotics /
Daniele Benedettelli.
Description: San Francisco : No Starch Press, Inc., [2019].
Identifiers: LCCN 2018044423 (print) | LCCN 2018045999 (ebook) | ISBN 9781593279332 (epub) | ISBN 1593279337 (epub) | ISBN 9781593279325 (print) | ISBN 1593279329 (print) | ISBN 9781593279332 (ebook) | ISBN 1593279337 (ebook)
Subjects: LCSH: Robotics--Juvenile literature. | LEGO toys--Handbooks, manuals, etc.--Juvenile literature.
Classification: LCC TJ211.2 (ebook) | LCC TJ211.2 .B46 2019 (print) | DDC 629.8/920228--dc23
LC record available at https://lccn.loc.gov/2018044423

To Lucia with love

about the author

Known worldwide for his LEGO MINDSTORMS creations, Daniele Benedettelli has been collaborating with The LEGO Group in testing and developing LEGO MINDSTORMS products for the last 12 years. In 2012, he was hired as an external programmer for LEGO Education, and he developed the programs for the LEGO MINDSTORMS Education EV3 Core Set models. He is the author of *Creating Cool LEGO MINDSTORMS NXT Robots* (Apress, 2008), *LEGO MINDSTORMS NXT Thinking Robots* (No Starch Press, 2010), and *The LEGO MINDSTORMS EV3 Laboratory* (No Starch Press, 2013).

As a freelance LEGO designer, Daniele creates models based on LEGO Education products for companies that run after-school and enrichment programs. He also creates complex working models of industrial automation plants for large, multinational companies, such as CEA Technologies, Reply, and ABB Robotics. He has participated in many LEGO events, and he's been invited to give lectures and hold workshops in many countries. Currently, Daniele works as a tenured high school robotics teacher in Tuscany, Italy. His YouTube channel boasts millions of views, and his creations have been featured on many TV shows around the globe.

You can learn more about his work at his website, *https://robotics.benedettelli.com/*, and his Facebook page, *http://www.facebook.com/robotics.benedettelli/*.

about the technical reviewer

Xander Soldaat is a former Mindstorms Community Partner for LEGO MINDSTORMS. He was an IT infrastructure architect and engineer for 18 years before becoming a full-time software engineer, first for Robomatter and currently for VEX Robotics. For the past five years, he has been working on developing firmware and programming environments for various robotics platforms in the field of education. In his spare time, he likes to tinker with robots and 3D printing, as well as assemble and paint wargaming miniatures.

acknowledgments

When a new LEGO product like LEGO BOOST comes out, it's hard to resist writing a new book about it, but man, it's tough work! There are many people I need to thank for making this possible. First, thanks to my extraordinarily patient wife, Lucia, for bearing with me and understanding that, after all, sometimes I *work* with LEGO toys rather than just *play* with them. Thanks to our lovely Maria Sole, who helped crash-test all the robots in this book with her chubby little hands.

Thanks to Marco Agostini, a smart kid who helped me test the book's content and gave me ideas for future projects. Also, thanks to Beatrice Grasso, a bright, creative girl, for her suggestions on how to make the building instructions clearer.

Thanks to the No Starch Press team, especially to Bill Pollock for opening his door when I come knocking with a new idea, and to Annie Choi and Meg Sneeringer for their support, reviews, and suggestions.

A big thanks to Xander Soldaat, a long-time LEGO colleague, who is as sound and serious technical reviewer as he is a witty friend when hanging out in person or remotely.

A huge thanks to all the LDraw community members who developed the bits and tools to create high-quality building instructions. Special thanks to master builder and book author Philippe Hurbain (Philo), a master in modeling 3D LEGO elements; to Roland Melkert for his awesome LDCad software; to Travis Cobbs for creating LDView; and to Trevor Sandy for his work on developing LPub3D, built from the ashes of Kevin Clague's original software.

Thanks to my dear photographer friend Francesco Rossi (*http://www.fr-ph.com/*) for the great photo on the book's cover. Francesco, this time it was easy, wasn't it?

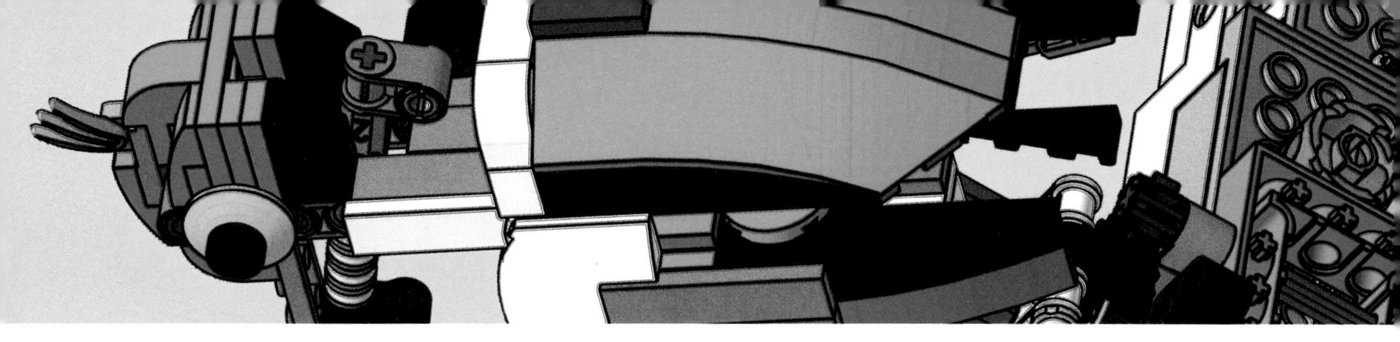

brief contents

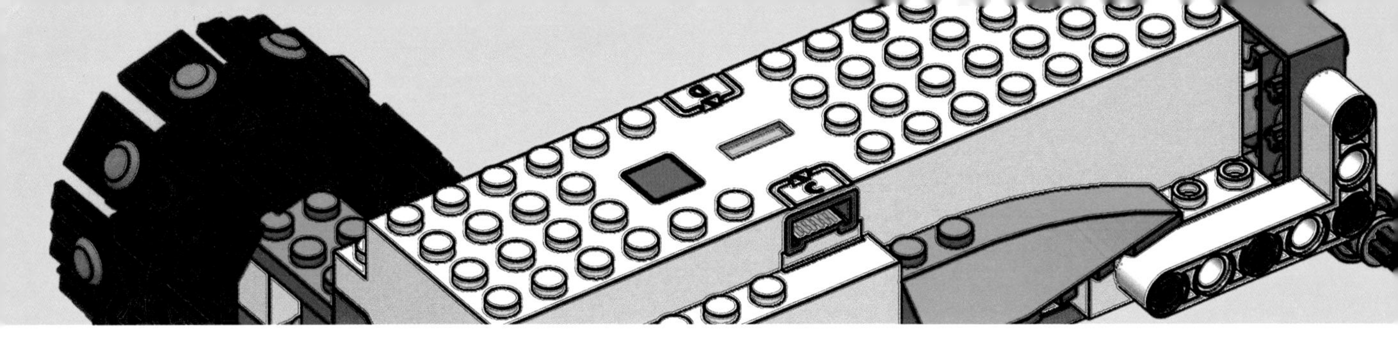

contents in detail

PART II: intermediate techniques

PART III: BrickPecker

PART IV: CYBOT

introduction

The LEGO BOOST set (#17101) is called a "Creative Toolbox" for a reason. Its large assortment of LEGO elements and electronic devices allows you to bring your LEGO creation to life! The BOOST set and its companion app were designed to teach programming and robotics to kids with a smooth learning curve. With LEGO BOOST, you can build and program your own robots or *boost* any of the LEGO models you already have by adding motors and sensors to them.

why this book?

Coding has become a buzzword in schools around the world because programming is considered a fundamental skill of the 21st century. Exploring robotics with LEGO BOOST is a great way to introduce programming to kids of all ages, even young ones.

Although the LEGO BOOST set includes ready-made programming blocks that allow you to do complex things, there's no manual in the box to show you how to get started or to create and program your own robots from scratch. That's where this book comes in.

The LEGO BOOST Activity Book uses a fun, hands-on approach to introduce you to the LEGO BOOST set and teaches you how to use it to build and program your own robots. It covers how the BOOST set works, general LEGO building techniques, and thoroughly introduces you to robot programming in a way that you won't find inside your BOOST set by itself. You'll learn how to use the BOOST app's programming blocks to program your own creations. You'll also find building instructions for three different robots!

NOTE: *For the sake of clarity and ease of reference, I've modified the official names of some of the programming blocks.*

As you work through the book, you'll find detailed descriptions of each program that will show you how to build it from scratch. When you understand how and why we make certain choices in programming, you'll start thinking like a programmer. If you'd like to go deeper into a particular topic, keep an eye out for the green "brain BOOSTer" boxes scattered throughout the book.

prerequisites

In order to use this book, you'll need the following:

- LEGO BOOST set #17101
- The LEGO BOOST app (included with the set)
- A BOOST-compatible device, such as one listed here: *http://www.lego.com/en-us/service/device-guide/boost/*
- At least six fresh AAA batteries (I recommend rechargeable batteries)
- A screwdriver to open the LEGO BOOST Move Hub battery box

For this book, we'll assume that you're already familiar with the LEGO BOOST app and that you've built and programmed the official models that come with the set.

about this book

In this book, you'll learn by doing. If you're brand new to programming, you should start from the beginning of this book. If you skip ahead, you might miss some concepts you'll need to know for later chapters. If you're more experienced, use the index to find the topic you want to explore, or jump ahead to build and program the more advanced robots.

The first part of the book introduces you to the BOOST set and some of the programming blocks available in the Creative Canvas that you'll use right away. You'll also meet your new friend MARIO, an easy-to-build wheeled robot that you'll later equip with modular tools and sensor attachments.

You'll start by making MARIO move with just one programming block, but you'll gradually increase its capabilities. Eventually, you'll program MARIO to move precisely, repeat actions, talk and play sounds, explore its surroundings, follow lines on the ground, follow walls, scan and look for targets to shoot down, and follow your hand. You'll even be able to control it by showing it colors, talking to it, and using the BOOST app as a remote!

At the end of Part II, you'll learn more about the LEGO system and some specific building tips and tricks using the parts included in the LEGO BOOST set. Special building techniques and design choices are highlighted in the building instructions of all the robots in the book. Experiments in each chapter will help you review what you've learned.

In the last parts of the book, you'll find the building and programming instructions for two robots, a brick-sorting bird named BrickPecker and a walking humanoid robot named CYBOT. You'll program BrickPecker to sort bricks by color, and you'll make CYBOT walk, talk, and respond to your voice commands.

Here's what you'll find in each chapter:

part I: programming basics

Chapter 1: your LEGO BOOST ceative toolbox describes the contents of the LEGO BOOST set.

Chapter 2: it's me, MARIO! shows how to build and program MARIO, a simple wheeled robot that you'll use throughout the book.

Chapter 3: getting around with Motor blocks shows how to use Motor blocks to control MARIO.

Chapter 4: moving your robot precisely shows how to move and steer your robot.

Chapter 5: repeating actions with loops shows how to reuse your code to have your robot repeat actions.

Chapter 6: "Hi, I'm an explorer!" shows how to add the BOOST sensor to your robot to allow it to detect and react to objects.

Chapter 7: detecting colors shows how to use colored tiles to control MARIO.

part II: intermediate techniques

Chapter 8: a line-following robot explains how to program MARIO to follow lines.

Chapter 9: following walls shows how to program MARIO to travel along walls and negotiate corners.

Chapter 10: a voice-activated robot shows how to interact with your robot by voice or by tilting it.

Chapter 11: taking a look around shows you how to build a scanner head for MARIO, which allows it to scan the environment and decide where to go.

Chapter 12: playing darts teaches you how to control your robot remotely and how to build a shooter that MARIO can use to play darts.

Chapter 13: building techniques discusses some basics of the LEGO building system, as well as advanced building techniques such as bracing and SNOT (Studs Not On Top). You'll also learn how to use gears to transform the motion of the motors.

part III: BrickPecker

Chapter 14: BrickPecker, a Brick-Sorting Bird shows how to build a bird robot called BrickPecker.

Chapter 15: programming BrickPecker shows how to program the BrickPecker to sort bricks by color.

part IV: CYBOT

Chapter 16: building CYBOT shows you how to build a humanoid robot called CYBOT.

Chapter 17: programming CYBOT covers how to program CYBOT to walk, move its head and arms, talk, shoot objects, and execute voice commands.

experiment answer key: This appendix contains solutions to the experiments in each chapter.

online resources

The LEGO BOOST world is ever changing. To get updates, find additional information, or troubleshoot any problem, you can use the following online resources:

- The official LEGO BOOST web page, *http://www.lego.com/en-us/themes/boost/*, includes the latest product-related news, and links to LEGO's online support and troubleshooting guide.
- On *http://www.lego.com/en-us/service/device-guide/boost/*, you can find a list of all the devices that will run the LEGO BOOST app.
- No Starch provides a companion page to the book, *https://nostarch.com/lego-boost-activity-book/*, that contains useful links.
- The author's website, *https://robotics.benedettelli.com/lego-boost-activity-book/*, offers additional tips and tricks, instructions, and errata. You'll also find the **"Complete Part Reference"** guide that describes each LEGO BOOST element's function in order to help you best use them in your own models.

PART I

programming basics

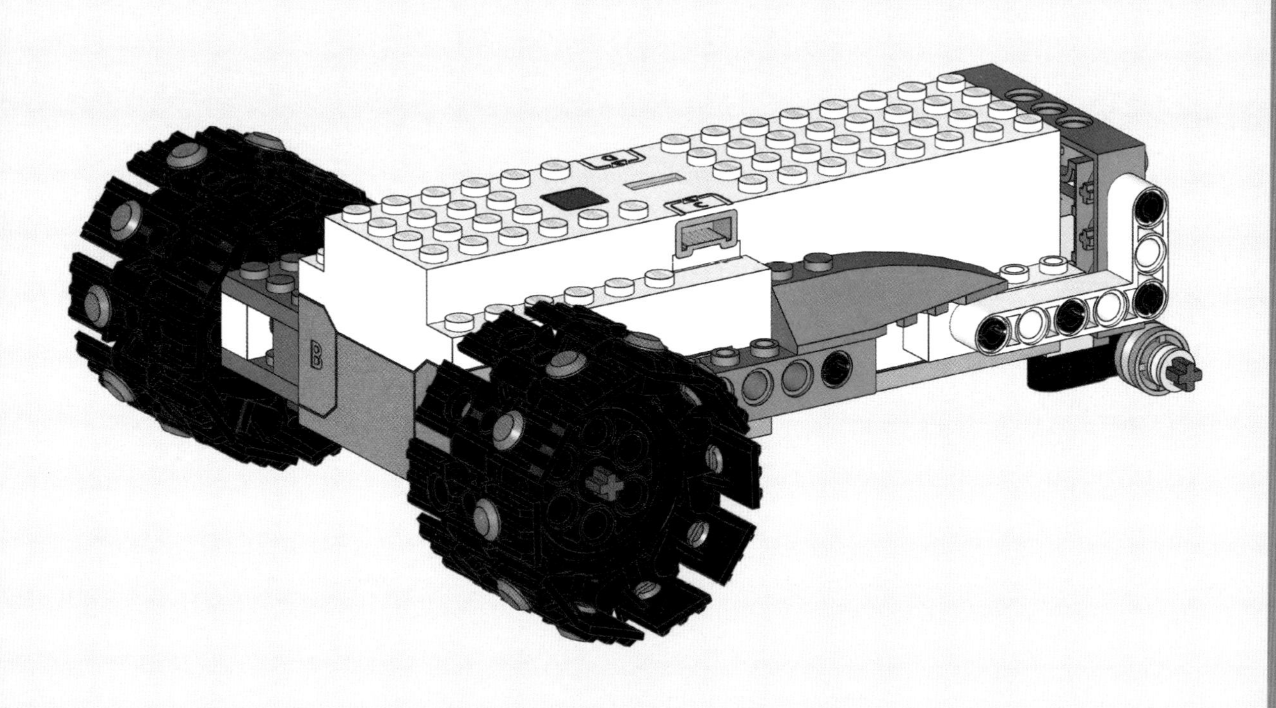

1

your LEGO BOOST creative toolbox

Your LEGO BOOST set includes an amazing assortment of colorful LEGO elements, ranging from plain bricks, plates, and tiles to Technic bricks and beams, axles, pins, gears, wheels, treads, and weird decorative elements. It also includes the LEGO BOOST Move Hub, the external motor and sensor that make this set unique!

If you haven't already done so, open your box. As you see in **FIGURE 1-1**, you'll find 11 numbered bags, an extra bag of pieces, a white box holding the LEGO BOOST Move Hub, and the LEGO BOOST cardboard playmat.

FIGURE 1-1 The LEGO BOOST set 17101 contains LEGO parts, electronic elements, and a cardboard playmat.

speaking LEGO

Imagine that you're building a LEGO BOOST creation with your friends and you need a part. But all you can muster is "Hey, would you pass me that . . . something . . . whatchamacallit . . . *thingy*?"

It's much easier to master LEGO building techniques—and talk about them with others—if you know how to classify, name, and measure LEGO parts. You can't write a novel if you don't know grammar and vocabulary, and the same holds true for making LEGO creations. You've got to learn how to speak LEGO.

The pieces in the LEGO BOOST set can be divided into these categories:

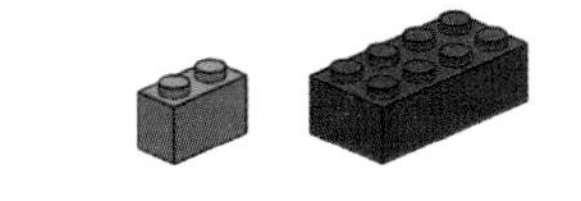

bricks These are the basic building blocks. You can measure them by counting the *studs* on top, and you name them by their studs. You'd say "2 by 4 brick" or see in print "2×4 brick."

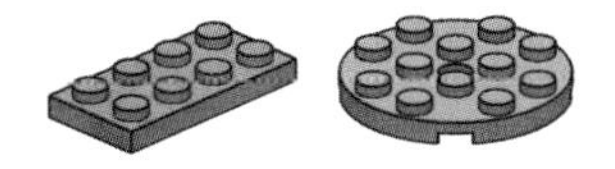

plates and flat tiles These thin pieces are one-third the height of a brick.

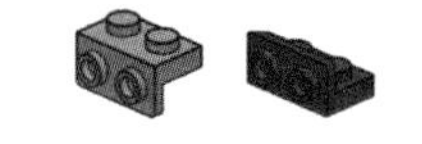

SNOT elements SNOT stands for *Studs Not on Top*. These elements have studs also on their sides, allowing you to build in different directions.

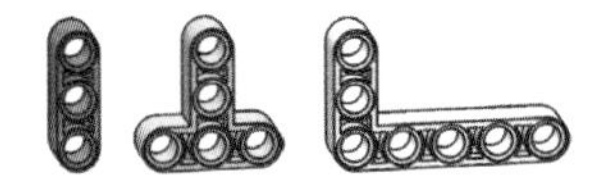

beams These Technic elements can be joined with connectors. You can measure these parts by counting their holes, just as with bricks.

axles These rods can spin freely or can be used to join elements fast together.

pins Pins come in two varieties: one with friction that holds fast and one without friction designed to spin freely. Try connecting beams with different kinds of pins to feel the difference.

hinges These pieces add joints to your models.

gears These pieces transmit motion.

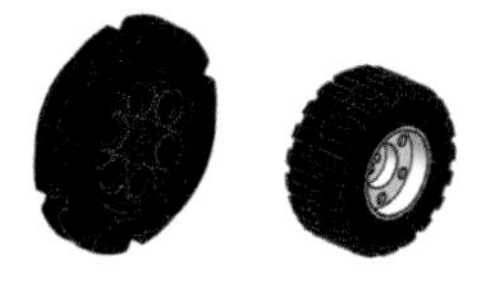

wheels These pieces come in a variety of sizes.

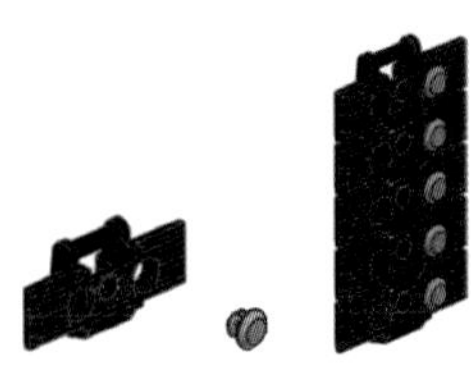

treads Use these for a tank or a bulldozer, and change the length by adding more pieces. The orange pads add grip to the tread.

Your LEGO BOOST set comes with three electronic components, shown in **FIGURE 1-2**.

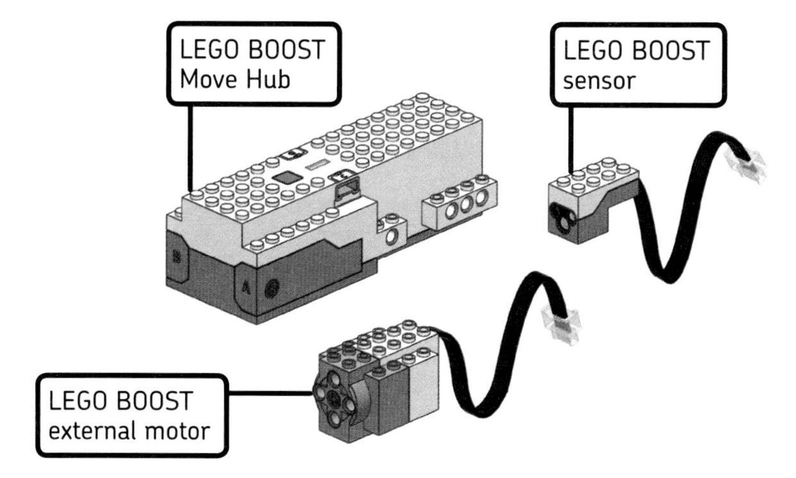

FIGURE 1-2 The electronic pieces

Move Hub Also called the *drivebase*, this is the "brain" of the BOOST set, and it communicates with your device using Bluetooth. The Move Hub has two motors, a built-in tilt sensor, and a multicolored light. You can connect the external motor and the sensor to its two ports. To power it, use 6 AAA batteries. (You might want to buy rechargeable batteries. The Move Hub is a real power hog that will drain a full set of batteries in few hours.)

motor When it's connected to the Move Hub, you can control this motor with precision.

sensor This sensor can detect colors, measure how far away objects are, and more.

Try playing around with these elements to get a better sense of what they do and how they work. Want to really geek out and get an exact inventory of every piece in the LEGO BOOST set? Check out the Complete Parts Reference at *https://nostarch.com/lego-boost-activity-book/*.

programming your robots

Programming a robot means telling your robot exactly what to do. To program the LEGO BOOST Hub, you'll need to download the LEGO BOOST app. The app allows you to *code*, or give your robot instructions in its own language. Download the LEGO BOOST app from the Google Play Store if you have an Android device, from the App Store if you own an Apple device, or from the Windows Store if you have a Windows 10 computer.

LEGO provides a list of compatible devices at *https://www.lego.com/en-us/service/device-guide/BOOST/*. Also, an ever-growing unofficial list of tested, compatible iOS and Android devices is published by the Facebook Unofficial LEGO BOOST Community Group (*https://www.facebook.com/groups/BOOSTcommunity/*).

how to use the brick separator

The BOOST set includes a handy tool, the LEGO brick separator, which looks a little like a crowbar. You can use this tool to separate a plate from the top (**A**) or bottom (**B**) of another plate, to lift tiles by their groove (**C**), or to push pins and axle pins out of the holes and cross holes of gears (**D**) or bricks (**E**).

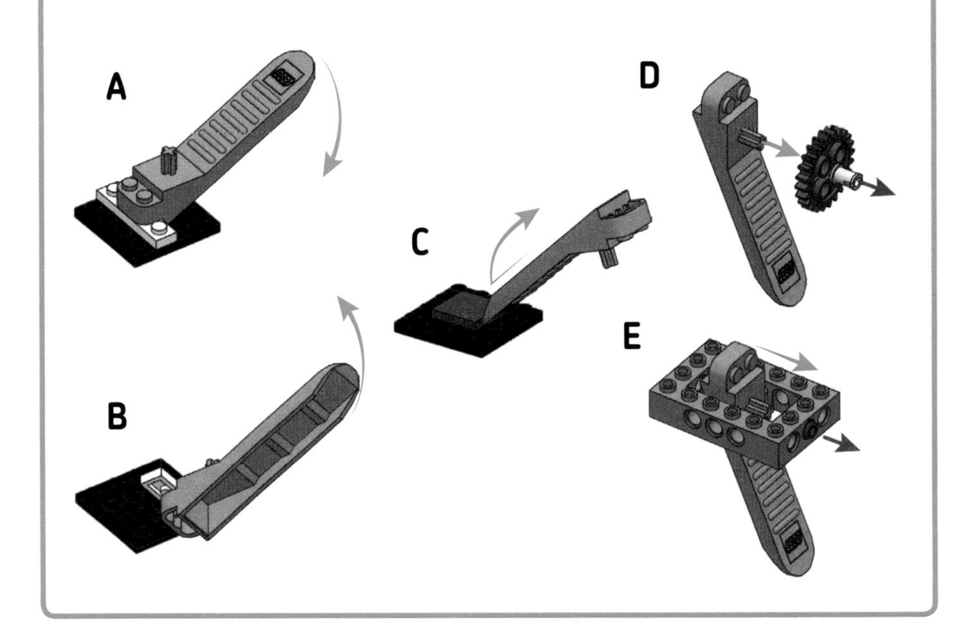

let's build a robot!

Now that you've seen a preview of the elements of the LEGO BOOST set and installed the app to control your robots, let's build a simple robot that moves so you can start exploring the world of robotics.

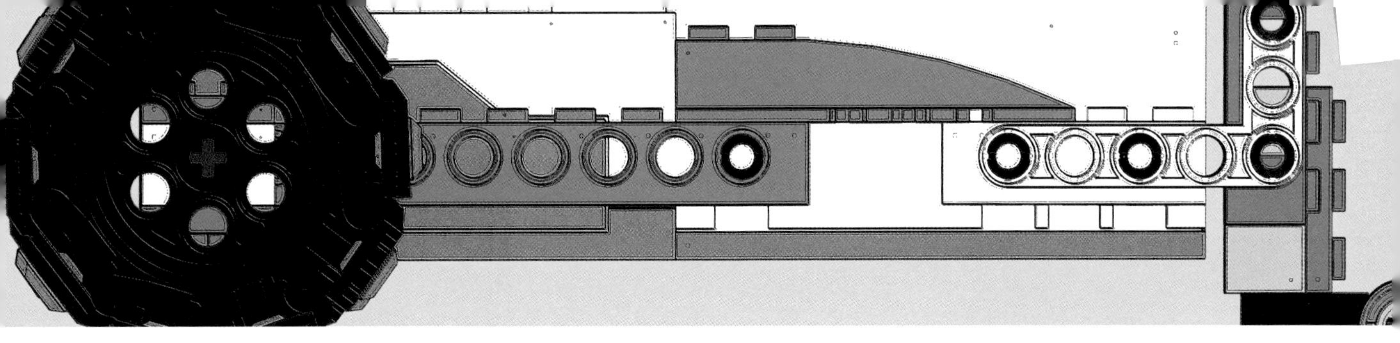

2

it's me, MARIO!

In this chapter, you'll build a wheeled robot and make your first program using the *Creative Canvas* programming environment, a section of the LEGO BOOST app that lets you program your own inventions from scratch.

Let's build a simple robot called **MARIO** (see **FIGURE 2-1**). MARIO stands for **Multi-Accessory Robot Is Obligatory**. Its name means we want to build a robot that we can equip with many accessories to make it do a lot of cool things! In later chapters, we'll improve MARIO by attaching new accessories to it.

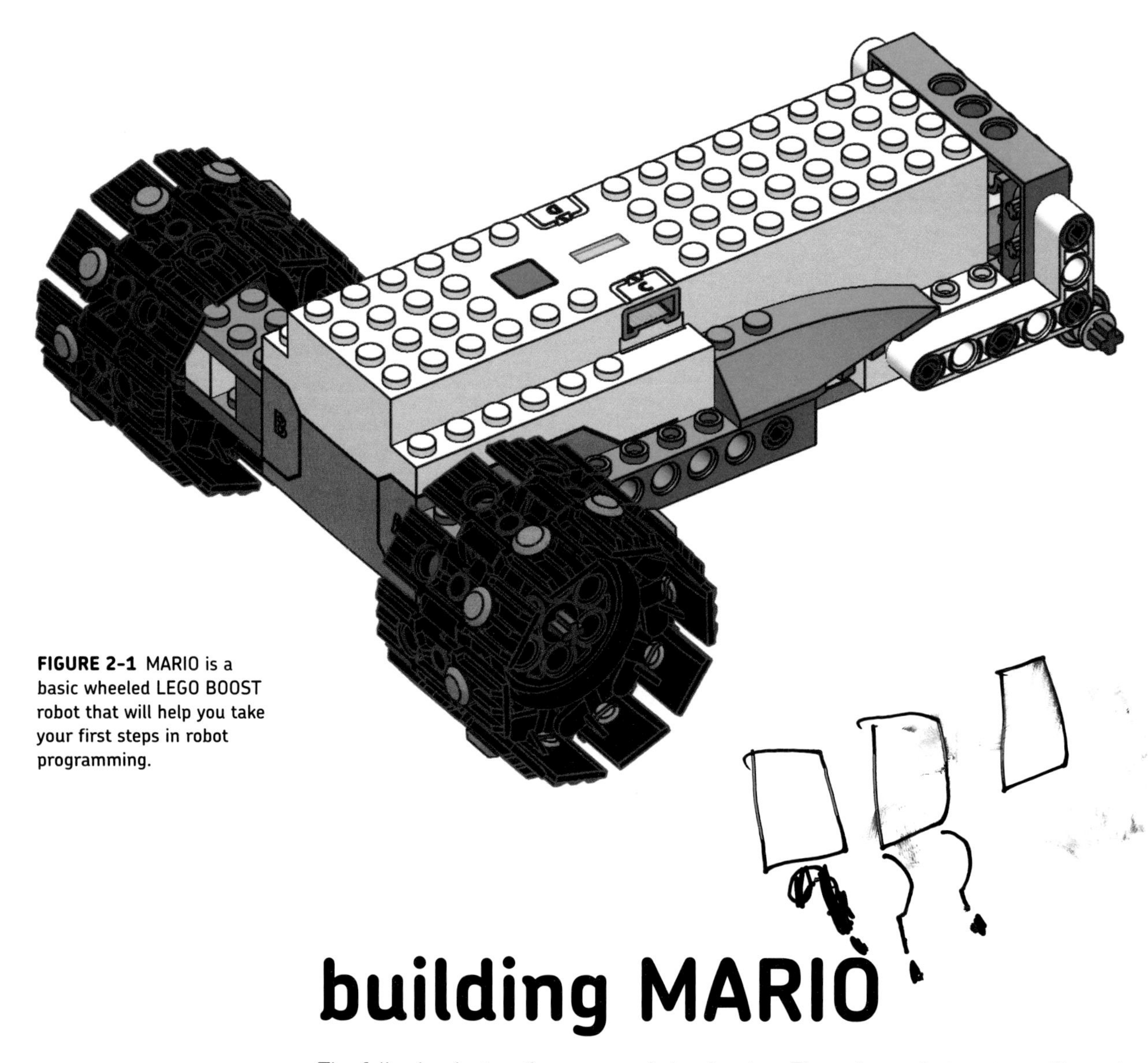

FIGURE 2-1 MARIO is a basic wheeled LEGO BOOST robot that will help you take your first steps in robot programming.

building MARIO

The following instructions proceed step by step. They show what parts you'll need for each step. For some parts, such as axles, I give the length in terms of LEGO units so you'll know which size to use. You can also measure axles by putting them next to a Technic brick and counting the studs, as shown in **FIGURE 2-2**.

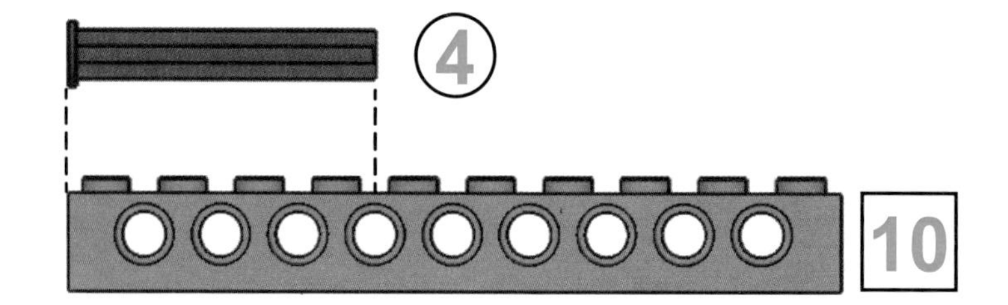

FIGURE 2-2 You can determine a brick's length by counting the studs. A LEGO axle doesn't have studs, so place it next to a brick and count the studs on the brick for the length of the axle.

1

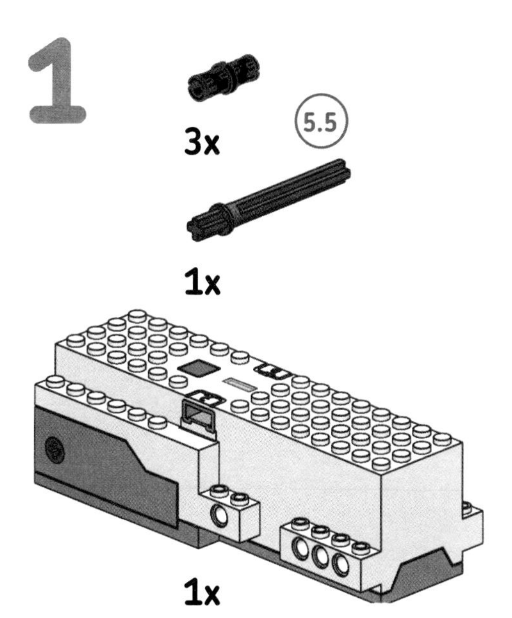

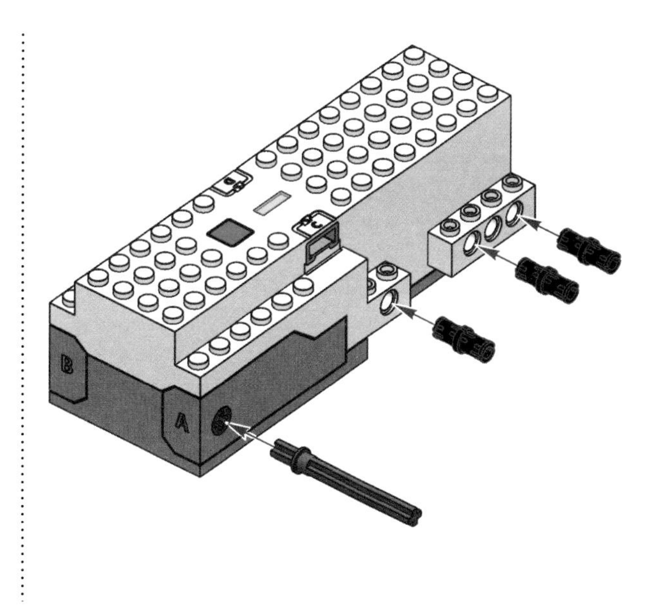

2

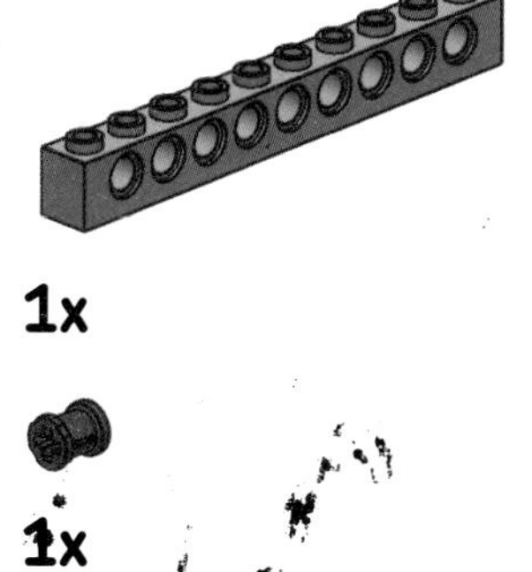

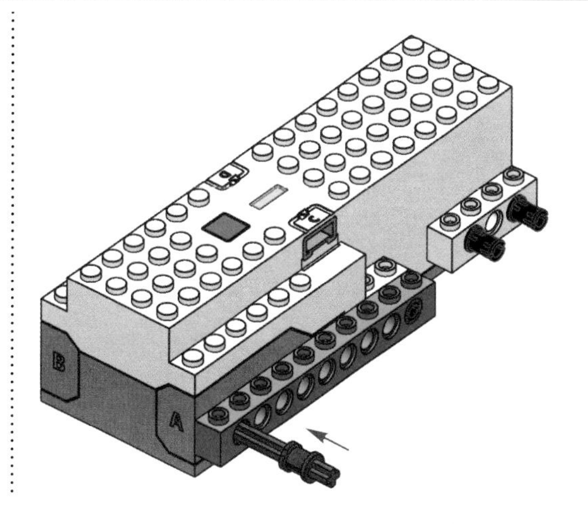

3

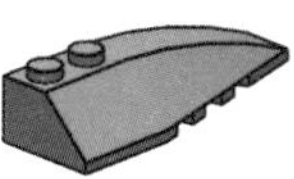

1x

1x

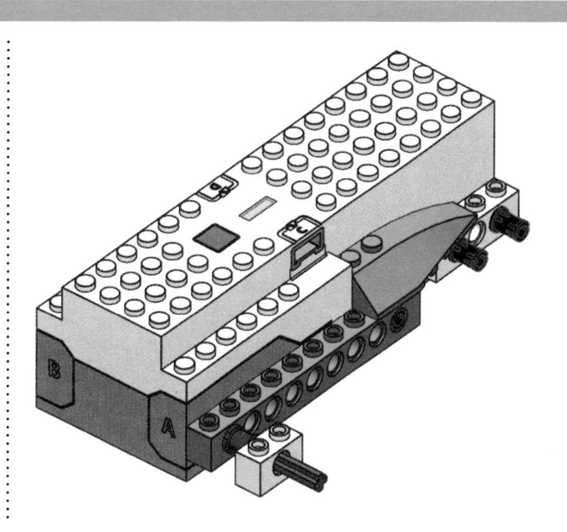

4

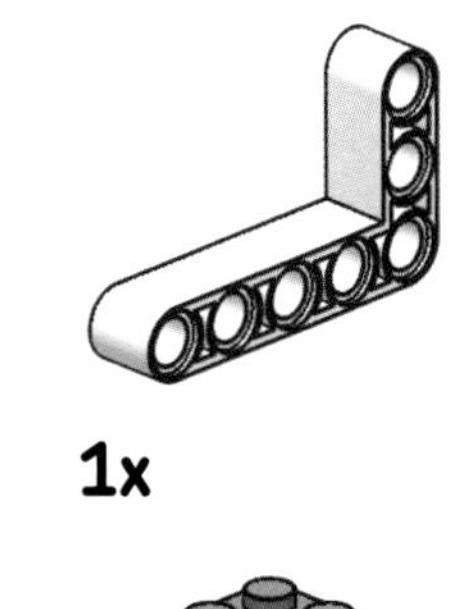

1x

2x

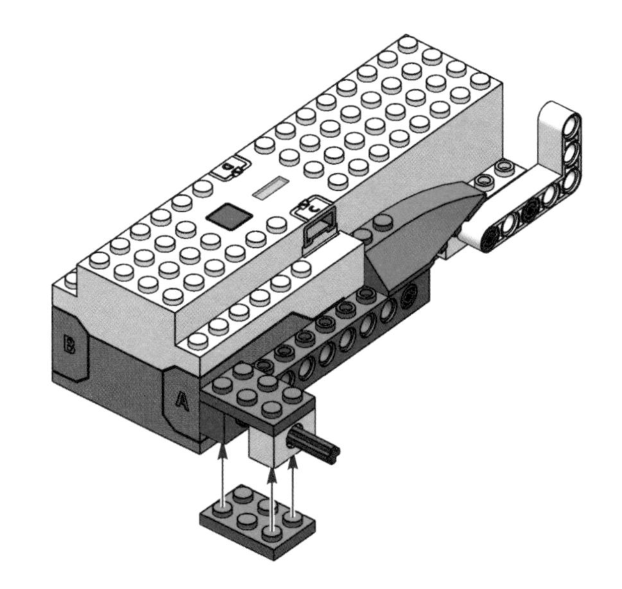

5

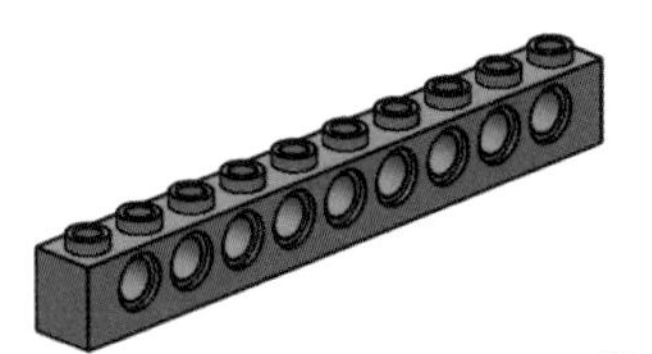

1x

1x 1x

2x 1x

1x

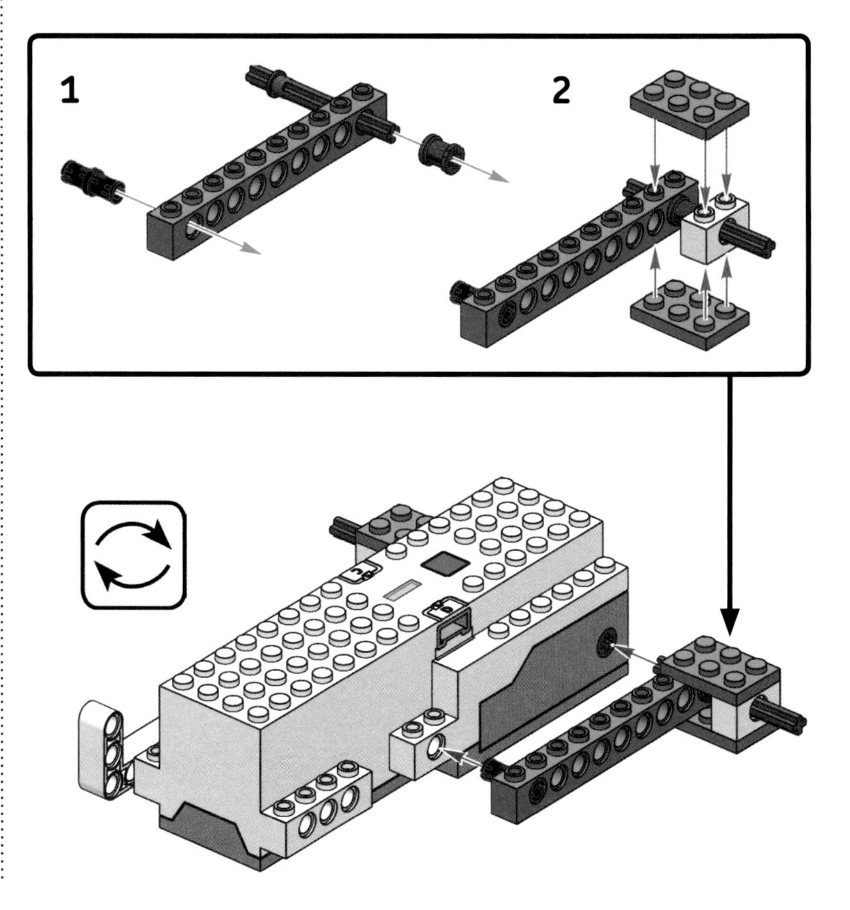

6

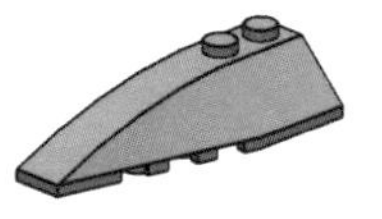

1x

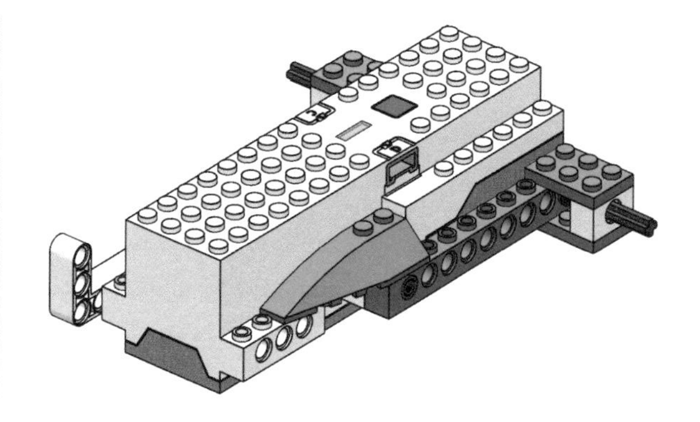

7

2x

2x

1x

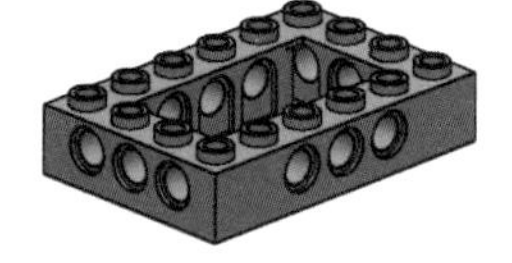

1x

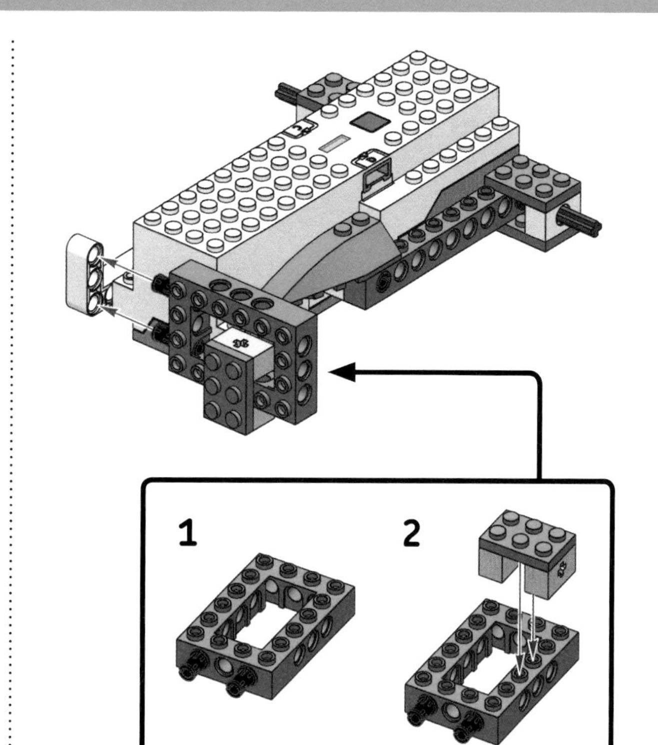

8

4x

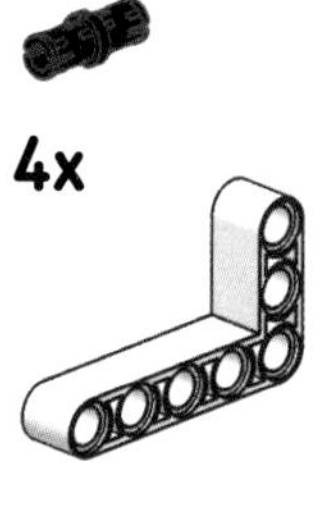

1x

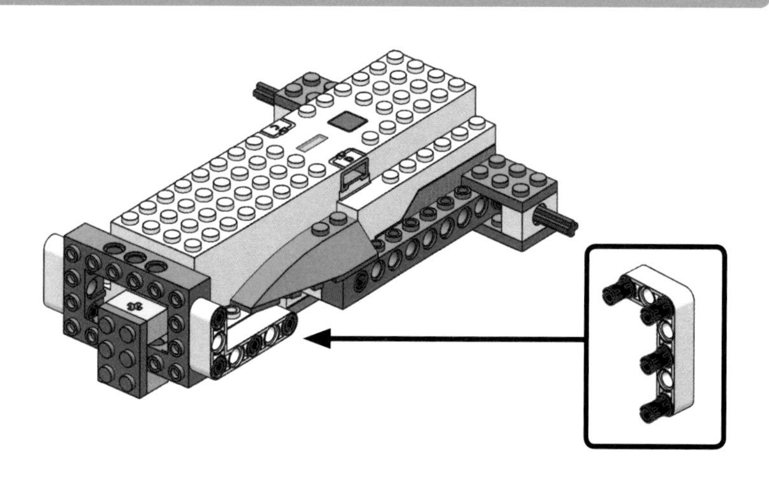

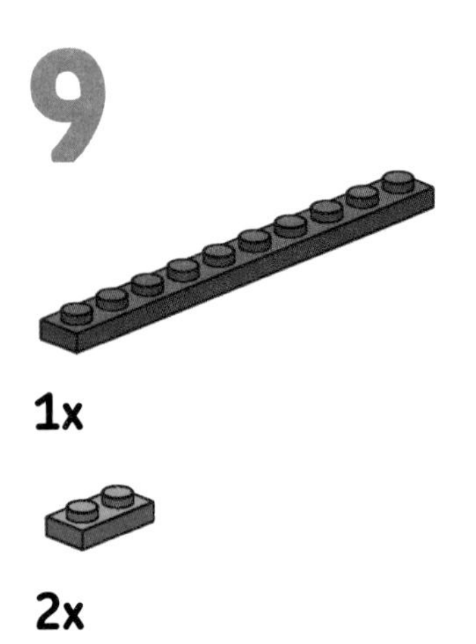

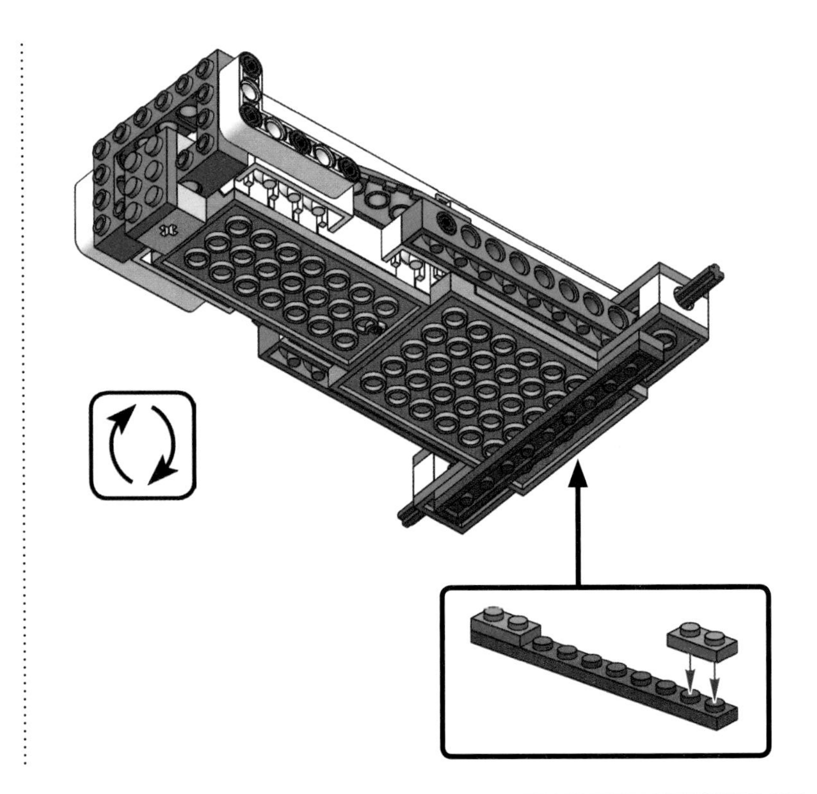

10

1x

2x

1x

2x

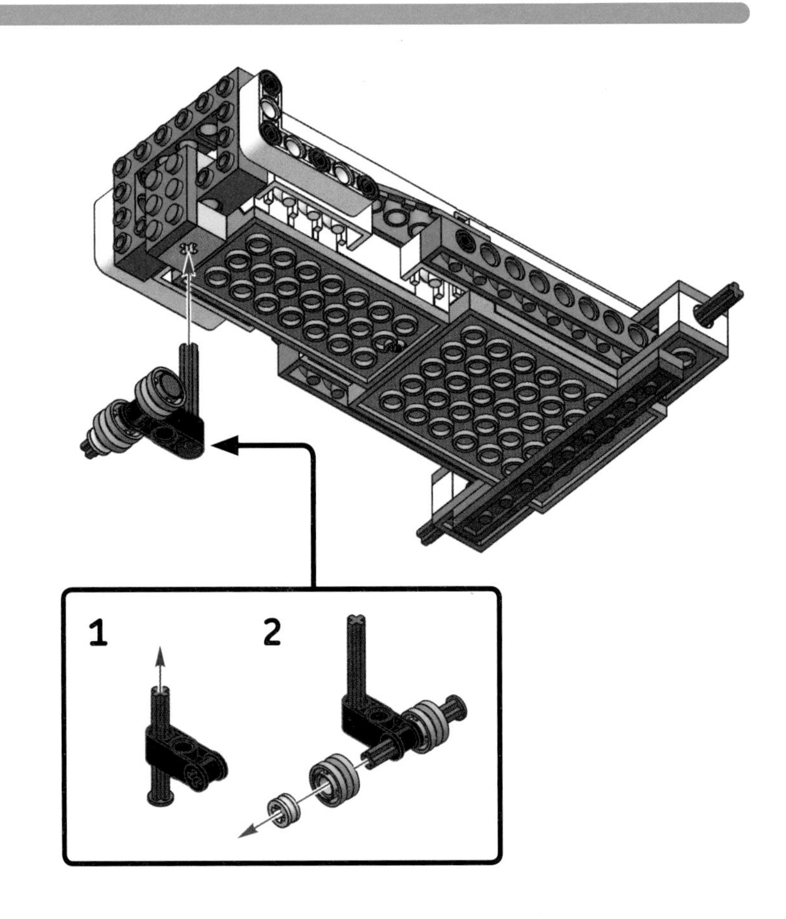

11

20x

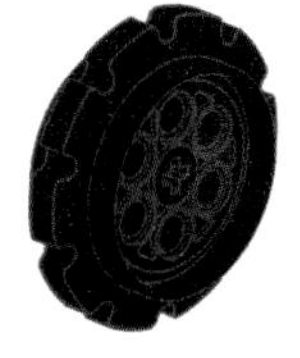

2x

20x

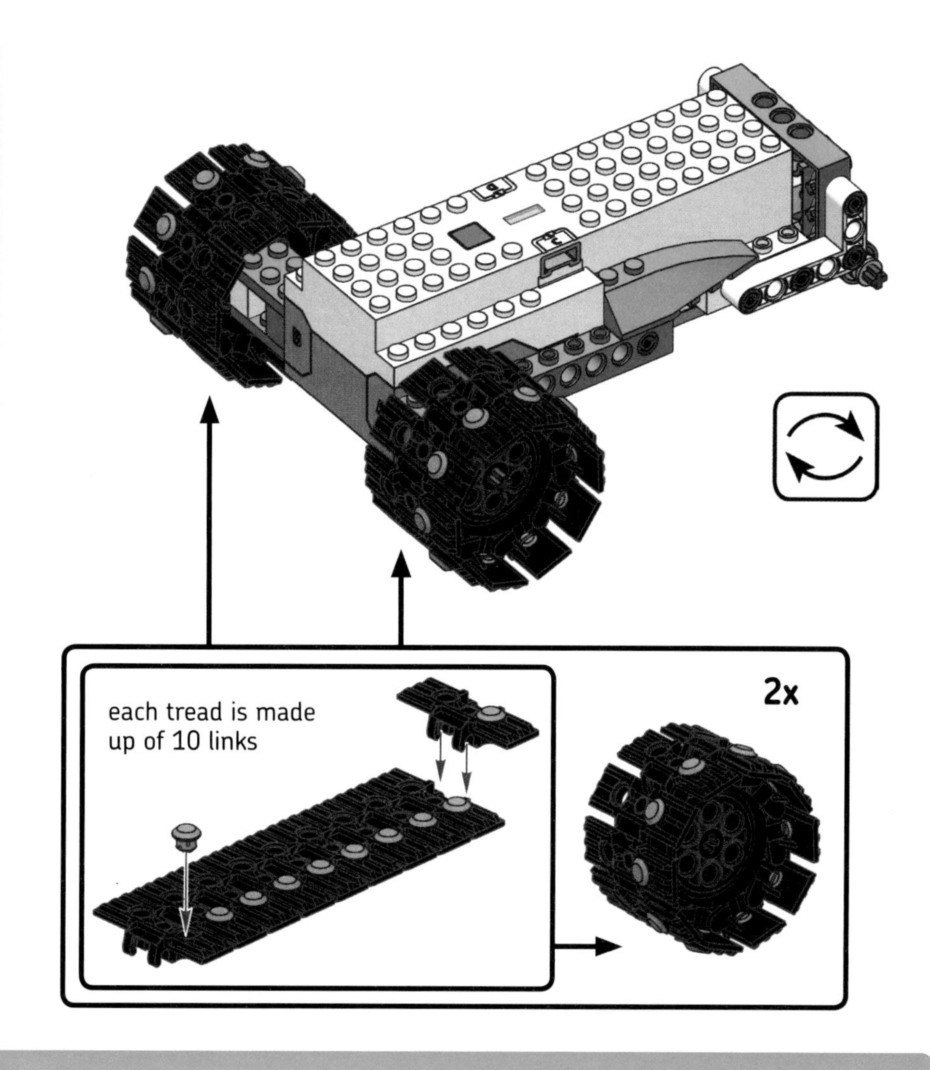

the Creative Canvas

The LEGO BOOST Creative Canvas allows you to program your robots from scratch to control every detail of their behavior.

NOTE:
This book is based on the LEGO BOOST app version 1.5. Since the writing of this book, the appearance of the app may have changed, and new functionality may have been added.

To get started, follow these steps, using the pictures as a guide:

Step 1: To enter the Creative Canvas, scroll down to the end of the main lobby screen on the left. You should see a window covered by a curtain. Tap the curtain to roll it up.

Step 2: Tap the spiral, which is a bit like the portal in *The LEGO Movie*.

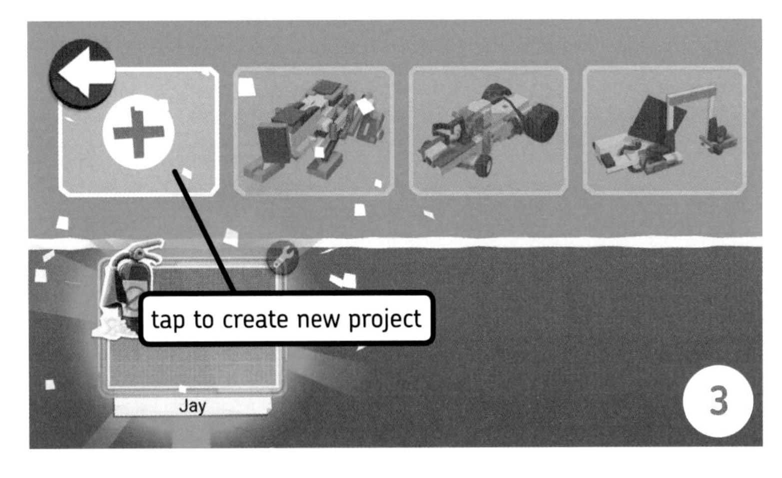

Step 3: The next screen is the Creative Canvas Lobby, and it is split in two. There are four buttons on top. One has a plus sign and is used to create a new blank project. One creates a project based on the *Walking Base*, another makes a project based on the *Drive Base*, and the last creates a project based on the *Gate Base*. These bases are three extra models that you can build and customize.

Because we're creating something entirely new, tap the button with a plus sign on it. The app creates a project with a random name and image and automatically opens it.

Step 4: You're now inside the Creative Canvas. Let's change the icon and the name of the project. Tap the Back arrow to go back to the Creative Canvas Lobby.

Step 5: Once you're back in the Creative Canvas Lobby, you can edit the project image and name by tapping the wrench icon.

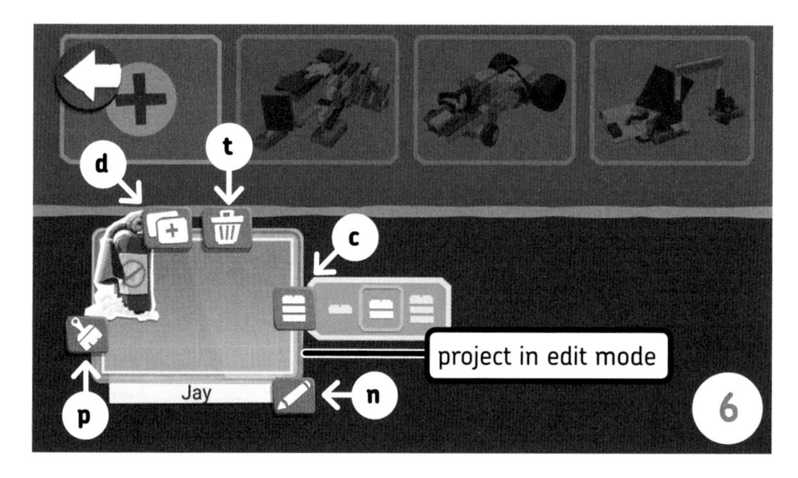

Step 6: The project is now highlighted, and five options appear:

- Duplicate the project by tapping the button labeled **d**.
- Delete the project by tapping the trash can icon, labeled **t**, and tapping again when it turns green to confirm. If you change your mind, tap anywhere else to cancel.
- Change the project picture by tapping the button with the brush icon labeled **p**.
- Rename the project by tapping the pencil icon, labeled **n**, and typing a name. The name can't be more than 11 characters long.
- Select the Blocks palette complexity level by tapping the button with the stack icon labeled **c**.

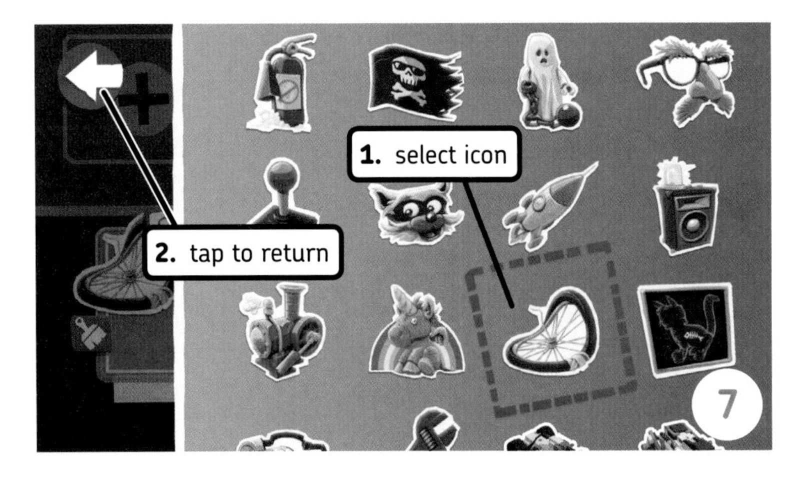

Step 7: Now, tap the stack button shown in Step 6 and select the *intermediate* programming level (two stacked bricks). Next, tap the brush button labeled **p** and change the project image to the *broken bike wheel*, then tap the Back arrow at the top left to return to the previous screen.

Tap the pencil icon, labeled **n**, and enter the name `MARIO1`. Then press ENTER on the keyboard.

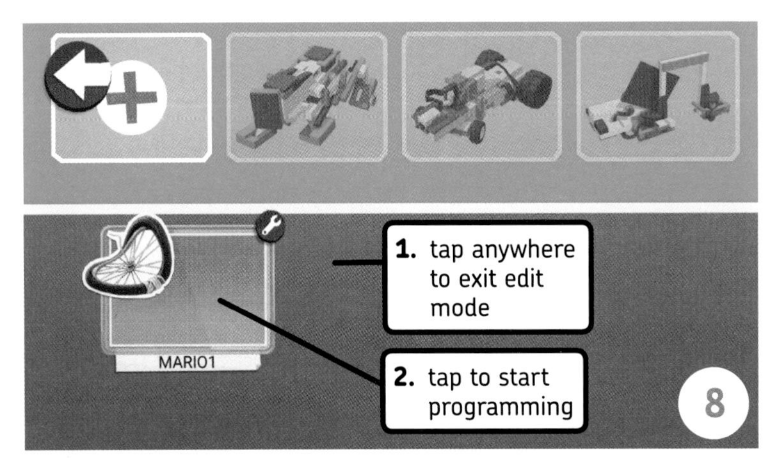

Step 8: To finish editing the project properties, tap anywhere on the screen and then tap the project image.

You are ready to start programming!

MARIO's first program

NOTE: *This book describes the programming blocks available in the* intermediate *level (two stacked bricks). You can access more advanced programming blocks by selecting the advanced level (three stacked bricks).*

Once the app finishes loading, you should see a blank canvas. A pop-up should invite you to turn on the Move Hub by pressing its green button. Follow the onscreen instructions to connect the Move Hub to your device. If you have any problems, see the official support pages at *https://www.lego.com/en-us/boost/support/* and *https://www.lego.com/en-us/service/help/products/electronics-robotics/boost/*.

Before creating your first program, let's take a tour of the programming area (**FIGURE 2-3**).

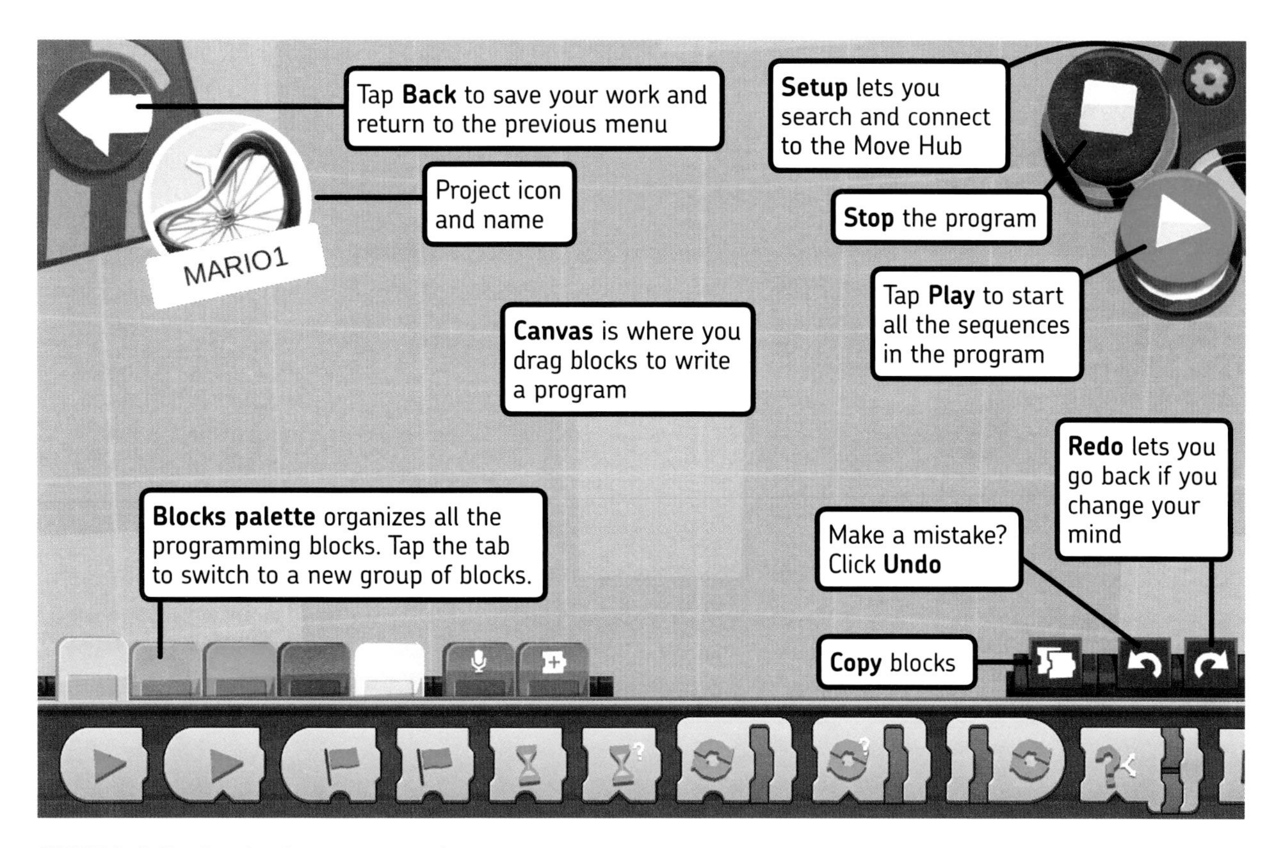

FIGURE 2-3 The Creative Canvas programming area

You can read the official names of the programming blocks and a brief description of what they do by pressing down on the blocks in the palette or in the programming canvas. Let's write a short program. Follow these steps, using the pictures to help find the blocks:

Step 1: The first palette on the far left contains the **Flow Control** blocks. Tap it to use these blocks.

Step 2: Drag and drop the **Start** block onto the canvas. This block starts your code sequence.

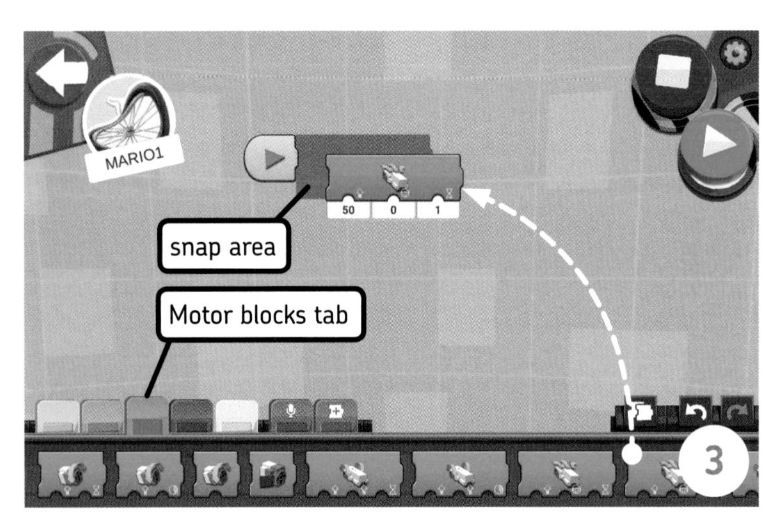

Step 3: Switch to the Motor blocks palette by tapping the green tab, and then drag and drop the **Drivebase Move Steering for Time** block onto the canvas. It has a steering wheel icon and an hourglass icon at the bottom. (There are four blocks that look similar, so be careful to select the right one.) When you drag the block to a place where it can snap to the previously placed block (the **Start** block), a grey area should appear.

Step 4: The **Drivebase Move Steering for Time** block has three values that you can change to affect your robot's behavior. The number on the left controls the speed of your robot. It is set to 50 by default.

To slow down your robot, try changing 50 to 20. Tap the number, and a numeric keypad or slider should appear (see **FIGURE 2-4**). Input **20** and then tap somewhere away from the interface to close it.

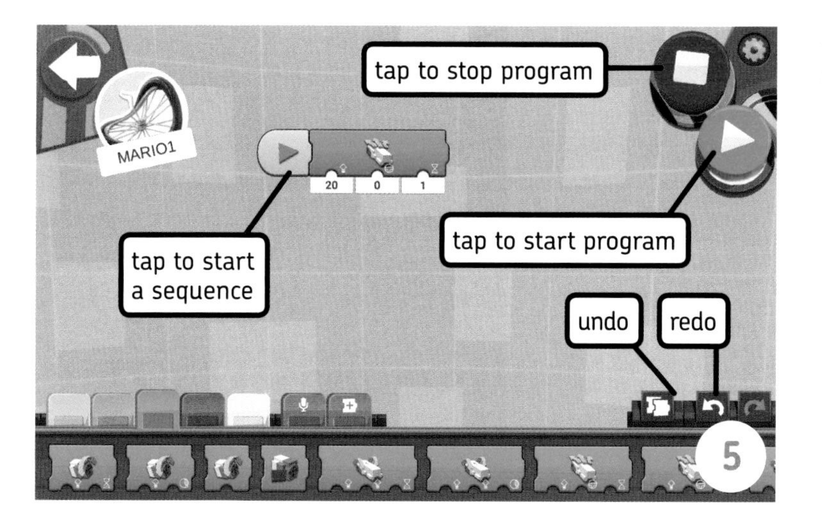

Step 5: To start the program, tap the **Start** block in your code.

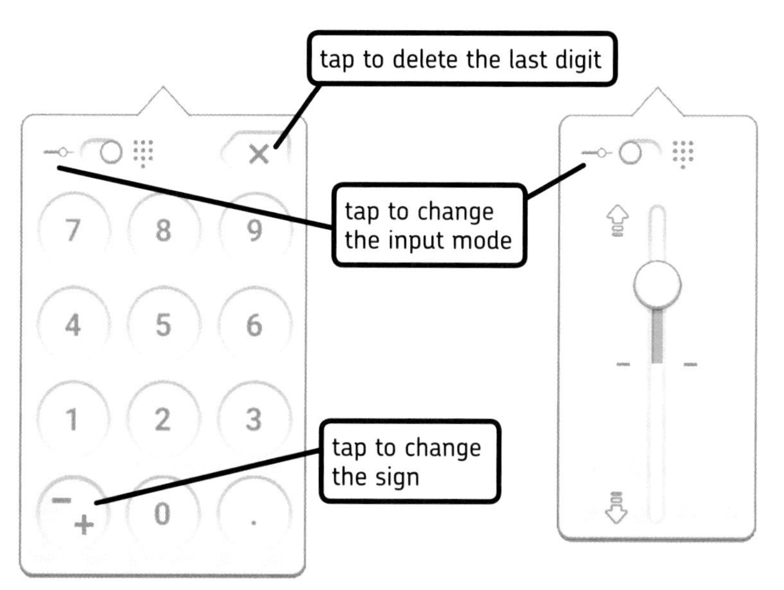

FIGURE 2-4 Edit the speed using the numeric keypad or the vertical slider. Switch between the keyboard and slider by tapping the button at the top left of the interface.

FIGURE 2-5 shows the finished program.

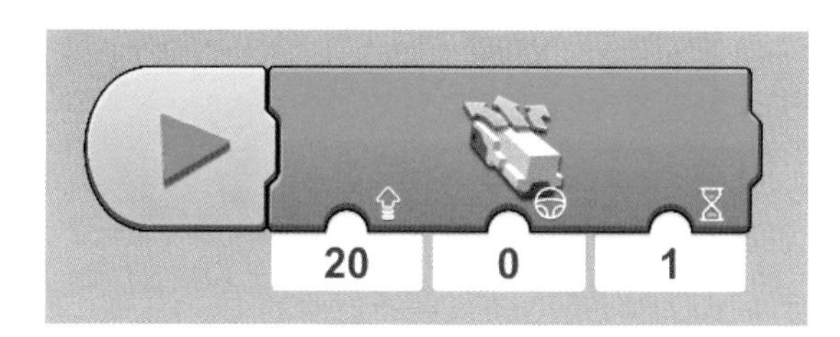

FIGURE 2-5 The first program for the robot MARIO

When you start the program, MARIO should travel straight ahead at speed 20 for 1 second.

Does your program work? Congratulations! You've taken your first step into the fantastic world of robot programming.

If your program doesn't work, double-check that the Move Hub is connected and that the blue LED on the Move Hub is lit up. To troubleshoot connection problems, see the online troubleshooting guides at *https://www.lego.com/en-us/themes/boost/support/* and *https://www.lego.com/en-us/service/help/products/electronics-robotics/boost/*. (If the robot does not travel straight ahead as expected, your Move Hub's batteries may be low.)

what you've learned

In this chapter, you built MARIO, a simple wheeled robot, which will be your companion as you take your first steps into the world of coding. In making MARIO, you learned how to enter the Creative Canvas environment and how to create projects and edit their properties, such as the project name and icon. You also wrote your first program using the **Start** block and the **Drivebase Move Steering for Time** block.

In the next chapter, you'll learn about other Motor blocks and how to change their parameters to make MARIO drive around!

experiment 2-1

You can change the Speed value to make the robot move slower or faster. What happens if you set the speed to a *negative* value?

When you're ready to check your answer, turn to the appendix on page 239, where you'll find the answer key.

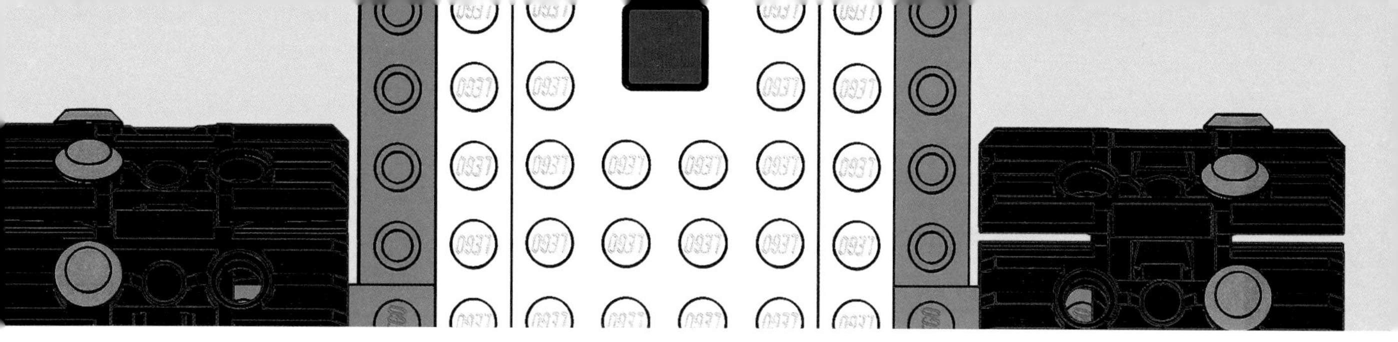

3

getting around with Motor blocks

In this chapter, we'll expand the basic program you made in Chapter 2 to make MARIO travel forward, turn, and come back. You'll learn everything you need to know about the Motor blocks that control the Move Hub's motors. These blocks are found in the palette with the green tab (see **FIGURE 3-1**).

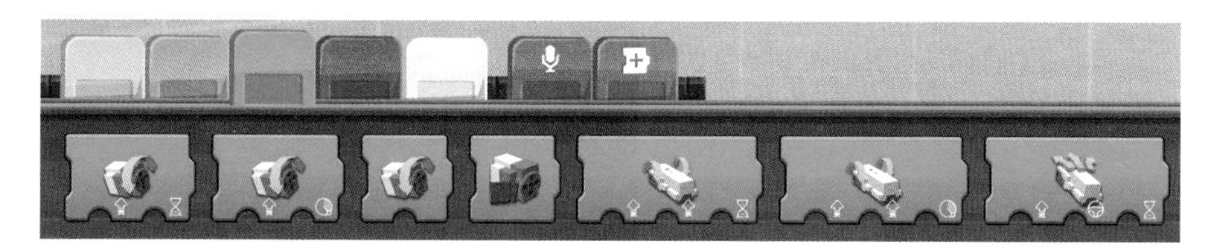

FIGURE 3-1 The Motor blocks

there and back

Before beginning to program, it's very helpful to write down what you want your robot to do. (This is how professional programmers work, too!) You might not know exactly how the LEGO BOOST programming language works yet, but you probably have some ideas about what you'd like your robot to do.

using pseudocode to plan your program

You can write a kind of rough draft of a program using *pseudocode*. Pseudocode is a detailed description of a program that a human can readily understand, with each action written on its own line to keep things tidy. Using pseudocode is a great way to break a big task into small steps, allowing you to plan your program before starting to code. For example, here's how you could tell MARIO to travel forward, turn around, and then travel back to its starting point in pseudocode:

```
Slowly move straight forward for 1 second
Slowly spin in place for 1 second
Slowly move straight forward for 1 second
```

If you knew how the LEGO BOOST language worked, you might add some details to your instructions, like so:

```
Move at speed 20 with steering at 0 for 1 second
Move at speed 20 with steering at 100 for 1 second
Move at speed 20 with steering at 0 for 1 second
```

Let's look at the BOOST programming environment to understand the meaning of "steering at 0" and "steering at 100."

coding with BOOST

To write the program on the LEGO BOOST app, follow these steps.

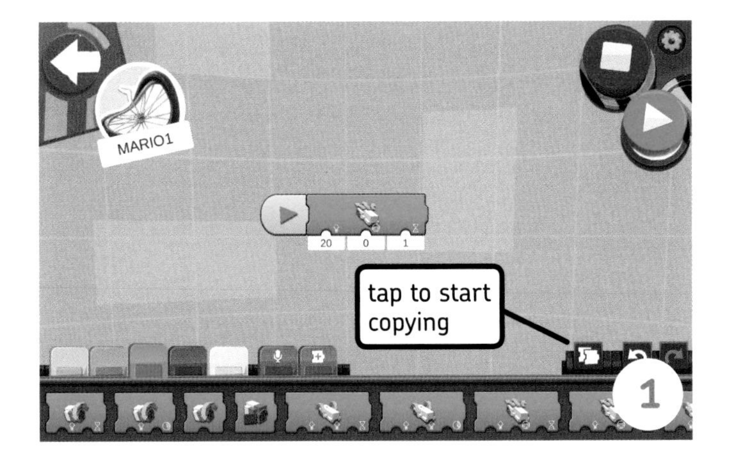

Step 1: Open the program MARIO1 you made in Chapter 2 (or create it now, and add a **Drivebase Move Steering for Time** block with inputs set to 20, 0, 1) and then tap the Copy button as shown at the left. The icon should turn light blue, indicating that you are ready to copy blocks.

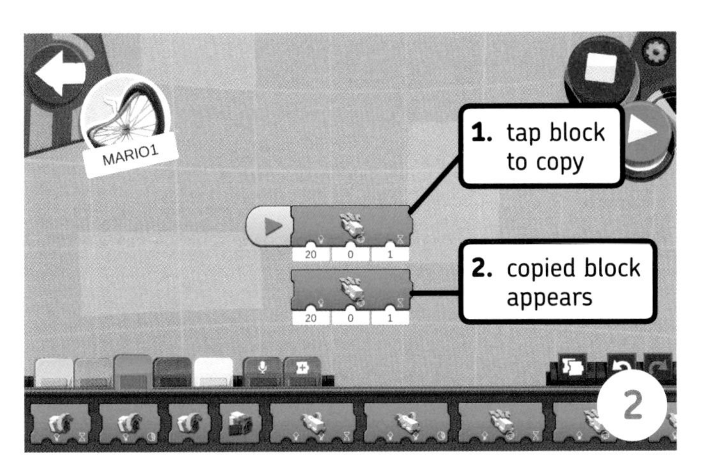

Step 2: Tap the green **Drivebase Move Steering for Time** block to copy it. The copied block should appear right under the original block.

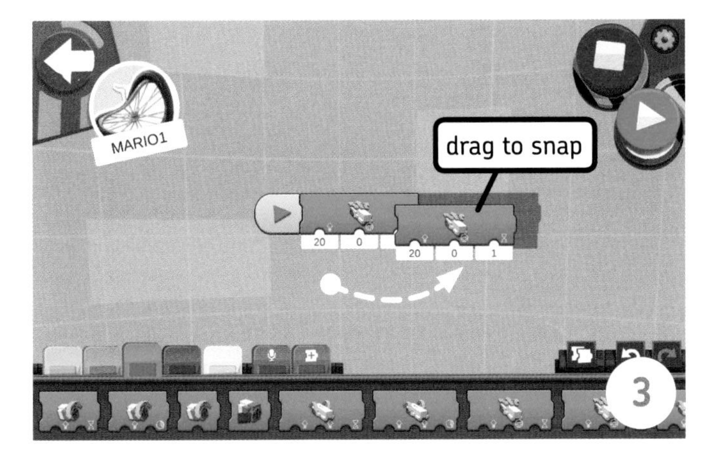

Step 3: Drag the new Move block after the first one and snap it into place.

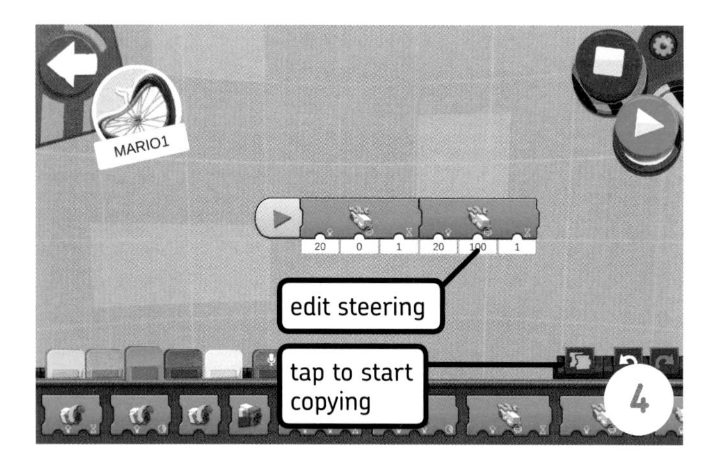

Step 4: Now tap the Steering input of the second Move block and change it from 0 to 100 (see **FIGURE 3-2**). Once you've finished editing, tap the Copy button.

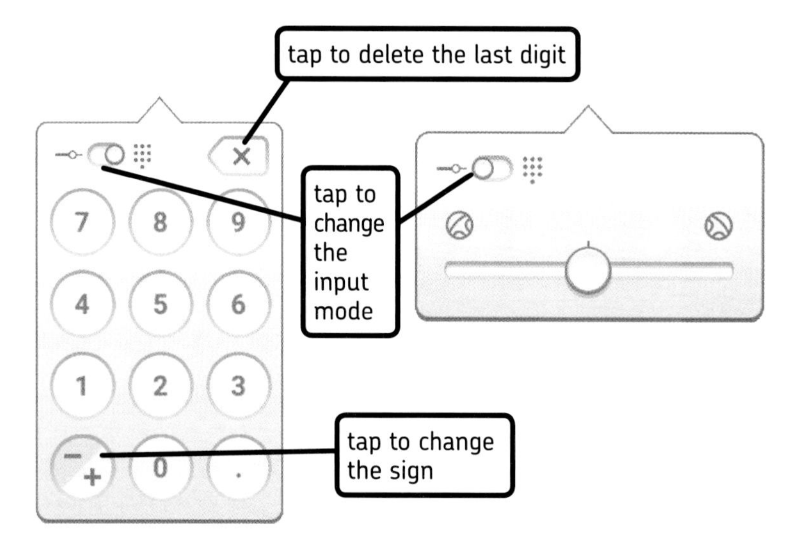

FIGURE 3-2 You can edit the Steering input with the numeric keypad or the horizontal slider.

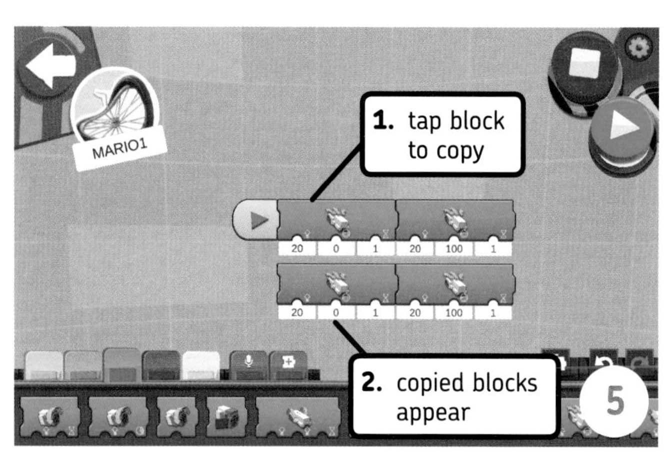

Step 5: Tap the first Move block and both the first and second blocks should be copied. (When you use Copy, all the blocks attached to the right of the block you tap should be copied.)

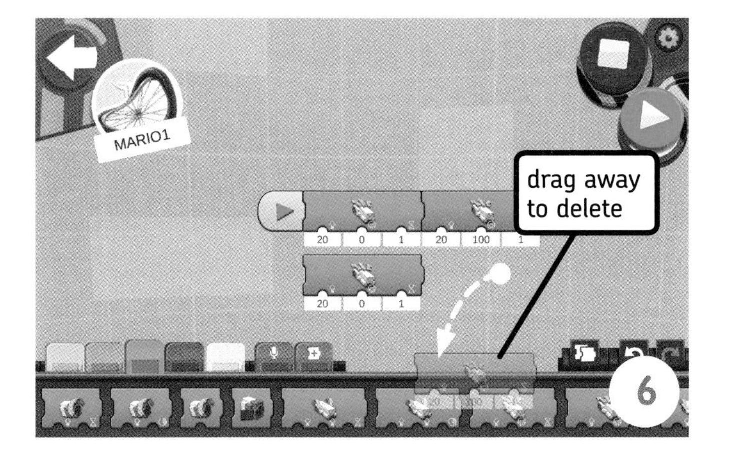

Step 6: Since we need only three blocks, let's delete the fourth block (the copy of the one with steering set to 100) by dragging it away from the sequence, down to the palette. When the block becomes transparent, drop it and it should disappear.

Step 7: Drag the disconnected Move block and drop it at the end of the sequence. The program should now have three **Drivebase Move Steering for Time** blocks.

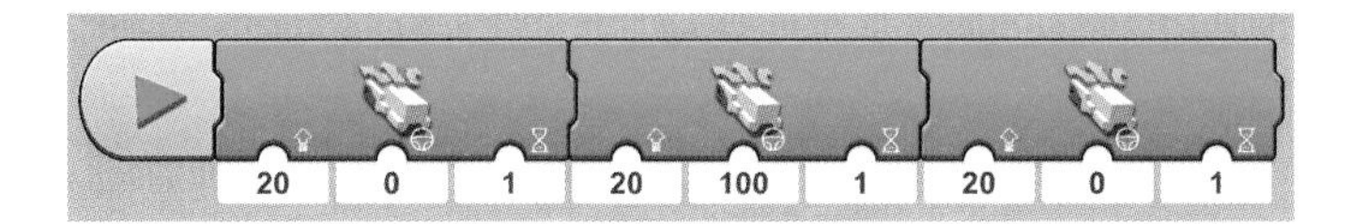

Step 8: Try running your code by tapping the big green **Play** button. MARIO should travel forward for 1 second, spin in place by about half a turn, and then return to its starting point.

differential drive robots

The LEGO BOOST moving robots—including the Getting Started Vehicle, Vernie, and MARIO all have two motors, each of which drives a wheel. The robots change direction like bulldozers or tanks, and can also spin in place. Such robots are called *differential drive* robots, because their movement depends on the *difference* between the speed of their wheels.

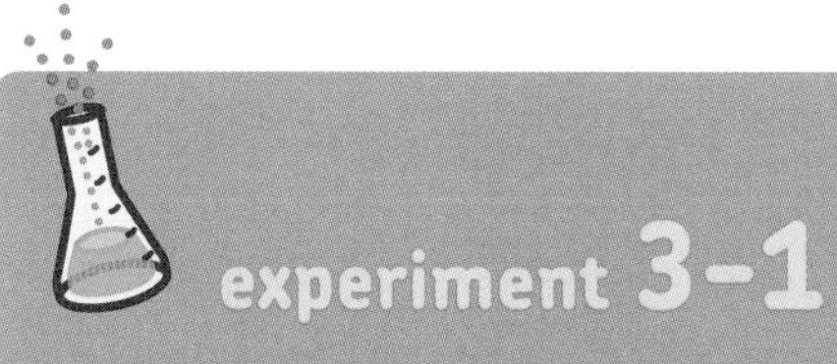

experiment 3-1

Try running some of these blocks yourself to better understand how to steer your robot. Can you guess how to make it turn left?

When you're ready to check your answer, see the answer key on page 239.

Drivebase Move Steering for Time vs. Drivebase Move Tank for Time

The **Drivebase Move Steering for Time** block is intuitive to use because it allows you to control your robot as if you were turning a steering wheel. The Move Hub computes the motor speeds necessary to steer your robot in the direction you want. On the other hand, sometimes you might want to control the speed of each wheel individually. The **Drivebase Move Tank for Time** block allows you to do that. **FIGURE 3-3** shows the two Move blocks side by side.

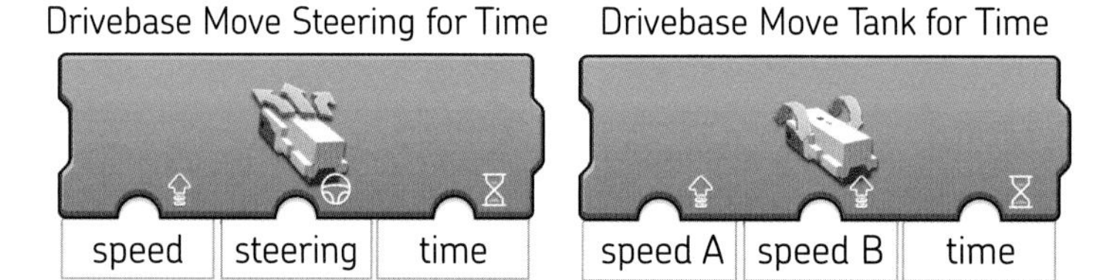

FIGURE 3-3 The Move Steering block and Move Tank block give you two ways to control the robot's movement.

FIGURE 3-4 and **TABLE 3-1** summarize how these two blocks work.

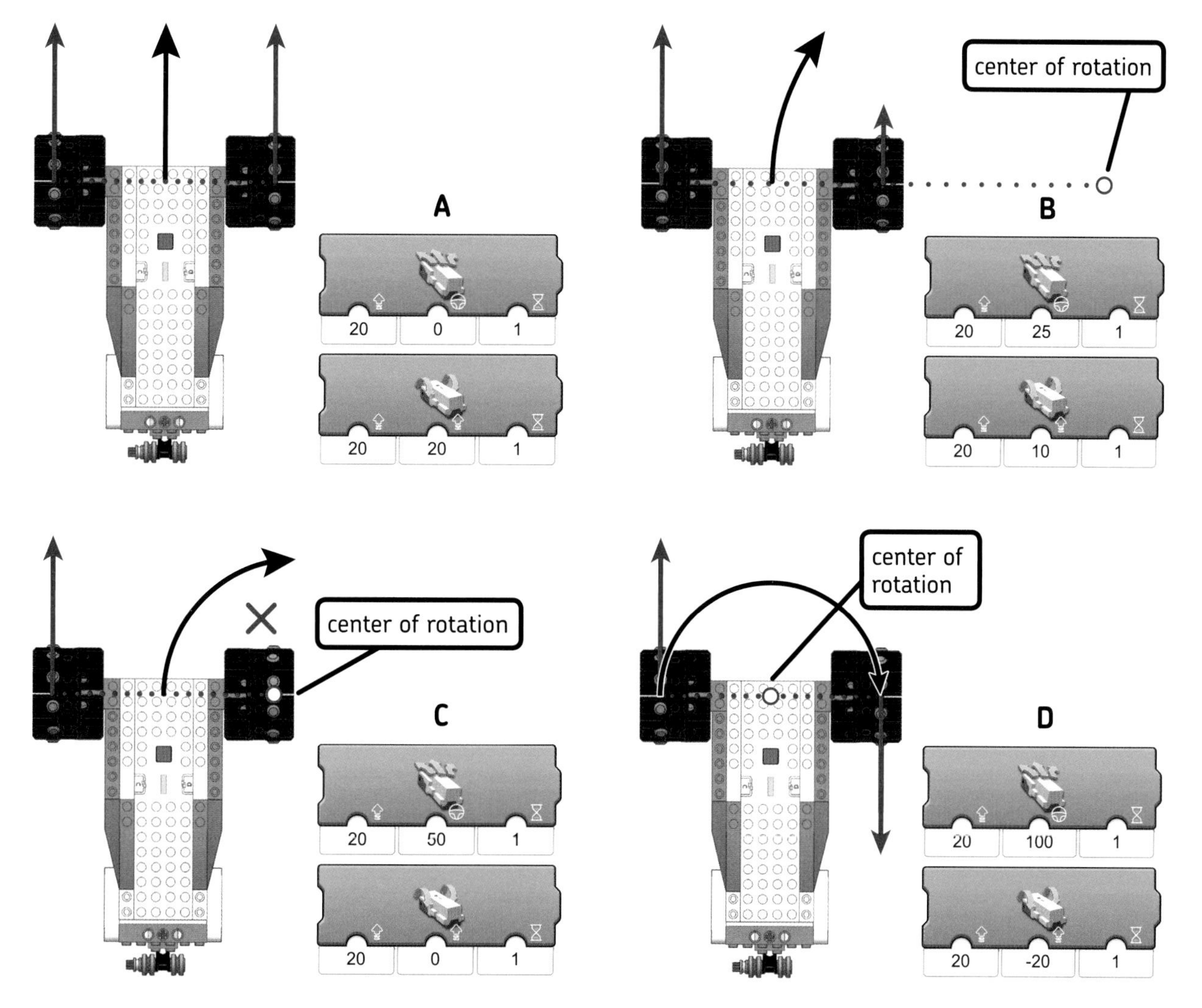

FIGURE 3-4 Setting the parameters of the Move Tank and the Move Steering blocks to achieve the same movement. The red arrows indicate the speed of the wheels' rotation, the black arrow shows the resulting direction of the robot, and the white circle with the red border indicates the center of rotation.

TABLE 3-1 how the Move Steering and Move Tank blocks work as shown in Figure 3-4

	DRIVEBASE MOVE STEERING FOR TIME	DRIVEBASE MOVE TANK FOR TIME
A Full speed ahead	Steering is 0%	Speed A and Speed B are equal
B Slight turn	Steering is 25%	Speed A is double Speed B
C Hard turn—right wheel is stationary, and robot moves to the right	Steering is 50%	Speed A is greater than zero while Speed B is zero
D Spinning in place—wheels turn at the same speed in opposite directions, and robot spins clockwise	Steering is 100%	Speed A and Speed B are of equal magnitude, but Speed A is positive while Speed B is negative

FIGURE 3-5 shows how setting the Steering input value affects the direction of the robot. Take a look at the **Drivebase Move Steering for Time** blocks. When the Steering value is positive, the robot turns right, and when the Steering is negative, it turns left. When the Speed is positive, the robot moves in the direction indicated by the red arrows, and when the Speed is negative, it moves along the blue arrows.

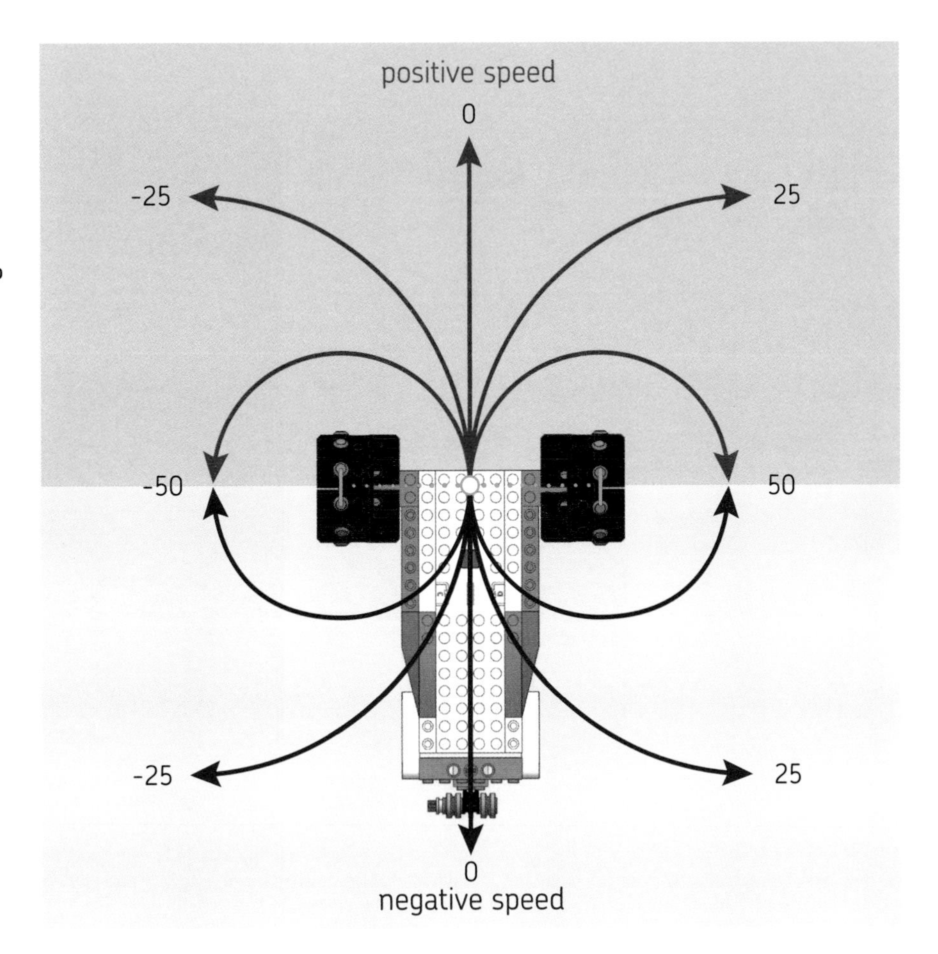

FIGURE 3-5 How to set the Steering and Speed inputs of the Drivebase Move Steering for Time block so your robot travels in various directions. The positive and negative numbers correspond to the Steering values, and the red and blue arrows correspond to positive and negative values of the Speed, respectively.

experiment 3-2

In the program shown in step 6 on page 25, the combination Speed = 20, Steering = 100, and Time = 1 makes the robot spin in place by about half a turn. If you set the Steering to 50, how should you change the Time parameter of the second block if you want to achieve the same result?

three new Move blocks

Let's explore in more detail how the **Drivebase Move Steering for Time** and **Drivebase Move Tank for Time** blocks work. These blocks are actually shortcuts. Each is equivalent to a **Drivebase Move Steering Unlimited** block (or to a **Drivebase Move Tank Unlimited** block) followed by a **Wait for Time** block and a **Drivebase Stop** block.

The **Wait for Time** block pauses the program for a set number of seconds. You'll find this block together with the **Start Sequence** block in the Flow Control blocks palette (yellow tab). The **Drivebase Stop** block stops the BOOST Hub motors. You'll find it together with the other Move blocks in the Motor blocks palette (green tab).

If you run a program with just a **Drivebase Move Tank Unlimited** or a **Drivebase Move Steering Unlimited** block in it, the robot will start moving and won't stop until you press the round red **Stop** button, turn off the screen device, or remove the batteries from the Move Hub. Try the programs shown in **FIGURE 3-6** to verify that they make the robot move the same way.

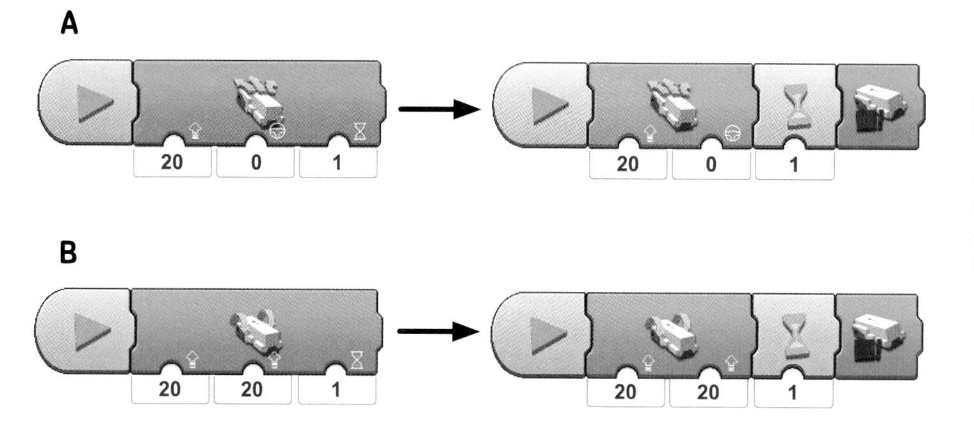

FIGURE 3-6 Drivebase Move Steering for Time blocks (A) and Drivebase Move Tank for Time blocks (B) are shortcuts that are equivalent to a Move Unlimited block followed by a Wait for Time block and a Stop block.

The **Wait for Time** block shown in **FIGURE 3-7** should pause the running of the program for 1.5 seconds. You can enter its parameter using the keypad. The lowest value you can input is `0.01`, a hundredth of a second. The highest value you can input is `9999.99` seconds, which is almost three hours (much longer than your Move Hub batteries will last).

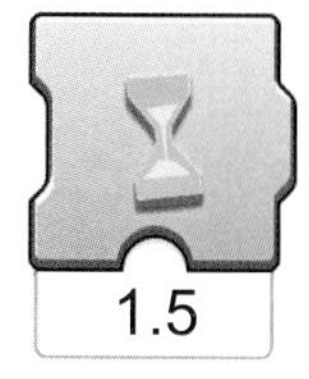

FIGURE 3-7 The Wait for Time block

what you've learned

In this chapter, you learned how to control a robot with two driving wheels, using either the **Drivebase Move Steering** block or the **Drivebase Move Tank** block. You also learned about the **Drivebase Move Steering Unlimited**, **Drivebase Move Tank Unlimited**, **Wait for Time**, and **Drivebase Stop** blocks. In Chapter 4, you'll learn how to tell a robot to drive for a precise distance, turn by a precise number of degrees, and repeat actions.

experiment 3-3

How should you change the Steering and Time parameters to make the robot spin counterclockwise by a quarter of a turn (90 degrees)?

4

moving your robot precisely

In this chapter, you'll use Motor blocks to turn the motors by a certain angle instead of for a certain amount of time. You'll learn what an angle is, how it's measured, how to use degrees to move your robot an exact distance, and how to steer it. Once you've finished this chapter, you should be able to control your robot's movements much more precisely!

rotation sensors

Sensors allow robots to be aware of the world around them, just like your senses tell you what's going on around you. A robot's sensors communicate their readings to the robot's processor (for BOOST, that's inside the Move Hub), just like your brain processes what you touch and smell.

The LEGO BOOST Move Hub has two built-in motors, each with a *rotation sensor* that lets you measure how much the motor turns. The external motor includes a rotation sensor, too. The rotation sensor measures the angle of a motor so that the Move Hub can precisely control the position and speed of the motors. Let's explore what that means for our robot.

the Drivebase Move Steering for Angle block

Let's look at the blocks that control motor behavior. **FIGURE 4-1** shows the **Drivebase Move Steering for Angle** block, which lets you control how far in degrees the motors should turn.

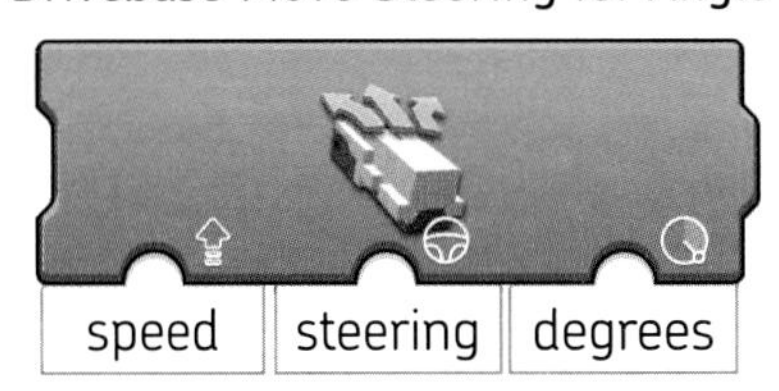

FIGURE 4-1 The Drivebase Move Steering for Angle block

Edit the Degrees input in the **Drivebase Move Steering for Angle** block by tapping the white label and entering the number of degrees you want the motor to turn. Use either the keypad or the dial to enter the number, as shown in **FIGURE 4-2**.

The examples in **FIGURE 4-2** show three different angles of rotation. The first angle on the left is 360 degrees, which represents a circle (or one full rotation). Notice that the counter in the center of the dial reads 1, for one complete rotation. The middle angle is 354 degrees, just 6 degrees shy of a full circle. The third angle on the right is 918 degrees, which means just a little more than two and a half rotations.

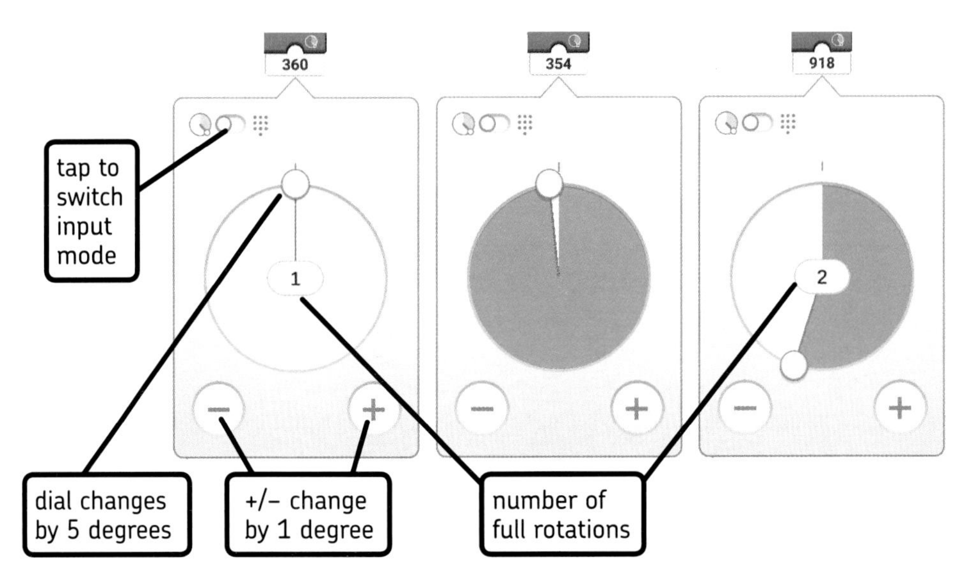

FIGURE 4-2 You can edit the Degrees input in one of two ways: using the numeric keypad or using the dial.

visualizing angles of rotation

Let's use MARIO to see how to use the Degrees input to control the robot's wheels. First, insert a peg in MARIO's wheel to make it easy to see how much the wheel has rotated (as shown in **FIGURE 4-3**). Now, before starting the program, manually rotate the wheel so that the peg is in the topmost position (the starting position) and hold the robot off the ground so it doesn't go anywhere.

FIGURE 4-3 Insert a peg into MARIO's wheel so you can track how the wheel spins.

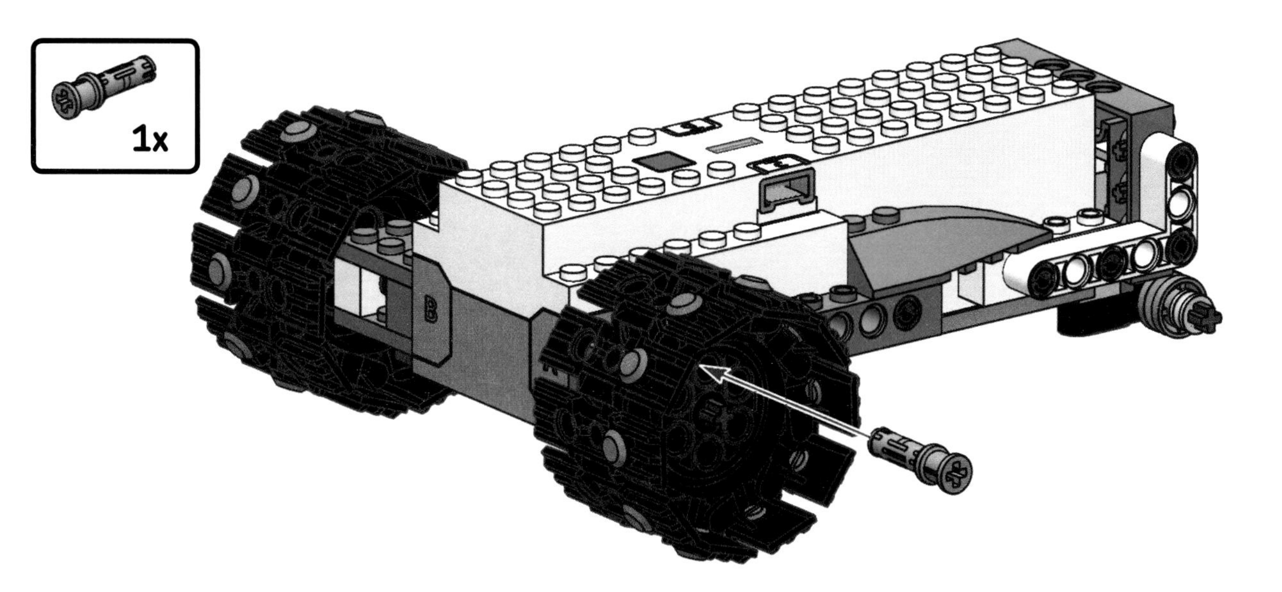

As you change the Degrees inputs, watch the position of the pin. Now, enter different values into the **Drivebase Move Steering for Angle** block's third input, as shown in **FIGURE 4-4**, to see how much the wheel rotates. For example, when you enter 360 degrees, the motor should go through a full rotation. A value of 180 should turn the motor halfway, and 90 should produce a quarter of a turn.

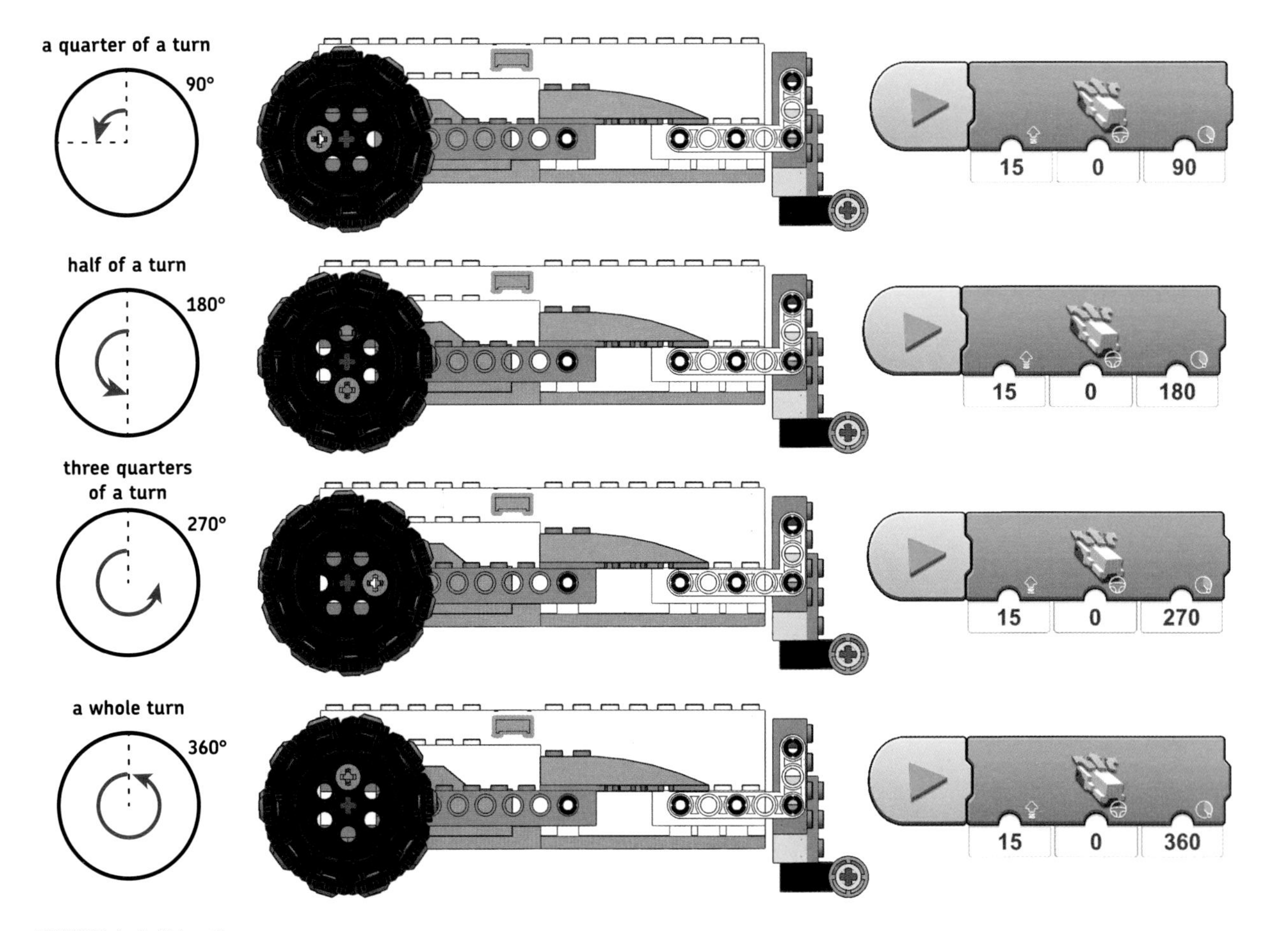

FIGURE 4-4 Using the Degrees input to control the rotation of the motor

moving a precise distance

We know how to use the Degrees input to tell the *motors* how much to turn, but that doesn't tell you how far the robot will actually *travel*. Say we want MARIO to move exactly one cell on the playmat, which is 157 mm (or 6.18 inches). How many degrees should the motor turn?

To answer this question, let's do a little math. **FIGURE 4-5** shows how to measure the wheel diameter, indicated by the letter *D*. It's 51 mm (2 inches). The distance we want the robot to travel is indicated by the letter *X*.

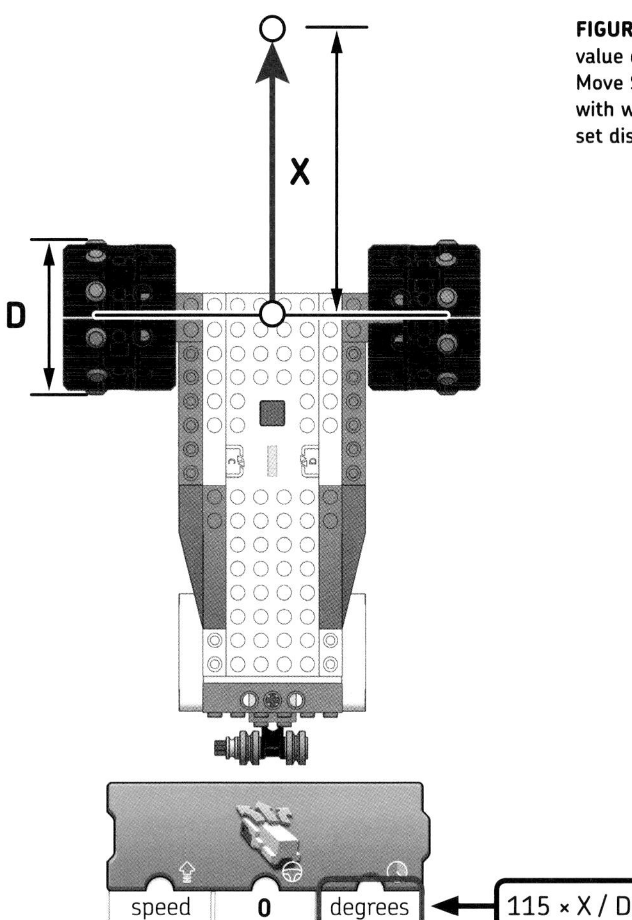

FIGURE 4-5 Use this formula to compute the value of the Degrees input of the Drivebase Move Steering for Angle block to make a robot with wheels of diameter *D* drive straight by a set distance *X*.

calculating the Degrees input to move precisely

Here's the formula to calculate the number of Degrees we should have the motors turn:

❶ motorDegrees = 115 × distanceToTravel / wheelDiameter

To find the value of the Degrees input to make MARIO travel any distance *X*, follow these steps, using **FIGURE 4-6** as reference:

Step 1: Multiply the distance to travel *X* (157 mm) by the constant number **115**. On the calculator, type **115 × 157**.

Step 2: Now, divide the resulting number by the wheel diameter *D*. On the calculator, continue typing **÷ 51** and press **=** to get the result, which is **354**, if you ignore decimals.

1 1 5 ×
1 5 7 ÷
5 1 =
354.01960

FIGURE 4-6 How to compute the Degrees input using a calculator

NOTE:
The formula works whether you measure the diameter D and the distance X in millimeters or inches, but you must use the same measurement unit for both dimensions.

To move MARIO by 157 mm, the motors have to rotate by 354 degrees. Test the program on the LEGO BOOST playmat, using the cell grid as reference. If the distance MARIO traveled was not exactly the size of a cell, you might have to fine-tune the value of the Degrees input. Conditions like bumpy or slippery ground might cause MARIO to not travel exactly the way you expect.

Try performing this calculation for other distances you want MARIO to travel! If you're using a robot with bigger or smaller wheels, they'll have a bigger or smaller diameter, but follow the same steps to calculate the degrees.

brain BOOSTer!

Where does the formula ❶ on page 35 come from? The figure below shows how we can measure the *diameter* of MARIO's wheels and then use that number to calculate their *circumference*.

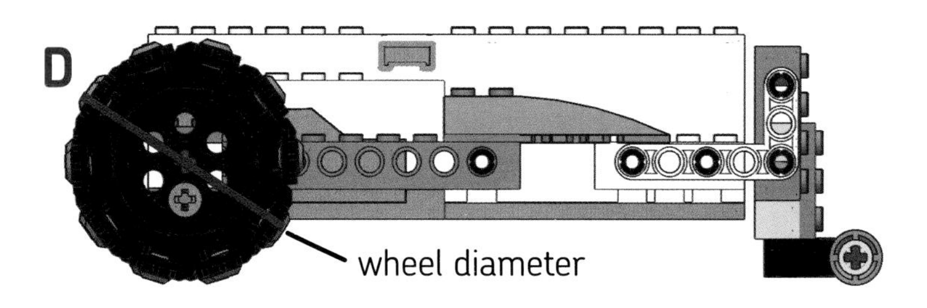

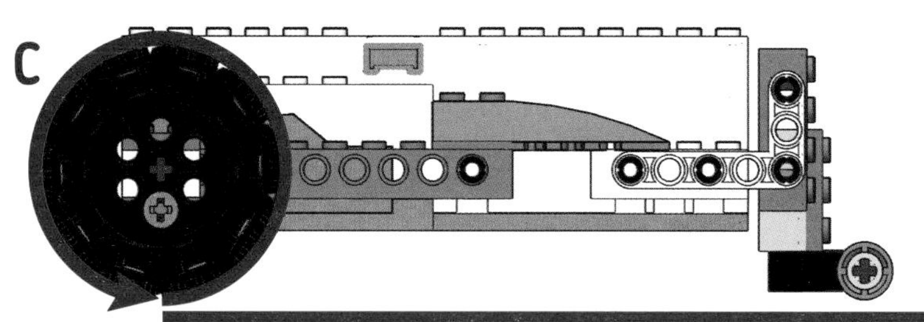

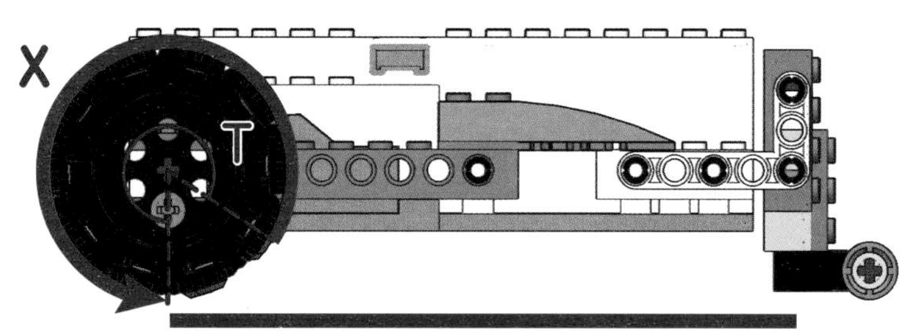

(continued)

Here's the equation we'll use, where C is the circumference, D is the diameter, and π (pi) is a constant approximately equal to 3.14.

$$C = \pi \times D$$

We measure the diameter as 51 mm. When we plug 51 for D into our equation, we discover that the wheel's circumference is 160 mm. This tells us that every time the robot's wheels travel 360 degrees, MARIO will move forward by 160 mm!

Let's make things a little more general so that we can calculate the degrees we would input to make MARIO travel any distance. Let's call the distance we want MARIO to travel X and call the degrees we need the motors to turn T. Now, let's set up a *proportion* comparing the degrees we tell the motors to turn and the distance MARIO goes. We know that inputting 360 degrees makes MARIO travel a distance equal to the circumference of the wheel ($\pi \times D$), so we'll put that relationship on the right and set it equal to T degrees over X distance:

$$\frac{T}{X} = \frac{360}{\pi \times D}$$

To get T, we multiply both sides by X:

$$T = X \times \frac{360}{\pi \times D}$$

Regrouping the terms, we get the final formula:

$$T = \frac{360}{\pi} \times \frac{X}{D}$$

The number 115 in the formula ❶ approximates the constant $360 / \pi$.

turning by a set angle

Let's use the **Drivebase Move Steering for Angle** block to make MARIO turn precisely. First, we'll program MARIO to make a right-angle turn by spinning in place (see **FIGURE 4-7**). Let D be the wheel diameter, and L be the distance between the points where wheels touch the ground. We need to determine the value of the Degrees that we need to input in order to make the robot turn by an angle A.

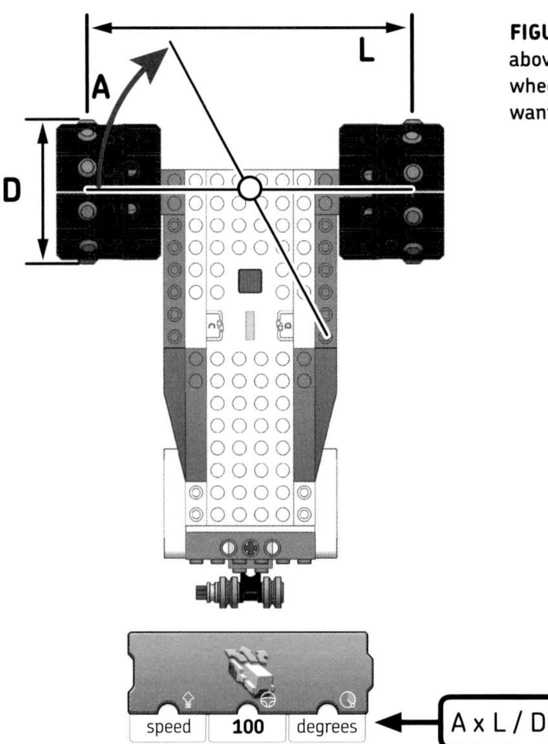

FIGURE 4-7 MARIO as shown from above, showing wheel diameter *D*, wheel distance *L*, and the angle we want the robot to turn, *A*

You can get *L* by measuring the distance between the points where the wheels touch ground (in this case, the rubber pads on opposite wheels). For MARIO, *L* is equal to 120 mm. The wheels diameter (including the rubber pads) is equal to 51 mm.

WARNING:

This formula ❷ works only with Steering input values set to 100 and 50. The formula works whether you measure the diameter D and the distance L in millimeters or inches, but you must use the same measurement unit for both dimensions.

calculating the Degrees input to turn precisely

For example, let's compute the Degrees input value to make MARIO turn by a quarter of turn, which corresponds to 90 degrees. Here's the formula to compute the Degrees input of the **Drivebase Move Steering for Angle** block:

❷ motorDegrees = angleToTurn × distanceBetweenWheels / wheelDiameter

To find the value of the Degrees input, follow these steps:

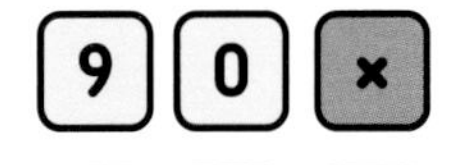

1 2 0 ÷

5 1 =

211.76470

Step 1: Multiply the angle to turn *A* by the distance between the wheels *L*. On the calculator, type `90 × 120`.

Step 2: Divide the result by the wheel diameter *D*. On the calculator, continue typing `÷ 51` and press `=` to get the result, which is about `212` when you round to the nearest integer.

Try performing this calculation for other angles you want MARIO to turn. To make your robot pivot on one wheel, set the Steering input to 50. To have it spin in place, set the Steering to 100. To turn or spin counterclockwise, either change the sign of the Steering input or the sign of the Degrees input.

brain BOOSTer!

How does the formula ❷ on page 38 compute the Degrees input for turning a precise angle work? The figure below shows MARIO turning angle *A* by pivoting on a stationary right wheel. The robot moves like this when you set the Steering input to 50. The result is the same as if the robot were spinning in place with the wheels turning in opposite directions by half the distance (as shown in **FIGURE 4-7**).

In the equations below, *D* is the diameter of MARIO's wheels, and *L* is the distance between the points where the wheels touch the ground.

Use this formula to compute the distance the wheel will travel, where *T* is the angle in degrees that the wheel turns:

$$Y = \frac{\pi}{360} \times D \times T$$

Use this formula to compute the arc length *K*, given the angle *A* in degrees and the radius of the circle *L*:

$$K = \frac{\pi}{360} \times A \times L$$

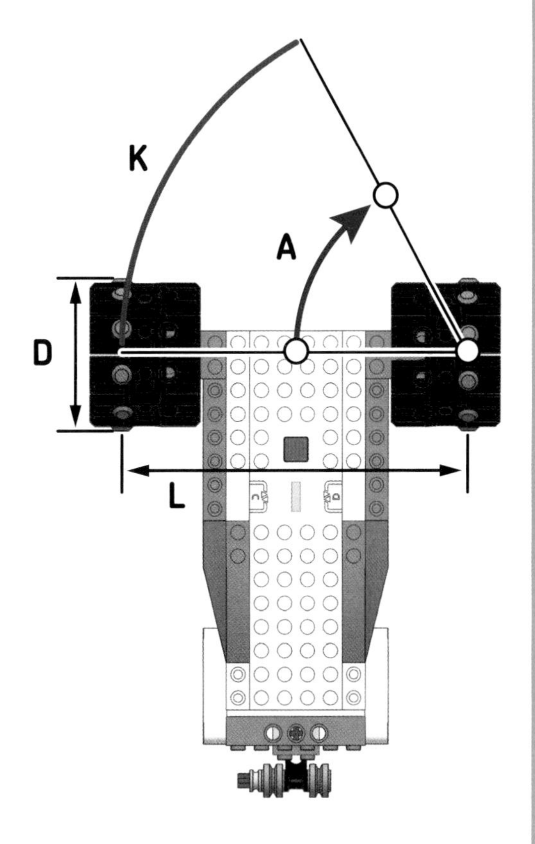

As you can see on the right, the length of the arc *K* must be equal to the path Y traveled by the left wheel. By making the values equal, we get:

$$\frac{\pi}{360} \times D \times T = \frac{\pi}{360} \times A \times L$$

Dividing both sides by (π / 360), we get this:

$$D \times T = A \times L$$

We want to compute *T*, the degrees the wheel should turn. To do so, we divide both sides by *D* to get the final formula, which is the same as formula ❷:

$$T = \frac{A \times L}{D}$$

why don't wheeled robots move exactly as expected?

If you've been playing around with MARIO and trying out these programs, you may have found that the robot doesn't always travel *exactly* the distance you calculated or turn at precisely the angle you expected. The real world is the reason, namely:

- *Friction* is the resistance when two objects rub against each other. Friction can be useful or a problem. On the one hand, friction allows you to grab things, and it's what holds LEGO bricks together. Robot wheels are usually equipped with rubber tires or other rubber elements that increase the grip on the ground (that is, increase the amount of friction) to help the robot push against the ground and move. On the other hand, friction can work against the robot's motion and result in a loss of energy. There's a bit of friction even when smooth objects rub against each other—for example, when LEGO axles turn inside Technic holes. Real-life robots use things like grease or ball bearings to minimize friction in their mechanisms.
- *Wheel slippage* happens when a wheel loses contact with the ground. The wheel keeps rotating, but the robot doesn't move. Even if slippage lasts only an instant, the robot's path will be affected. If just one wheel slips, the robot might not travel straight. If both wheels slip, the robot might not travel as far as you wanted it to.
- *Bumps* and uneven ground can also affect the robot's motion. When traveling across a bump, a wheel has to travel a slightly different distance than it would on a perfectly smooth surface.

NOTE:
Remember that these values are valid only for MARIO. If your robot has wheels that are a different size than MARIO's or has a different wheel distance, you have to compute new values using the formula ❷ on page 38.

TABLE 4-1 shows Degrees values corresponding to common MARIO turning maneuvers. For example, to make MARIO turn (180 degrees), set the Degrees input of the **Drivebase Move Steering for Angle** block to 424.

TABLE 4-1 degrees to input for common MARIO direction changes

DIRECTION CHANGE	DIRECTION CHANGE IN DEGREES	DEGREES INPUT VALUE
1/8 turn	45	106
1/4 turn	90	212
1/2 turn	180	424
3/4 turn	270	636
Full spin	360	848

what you've learned

In this chapter, you learned the math behind the number of degrees the robot's wheels should turn to make it move a precise amount. You can use the equations in this chapter to compute the Degrees input of the **Drivebase Move Steering for Angle** block to make any wheeled robot drive a set distance and turn by set angles.

5

repeating actions with loops

We'll explore loops in this chapter. You can use a loop to repeat a sequence of actions in your program to save time, make your program more efficient, or create different effects. You'll find the Loop blocks together with the Start blocks in the yellow tab on the Creative Canvas Palette.

traveling along a square path

Let's make MARIO travel along the square grid of the LEGO BOOST playmat, as shown in **FIGURE 5-1**. In order to travel along the square and return to where it started, MARIO has to move straight by 157 mm (6.18 inches) and turn right (90 degrees) four times. That means that we'll need to repeat a sequence of two blocks four times.

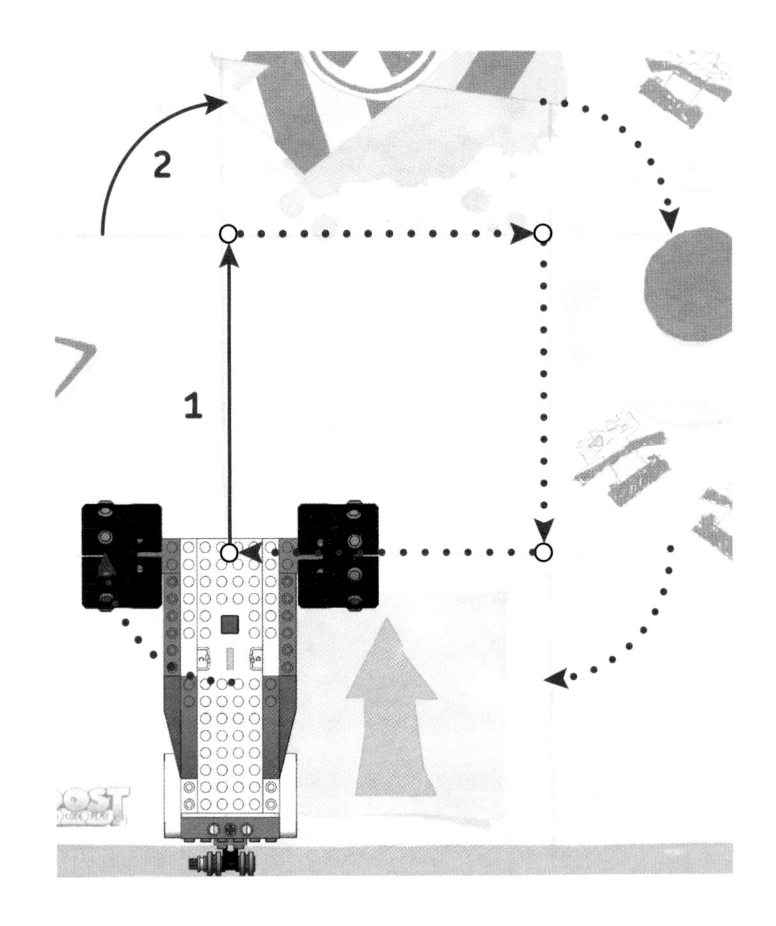

FIGURE 5-1 MARIO travels along a square path around the edge of a cell on the BOOST playmat.

To make your robot travel *straight* for 157 mm, you need a **Drivebase Move Steering for Angle** block with the Steering parameter set to 0 and the Degrees parameter set to 354. Then, to have it *turn* clockwise by a quarter of turn (or 90 degrees), you need another **Drivebase Move Steering for Angle** block with Steering set to 100 and Degrees set to 212.

Go ahead and make the program to have MARIO travel along the square grid of the BOOST playmat. **FIGURE 5-2** shows the solution. (Don't peek!)

As you can see in the figure, the complete program is very long. What if you had to repeat the same sequence, say, 10 times? That would be pretty annoying, but there is a better way. We'll use loop blocks!

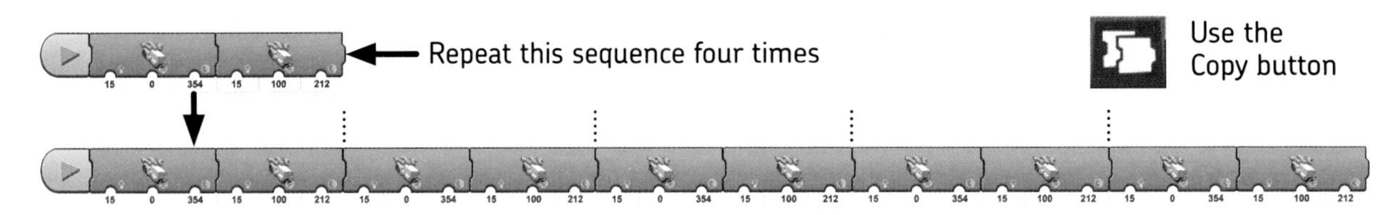

FIGURE 5-2 This program makes MARIO travel along a square path.

Loop blocks

There are three types of Loop blocks:

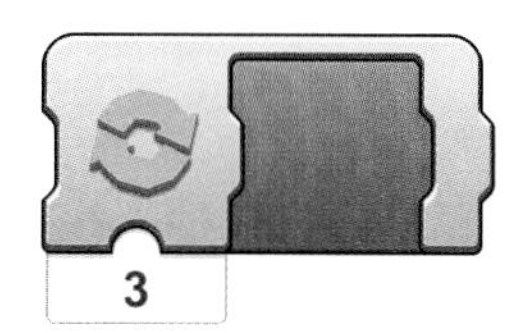

- The ***Loop for Count*** block repeats the inner sequence of blocks for the number of times specified.

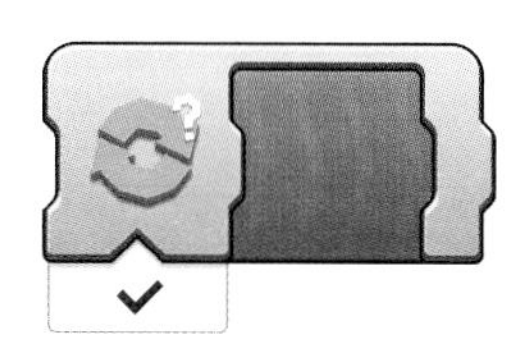

- The ***Loop While True*** block repeats the inner sequence while a condition is *true*.

- The ***Infinite Loop*** block repeats the inner sequence until the batteries run out or the program is stopped.

When you drag and drop sequences of blocks into a Loop block, the block will automatically change its size to accommodate the sequence you place inside it.

FIGURE 5-3 shows how we might use a Loop block in a program. The **Loop for Count** block shown repeats the base sequence of two Move blocks four times. Doesn't the resulting program look much better than the one shown in **FIGURE 5-2**?

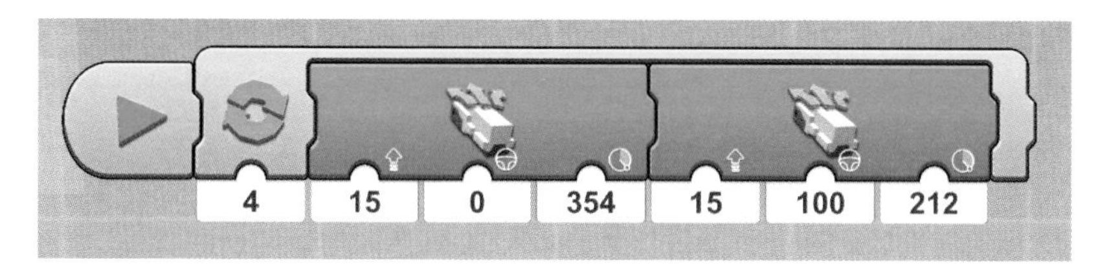

FIGURE 5-3 A program that uses a Loop block to make MARIO travel around a square cell of the BOOST playmat

experiment 5-1

Make MARIO patrol back and forth forever. Hint: Adapt the program shown in **FIGURE 5-2** and use an **Infinite Loop** block.

what you've learned

In this chapter, you learned how to use the Loop blocks to write programs to make your robot repeat actions. In Chapter 6, you'll give MARIO the ability to sense his environment by attaching the LEGO BOOST sensor to the LEGO BOOST Move Hub.

experiment 5-2

Make MARIO travel along a triangular path by copying and modifying the program shown in **FIGURE 5-3**. If you keep the side of the triangle 157 mm long, what Degrees input value for the Move block will make the robot turn, and how many times should the loop repeat? Hint: review how to make the robot turn by a precise number of degrees in Chapter 4.

experiment 5-3

Make MARIO travel along a hexagonal (six-sided) path by copying and modifying the program shown in **FIGURE 5-3**. Keeping the side of the hexagon 157 mm long, how should you change the Degrees input for the Move block to make the robot turn and how many times should the loop repeat?

6

"Hi, I'm an explorer!"

In this chapter, we'll attach the LEGO BOOST sensor to your robot, using a poseable, adjustable head that will allow you to point the sensor forward, sideways, or down, depending on the task at hand. You'll also learn how to make your robot react to what it senses, and how to make it play prerecorded sounds from the sound library and ones that you record yourself.

the LEGO BOOST sensor

The LEGO BOOST sensor (shown in **FIGURE 6-1**) detects distance and color, and can:

- Detect an object's relative distance to the sensor with values ranging from 0 (nearest) to 10 (farthest). (This number has no unit—it is not in centimeters or feet, for example.)
- Determine whether an object is present and detect the colors black, blue, green, yellow, red, and white.
- Measure the amount of light reflected by an object, returning a value from 0 (darkest) to 10 (lightest).
- Display a red, green, blue, or white light.

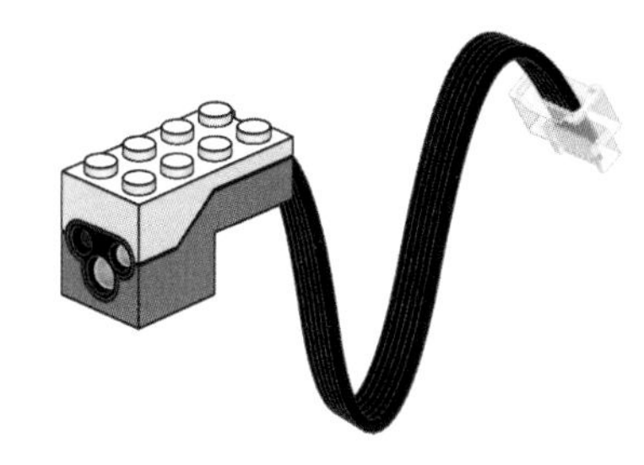

FIGURE 6-1 The LEGO BOOST sensor

building the sensor head

Follow the instructions below to build the sensor attachment for MARIO and attach it to port C of the Move Hub.

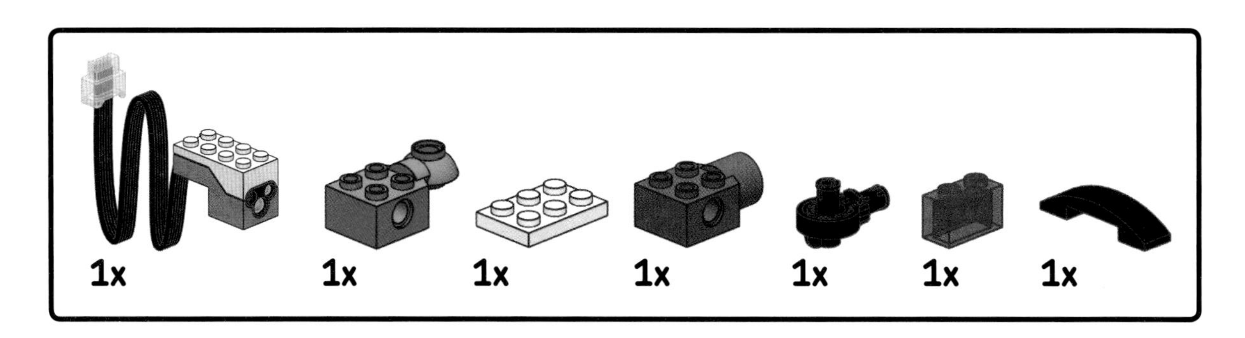

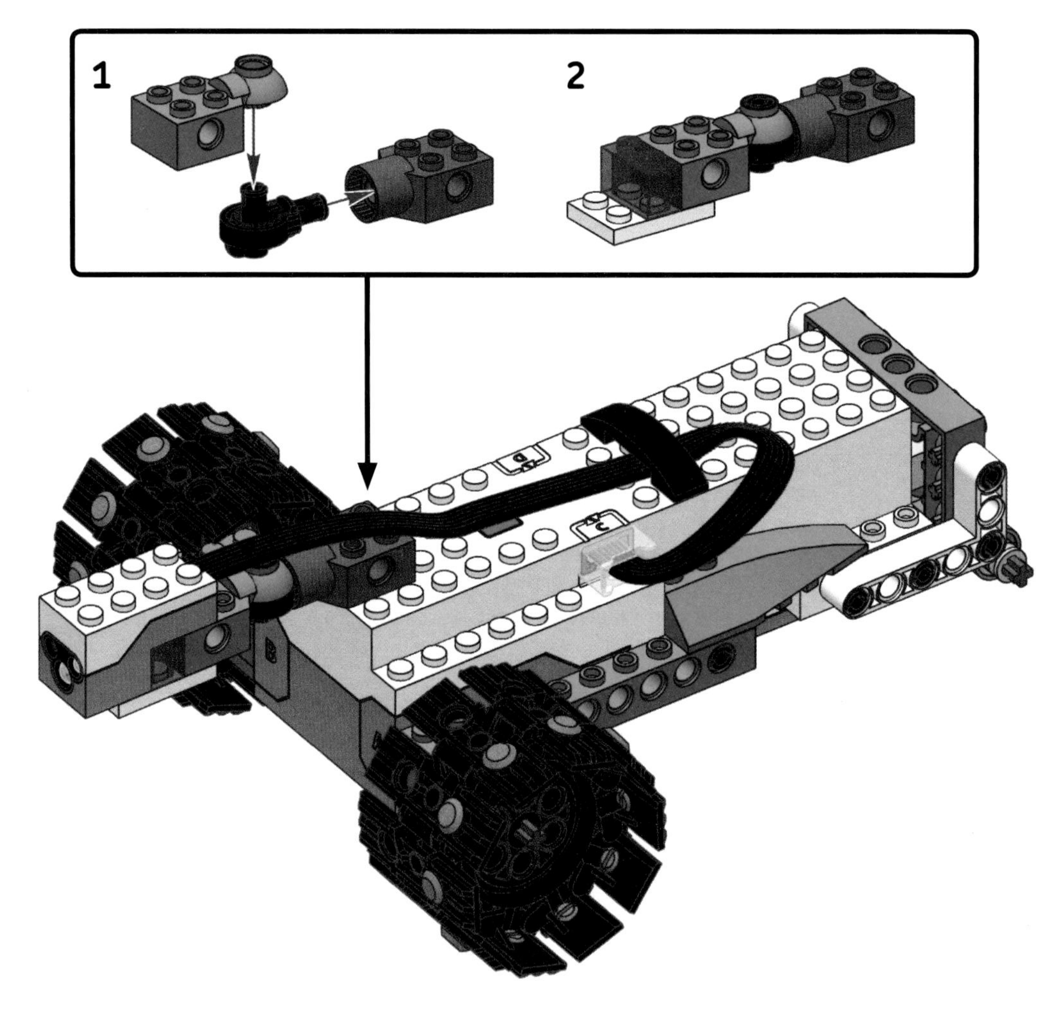

measure distance with Sensor blocks

The Sensor blocks let you measure distance to an object:

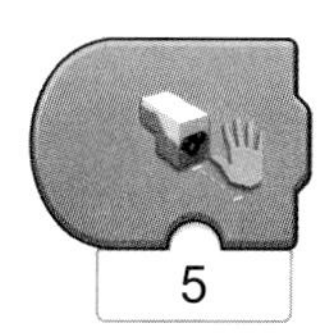

- When the **Trigger on Distance** block is placed at the beginning of a sequence, it executes the sequence whenever the sensor measures the distance to an object that is less than or equal to a number you specify (from 0 to 10).

- The **Wait for Distance** block pauses the program until the sensor measures the distance to an object as less than or equal to a number you specify (from 0 to 10).

- The **Sensor Distance Reporter** block returns the distance to an object as a number from 0 to 10 in real time. You can place this block anywhere on the canvas to monitor the distance to an object, but you can't place it directly into a programming sequence; it must be attached to the bottom of other blocks.

avoiding obstacles

In Chapter 3, you used the **Drivebase Move Steering for Time** block to program MARIO to move straight ahead for a certain amount of time. What if you want MARIO to explore a room? Say you want it to go straight until it detects an obstacle, maneuver to avoid it, and then repeat those actions. In this way, we can have MARIO make its way around a room, avoiding obstacles as it goes, rather than just moving ahead for a fixed amount of time.

The pseudocode for this program might look something like this:

```
Infinite loop begins
    Slowly move straight forward
    Wait for the sensor to measure a distance less than or equal to 5
    Go backward and turn for a set number of degrees
Go back to the start of the infinite loop
```

Let's try coding this program on the LEGO BOOST app's Creative Canvas. Create a new project and call it `explore`, and then make a program sequence like the one shown in **FIGURE 6-2**.

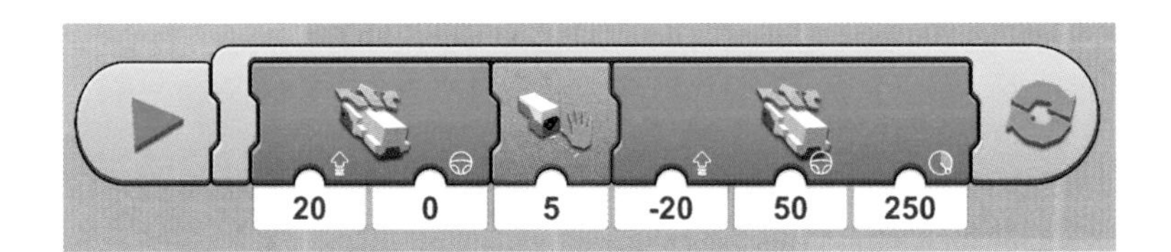

FIGURE 6-2 The obstacle avoidance program in the *explore* project

This program begins with a **Drivebase Move Steering Unlimited** block to make the robot drive forward (Steering at 0) at Speed 20. Next, we use the **Wait for Distance** block from the Sensor blocks palette (orange tab). This block pauses the sequence and asks, "Is the sensor measuring a distance less than or equal to 5?" When the answer to this question is *yes*, the program can continue. In essence, this Sensor block controls program's flow by pausing it until the condition becomes *true*. When this block lets the program continue, the **Drivebase Move Steering for Angle** block makes the robot turn to avoid the obstacle. Because it's included in an **Infinite Loop** block, this sequence is repeated forever.

Once you've built your program, start it by tapping the **Start Sequence** block, and you should see MARIO begin to explore the room while avoiding obstacles. Now, change the parameters of the **Wait for Distance** block to see how the robot's behavior changes. If you set the distance to 9, MARIO should change direction when the obstacle is far away. Setting the distance to 1 could be risky, as MARIO could react too late and hit the obstacle before turning. (Chapter 8 will show you how to use different conditions for more control.)

triggering actions

Use the **Trigger on Distance** block to make MARIO react to a particular sensor reading. The block looks like the Start block, and it starts a sequence of blocks when the sensor measures a distance less than or equal to a specific number. Let's test this out.

Create a project called `trigDist` and then build the sequence shown in **FIGURE 6-3**. Now, tap on the **Trigger on Distance** block, and it should start flashing. The robot shouldn't do anything until the sensor measures a distance less than or equal to 5.

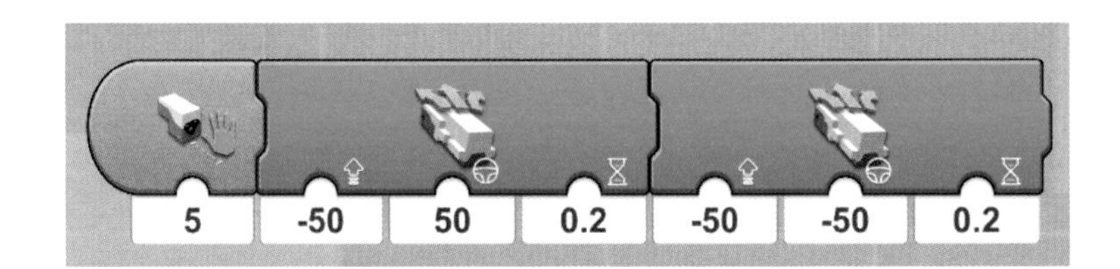

FIGURE 6-3 The sequence in the *trigDist* project begins with a Trigger on Distance block.

Next, place your hand in front of the sensor, and the **Trigger on Distance** block should flash. MARIO should now move backward two steps. If you keep your hand near the sensor, the sequence should be triggered again. If you hold your hand still, MARIO should move backward until it detects that the distance from your hand is greater than 5.

To stop the program, tap the red **Stop** button at the top right of the screen.

trigger conflicts

When two blocks or sequences try to control the motors in different ways, it creates a trigger conflict. Let's try a little experiment. Add another sequence to the Canvas, again starting with a **Trigger on Distance** block, but set the threshold to 2, as shown in **FIGURE 6-4** (sequence 2). Instead of having the robot back up, this sequence should move MARIO forward for 2 seconds.

When you start the program by tapping the green Start button, and if the sensor reads a value greater than 5, both **Trigger on Distance** blocks should start blinking, as you can see in the top part of **FIGURE 6-4**. Now, try placing your hand in front of the sensor so that it reads less than 5 but greater than 3. Only sequence 1 should execute, and MARIO should start to back up.

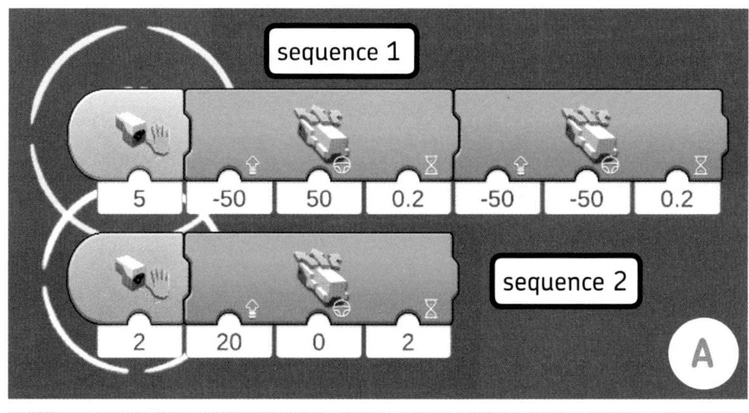

FIGURE 6-4 Sequence 1 and sequence 2 are trying to move the motors backward and forward at the same time, creating a conflict.

As you get closer to the robot, the sensor will read a value of 2 or less, activating both Trigger blocks at the same time, as shown in the lower part of **FIGURE 6-4.** This happens because the value read by the sensor satisfies both conditions: it's both less than or equal to 2 and less than 5.

This causes MARIO to behave strangely: it might go backward a little (sequence 1) and then go forward (sequence 2). To avoid this kind of conflict, don't place two **Trigger on Distance** blocks on the same canvas.

playing sounds

Making your LEGO BOOST play a sound is easy. (Your device that runs the BOOST app will actually play the sounds, since the Move Hub doesn't have speakers.) Use the Sound blocks to play one of over 500 prerecorded sounds in the BOOST sound library, or import and play your own recordings. You'll find the Sound blocks in the palette with the violet tab.

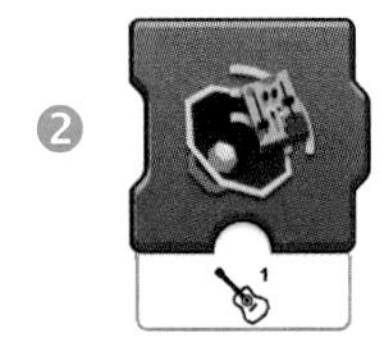

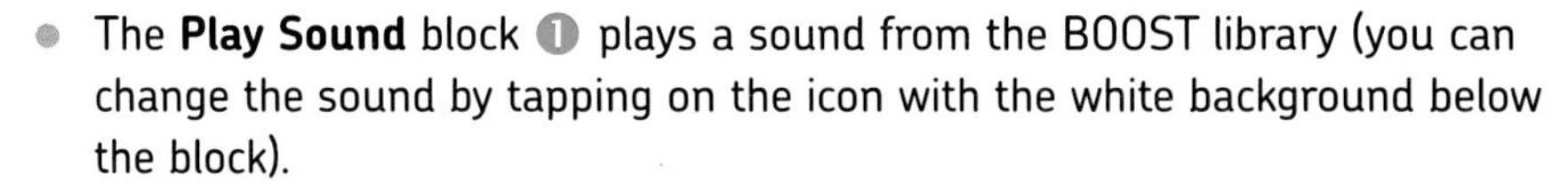

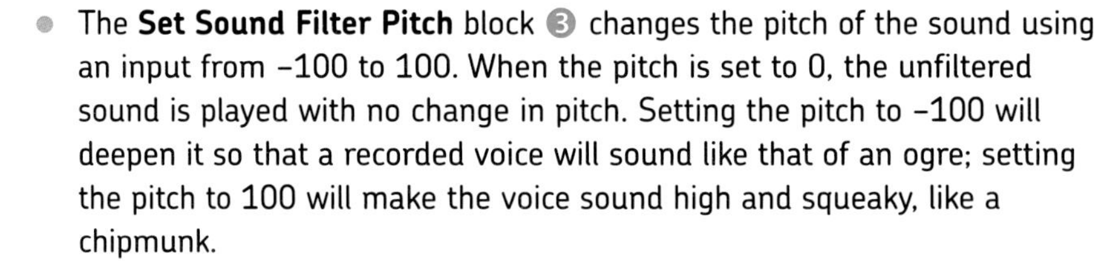

- The **Play Sound** block ❶ plays a sound from the BOOST library (you can change the sound by tapping on the icon with the white background below the block).
- The **Play Sound with Filters** block ❷ plays a sound from the BOOST library with filters applied.
- The **Set Sound Filter Pitch** block ❸ changes the pitch of the sound using an input from –100 to 100. When the pitch is set to 0, the unfiltered sound is played with no change in pitch. Setting the pitch to –100 will deepen it so that a recorded voice will sound like that of an ogre; setting the pitch to 100 will make the voice sound high and squeaky, like a chipmunk.
- The **Set Sound Filter Distortion** block ❹ controls the amount of distortion applied when a sound is played. When set to 0, there is no distortion. When set to 100, the played sound will be croaky and scratchy, like an electric guitar at full volume.
- The **Set Sound Filter Echo** block ❺ adds echo to a sound, with the volume decreasing each time the sound is played, just like a real echo. To control the delay between repetitions and how long it takes for the sound to fade away, enter a number from 0 to 100.
- The **Reset Sound Filter** block ❻ disables all applied filters.

testing sound effects

In this section, we'll play with the pitch, distortion, and the echo filters to give you a sense of their effects. Create a project called `filters` and then fill it with the sequences shown in **FIGURE 6-5**. Now, drop a **Play Sound** block onto each sequence. Change the sound by tapping on the block's input label to open the sound library and choose a sound.

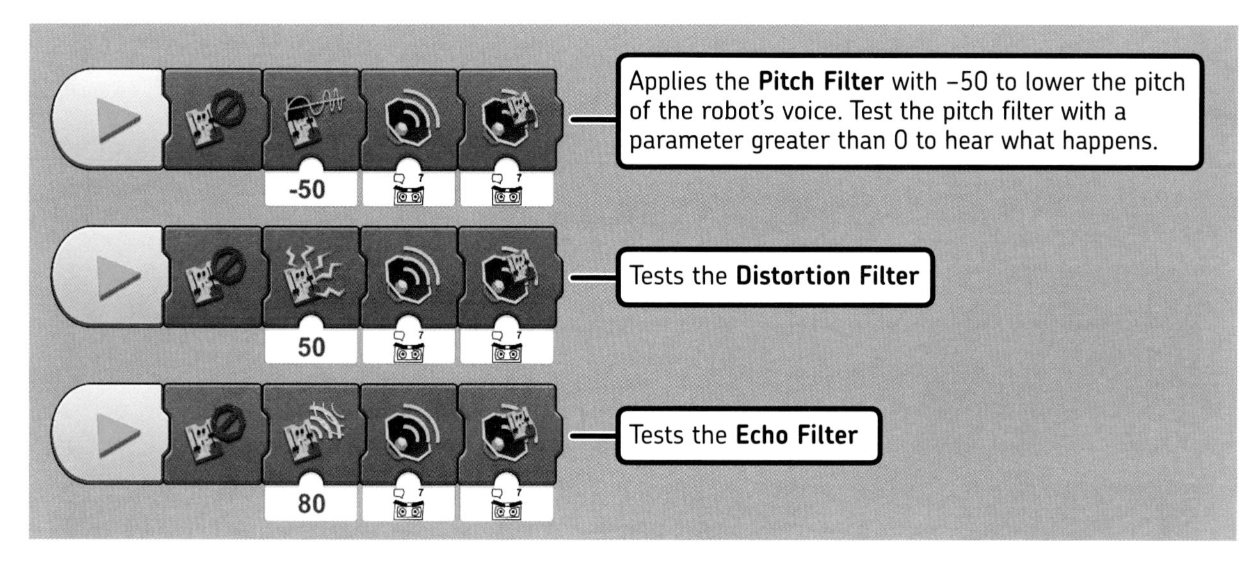

FIGURE 6-5 With this program, you can test all the sound effects.

Tap each **Start Sequence** block to hear how the filters produce various sound effects. To have only one filter active at a time, place a **Reset Sound Filter** block at the beginning of each sequence.

A **Play Sound** block in each sequence plays the sound from the library without filters, and a **Play Sound with Filters** block plays it with the current filters applied.

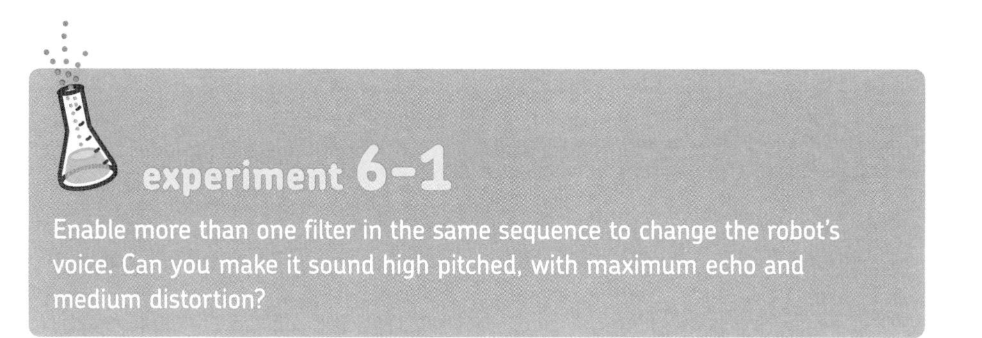

experiment 6-1

Enable more than one filter in the same sequence to change the robot's voice. Can you make it sound high pitched, with maximum echo and medium distortion?

triggering a sound

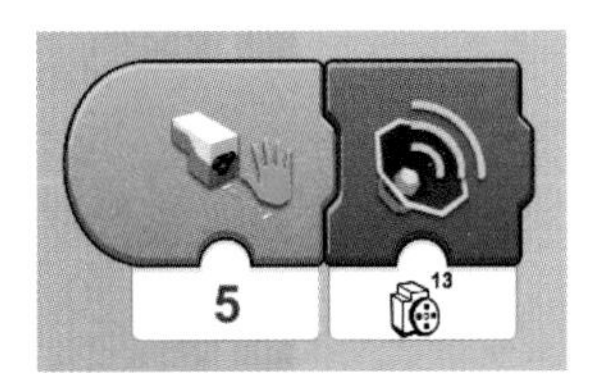

FIGURE 6-6 This sequence plays a motor sound when the sensor reads a distance less than or equal to 5.

Let's make MARIO react to changes reported by the distance sensor by playing a sound. Create a project called **sounds** and then fill it with the simple sequence shown in **FIGURE 6-6**. The **Trigger on Distance** block will execute the **Play Sound** block when the sensor reports a distance less than or equal to 5.

Once you drop the **Play Sound** block onto the sequence, change the sound played by the block by tapping on its label to open the sound library. Select the **Motor sounds** category and then choose sound number **13** ( ).

To test your program to see whether a change in an object's distance from the sensor will trigger a sound, start the program, put your hand in front of the sensor, and you should hear a motor sound. If you don't move your hand, the sound should loop. Notice that the program waits for the **Play Sound** block to finish playing the sound before continuing.

Change the sound and have fun exploring the vast sound library included with the BOOST app!

recording sounds

In addition to playing sounds from BOOST's library, you can record your own voice and use it to make your creation talk! Follow these steps to make a recording that will have MARIO introduce itself when you approach.

1: Tap the blue tab with the microphone icon in the Blocks palette (**FIGURE 6-7**). This is the **Custom Sounds** palette.

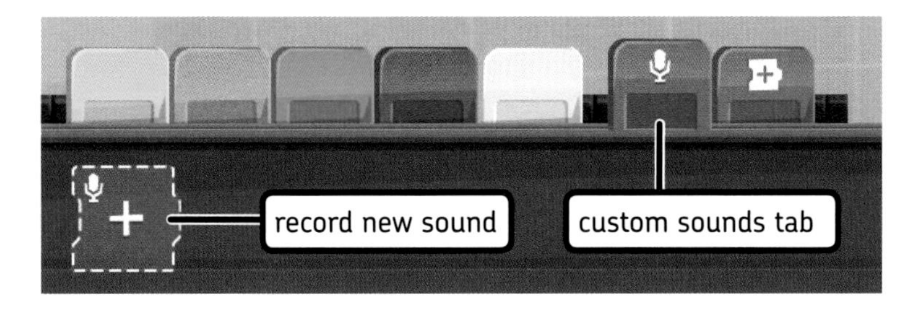

FIGURE 6-7 The Custom Sounds palette

2: Tap the icon with the plus sign and the one with the microphone to open the sound-recording interface as shown in **FIGURE 6-8**.

3: Tap the **Record** button and say, "It's me, Mario!" You can record up to about six seconds of sound. When you've finished your recording, tap the **Stop** button.

4: Play the sound using the **Play** and **Stop** buttons. If you're not happy with it, tap **Record** to record it again.

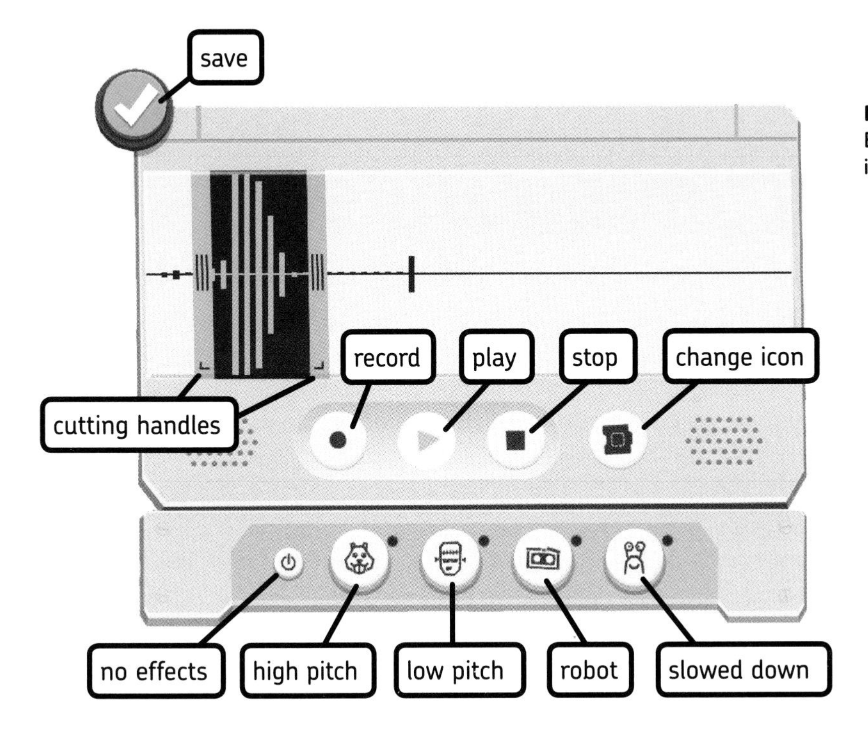

FIGURE 6-8 The LEGO BOOST sound-recording interface

5: Once you like the sound, you can drag the **cutting handles** to shorten the sound, removing unwanted heading and trailing noise from the sound.

6: Use the buttons at the bottom of the sound-recording interface to apply effects to your sound. You can have only one effect active at a time. Here's what those effects do:

- No effects: plays the original recorded sound without applying any effect.
- The high- and low-pitch buttons make a sound sound higher or lower, like a chipmunk or a monster.
- The robot button makes the sound metallic, like an old-school robot.
- Slowed down makes a sound very slow and low pitched.

7: Tap the **high pitch** button to enable that effect.

8: Use the **change icon** button to change the icon for your custom sound block. Clicking the button should open the icon library. Select the **Loudspeaker** icon to make the block look as shown in **FIGURE 6-9**.

9: Tap **Save** to save your sound and return to the programming canvas. Complete your program by attaching your newly created Sound block to a **Trigger on Distance** block, as shown in **FIGURE 6-9**. If you have an old Sound block on your canvas, delete it by dragging it down to the Blocks palette and then attach the new Sound block to the Trigger block.

10: To complete your program, tap the **Trigger on Distance** block to enable it to check for distance sensor values. When you put your hand in front of it, MARIO should now say the phrase that you recorded.

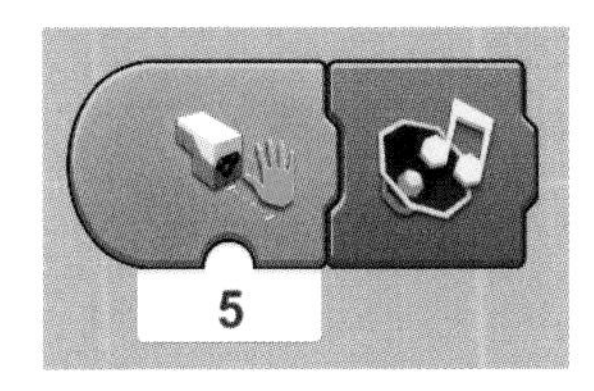

FIGURE 6-9 The program that makes MARIO say a greeting when you approach

editing and deleting custom sounds

To edit or delete a Custom Sound block, tap on its icon in the Custom Sounds palette to select it and then modify or delete it from the Sound Recording interface.

Before you can delete a Custom Sound block, you must delete all of its instances from the program first. The Trash Can icon shown in **FIGURE 6-10** will tell you whether you can delete a block. If a block is being used somewhere in the program, the Trash Can icon is faded (as shown in **FIGURE 6-10**), and the block cannot be deleted.

If the block can be deleted, the Trash Can icon should be bright red, and you should be able to delete it by tapping the Trash Can. When you tap the Trash Can, it should turn green. Tap it again to delete the block or tap anywhere else to cancel deletion.

WARNING!

Deleting a block is an action that cannot be undone, so be careful.

FIGURE 6-10 Use the Trash Can icon to delete a Sound block. The faded Trash Can means that the block is used in the program and can't be deleted. Red means you can delete the block. The Trash Can turns green once you tap it. Tap it again to delete the block.

what you've learned

In this chapter, you learned how to use the Sensor blocks to detect and respond to an object close by or to trigger a sequence of actions. You learned how to play sounds from the sound library, apply effects to them, and record and play your own custom sounds. In Chapter 7, you'll learn how to use color detection.

experiment 6-2

How about trying to give MARIO some personality? Can you make him look annoyed by having him turn his back on you when you approach? Build a program to give it this behavior. Hint: use the **Trigger on Distance** block and Move blocks.

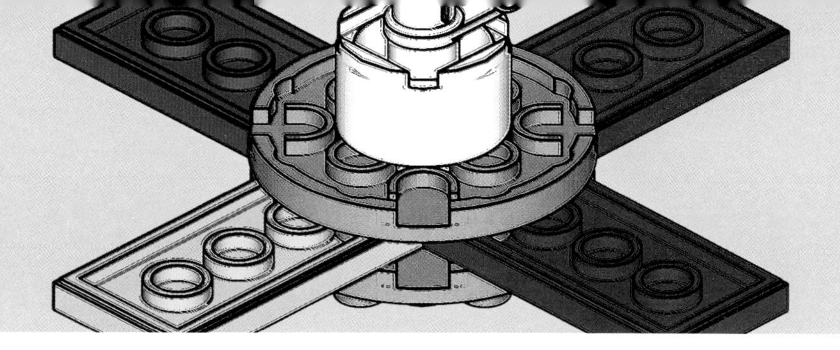

7

detecting colors

In this chapter, you'll learn how to give MARIO commands by showing colored tiles to the BOOST sensor.

color detection tips

The LEGO BOOST sensor can detect six colors (black, blue, green, yellow, red, white, and *no color*, which means no object is detected) as long as the object is really close to the sensor. How close? As shown in **FIGURE 7-1**, objects must be within 0.3 cm to 2 cm (0.1 to 0.8 inches). The object's face also has to be at a right angle to the sensor.

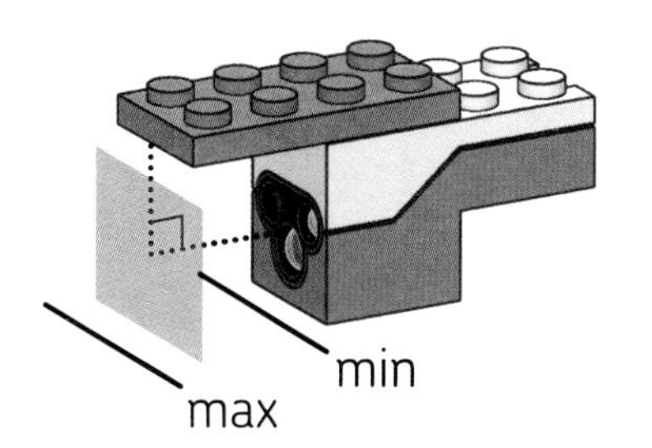

FIGURE 7-1 The BOOST sensor can detect the color of objects placed close to and at a right angle to the color sensor. (That's about 0.5 to 2.5 LEGO units as you can see, using the orange plate on top of the sensor as reference.)

If an object is outside the range of the sensor, its color may not be detected correctly. A white object might be detected as yellow, for example.

Color Sensor blocks

There are three types of Color Sensor blocks:

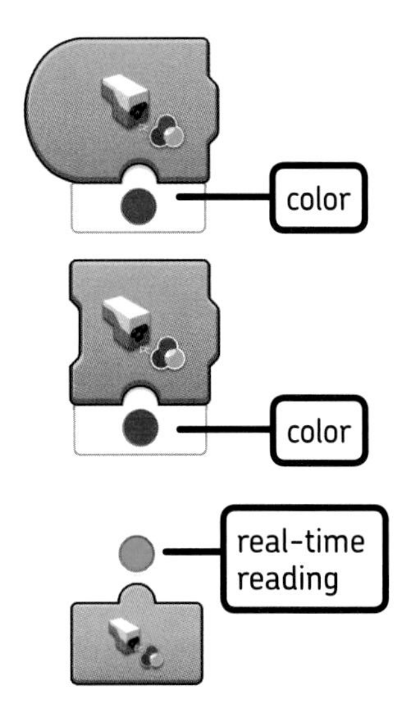

- When placed at the beginning of a sequence, the **Trigger on Color** block (orange) executes the sequence when the sensor detects a specific color.
- The **Wait for Color** block pauses the program until the sensor detects a specific color.
- The **Sensor Color Reporter** block reports the color detected by the sensor. You can place this block anywhere on the canvas and directly into a programming sequence to monitor detected colors in real time, but it must be attached to the bottom of other blocks.

Tap on the color label of a Color block to choose another color, as shown below.

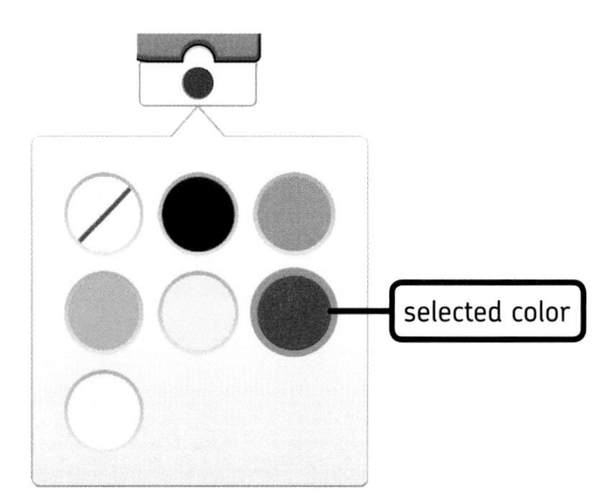

building the Color Controller

The following building instructions will show you how to assemble the Color Controller, which we'll use to control MARIO with its colored tiles.

1

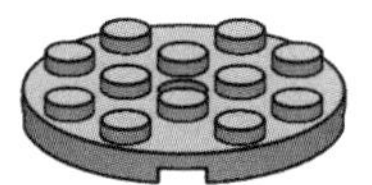

1x

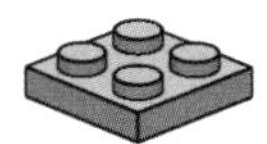

1x

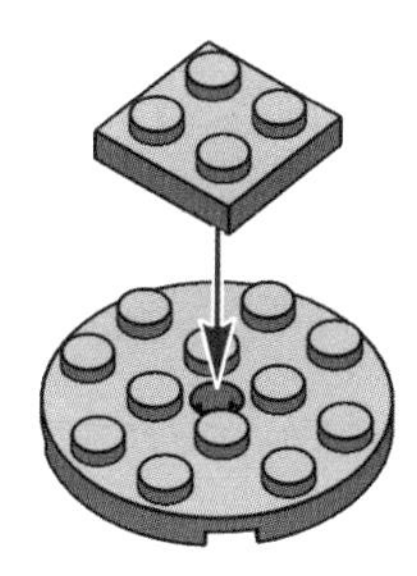

2

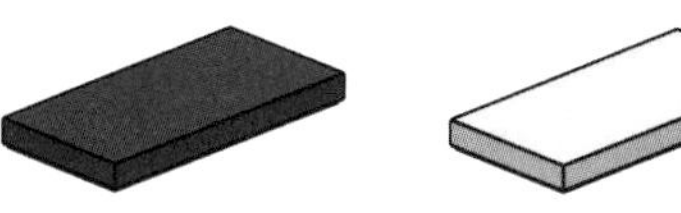

1x 1x

1x 1x

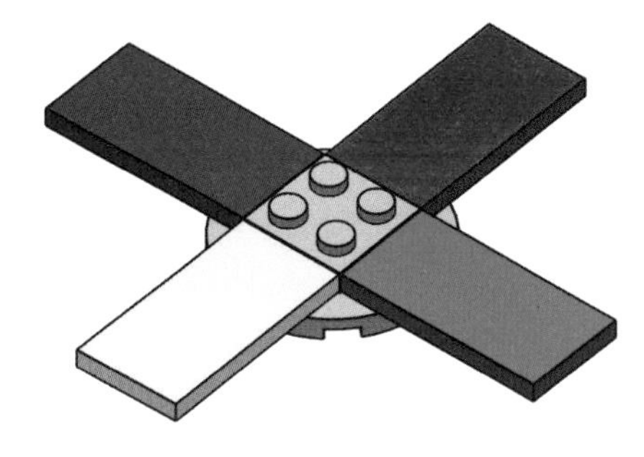

3

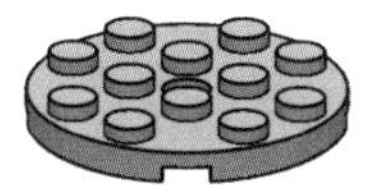

1x

1x

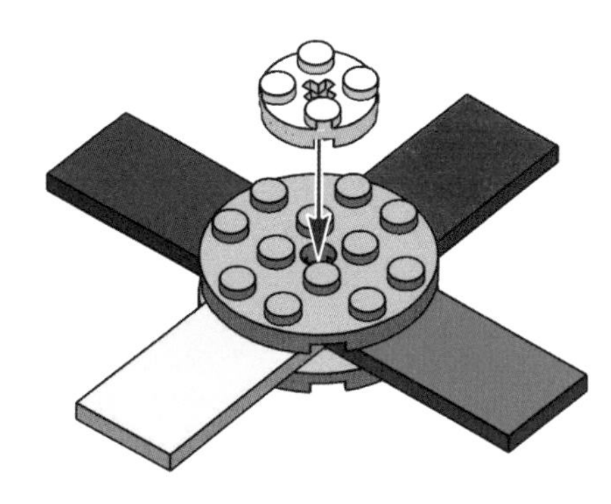

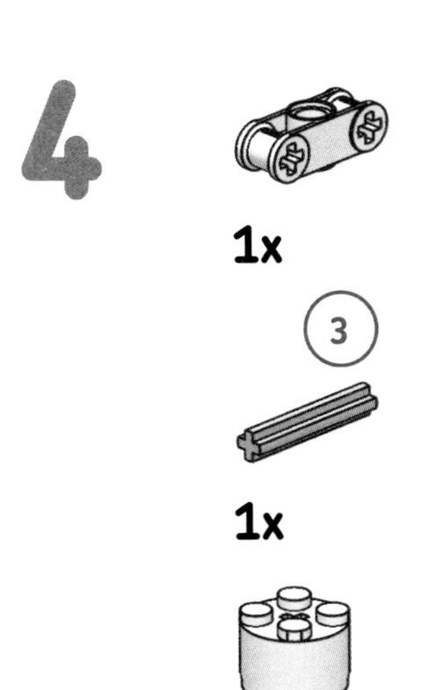

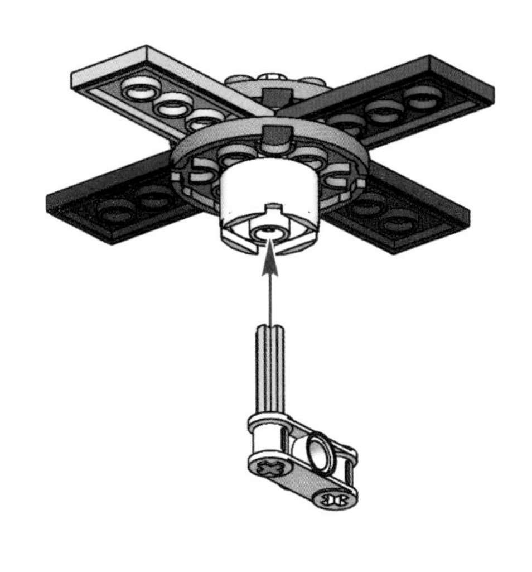

Flip up the poseable sensor head that you built in Chapter 6 to make it easy to show the robot a color.

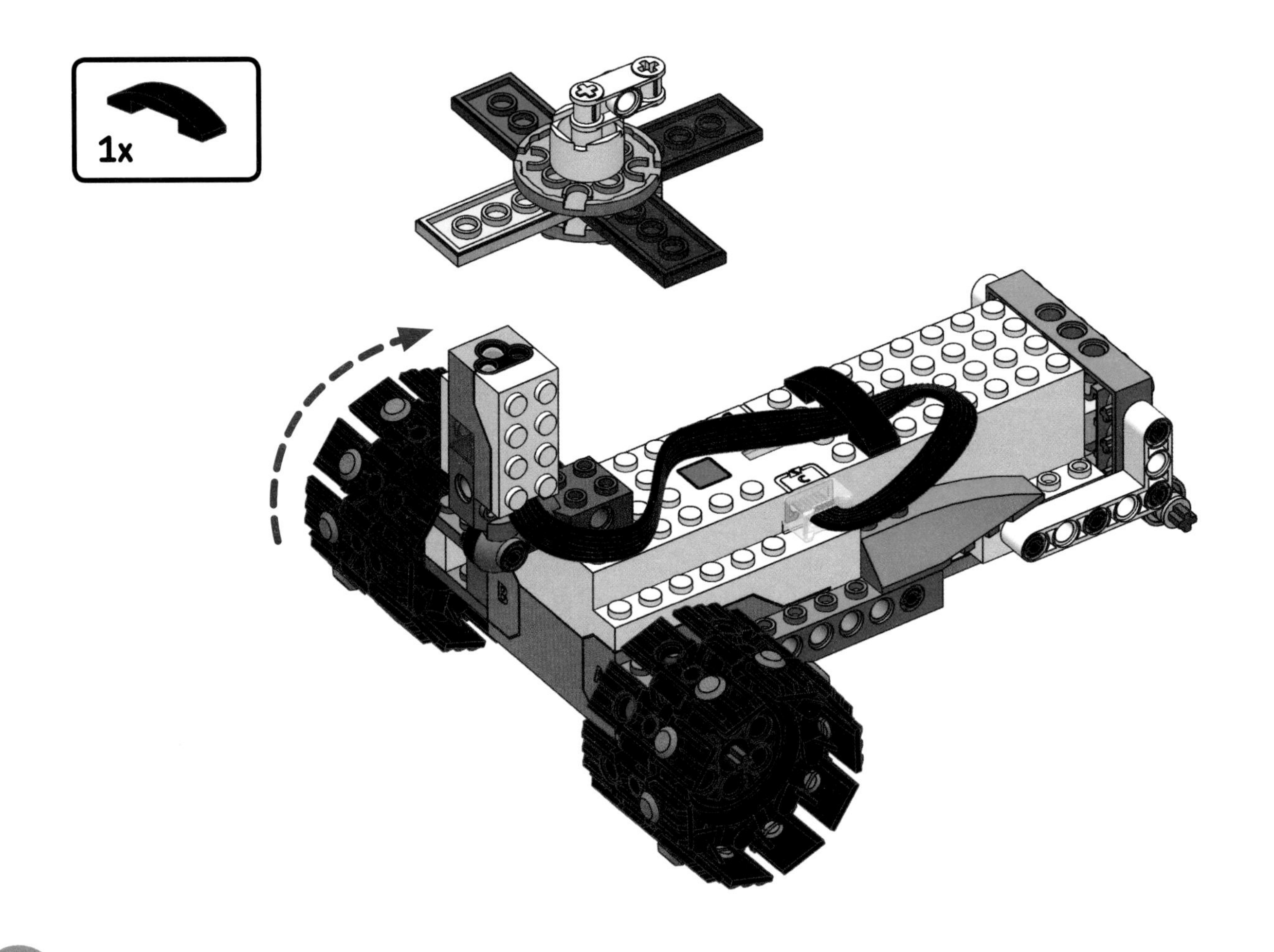

experiment 7-1

Let's place a **Sensor Color Reporter** block on the canvas to see the color that's detected in real time. Build the test rig shown below, attach a LEGO 2x4 colored tile, and check to see whether the sensor correctly detects the color of the tile by moving it around within the sensor's range. Now, answer these questions.

- Which colors are correctly detected even at relatively long distances?
- Which color can be correctly detected only within the 0.3 cm to 2 cm range?

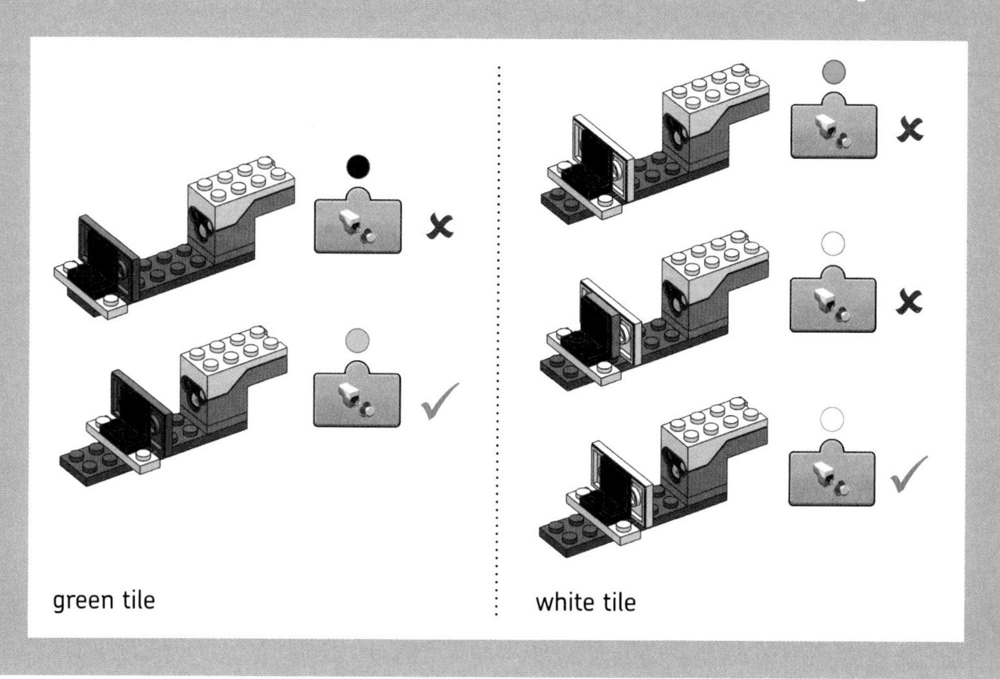

color commands

In this section, we'll create a program that will allow us to use our Color Controller to command MARIO to move across the BOOST playmat. **TABLE 7-1** shows a list of available colors and the commands we'll attach to them. For example, to make MARIO advance by one cell, we'll show the yellow tile of the Color Controller to the sensor. To have MARIO make a quarter turn to the right, we'll show it the green tile.

TABLE 7-1 color commands

COLOR	COMMAND
yellow	go forward one cell
red	go backward one cell
green	spin right by a quarter turn
blue	spin left by a quarter turn

program description

Create a project called `colorCmd` and then fill it with the program shown in **FIGURE 7-2**. I've noted the color of each block here.

- The **Trigger on Color** and **Wait for Color** blocks (orange) belong to the Sensor blocks palette.
- The **Wait for Time** block (yellow) belongs to the Flow Control blocks palette.
- The **Drivebase Move Steering for Angle** blocks (green) belong to the Motor blocks palette.

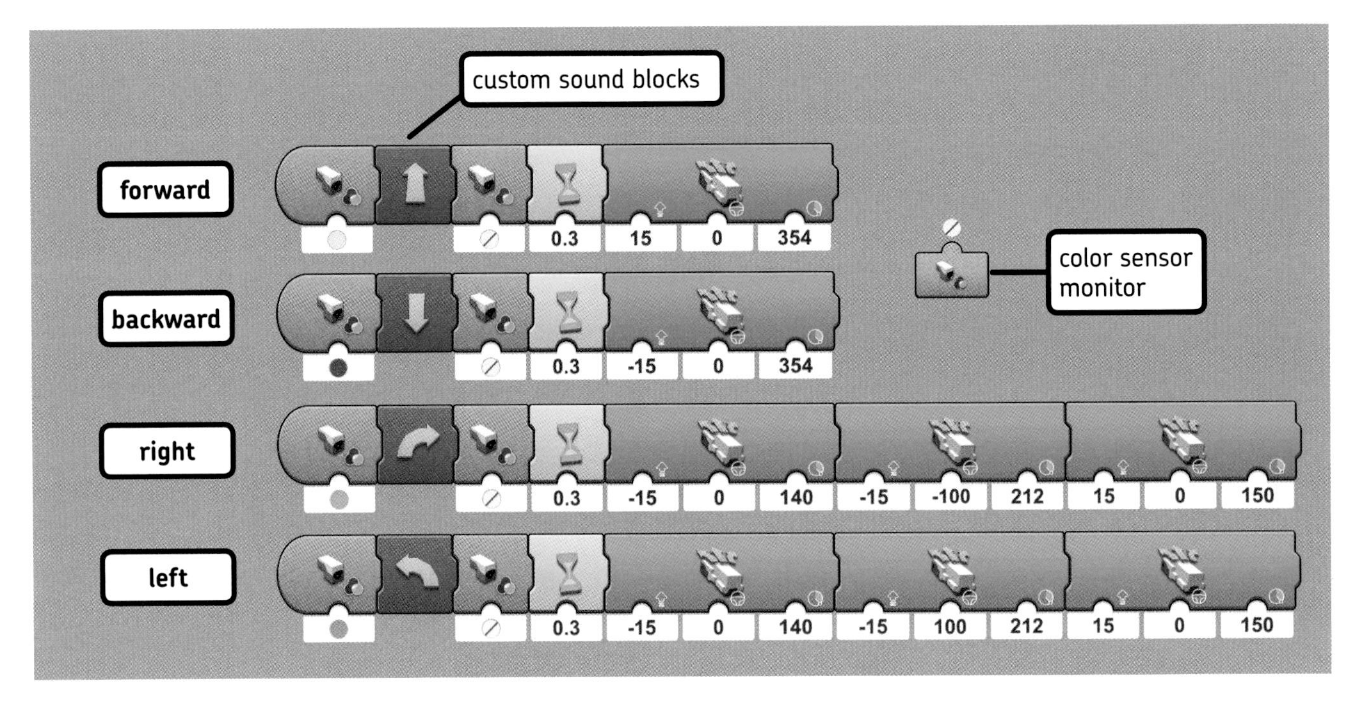

FIGURE 7-2 The *colorCmd* program shows the function of each sequence as triggered by the colors yellow, red, green, and blue, from top to bottom.

Notice in this code that there is no yellow **Start** block. All of the sequences begin with a **Trigger on Color** block whose color input differs for each sequence. We use the purple custom Sound block to have MARIO announce the action it will perform when it detects a specific color. Once a color is detected, MARIO should announce the action it will perform. Placing this Sound block in the program makes MARIO tell you when it "sees" the color. When you hear the sound, you can move the Color Controller away from the sensor. The **Wait for Color** block will detect when you do this, waiting for the sensor to read *no color*.

We use the **Wait for Time** block (set to 0.3 seconds) to make sure MARIO doesn't detect the wrong color while the Color Controller is being moved away. When you move the Color Controller away, the **Drivebase Move Steering for Angle** blocks run.

recording custom sounds

Each sequence starts with a custom Sound block. Try recording four custom sounds, saying “forward,” “backward,” “turn left,” and “turn right,” and then attach them to each movement (using the Movements category in the icons library), as shown in **FIGURE 7-3**. (See page 54 in Chapter 6.) To make MARIO sound a bit funnier, apply the high-pitch effect.

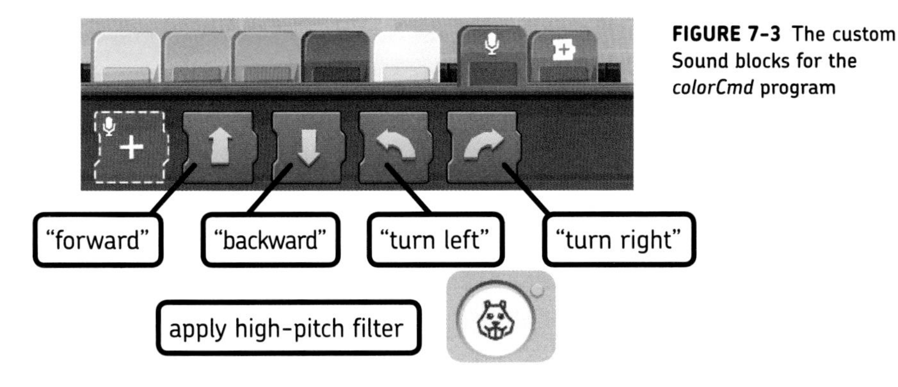

FIGURE 7-3 The custom Sound blocks for the *colorCmd* program

testing the program

After the program is complete, tap the green **Play** button to start it, and all of the **Trigger on Color** blocks should start blinking. Now, when you show the Color Controller tiles to the sensor, the corresponding Trigger block should flash and execute the sequence.

Once the program is running, try to use color to have MARIO reach the objects drawn on the LEGO BOOST playmat. For example, to reach the banana from the starting point (see **FIGURE 7-4**), MARIO should perform the following actions:

```
forward, forward, forward, forward, turn left, forward
```

These movements correspond to this color sequence:

```
yellow, yellow, yellow, yellow, blue, yellow
```

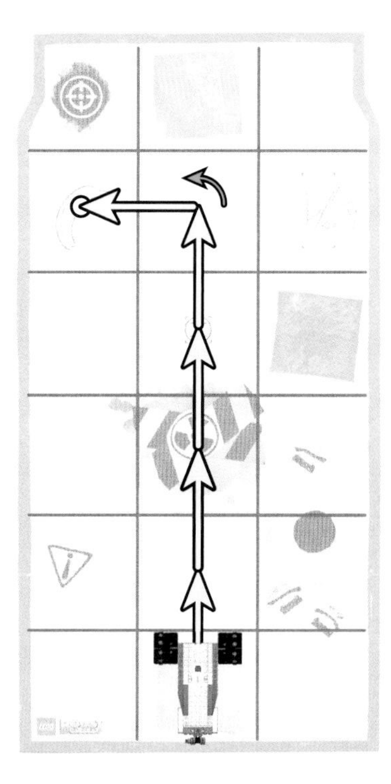

FIGURE 7-4 A mission on the BOOST playmat: reach the banana!

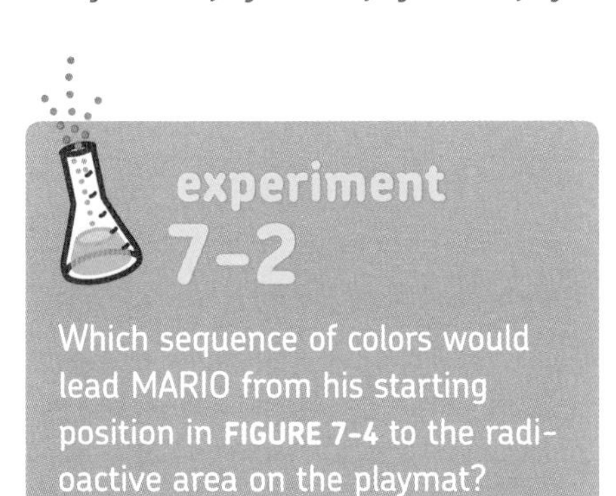

experiment 7-2

Which sequence of colors would lead MARIO from his starting position in **FIGURE 7-4** to the radioactive area on the playmat?

experiment 7-3

Which sequence of colors would lead MARIO to the fire on the playmat? What about the blue area?

what you've learned

In this chapter, you learned how to use color with the BOOST color sensor and our Color Controller to move MARIO across the playmat. In Chapter 8, you'll see how your robot can choose actions based on sensor readings.

experiment 7-4

Make a new program to have the robot say the name of the color it sees. Hint: record the color names and play them using custom Sound blocks as in the program shown in **FIGURE 7-3**.

PART II

intermediate techniques

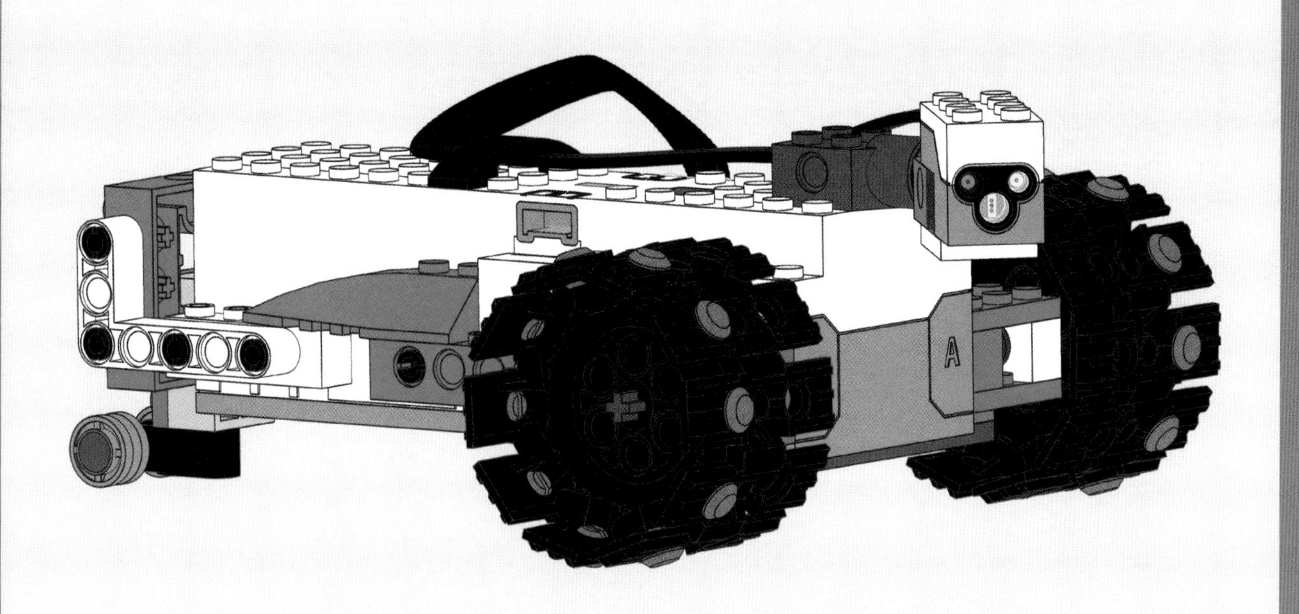

8

a line-following robot

In this chapter, you'll use the LEGO BOOST sensor to allow MARIO to follow a dark line on a light background. This is called line-following, and it's a true classic in robot programming!

a simple approach to robot navigation

The easiest way to program a robot to navigate from one point to another is to have it travel along a predetermined path by following a line on the ground. Line-following robots can follow painted lines on the ground by detecting them with cameras or by following metallic wires embedded in the pavement, which they detect with magnetic sensors. In fact, the LEGO Group itself uses robots like these in its factory!

MARIO can follow a line on the floor by using its sensor in a downward-pointing orientation. The sensor emits light and then senses the light reflected back from the surface. You can use either a dark line set against a light background or a light line on a dark background, but no matter what you choose, it must have enough contrast with the background. One simple way to create paths is to attach some black tape to a light floor or to print thick black paths on white paper.

the Switch block

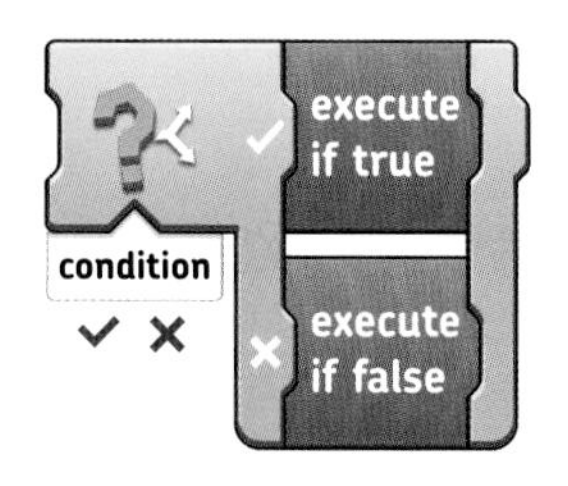

FIGURE 8-1 The Switch block

Some brainy folks have proven that every program can be written using only three main structures: *sequences*, *loops*, and *choices*. We already know how to make sequences of actions and how to repeat them in a loop. It's time to learn how to make your robot make choices based on certain conditions in its environment. A *condition* is like a yes or no question ("Is the distance read by the sensor less than 5?"). You can program your robot to do different things based on the answer to this question.

The **Switch** block in the Flow Control blocks palette (the yellow tab as shown in **FIGURE 8-1**) runs the top sequence of blocks in a program if a condition is true or the bottom sequence if the condition is false. In other words, this block allows your robot to appear to choose what to do based on whether or not a condition is met.

To better understand how the **Switch** block works, let's talk about *logic values* (also called *Boolean values*).

understanding data types

You use two kinds of data in the LEGO BOOST app: *numbers* and *logic values*. You used numbers with the Move and Sensor blocks. Logic values are ones that can only be *true* (✓) or *false* (✗). For example, consider the question "Is the sensor reading a distance less than 4?" If the sensor is reading 3, the answer is yes (✓). Otherwise, the answer is no (✗).

Unlike the rounded shape of numeric inputs ( ), the logic-based Switch block input is triangular shaped ( ), as you can see in **FIGURE 8-1**.

the Compare blocks

The *Compare* blocks compare two numbers and return a logic value of true or false. You'll find them in the *Math blocks palette* (white tab). For example, the **Compare Less Than** block compares two numbers and answers yes (✓) or no (✗) to this question:

```
Is the first number less than the second one?
```

Compare block inputs can be either a constant (a number that does not change its value) or the output of an orange Sensor block. For example, you might write a program that uses output from one block as input to a Compare block so that your robot can make a decision based on a certain condition. Here's a description of each type of Compare block.

- The **Compare Equal** block returns true (✔) if the inputs are the same. Otherwise, it returns false (✖).
- The **Compare Less Than** block returns true (✔) if the value of the first input is less than the value of the second input. For example, $3 < 3$ returns false, because 3 is equal to and not less than 3.
- The **Compare Greater Than** block returns true (✔) if the value of the first input is greater than the value of the second one. For example, $3 > 3$ returns false, because 3 is equal to and not greater than 3.
- The **Compare Not Equal** block returns true (✔) if the inputs are different. Otherwise, it returns false (✖).

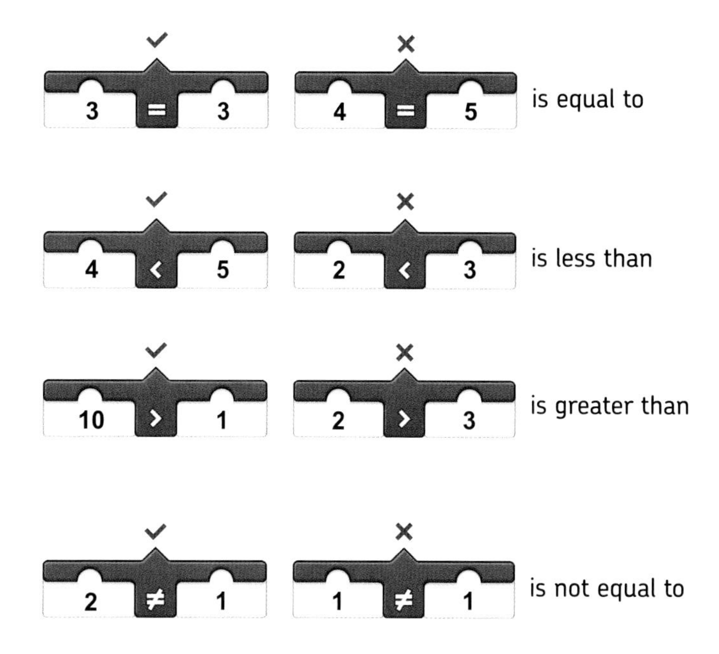

MARIO: line-following version

MARIO is ready to follow lines on the ground! Flip the sensor to look down (see **FIGURE 8-2**).

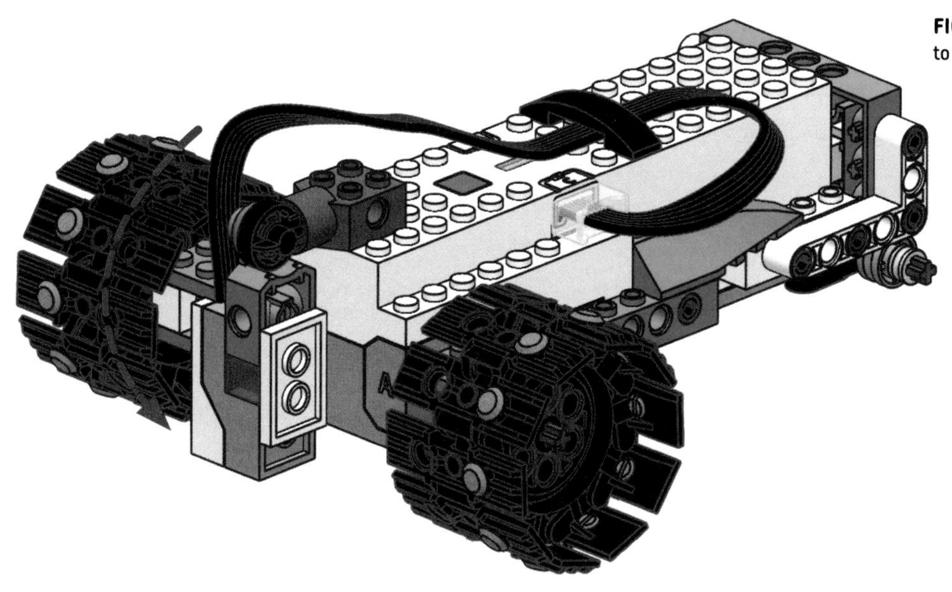

FIGURE 8-2 MARIO configured to follow lines on the ground.

line-following with one switch block

Think of the robot as following the boundary between light and dark, as shown in **FIGURE 8-3**. As the robot moves forward, it turns toward the dark line if the sensor sees a light color (**A**) or toward the light ground if the sensor sees a dark color (**B**). The result is a zigzagging motion along the right edge of the line (**C**).

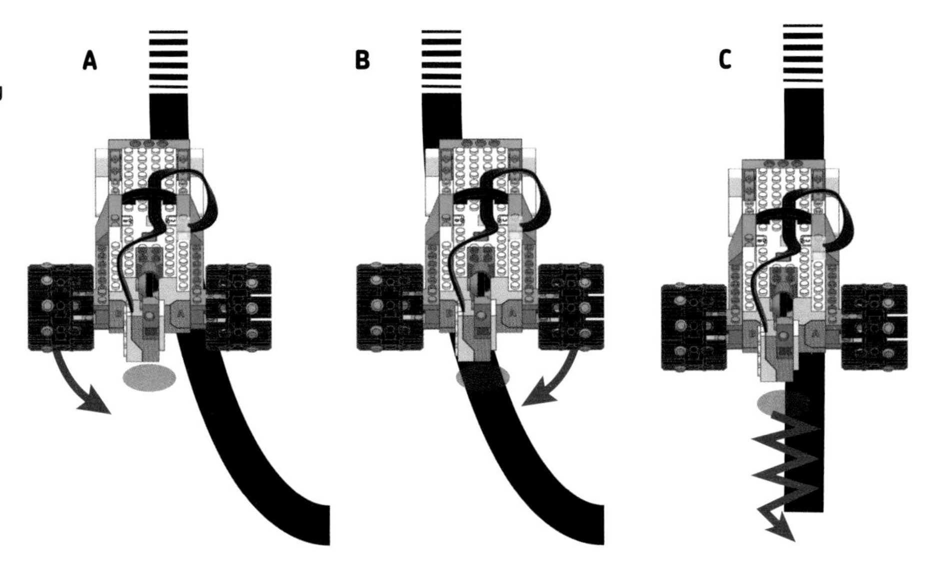

FIGURE 8-3 MARIO travels a zigzag path as it follows a dark line on a light surface by making a series of decisions.

This is the pseudocode for the line-following program:

```
Infinite loop begins
   If the sensor sees dark, then
      advance curving right (away from the line)
   Else
      advance curving left (toward the line)
Go back to the start of the infinite loop
```

FIGURE 8-4 shows how to turn our pseudocode into a line-following program in the LEGO BOOST app.

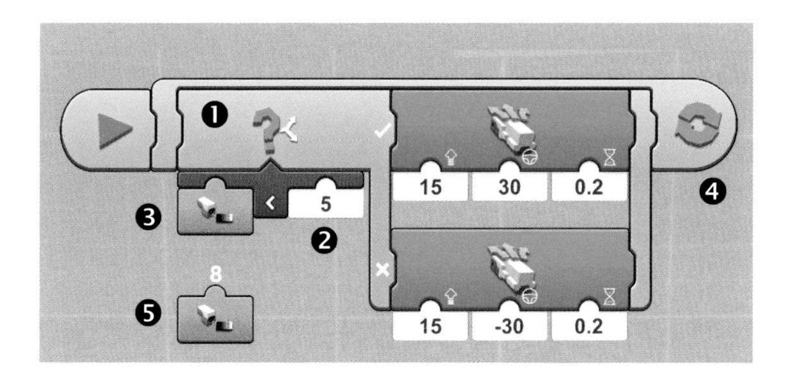

FIGURE 8-4 A simple line-following program

As you can see, this program uses a **Switch** block ❶ to decide whether the robot should curve left or right. A **Compare Less Than** block ❷ provides the condition for the Switch block. The **Compare Less Than** block compares the output of the **Sensor Light Level Reporter** block ❸ to the number 5. We'll call this number a *threshold*, because it's the value that we compare against the sensor reading for the condition to be met. The name is the same as the bottom of a doorway that you must cross to enter a place.

The **Switch** block is placed inside an **Infinite Loop** block ❹, which runs the sequence until you stop the program. Below the sequence, a copy of the **Sensor Light Level Reporter** block ❺ shows the value of the sensor in real time, a feature that will help when testing your robot.

The BOOST sensor measures the amount of light reflected by objects, returning a value from 0 (darkest) to 10 (lightest). Place the sensor on the edge of the line and set the value of the second input of the Compare block (the threshold value) equal to the value read by the sensor. A value of 5 should work, but just try a different value if it doesn't work.

Try changing the Speed, Steering, and Time inputs of the Drivebase Move blocks to see how the robot's line-following performance changes. Be careful! If you make the Speed value too high, MARIO may lose track of the line.

problems with communication delay

When you test out MARIO with this program, you'll find that his movement is a bit jerky because the **Drivebase Move Steering for Time** block brakes the motors after each movement. To make the robot's movement smoother, you could try using the **Drivebase Move Steering Unlimited** blocks instead by updating the steering to occur every 100 ms, as you can see in **FIGURE 8-5**.

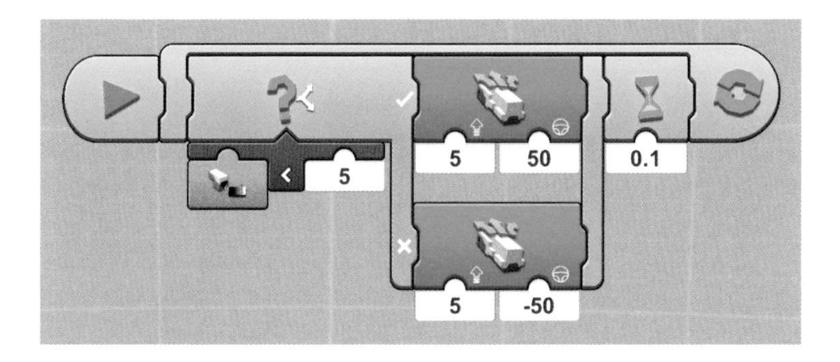

FIGURE 8-5 This line-following program does not work as intended because of slow communication over Bluetooth between the app and the Move Hub.

This program works in theory, but not in practice because the delay in Bluetooth communication between the app and the Move Hub is too high. The sensor readings come too late, which means the motor speed commands are sent too late, as illustrated in **FIGURE 8-6**.

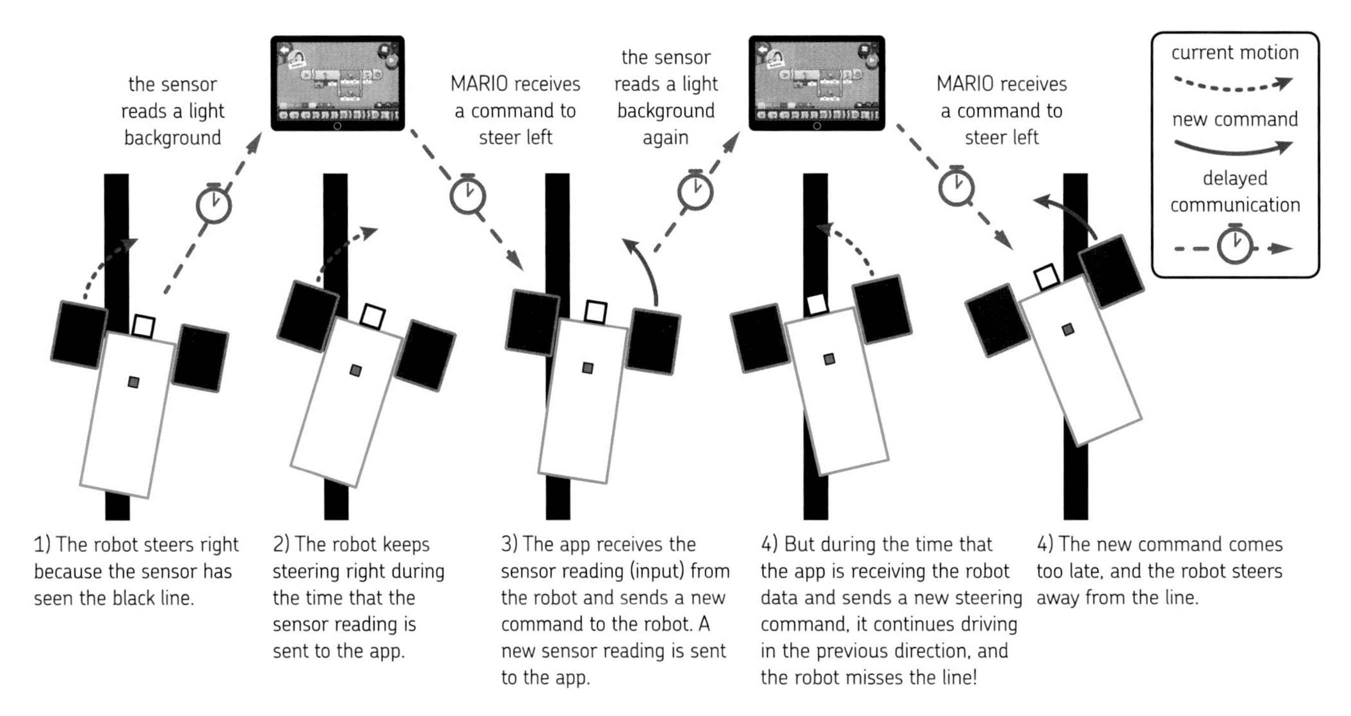

FIGURE 8-6 **The delay in communication between the robot and the app controlling it might cause the robot to lose the line.**

As you can see in **FIGURE 8-6**, these delays prevent the robot from keeping track of the line because, by the time new commands come in, the robot will have already veered off the path. Not even using the BOOST's lowest speed setting will completely solve the problem.

improving line-following with Switch blocks

In our current program shown in **FIGURE 8-4**, we determine whether the sensor is seeing the dark line by checking to see if its reading is below the threshold value 5. This time, we'll add code to respond to grey as well, which is a combination of the black line and the light background that the sensor sees when the robot is right on the edge of the black line. (The combination of colors results from the fact that the sensor measures a small area, not just a single point.) In other words, when the robot's sensor sees grey, it means it's on the edge of the line, and we can tell it to keep going straight instead of correcting its direction—thus making it go faster overall.

To handle three cases (light, dark, and grey), our revised program will need two conditions. Here's the pseudocode for the improved line-following program:

```
Infinite loop begins
   If the sensor sees dark, then
      advance curving right (away from the line)
   Else
      If the sensor sees very light, then
         advance curving left (toward the line)
      Else
         Go straight
      EndIf
   EndIf
Go back to the start of the infinite loop
```

FIGURE 8-7 shows how we can use two **Switch** blocks to handle these three conditions.

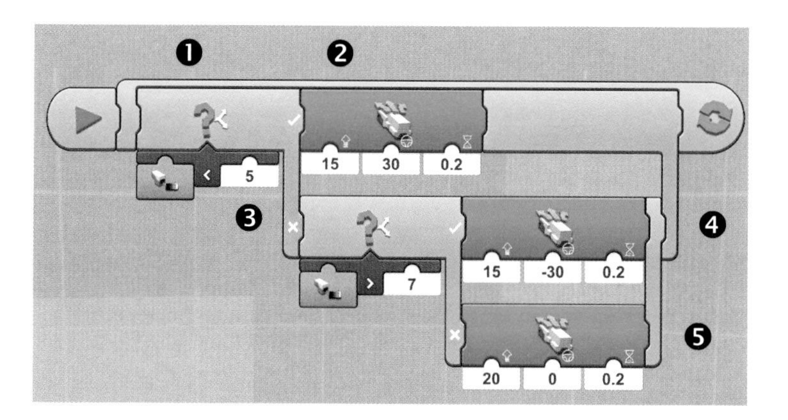

FIGURE 8-7 The line-following program with two Switch blocks

The first **Switch** block ❶ checks whether the sensor is seeing the black line. If so, the top Move block ❷ steers the robot away from the line. If the first condition is false, the second **Switch** block ❸ checks whether the sensor is seeing the light background. If so, the Move block ❹ steers the robot towards the line. If that condition is false too, it means that the sensor reading was between 5 and 7. This means it's seeing the grey edge of the line, and the Move block ❺ makes the robot go straight.

monitoring sensor values

To monitor the sensor value in real time, place a **Sensor Light Level Reporter** block anywhere in the canvas, leaving it floating. You can also attach it to the Compare blocks, as shown in **FIGURE 8-8**.

experiment 8-2

Imagine that MARIO is scared by nearby objects, and it goes backward fast when it sees them. Once it gets far enough away from the object, it stops. Make a program to make MARIO behave like this.

Hints: use a **Switch** block, a **Compare Less Than** block, and a **Sensor Distance Reporter** block. Position the sensor head facing straight forward.

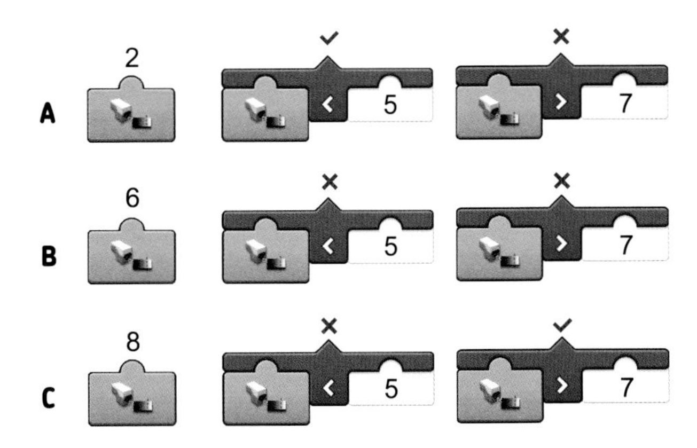

FIGURE 8-8 Monitoring the light sensor in real time

TABLE 8-1 monitoring the reflected light sensor and comparing its value to two thresholds

LABEL IN FIGURE 8-8	SENSOR POSITION	DISTANCE SENSOR READING	RESULT OF COMPARE LESS THAN 5	RESULT OF COMPARE GREATER THAN 7	LINE-FOLLOWING ACTION
A	On the dark line	2	✔	✖	Curve right, away from the line
B	On the edge of the line	6	✖	✖	Go straight, remain on the edge
C	On the light surface	8	✖	✔	Curve left, toward the edge

With the Move Hub connected to your device, place the sensor on a white surface or on the line. Then try to reproduce the results summarized in **TABLE 8-1**, which correspond to the three cases shown in **FIGURE 8-8** of the line-following program with two **Switch** blocks.

waiting for custom conditions

FIGURE 8-9 The Wait for True block pauses the program until the specified value becomes true.

The **Wait for Distance** block makes the robot wait until the sensor reads a distance less than a certain number specified. But what if you want your robot to wait for the sensor to read a distance *greater than* a certain number? For example, if you want MARIO to wait to act until an object moves away more than a certain distance.

To program MARIO to wait until a certain condition is met, we use the **Wait for True** block (**FIGURE 8-9**), which pauses program execution until that condition becomes true. For example, you can use it to make your robot wait for the sensor to read a distance greater than a certain number.

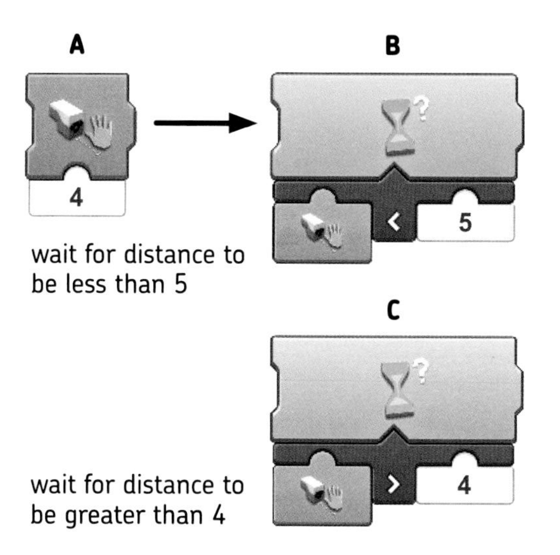

FIGURE 8-10 The Wait for Distance block (**A**) can be replaced with a Wait for True block with a Compare block on its input (**B**, **C**). The condition can be customized to your needs.

The **Wait for Distance** block (see **A** in **FIGURE 8-10**) waits for a certain condition to become true. The block shown here pauses the sequence and checks continuously: "Is the sensor measuring a distance *less than or equal to* 4?" Note that this is the same as asking whether the distance is *less than* 5, since the sensor returns values in whole numbers. When the answer to this question is *yes*, the program can continue. In effect, this sensor block controls the flow of the program.

You can replace the **Wait for Distance** block with a **Wait for True** block, which uses a **Compare Less Than** block to set the logic condition, as shown in **B** of **FIGURE 8-10**.

Notice that the first input of the **Compare Less Than** block in **B** of **FIGURE 8-10** is fed by the **Sensor Distance Reporter** block, which continuously returns the sensor reading. So, the pseudocode for the **Compare Less Than** block becomes the following:

```
Is the current distance reading less than 5?
```

When the output of the Compare block is attached to the input of the **Wait for True** block, the complete pseudocode becomes the following:

```
Wait until the distance reading is less than 5
```

Now, by changing the type of Compare block we're attaching as the input of the **Wait for True** block, you can customize the logic conditions you want the robot to wait for. For example, you can wait for the sensor to read a distance *greater than* 4 by attaching a **Compare Greater Than** block to the **Wait for True** block input, as shown in **C** of **FIGURE 8-10**.

experiment 8-3

Place MARIO on a light surface and make a "fence" with black tape around it. Now, create a program to keep MARIO inside the fence without escaping. (Hint: position the sensor so it looks down.)

experiment 8-4

Make a program that has MARIO travel straight until it sees an obstacle, then stop until the obstacle goes away. Once the obstacle is removed, MARIO should start moving forward again.

(Hint: use a **Wait for True** block with a **Compare Greater Than** block to wait for the obstacle to be removed.)

triggering sequences with custom conditions

FIGURE 8-11 The Start on True block starts a sequence when its logic input is true.

Say you want to trigger a sequence of blocks when a logic condition becomes true, using the **Start on True** block (**FIGURE 8-11**).

For example, the **Trigger on Distance** block starts a sequence when the sensor reads a distance less than or equal to the value specified as input (see **A** in **FIGURE 8-12**). The condition "less than or equal to" is fixed.

Now, say you want to start a sequence when the sensor measures a distance greater than 4. To handle a custom condition like this one, you would use the **Start on True** block (**C**) with a **Compare Greater Than** block attached to its input. As you can see in **FIGURE 8-12**, the **Start on True** block (**B**) behaves exactly like the **Trigger on Distance** block (**A**), starting a sequence when the distance of an object from the robot is 4 or less.

FIGURE 8-12 The Trigger on Distance block (**A**) can be replaced by a Trigger on True block with a Compare Less Than block on its input (**B**). The condition can be customized to meet your needs (**C**).

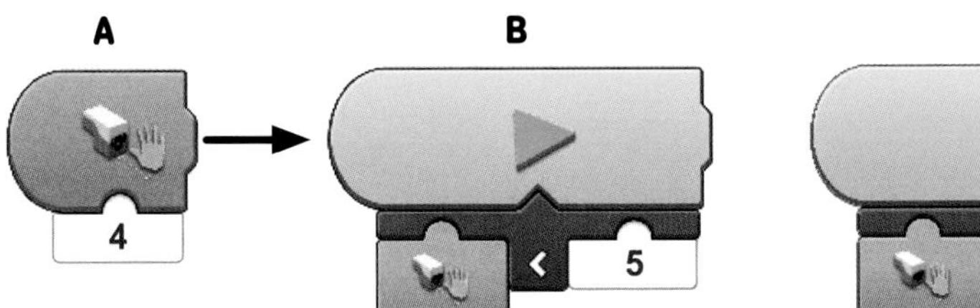

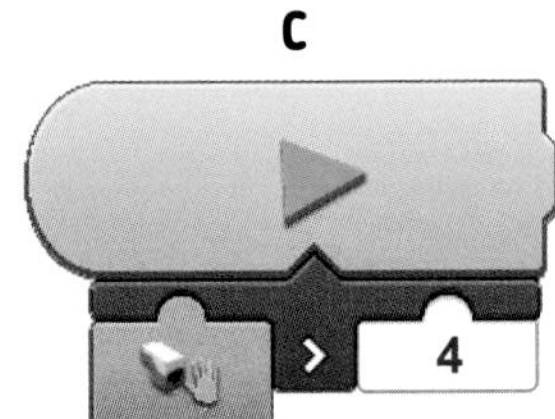

start the sequence when the distance is less than **5**

start the sequence when the distance is greater than **4**

experiment 8-5

Let's improve the obstacle-avoidance program we made in Chapter 6. Point the sensor straight ahead and then modify the program in **FIGURE 6-2** to make MARIO go forward slowly until it sees an obstacle within a distance of 7. When it does, make it go backward, pivoting on its right wheel until the distance between it and the obstacle is greater than 5.

comparing colors

The **Wait for Color** and **Trigger on Color** blocks activate when the color read by the sensor is *equal* to the one specified as input. If you'd like to handle custom color detection instead, for example to wait for a color other than red, you can combine the **Wait for True** and **Start on True** blocks with Compare blocks, as shown in **FIGURE 8-13**.

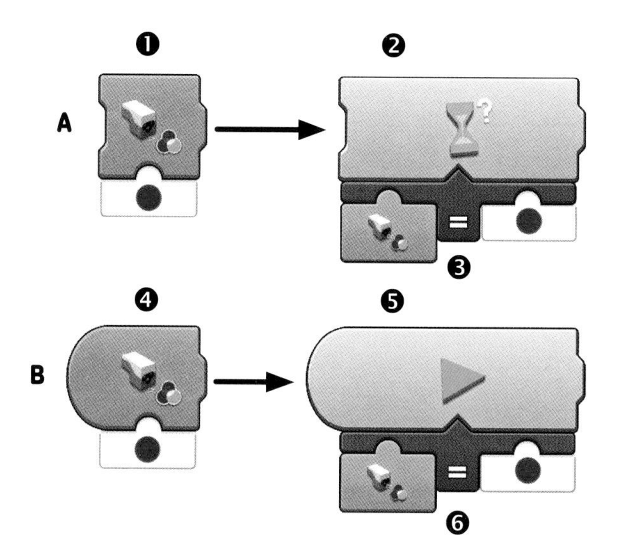

FIGURE 8-13 The Wait for Color block corresponds to a Wait for True block with a Compare Equal block attached to its input **(A)**. By the same token, the Trigger on Color block **(B)** works like a Start on True block with a Compare Equal block attached to its input. The combination of two blocks as shown in the right-hand column allow us to include custom color detection in our program.

The **Wait for Color** block ❶ works the same as a **Wait for True** block ❷ with a **Compare Equal** block ❸ attached to its input **(A)**. The **Trigger on Color** ❹ works the same as a **Start on True** block ❺ with a **Compare Equal** block ❻ attached to its input **(B)**.

When you attach a **Sensor Color Reporter** block to a Compare block, you will need to choose a color instead of a number for the input. Remember that colors are coded with a number (0 = no color, 1 = black, 3 = blue, 5 = green, 7 = yellow, 9 = red, and 10 = white).

You can choose to use the **Compare Equal** or **Compare Not Equal** blocks to determine whether a sensor reading is *equal* or *not equal* to a color. It doesn't make sense to make your robot wait for a color to be *less than* blue.

FIGURE 8-14 shows how to use a **Compare Not Equal** block to make the sequence wait for the color sensor to detect any color other than no color.

experiment 8-6

Make a program that makes MARIO get close to your hand whenever it feels you're too far and is looking for cuddles. (Hint: use a **Start on True** block.)

experiment 8-7

Place MARIO on the blue arrow of the BOOST playmat and make MARIO go straight ahead until the sensor sees any of the objects drawn on the paper. Then, have MARIO stop and play an alarm sound. (Hint: flip the sensor down and use a **Wait for True** block.)

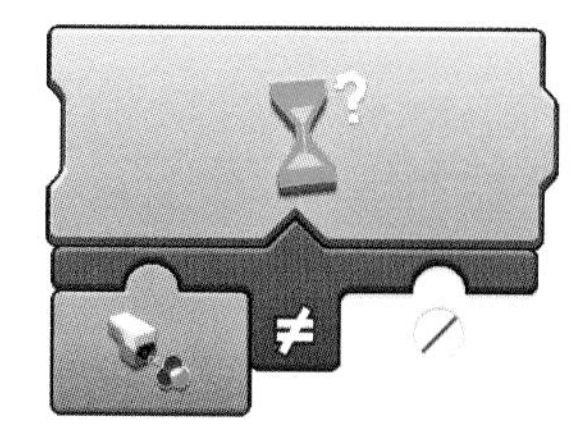

FIGURE 8-14 This Wait for True block waits for the sensor to see any color other than no color.

experiment 8-8

Create a program that makes MARIO play a sound whenever you show an object of any color to its sensor. (Hint: use a **Start on True** block.)

experiment 8-9

Extend the program described in experiment 8-5 to make MARIO play two sounds in a loop while looking for objects on the playmat. (Hint: use a **Loop While True** block to repeat Sound blocks until the condition is met.)

repeating actions while a condition is true

The **Loop While True** block shown in **FIGURE 8-15** repeats an included sequence *while* the input condition is true.

A Wait block just waits for something to happen (For example, it might wait for time to pass or for the sensor to read a certain value.) When you use the **Loop While True** block instead, you can have your robot do something interesting while it waits for something else to happen. The pseudocode for this action might look like this (with the condition in parentheses):

```
... previous code
While (this condition is true)
    ... do something
End While
... following code
```

FIGURE 8-15 The Loop While True block repeats the included sequence while the input condition is true.

what you've learned

In this chapter, you learned how to make a robot follow lines on the ground. In order to do so, you used the light reading from the sensor with the **Switch** block to allow your robot to choose what to do based on sensor readings. You learned how to compare two numbers with the Compare blocks and how to work with logical values such as *true* and *false*. Finally, you saw how to use various Flow Control blocks that accept a logic condition as input, such as the **Wait for True**, **Start on True**, and **Loop While True** blocks, to make your robot respond to changing conditions.

experiment 8-10

Make a program that lets MARIO play a guitar serenade to anyone nearby. If no one is in sight, it should spin around until it detects a potential listener and then start its serenade again. (Hint: use a **Loop While True** block to repeat Sound blocks until the condition is met.)

9

following walls

In this chapter, you'll teach MARIO to explore different rooms in your home before returning to its starting point. To accomplish this, by the end of this chapter, you'll create an elegant wall-following program to help MARIO travel along each wall while negotiating corners.

The wall-following programs in this chapter are examples of *feedback controllers*. A *controller* is a device (or, more frequently, a piece of software) that monitors and changes the behavior of a system (your robot). To keep the robot at a constant distance from a wall, we'll use the distance sensor as the input channel providing feedback to the controller. The Move Hub motors that drive the robot are the *output*.

The first and second wall-following programs you'll create in this chapter implement a *Bang-Bang controller*, or *On-Off controller*, so called because the control command (the steering amount) switches abruptly between two states. The last wall-following program uses a proportional feedback controller, which adjusts the steering depending on MARIO's distance from the wall.

To begin, orient MARIO's sensor head as shown in **FIGURE 9-1**.

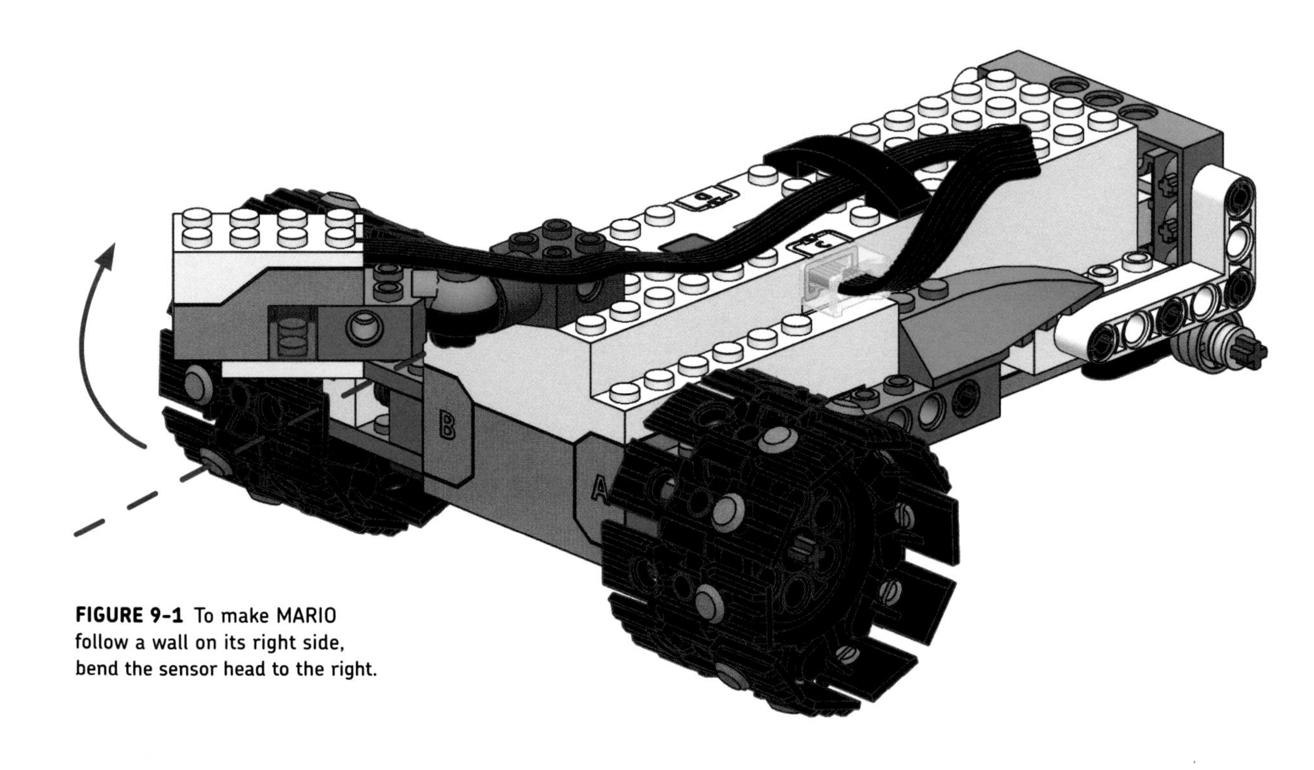

FIGURE 9-1 To make MARIO follow a wall on its right side, bend the sensor head to the right.

Be sure to rotate the sensor head three clicks clockwise so that it points at a 45-degree angle from the front, as shown in **FIGURE 9-2**. This orientation will allow MARIO to see objects slightly to the right.

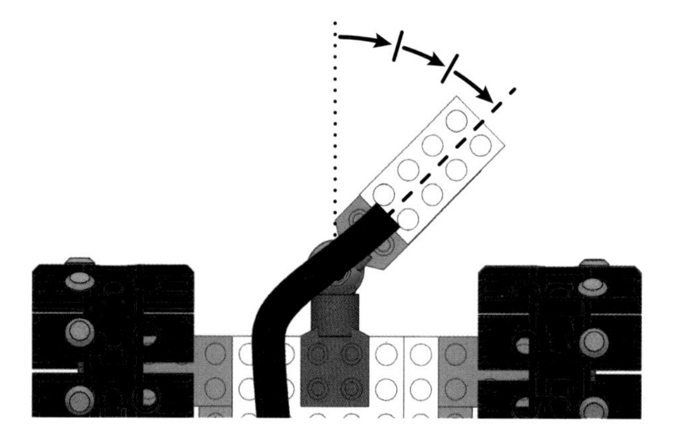

FIGURE 9-2 Turn the sensor three steps to the right to make MARIO follow walls.

MARIO will use its sensor to stay a constant distance from walls or any other obstacles as it explores its environment, as shown in **FIGURE 9-3**.

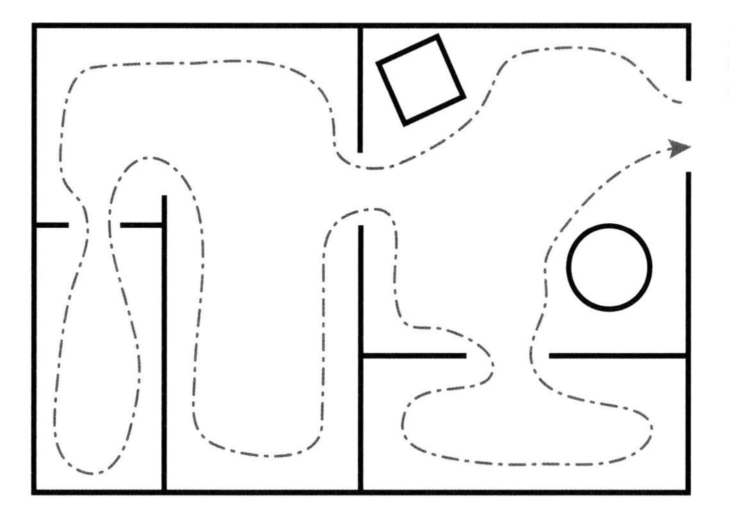

FIGURE 9-3 MARIO can explore your entire home.

FIGURE 9-4 shows how MARIO will use its sensor to follow walls just as it would follow a line. As shown in **FIGURE 9-4**, the distance between MARIO and the wall eventually drops below a certain number (the threshold) as MARIO moves toward a wall—at which point MARIO turns away from the wall until the distance between it and the wall rises above another threshold. Although these movements make MARIO wiggle, the average distance between your robot and the wall remains constant, and MARIO keeps its distance from the wall and any corners or edges.

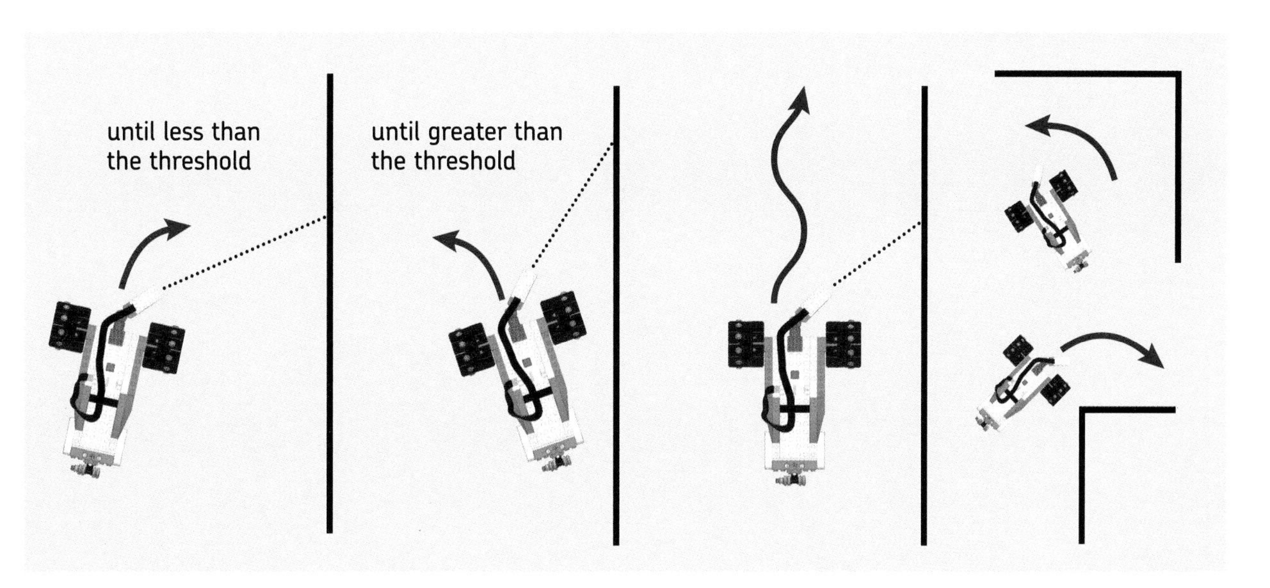

FIGURE 9-4 How MARIO navigates along walls and around corners

solving the wall-following problem

As you've seen, there is often more than one way to solve the same problem in robotics or to achieve the same behavior. In the following sections, I'll show you various ways to use the Flow blocks to improve your wall-following robots.

using Wait blocks

But before we dig into this challenge, let's write the pseudocode that implements the behavior shown in **FIGURE 9-4** above. Here it is.

```
Infinite loop begins
   Advance curving to the right (toward the wall)
   Wait for the distance to be less than 8
   Advance curving to the left (away from the wall)
   Wait for the distance to be greater than 8
Return to the start of the infinite loop
```

Using the Wait for True blocks

In Chapter 8, you used **Wait for True** blocks to trigger actions based on specific conditions. When creating MARIO's wall-following behavior, you use **Wait for True** blocks to have your robot wait for the distance between it and the wall to fall either above or below a certain threshold before having the robot take action.

To experiment with the **Wait for True** blocks, create a new project called `wallFollow` and then fill it with the program shown in **FIGURE 9-5**. This program will allow MARIO to navigate along a wall.

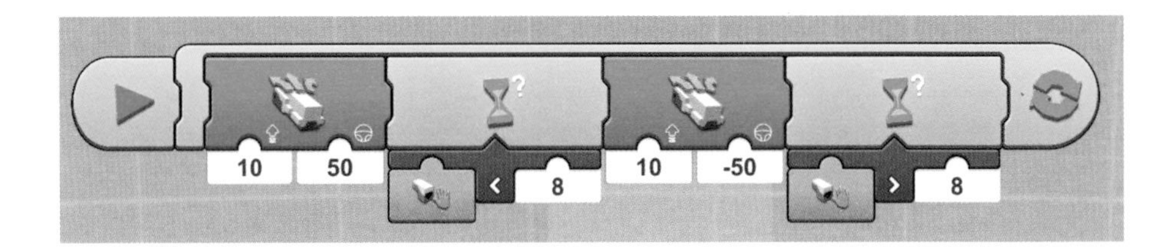

FIGURE 9-5 Wall-following program using Wait for True blocks to wait for changes in distance from the wall

Test the program by placing MARIO near a wall, with the wall on its right. Start the program. What happens?

experiment 9-1

How well does MARIO deal with corners and edges when running the program in **FIGURE 9-5**? Does it get stuck? Try lowering the threshold from 8 to see how its movement changes. Is it better or worse?

using the Switch block

You can program the same wall-following behavior using a **Switch** block instead of Wait blocks. In the program shown in **FIGURE 9-6**, the robot chooses which direction to turn based on the distance read by its sensor.

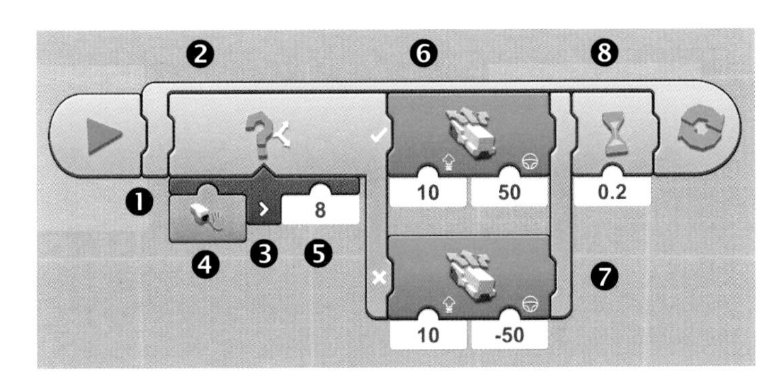

FIGURE 9-6 This wall-following program uses a Switch block to choose what to do, according to sensor readings.

Inside an **Infinite Loop** ❶, a **Switch** block ❷ makes the robot decide how to move, based on the result of the comparison performed by **Compare Greater Than** block ❸ that compares the value reported by the **Sensor Distance Reporter** block ❹ and the threshold ❺. If the result is true, it tells MARIO to steer right ❻ or left ❼ using the **Drivebase Move Steering Unlimited** block.

Notice that in this program I use a **Wait for Time** block ❽ to pause the execution by 0.2 seconds to slow down the loop. This pause makes the robot drive for 0.2 seconds before changing its direction in the next run of the loop. If we didn't add the pause, the loop would run at maximum speed, and the app would send commands to the Move Hub so often that it might overwhelm the Hub, causing the robot to behave unpredictably.

Notice too that we don't use a **Drivebase Move Steering for Time** block, because doing so would brake the motors once the specified time has elapsed, producing interrupted movement. Instead, we use the **Drivebase Move Steering Unlimited** block followed by a **Wait for Time** block to make sure the motors continue to run until a new Move block overrides the old command with new steering or speed values.

NOTE:

When you have two sequences in the same canvas but want to execute just one of them, tap the Start Sequence block attached to the sequence you want to run and not the round green Play button.

using Start on True blocks

You can also make a wall-following program using **Start on True** blocks, as in **FIGURE 9-7**.

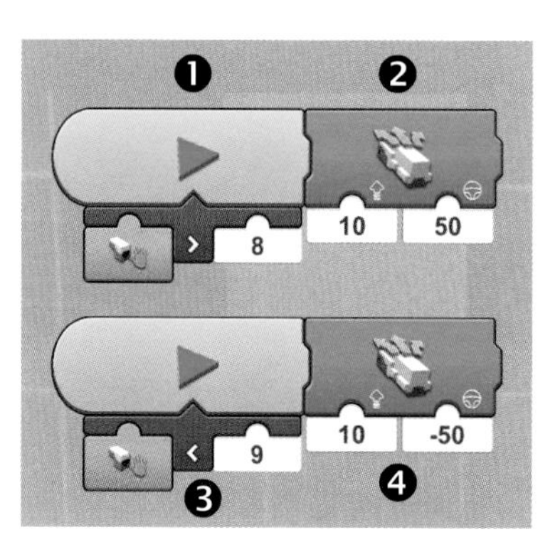

FIGURE 9-7 This wall-following program uses Start on True blocks to change the robot's direction based on the distance readings.

NOTE:

Although this wall-following program looks like it's running two sequences at the same time, it's actually running only one at a time. When the first condition is true (the distance is greater than 8), the other has to be false (with a distance less than 9), and vice versa. This means that both sequences can never run at the same time.

The program in **FIGURE 9-7** shows how you can use **Start on True** blocks to create a wall-following program. Here, we use a **Start on True** block ❶ to wait for the sensor to measure a distance greater than 8, which tells the robot it has strayed too far from wall.

Once we get this reading, we use the **Drivebase Move Steering Unlimited** block ❷ to make the robot steer to the right toward the wall.

Another **Start on True** block ❸ makes the robot wait for the sensor to measure a distance less than 9 to check whether the robot is too close to the wall. If the robot is too close to the wall, we steer it to the left, away from the wall, using the **Drivebase Move Steering Unlimited** block ❹. To start this program, tap both **Start on True** blocks ❶ and ❸, one after another.

a smoother wall-following program with math

All of our wall-following programs so far switch between two steering directions depending on the distance read by the sensor, but that results in jerky motion. To make the robot's movement smoother, we'll vary the amount of steering based on the sensor distance reading with the help of Math blocks.

FIGURE 9-8 shows the Math blocks, which you'll find in the Math blocks palette (white tab), together with the Compare blocks. You can use these blocks to add, subtract, multiply, or divide two numbers. We'll use Math blocks to compute the value of the Steering input for a Move block starting from the value read by the sensor.

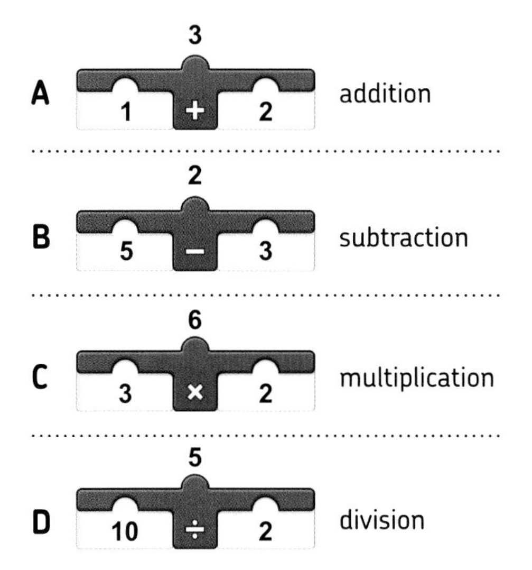

FIGURE 9-8 The Math blocks

proportional steering

The wall-following sequence shown in **FIGURE 9-9** uses the reading from the sensor to gradually vary the amount that the robot steers depending on the robot's distance from the wall. When the robot is at about the desired distance from the wall, the wall-following part of the sequence of **FIGURE 9-9** will make only minor correcting steering adjustments. But when the robot is too far from the wall or too close to it, the steering will be stronger.

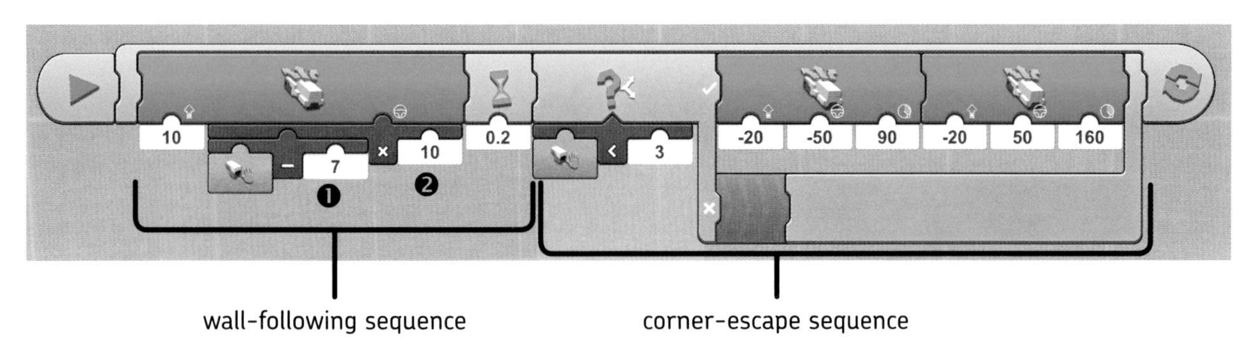

FIGURE 9-9 This program controls the amount of steering according to the distance sensor reading so that the robot follows the wall smoothly.

Engineers call this piece of code a *proportional controller*, because it produces a command for a robot that is proportional to the reading of a sensor. "Proportional" means that the Steering level is big if the robot is far from the desired reference distance ❶ from the wall, and there's very little steering (or none) when the robot is close to the desired distance from the wall. We use the number 10 ❷ to control the strength of the robot's steering. (The program also activates an emergency maneuver in case the robot gets much too close to the wall.)

Follow the steps shown in **FIGURE 9-10** to make the proportional controller.

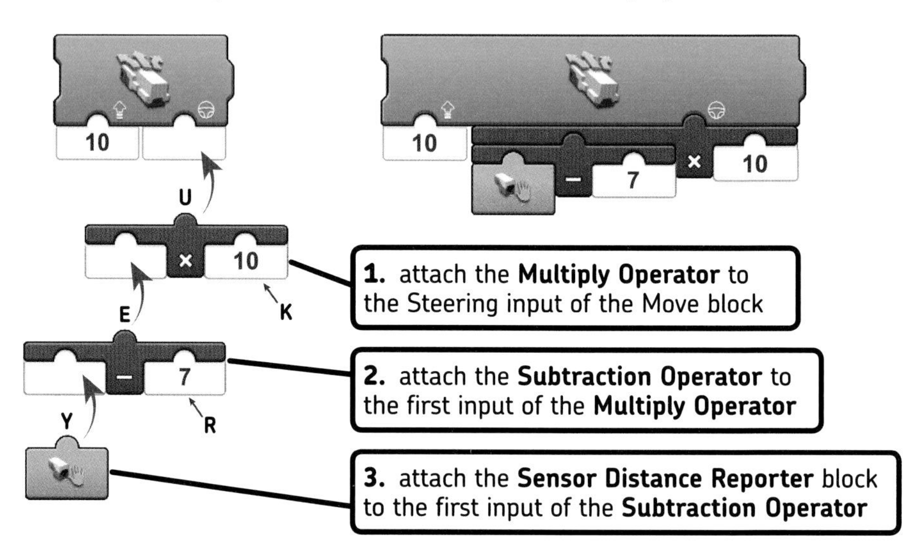

FIGURE 9-10 The steps to build the proportional controller

The Math blocks are key to making this work. First, we use a **Subtraction Operator** to compute the error **E**, which is the difference between the measured distance **Y** and the *desired* distance from the wall **R**.

```
E = Y - R
error = measurement - reference
```

The values for **Y** returned by the sensor range from 0 to 10. Since we want **R** to be 7, the difference **E** can range from –7 to 3.

But we have a bit of a problem. The Steering parameter of the **Drivebase Move Steering Unlimited** block can range from –100 to 100, which tells us that small values like –7 or 3 will have almost no effect on the steering. To make **E** effective as a steering parameter, we'll make it bigger by multiplying by a constant called *gain* (**K**). The result is the final steering command **U**, which we feed to the Steering input of the **Drivebase Move Steering Unlimited** block, like this:

```
U = K × E
steering command = gain × error
```

NOTE:

The distance measured by the sensor (Y) should never be 0, because that would mean the robot has crashed into the wall! For this reason, will never be as low as –70).

Multiplying **E** by a factor of 10 gives an effective steering command **U** in the range of –70 to 30.

The greater the difference between the measured and the desired distances, the stronger the steering will be! For example, when the robot is at the right distance from a wall, the steering command value will be a small number, and the robot will move almost straight ahead, making only small adjustments to its path. But when the robot is very close to a wall, E will be bigger, and the steering will also be greater in order to move the robot away from the wall.

After the **Drivebase Move Steering Unlimited** block, there's a **Wait for Time** block. As we've done before, we use it to pause the loop for a fraction of a second to avoid updating the motor command more often than the Move Hub can process it.

adjusting R and K

You can adjust the desired distance between the robot and the wall by changing the reference value R ❶ in **FIGURE 9-9**. We use the gain K ❷ to control the strength of the robot's reaction.

As shown in **FIGURE 9-10**, the larger the number we set for the gain, the more sensitive our robot will be, resulting in jerky movements. The smaller the number, the weaker the steering action will be, giving us less control over the robot (especially around corners).

You'll need to think about the trade-off between smoothness and responsiveness when changing the value of this number.

This wall-following program has a few limitations. The first is that our robot can only follow walls on its right side. However, you can modify the sensor assembly and the program to let the robot follow walls on its left. Another limitation is that this program will fail if the robot is too far from the wall; the program will make it spin in place with no chance of finding the wall again.

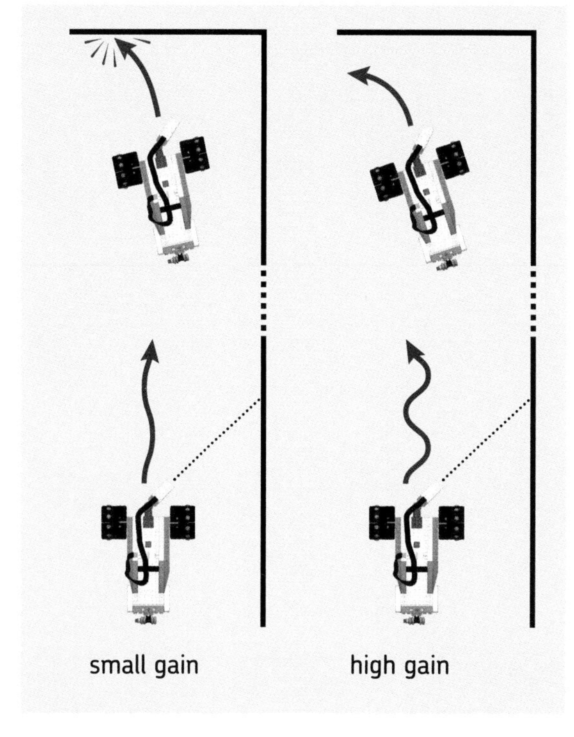

FIGURE 9-11 How changing the gain value affects the wall-following behavior

backing out of corners

With the current values for K and R, MARIO should be able to turn without getting its right wheel stuck in the corner of a wall. However, when it comes to negotiating corners, the proportional controller alone might not be effective: the robot might hit the wall in front of it before the steering command becomes strong enough to turn the robot sharply away from the wall.

To solve this problem, we'll use a **Switch** block to activate an escape maneuver (see **FIGURE 9-12**) when the distance measured by the sensor is less than 3.

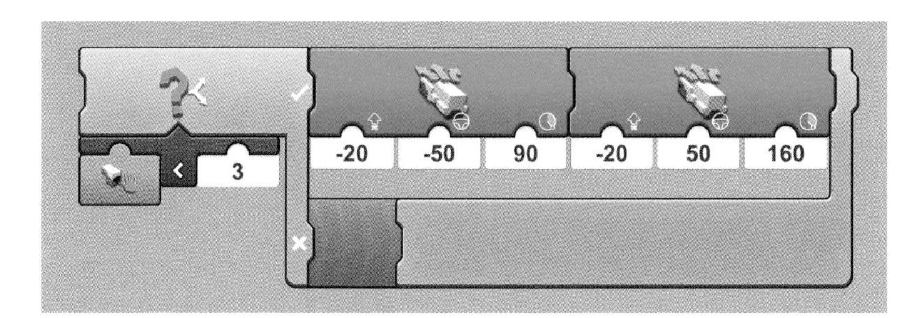

FIGURE 9-12 The corner-escape sequence

experiment 9-2

Rotate the sensor to look ahead to the left, and change the program shown in **FIGURE 9-9** to make the robot follow the wall on its left.

The escape sequence uses two **Drivebase Move Steering for Angle** blocks to make the robot back out of the corner while turning left. This creates enough distance from the wall so that once the robot negotiates the corner, the proportional controller can continue working in its safe range of distance values.

what you've learned

In this chapter, you learned how to make a robot that can explore an enclosed space while following walls at a safe distance. You did this in four different ways, using **Wait for True** blocks, a **Switch** block, **Start on True** blocks, and a proportional feedback controller. Along the way, you also learned how to use Math blocks to do math operations, which you used to control the robot's steering level based on its distance from the wall.

In Chapter 10, you'll learn how to control your robot by clapping and with voice commands!

experiment 9-3

Build a frame to hold a video camera or a smartphone facing forward. Switch on recording and let MARIO explore a room by following the walls. When your robot returns, you'll have a video of the trip. If you use video chat software, such as Skype or Hangouts, you can even stream the live video of MARIO exploring its environment!

experiment 9-4

Make a program that allows you to control MARIO without touching it. For example, when you place your hand in front of the sensor, the robot should keep a distance equal to 5 from your hand. (Hint: use a proportional controller that produces a Speed input for a Move block.)

10

a voice-activated robot

In this chapter, you'll learn how to use the Sound Sensor blocks to control MARIO with your voice or by clapping your hands. Then, you'll learn how to use the Tilt Sensor blocks to make MARIO react to pokes and to being moved. Finally, you'll learn how to program MARIO to play scripts and even tell jokes!

Sound Sensor blocks

Because the Move Hub lacks a built-in microphone, the LEGO BOOST app measures the sound level detected by the microphone of the device that you're using to program it, like your tablet or desktop computer.

You can use the Sound Sensor blocks shown here to make your robot measure and react to changes in the sound level.

- The **Trigger on Sound Level** block (**A**) starts the sequence when the sound level is greater than the input number.
- The **Wait for Sound Level** block (**B**) pauses the programming sequence while it waits for the sound level to exceed the input number.
- The **Sound Level Reporter** block (**C**) shows you the currently detected sound level. It reports the sound level with a number ranging from 0 (silence) to 10 (loud noise).

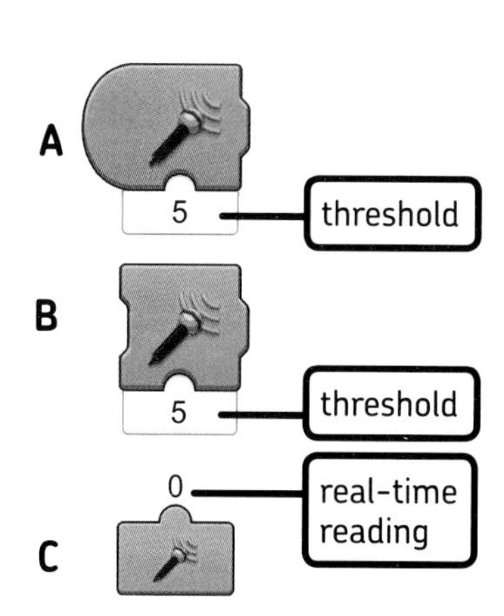

Let's write a program to make your robot respond to a sound.

clapper switch

Create a project and name it `clapper`, and then fill it with the programming sequence shown in **FIGURE 10-1**.

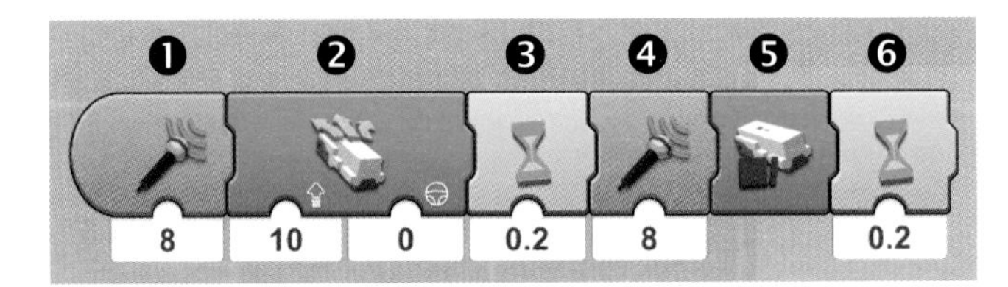

FIGURE 10-1 Use this program to start and stop MARIO with your voice or by clapping your hands.

This sequence lets you start and stop the robot by clapping your hands or by saying something aloud, like "Start" or "Stop." Actually, any loud enough noise will do.

(The BOOST app doesn't actually recognize speech, like Google Assistant, Siri, or Alexa. You can say "Stop" when you want MARIO to start moving, and the program will work just the same.)

Let's take a walk through this programming sequence. A loud enough sound activates the first block, **Trigger on Sound Level** ❶, and allows the execution of the blocks attached to it. The **Drivebase Move Steering Unlimited** block ❷ then starts the motors, making MARIO go forward. Next, we use the **Wait for Time** block ❸ to pause the sequence for 0.2 seconds. This prevents the **Wait for Sound Level** block ❹ from detecting the first sound again, which would have MARIO stop at once. When the second sound is detected, the **Drivebase Stop** block ❺ stops the Move Hub motors, and MARIO stops moving. We use a second **Wait for Time** block ❻ at the end of the sequence to avoid having the second sound, the one that stopped the motors, activate the Trigger block ❶ again. This problem of successive **Wait for Sound Level** blocks reacting to sounds not meant for them is especially common when the sounds are long, such as if you sang "Maaaar-i-ooo!"

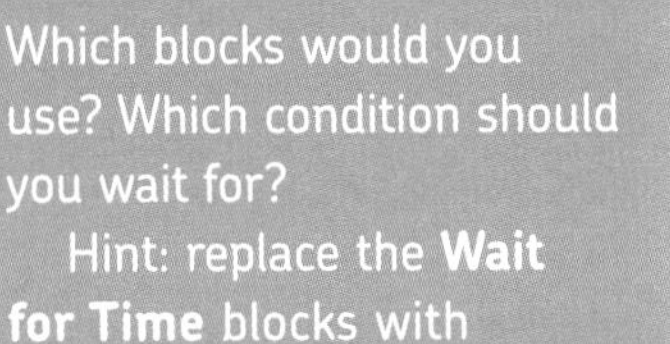

experiment 10-1

Change the `clapper` program in **FIGURE 10-1** to use something other than the **Wait for Time** block to avoid double detection. Which blocks would you use? Which condition should you wait for?

Hint: replace the **Wait for Time** blocks with **Wait for True** blocks, each with an attached **Compare Less Than** block comparing the current sound level (from the **Sound Level Reporter** block) to 2.

clapper navigator

Now, let's use sounds to make MARIO switch between straight and curved movements. For example, the robot should move straight until a sound is detected, then turn when another sound is detected, and then alternately go straight or turn in a continuous loop. The pseudocode for this program looks like this:

```
Infinite loop begins
    Go straight
    Wait for a sound level greater than 8
    Curve backward, pivoting on the right wheel
    Wait for a sound level greater than 8
Go back to the start of the infinite loop
```

FIGURE 10-2 shows the LEGO BOOST program that corresponds to this pseudocode.

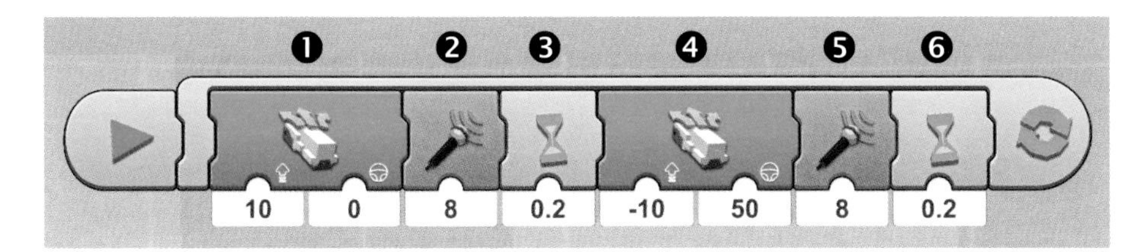

FIGURE 10-2 Use this program to make MARIO go straight or turn by using your voice or by clapping your hands.

In this program, the sequence of blocks loops forever. The **Drivebase Move Steering Unlimited** block ❶ makes the robot move straight forward. The **Wait for Sound Level** block ❷ allows the robot to continue moving until the microphone of your device detects a sound level greater than 8. The **Wait for Time** block ❸ pauses the program for 0.2 seconds to prevent the **Wait for Sound Level** block ❺ from detecting the first sound so that the robot will continue turning.

The second **Drivebase Move Steering Unlimited** block ❹ makes the robot back up and turn. Thanks to another **Wait for Sound Level** block ❺, the robot continues steering until another sound is detected. Another **Wait for Time** block ❻ prevents the **Wait for Sound Level** block ❷, executed when the loop restarts, from detecting the sound that made MARIO stop turning. Without this block ❻, the robot would immediately stop going forward and keep turning forever.

experiment 10-2

Change the `clapper` program in **FIGURE 10-2** to avoid the double-detection problem even when sounds are longer than 0.2 seconds (for example, if someone claps repeatedly). Hint: the solution is similar to the one for experiment 10-1.

Tilt Sensor blocks

One particularly cool thing about the LEGO BOOST Move Hub is that it has a tilt sensor that can measure how the brick is oriented, and it can report the tilt angles along the X and Y axes, as shown in **FIGURE 10-3**.

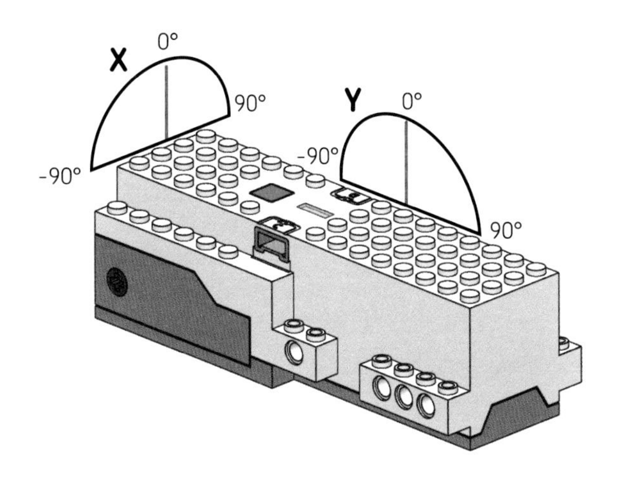

FIGURE 10-3 The built-in tilt sensor can measure the angle at which the brick is tilted along along the X and Y axes.

You can use the Tilt Sensor blocks shown in **FIGURE 10-4** to make your robot react to changes in tilt. These blocks have special inputs, with small images (icons) rather than numbers.

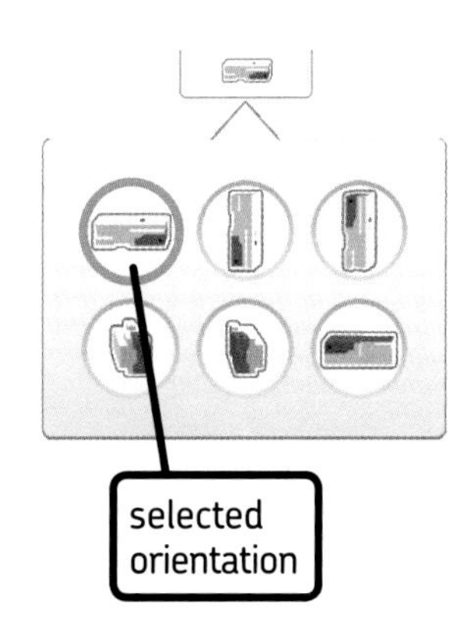

FIGURE 10-4 The Tilt Sensor blocks and the six possible Hub orientations

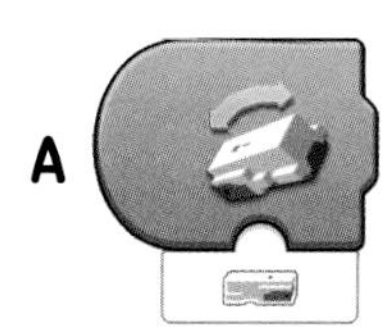

- The **Trigger on Hub Orientation** block (**A**) starts the sequence when the Move Hub is oriented a certain position, shown by the icon at the bottom of the Tilt Sensor block.

- The **Wait for Hub Orientation** block (**B**) pauses the sequence, waiting for the Move Hub to be oriented as specified by the icon.

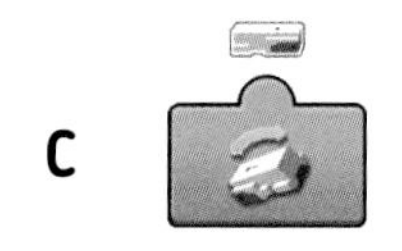

- The **Hub Orientation Reporter** block (**C**) displays the current Move Hub orientation (see **FIGURE 10-4**).

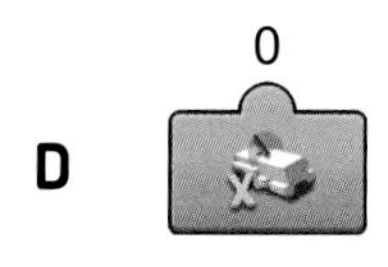

- The **Hub Tilt X Reporter** block (**D**) displays the current tilt angle of the Move Hub along the X axis, showing whether it's leaning to the left or right.

- The **Hub Tilt Y Reporter** block (**E**) displays the current tilt angle of the Move Hub along the Y axis, showing whether it's leaning forward or backward.

"hey, put me down!"

Let's use the tilt sensor to make MARIO stop its motors when it knows that you've lifted it from the ground and restart its motors when you put it back down. Here's the pseudocode that describes the program:

```
Infinite loop begins
    Go straight
    Wait for the Y angle to be greater than 10 (telling us
    that the robot is lifted)
    Stop the motors
    Wait for the Y angle to be equal to 0 (the robot is on
    the ground)
Go back to the start of the infinite loop
```

Now, turn this pseudocode into a program. Create a new project named `tilt sensor` and build the sequence shown in **FIGURE 10-5**.

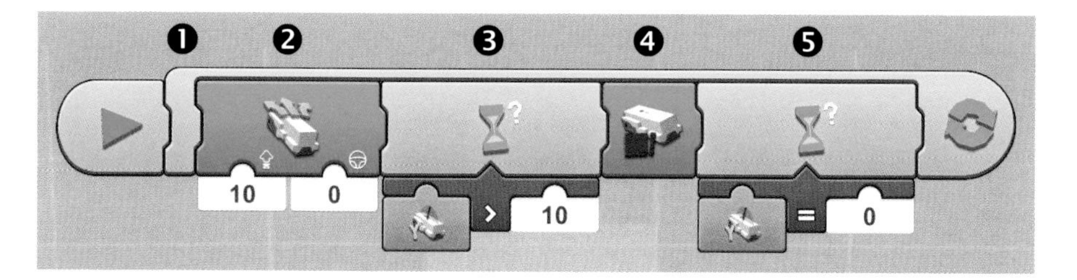

FIGURE 10-5 This program makes MARIO stop when it's lifted off the ground and continue moving when it's put back down parallel to the ground.

Inside an **Infinite Loop** ❶, we start the program with the **Drivebase Move Steering Unlimited** block ❷, which tells the robot to go forward. As it moves, a **Wait for True** ❸ waits for the Y angle to be greater than 10, a sign that the robot is leaning slightly backward as it's being lifted off the ground. When this occurs, the **Drivebase Stop** block ❹ tells the Move Hub Hub motors to stop.

Once the robot is put back down, the Y angle reported by the tilt sensor reads 0, and the last **Wait for True** block ❺ in the loop lets the program continue with the next repetition of the loop.

brain BOOSTer: the tilt sensor

The tilt sensor inside the Move Hub is actually a two-axis accelerometer, which measures the *acceleration*, or the change in speed of an object, along two directions. When the object is sitting still, the accelerometer measures the intensity of gravity, also known as acceleration due to gravity. Using the acceleration values, the accelerometer computes the orientation of the Move Hub. (Your tablet or smartphone uses the same kind of sensor to change the orientation of its screen.)

We also use accelerometers in cars to trigger airbags upon impact, as well as in airplanes as an essential part of their automatic guidance system. Humans use acceleration too: special organs in the ears measure acceleration and allow us to keep our balance while moving around.

experiment 10-3

Make a program that plays guitar chords 42 to 45 in the Sound Library triggered by different orientations of the Move Hub. Try to play the guitar riff that introduces "Smoke on the Water" by Deep Purple.

detecting a sudden hit

When the Move Hub bumps into something, is poked, or is hit, the value of the X and Y angles changes sharply because of the sudden change in acceleration. We can use these features of the Move Hub's angle estimation to make a robot react to being struck. **FIGURE 10-6** shows what happens to the Y tilt value when you hit the Move Hub.

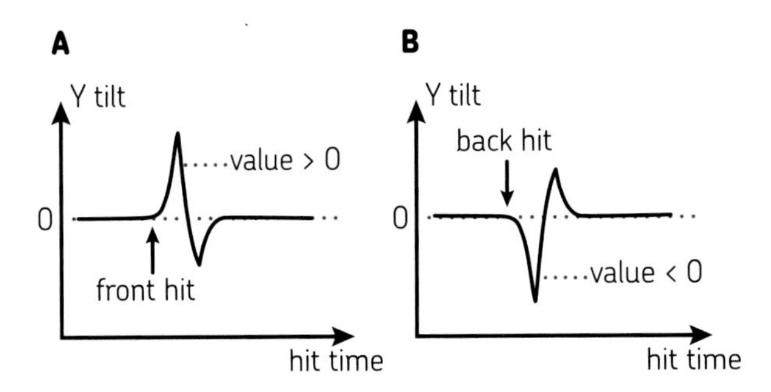

FIGURE 10-6 The graphs plot the value of the Y angle against time when the robot is hit from the front (A) and from the back (B).

The Move Hub must be still and *perfectly horizontal* for the poke detection to work. When you hit the Move Hub from the front, you get a positive spike. When you hit it from the back, you get a negative spike.

Now, let's create a program to detect when MARIO is struck, as shown in **FIGURE 10-7**.

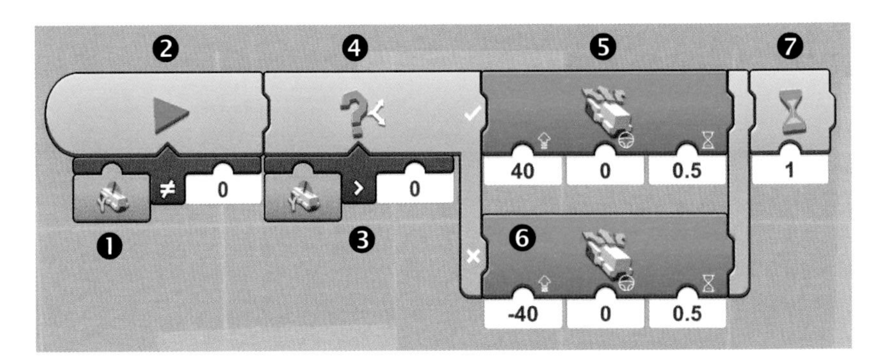

FIGURE 10-7 This program allows MARIO to detect if it's been hit from the front or back, and to react accordingly.

Place MARIO perfectly horizontal so that the **Hub Tilt Y Reporter** block ❶ returns 0. You can place a copy of this block on the canvas without attaching it to anything to display real-time readings of the Y angle. The **Start on True** block ❷ is activated when the Y angle is not 0, which happens if you poke the robot.

If the value of the Y angle is greater than 0, it means the robot was poked from the front; otherwise, it was poked from behind. The **Compare Greater Than** block ❸ allows the **Switch** block ❹ to distinguish where MARIO was struck.

If it was hit from behind, the **Drivebase Move Steering for Time** block ❺ makes MARIO go forward for 0.5 seconds; if MARIO was hit from the front, the **Drivebase Move Steering for Time** block ❻ makes MARIO go backward for 0.5 seconds. We use the **Wait for Time** block ❼ at the end of the sequence to prevent the **Start on True** block ❶ from starting the whole sequence again when detecting the sudden change in acceleration caused by the robot braking at the end of the movement.

Light blocks

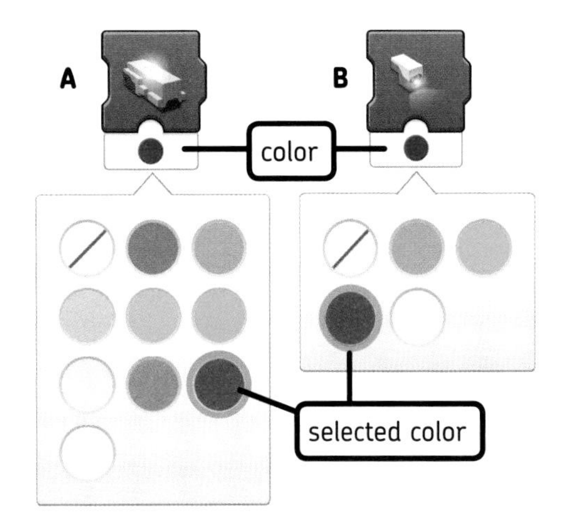

The LEGO BOOST can change the color of its RGB LED (red-green-blue light-emitting diode), as well as the color of the sensor light.

The violet colored Light blocks are in the same palette as the Sound blocks.

- The **Set Hub LED Color** block (**A**) sets the color of the Move Hub RGB LED. You can pick one of the colors shown below it.
- The **Set Sensor LED Color** block (**B**) sets the color of the sensor. You can choose from the colors shown.

random actions

To make your LEGO BOOST creations behave in more interesting ways, you can make them perform random actions.To do this, you'll generate random numbers and then execute different sequences according to the generated values.

random numbers

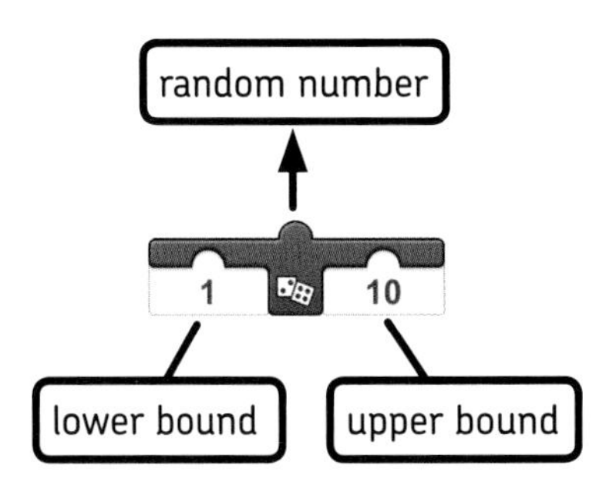

FIGURE 10-8 The Random Number block, in the Math blocks palette, generates random whole numbers within a set range.

You can use the **Random Number** block (**FIGURE 10-8**) to generate a random number within a set range. You can find the Random block inside the Math blocks palette (white tab). The random number will fall somewhere between the lower and upper bounds of the range, inclusive. For example, if you set the lower and upper bounds to 1 and 10, the random number could be 1, 10, or anywhere in between.

The numbers you input for the lower and upper bounds should be whole numbers. If you specify a bound as a decimal, the **Random Number** block will round it to the nearest whole number. For example, if you set the bounds to 1.5 and 4.4, the **Random Number** block would treat these as if they were 2 and 4, and the random values generated might be 2, 3, or 4.

NOTE:

If the lower bound is bigger than the upper bound, the Random Number block assumes that the bigger number is the upper bound and that the smaller number is the lower bound.

brain BOOSTer: random logic values

To have your robot randomly choose between two actions, feed a random logic value to a **Switch** block. To generate logic values, combine the **Random Number** block with Compare Math blocks, as shown here.

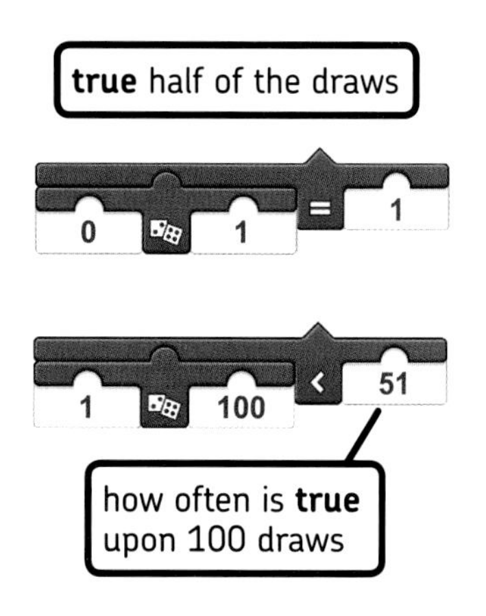

In the first example, the **Random Number** block has an equal chance of generating a 0 or a 1. By comparing its output value with 1, you get a logic value. There's a chance of getting a *true* logic value half the time you use this block, just as if you were tossing a coin and looking for heads or tails.

In the second example, the **Random Number** block generates random numbers from 1 to 100, and we check whether the random number is *less than* another number between 0 to 100. This number lets you decide how likely it is for an output to return *true* (its *probability* of being true). For example, if you set the number to 51, you'll get the same result as above (there are 50 values less than 51, and 50 is half of 100). But if you set the input to 21, the output logic value will be true only 20 times out of 100, since there are only 20 numbers out of a 100 that are less than 21. If set to 0, it will always be false because numbers between 1 and 100 will always be greater than 0. If set to 101, the result will always be true.

randomizing colors and sounds

You can attach the **Random Number** block to Light blocks or Sound blocks. When you do so, you'll see some icons instead of numbers. Each color, sound, and orientation icon has a corresponding numeric code that the program can understand, even though you won't see it.

We'll use **Random Number** blocks to make our robot generate random sounds and randomly change the color of the light when it detects movement of the Move Hub. Create a new project and name it `random`. Then build and run the program shown in **FIGURE 10-9**.

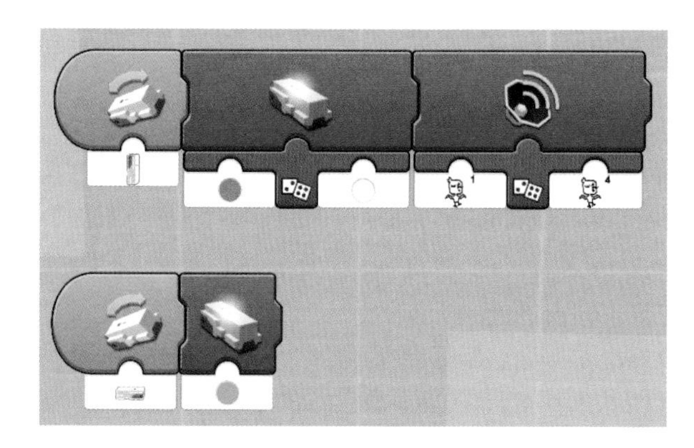

FIGURE 10-9 Generating random sounds and randomly changing the color of the light when the Move Hub is tilted upward

When the Move Hub is tilted, this program uses the **Random Number** block to tell the Move Hub light to randomly change color. We also use the **Play Sound** block to play a random sound in the range specified by the icons (in **FIGURE 10-9**, we're using animal sounds 1 to 4). When you set the Move Hub down again, the light on the Move Hub should return to its usual blue color.

experiment 10-4

Make a program that lets MARIO explore its surroundings by avoiding obstacles, but this time, randomize its steering direction and the duration of the steering.

Hint: use a **Random Number** block to generate a logic value to feed a **Switch** block, which will choose the steering direction. Use other **Random Number** blocks to feed the Time input of **Drivebase Move Steering for Time** blocks.

experiment 10-5

Modify the program of **FIGURE 10-9** to make MARIO produce random sounds whenever it's not lying flat on the ground. Hint: why don't you try some of the funny sounds?

starting parallel sequences

Until now, our programs have had just one sequence, or program flow. Each main sequence has started with the usual **Start Sequence** block and executed the blocks one after another. Even though we used multiple Trigger blocks on the same canvas, the sequences only ran one at a time, since each depended on conditions that were mutually exclusive (see **FIGURES 7-2**, **9-7**, and **10-9**). That is, if one condition was true, no other condition was true. The LEGO BOOST app allows you to run more than one sequence at a time. This is also called *multitasking*.

One way to run multiple sequences of blocks in parallel is to place multiple Start blocks on the canvas and start them all by tapping the round green Play button. Usually the program will stop when the last block of a sequence finishes.

If you tap a Trigger block, however, it will start blinking, listen to a sensor, or check a condition, and the program will continue to run until you tap the red Stop button.

Let's take a look at the *Flow* blocks that allow you to run multiple sequences of blocks in parallel. There are also Flow blocks that you can use to stop sequences.

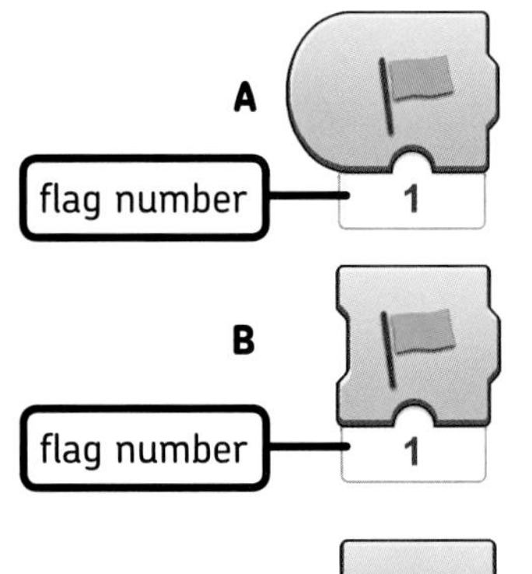

- The **Start on Flag** block (**A**) starts a sequence when the **Flag Trigger** block (**B**) is executed by another sequence. You can have more than one **Start on Flag** block with the same flag number; when the **Flag Trigger** block is executed, these blocks will all start their sequences in parallel.
- The **Flag Trigger** block (**B**) starts a sequence attached to a **Start on Flag** block with the same number.

- The **Stop All Other Sequences** block (**C**) stops all the sequences except the one that executes this block. The sequence attached after this block continues running.

- The **Stop All Sequences** block (**D**) stops the whole program, including the Trigger blocks, which no longer wait for new sensor events. (Notice that you cannot attach blocks after this one.) Using this block at the end of a sequence has the same effect as tapping on the app's round red Stop button.

the interrupting robot joke

Let's use what you've learned so far to make MARIO play its own version of a silly "interrupting cow" joke. Here's the script that we'll later transform into a LEGO BOOST program:

You: "MARIO, tell me a joke."

MARIO: "Knock! Knock!"

You: "Who's there?"

MARIO: "An interrupting robot named MARIO!"

You: "An interrupting . . . "

MARIO: "Ababababababababababa!" (moving like crazy, jeering at you)

You are very annoyed and pick MARIO up, trying desperately to stop it. MARIO stops moving and farts.

building the program

Create a new project, name it **joke**, and then build the program shown in **FIGURE 10-10**.

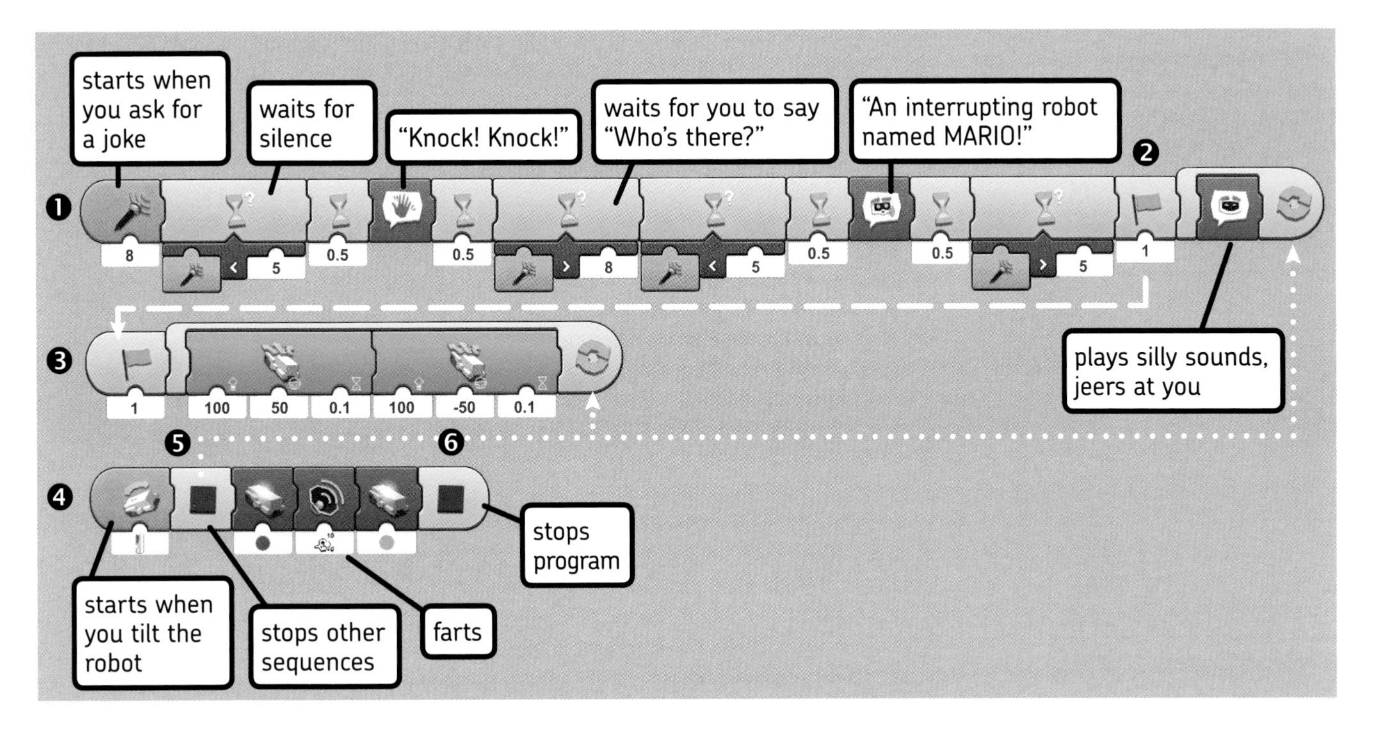

FIGURE 10-10 The program to play the interrupting robot joke

The main sequence at the top starts with a **Trigger on Sound Level** block ❶ that waits for you to ask MARIO for a joke. Then the program waits for you to finish the phrase, since we don't want the robot to interrupt you at this point, before playing the recorded sound "Knock! Knock!" The program waits for you to answer "Who's there?" and plays another recorded sound that says "An interrupting robot named MARIO!" Then, it waits for you to ask "An interrupting robot named MARIO who?" but won't let you finish the phrase. In fact, there's no Wait block to wait for the sound level to go below a threshold.

To start the program inside the loop and play the disturbing sound "ababa" at the same time, we use a **Flag Trigger** block ❷ that starts the **Start on Flag** block ❸ (notice they both have the flag number 1). The main sequence ends by playing the silly sound in a forever loop, while the parallel sequence makes the robot move forward in little steps.

Besides stopping the program with the round Stop button on the app, the only way to stop MARIO from going crazy is to tilt it all the way up. This activates the sequence starting with the **Trigger on Hub Orientation** block ❹ (the sequence at the very bottom of **FIGURE 10-10**). The **Stop All Other Sequences** block ❺ stops the other sequences and continues running, changes the Hub LED color, plays an obnoxious sound (a fart, a burp, or any other sound you find amusing), changes the light back to blue, and finally, terminates the program with the **Stop All Sequences** block ❻.

experiment 10-6

Use the **Wait for Sound** and custom Sound blocks to make your robot tell any joke you want. For example:

"What's a robot's favorite kind of music?"
"Heavy metal!"

"What would you say to your dead robot?"
"Rust in peace."

To see the joke in action, pick the robot up only when it's moving and jeering at you. However, you can pick the robot up to stop the program at any moment.

You'll need three custom sounds for this program (see **FIGURE 10-11**). To make things even sillier, apply the high-pitch effect to all the custom sounds you record using the sound-recording interface. (To review how to record and edit custom sounds, see Chapter 6.)

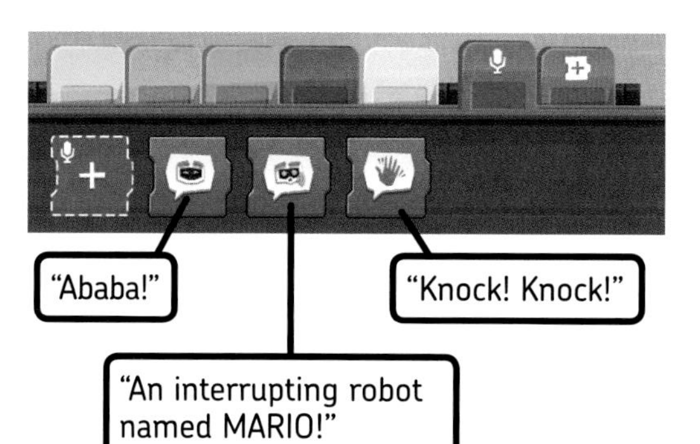

FIGURE 10-11 The three sounds needed for the interrupting robot joke program

what you've learned

Whew, we did a lot in this chapter! You learned how to use the Move Hub's built-in tilt sensor and the microphone of your device as a sound sensor. You also learned how to generate random numbers to create interesting and unpredictable behavior in your robot. You saw how to change the color of the Move Hub and sensor LEDs. Most importantly, you discovered MARIO's hidden comedic talents. In Chapter 11, you'll build a scanner head that will let MARIO explore open spaces and even follow your hand!

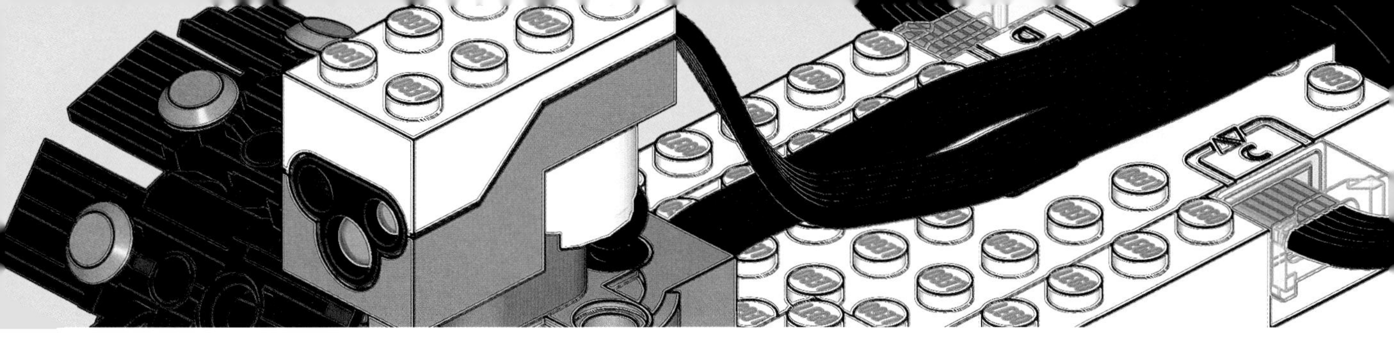

11

taking a look around

In this chapter, you'll build a motorized scanner head for MARIO as shown below. Your robot's scanner head will allow it to scan its environment, sense its surroundings, track moving objects, and much more!

As you build, you'll learn how to group sequences of actions to create *composite blocks* and how to allow your robot to store data.

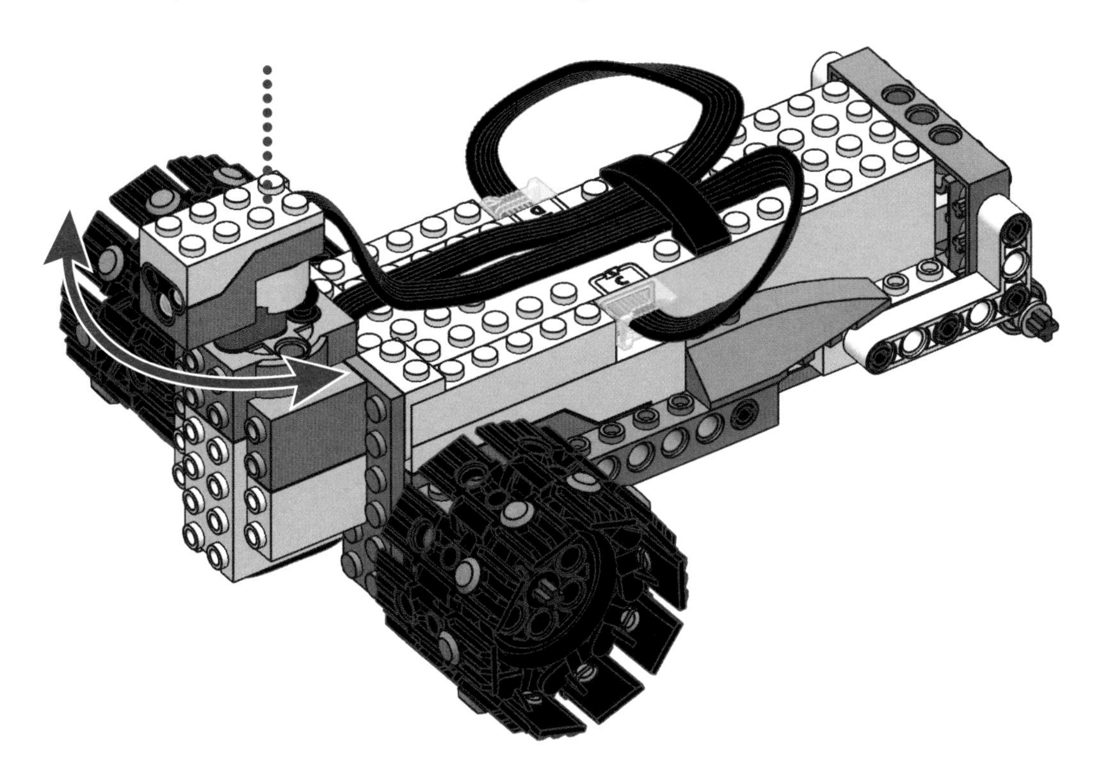

building the scanner head

Beginning with the base version of MARIO shown on page 8, follow the instructions below to build the scanner (first, you'll need to disassemble the sensor attachment you built previously).

1

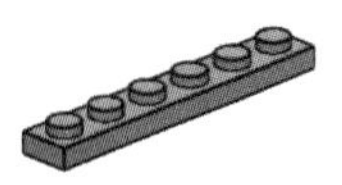

1x

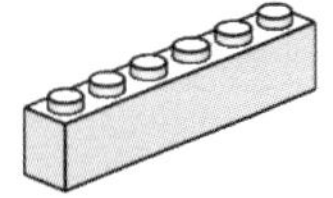

2x

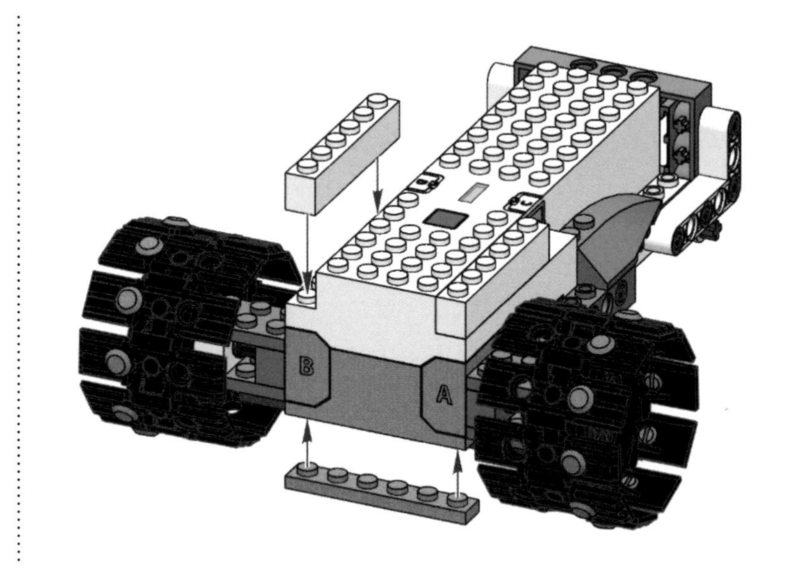

2

2x

2x

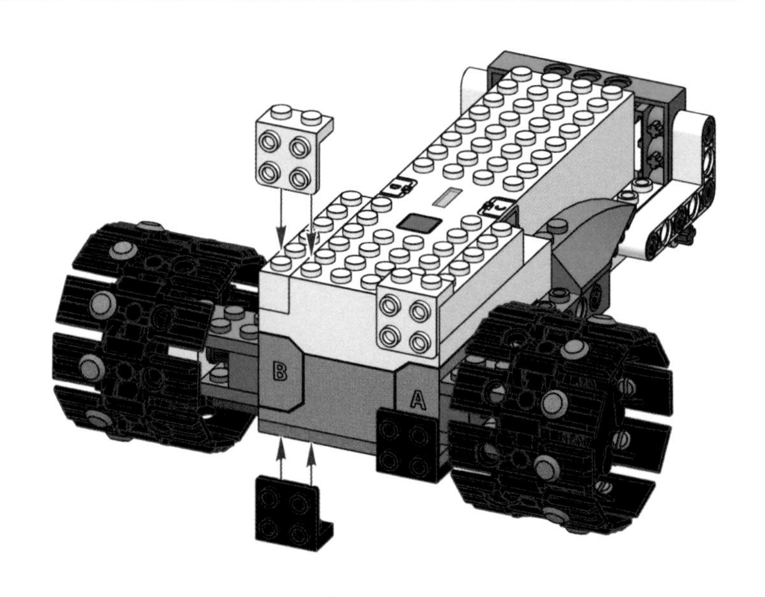

3

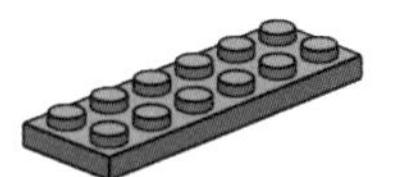

2x

This is SNOT building, with the 2x6 plates attached to the top and bottom brackets with their studs facing forward, allowing us to attach the motor with the shaft pointing up. We'll place the sensor on the motor's shaft to act kind of like the neck of our robot's scanner head.

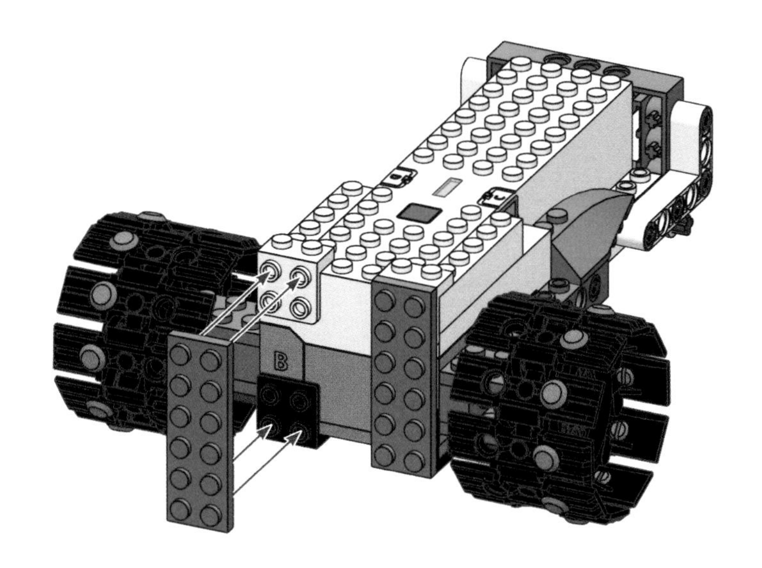

4

1x

1x

1x

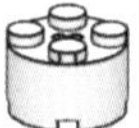

1x

1x

Pass the motor's cable between the bottom of the motor and the Move Hub, and through the little space between the two blue 2x6 plates.

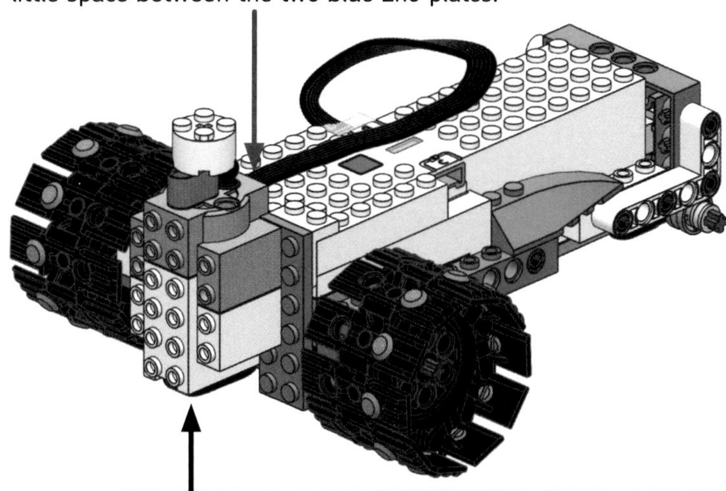

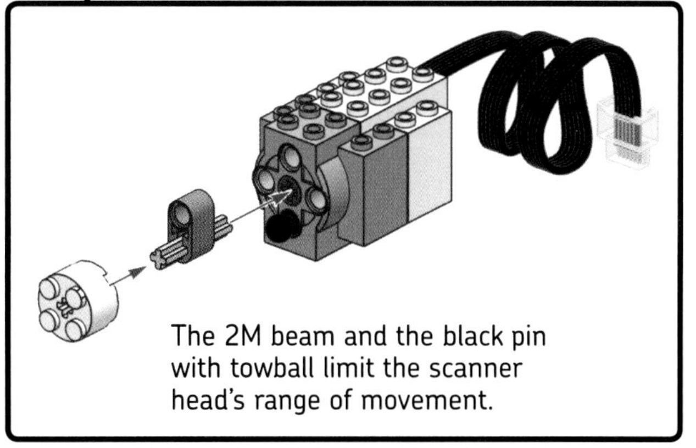

The 2M beam and the black pin with towball limit the scanner head's range of movement.

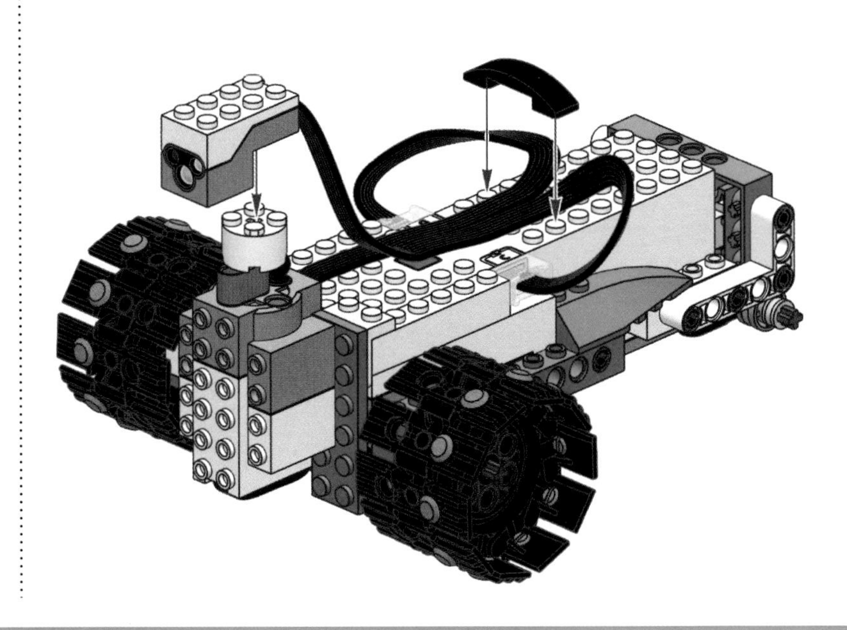

single-motor blocks

In this section, you'll learn how to control the three motors using the blocks shown in **FIGURE 11-1**.

FIGURE 11-1 Use these Motor blocks to tell a single motor what to do.

	time	angle	speed	stop
motor A	Motor A Run for Time (speed, time)	Motor A Run for Angle (speed, degrees)	Motor A Start (speed)	Motor A Stop
motor B	Motor B Run for Time (speed, time)	Motor B Run for Angle (speed, degrees)	Motor B Start (speed)	Motor B Stop
external motor	Ext. Motor Run for Time (speed, time)	Ext. Motor Run for Angle (speed, degrees)	Ext. Motor Start (speed)	Ext. Motor Stop

As you can see in the grid, you can make each motor move at a speed from –100 to 100 for a set number of seconds or a set number of degrees relative to the current shaft position. You can also set the motors to run forever at a certain speed or stop them altogether.

using the rotation sensors

You can use the Sensor blocks shown in **FIGURE 11-2** to read the speed (called the angular speed) of the spinning as well as the angle of the shaft in degrees (where 360 degrees is one full rotation). This speed reading is handy when, for example, you want to detect whether a motor shaft is blocked and can't move. You can use the reading of the shaft angle to determine the position of the motor shaft.

The rotation sensor counts the number of degrees the shaft has turned since the last time you set its value with the Preset Motor Angle blocks shown in the rightmost column of **FIGURE 11-2**. You'll usually set the value of the Preset blocks' input to 0. The Angle Reporter blocks in the middle column will measure the motor shaft's angle relative to this preset position.

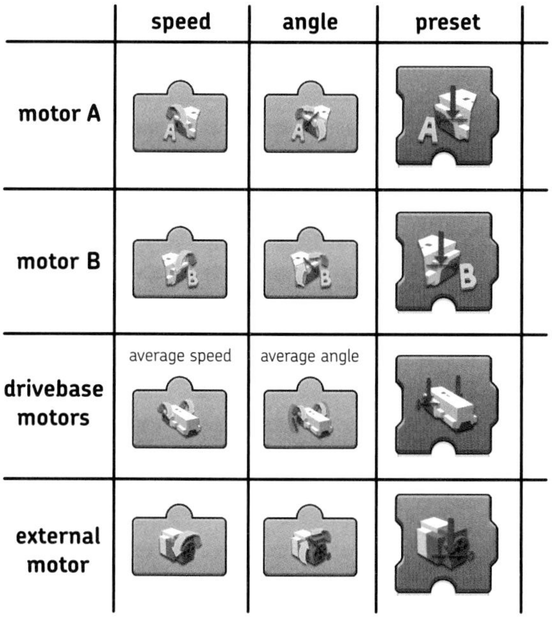

	speed	angle	preset
motor A			
motor B			
drivebase motors	average speed	average angle	
external motor			

FIGURE 11-2 The motor speed and position Sensor blocks

scanning

In this section, we'll build a program to have MARIO's scanner head turn 60 degrees to the right and left. Create a project named **scanner** and add three **External Motor Run for Angle** blocks to the sequence, as shown in **FIGURE 11-3**. (Be sure the scanner head is looking straight ahead before running this program.)

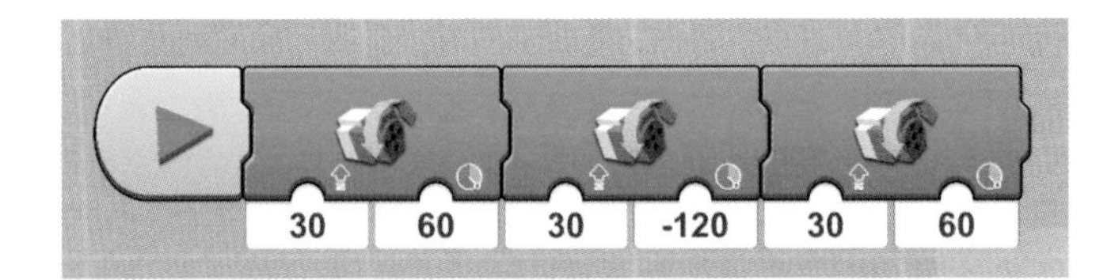

FIGURE 11-3 A sequence that makes the scanner head look right, left, and then straight ahead again

FIGURE 11-4 shows how the scanner head rotates, according to the program above.

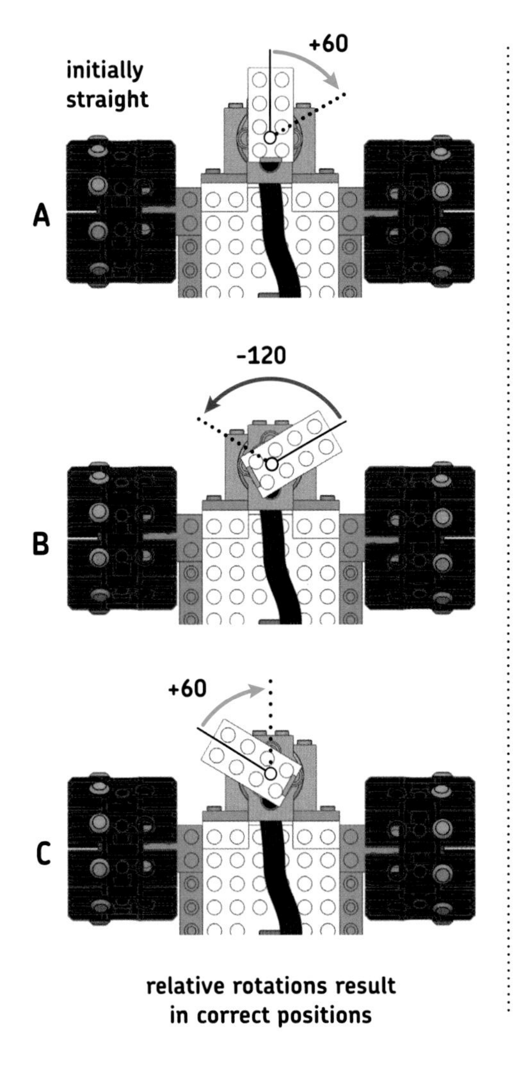

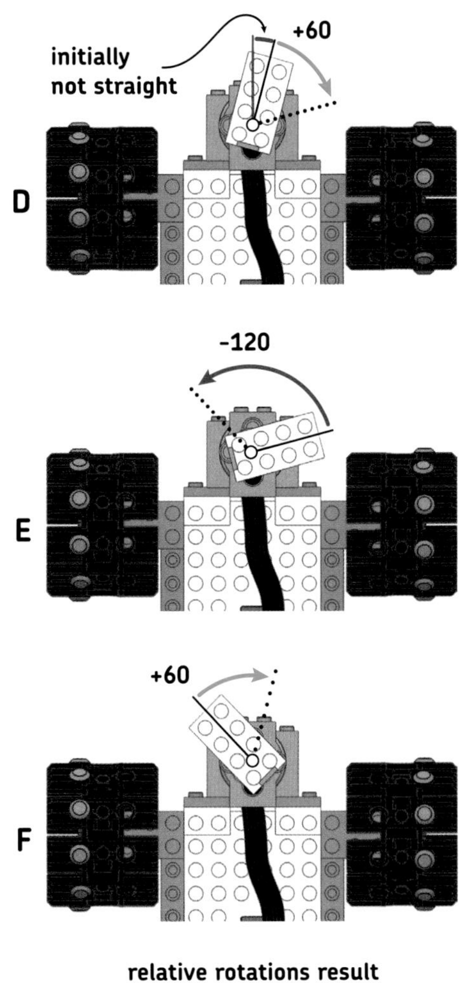

FIGURE 11-4 If the scanner head is not straight when the program starts, it won't rotate to the positions you want.

Before starting the program, be sure to manually align the scanner so that it is looking straight ahead or your measurements will be off. Set the first **External Motor Run for Angle** block input to +60, since that's how many degrees we want the head to turn right.

To have MARIO look left, we need it to move through 120 degrees: 60 degrees back to center and then another 60 degrees to the left. We enter the 120 degree value with a minus sign to make the motor turn in the opposite direction.

Finally, to return the scanner to the center, we set the Degrees input of the last block to +60 degrees.

Remember that each time the program executes an **External Motor Run for Angle** block, the value of the Degrees input is relative to the previous shaft position. Every time you want to rotate the scanner head to a new position, you must take into account its last position.

Illustrations (**D**), (**E**), and (**F**) in **FIGURE 11-4** show what happens if the scanner head is not facing straight ahead when the program begins. Since every movement is relative to the current position of the scanner, the robot's head will always be in a different position than you want.

Next, you'll learn how to set the target shaft angle, letting the program manage all the rest. After that, you'll see how to automatically bring the scanner head to the straight-ahead position so you don't have to do it manually.

moving relative to a zero position

Instead of running a motor by an angle relative to the current shaft position, it's much easier to refer to a known preset position for a motor's shaft. Let's see how to tell a motor to run to a position relative to the position it had when the shaft angle reading was set to 0 with a Preset block. Since the Degrees input of the **External Motor Run for Angle** block tells the motor how much to rotate from its current position, we *subtract* the current shaft angle (`where I am`) from the target angle (`where to go`) to determine where to head. Here's the corresponding formula:

```
way to go = where to go - where I am
```

To determine how much to move the sensor head, we'll use the **Subtraction Operator** block to calculate the difference between the target angle and the current angle:

```
distance = target angle - current angle
```

Use the **External Motor Angle Reporter** block to get the current shaft angle and attach it to one of the Subtraction block inputs, as shown in **FIGURE 11-5**.

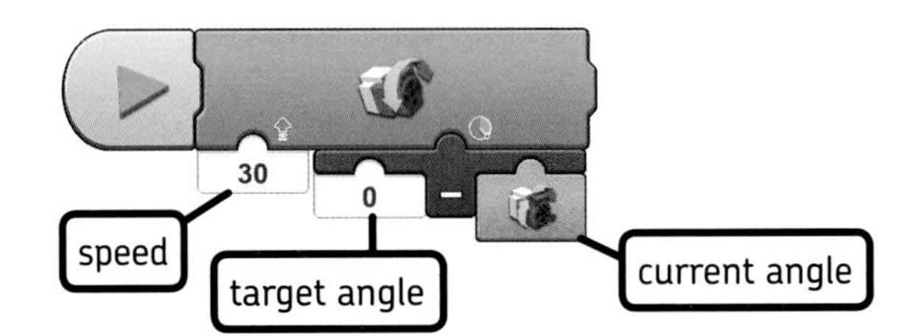

FIGURE 11-5 Use this block to determine how far to rotate the scanner head relative to the zero angle position.

FIGURE 11-6 shows some examples of how the program of **FIGURE 11-5** works. To test it for yourself, you have to make sure the scanner head was in the straight-ahead position when you connected the Move Hub to the app. If it was not, disconnect the Move Hub, manually rotate the scanner head to the straight-ahead position, and then reconnect the Move Hub to the app. Later, we will use the Preset block to do this automatically.

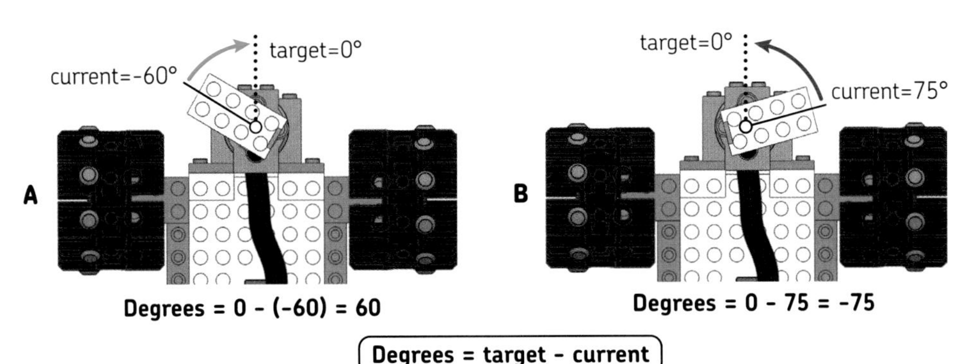

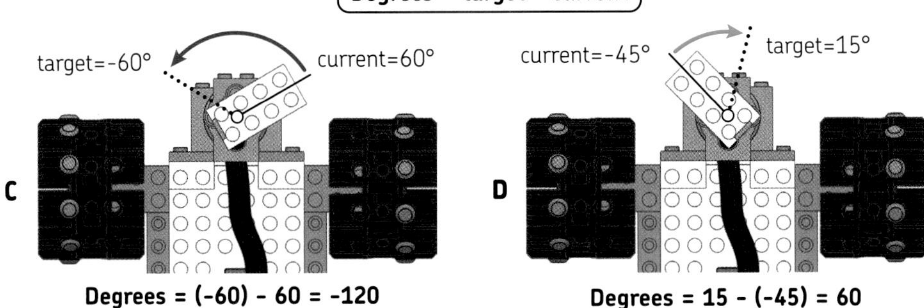

FIGURE 11-6 Examples of how the program of **FIGURE 11-5** works

experiment 11-1

Using the program shown in **FIGURE 11-5** as reference, make a program that works like the one shown in **FIGURE 11-3**. This time, make MARIO look 45 degrees to the right, 90 degrees to the left, and then straight ahead again. Which values will you need for the target angle each time?

Manually rotate the scanner head away from the straight-ahead position. When you run the program, the scanner will rotate back to its original position. Try manually rotating the scanner head to other positions and check that it always returns to its original position no matter whether you first rotated it to the right or to the left.

By setting target angles other than 0, you can make the scanner head rotate to any position relative to the straight-ahead position, without having to consider the current position of the motor shaft.

resetting the scanner head

To avoid having to manually align the scanner head, we'll write a sequence that automatically moves it to point straight ahead and that sets the value of the rotation sensor to 0. The scanner head has a limited range of motion because the 2M beam hits the black pin so it can't spin freely. Our goal here will be to program a sequence to rotate the scanner until it hits one of its limits and then rotate it back to the straight-ahead position.

Because the motor's rotation sensors read the angle of the motor's rotation relative to the last time they were reset, we'll preset the external motor rotation sensor to 0 so that we can refer to the straight-ahead position as the *zero position*.

To preset the scanner head position, we'll turn the motor until the beam hits the black pin. Since we can measure the angle of the scanner from the straight-ahead position to the position it has when it hits the pin, we know how many degrees the scanner should rotate in order to return to the straight-ahead position.

In order to move the motor right to the point where the scanner head hits the black pin, we set the motor to run slowly, wait for a fraction of a second for it to start moving, and stop it as soon as its measured speed becomes 0, which tells us that it's now blocked by the pin. **FIGURE 11-7** shows how to do this.

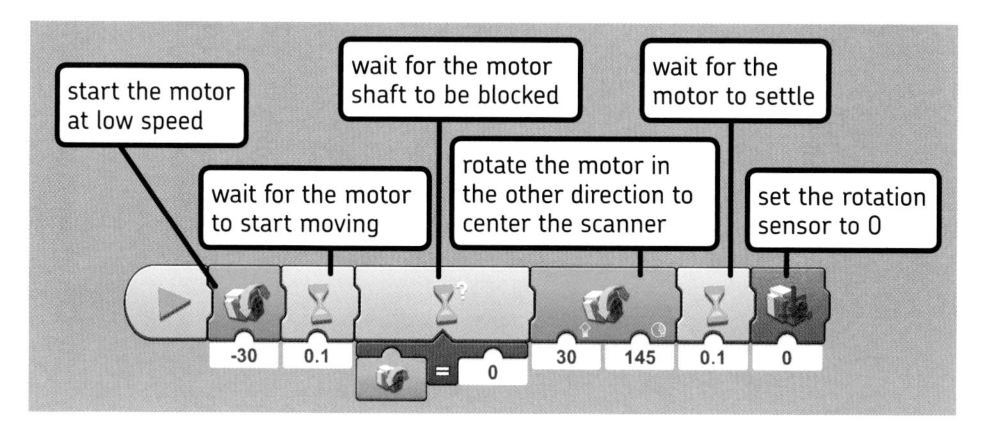

FIGURE 11-7 This sequence positions the scanner head to the straight-ahead position and sets the rotation sensor to 0.

First, we start the motor at a low speed, then once its speed is 0, instead of stopping the motor, we use an **External Motor Run for Angle** block to rotate the shaft in the opposite direction so that the scanner head returns to center. (You'll find the value of this **External Motor Run for Angle** block's Degrees input by trial and error, since it depends on your robot's structure.) After another short pause, we set the external motor rotation sensor value to 0.

Once you've made the sequence in **FIGURE 11-7**, test it to verify that the rotating head is properly positioned.

making composite blocks

When you have a sequence of blocks that you want to use repeatedly to perform a specific operation, you can group them into a composite block, or *c-block*, that you can then reuse in your program. This is a great way to organize your code, keeping it clean and readable.

If you've programmed any of the official robots in the BOOST app, you were coding using composite blocks. The **Spin Propeller** block shown below, and used in the first BOOST app activity for the Getting Started Vehicle, is one such block.

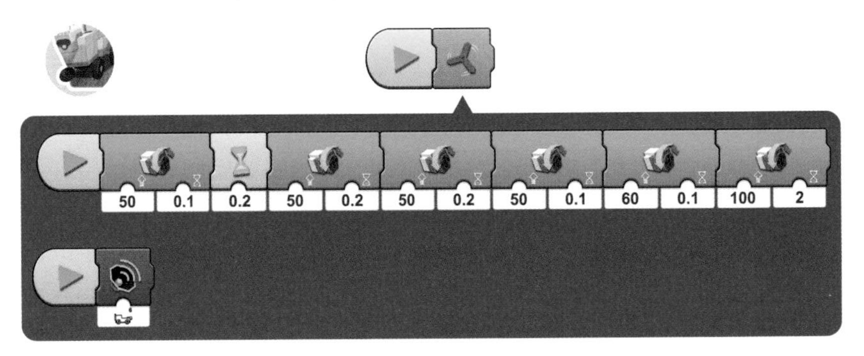

Follow these steps to make your first c-block for the scanner head reset procedure.

1: Switch to the Composite blocks palette (the grey tab) and tap the block icon with the plus sign and dashed outline.

2: You should see a light blue block with a random icon and the c-block preview frame with a dark blue background appear. Drag the sequence you created in **FIGURE 11-7** into the preview frame where the dashed arrow is pointing. To keep the original sequence in the main canvas, copy it before dragging.

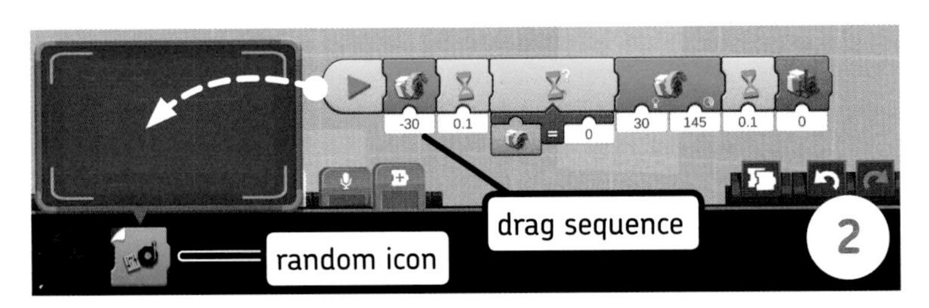

3: A tiny image inside the preview should show the sequence of your new c-block. Tap the preview frame to edit the c-block.

4: When you edit a c-block, the canvas background should change from pale to dark blue. Tap the block preview ❶ to replace its icon with one from the library (⊥). Tap the wrench ❷ to edit the c-block's background color. (Use a light blue, white, red, or purple color to distinguish your c-blocks from the regular orange and green blocks). Tap the red back arrow at the top-left corner of the screen ❸ to return to the main program.

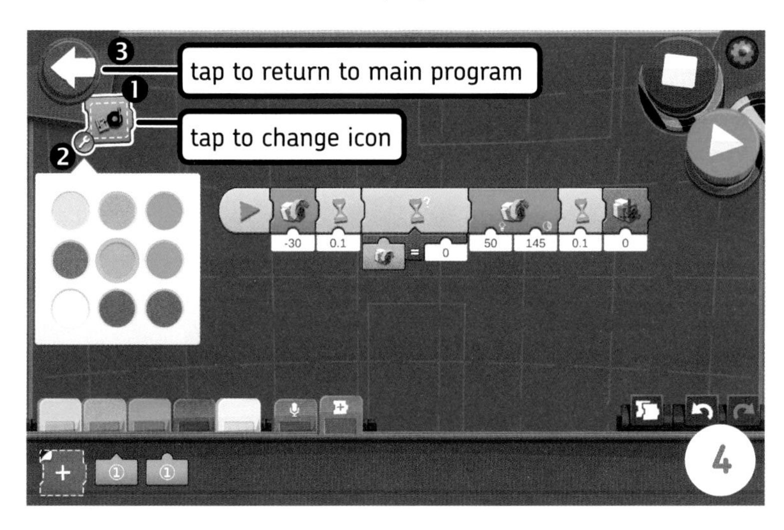

5: Once you're back in the main canvas, add a yellow Start block and attach your newly created **Reset** c-block to the sequence. Start the program to check that it still works.

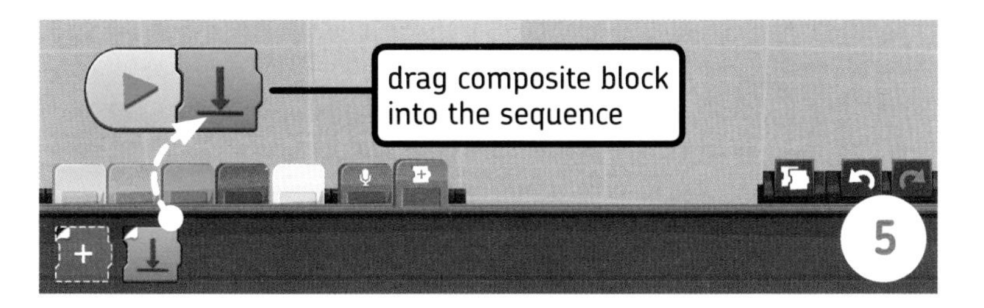

FIGURE 11-8 shows the final **Reset** c-block sequence.

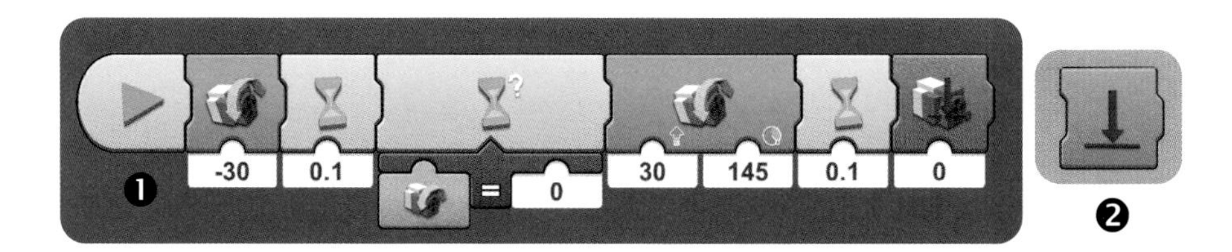

FIGURE 11-8 The complete Reset composite block sequence ❶ and what the c-block looks like in your program ❷

making composite blocks with inputs

The sequence you made to control the scanner head in **FIGURE 11-5** should work great, but packing it into a c-block that takes inputs would make it even better because the c-block uses much less space and makes the program easier to read. Follow these steps to create the **MoveAbs** c-block with inputs that will set the direction the scanner should point to.

1: If you haven't already done so, create the sequence shown in **FIGURE 11-5**. Next, switch to the Composite blocks palette and tap the icon with the plus sign to start creating a new c-block.

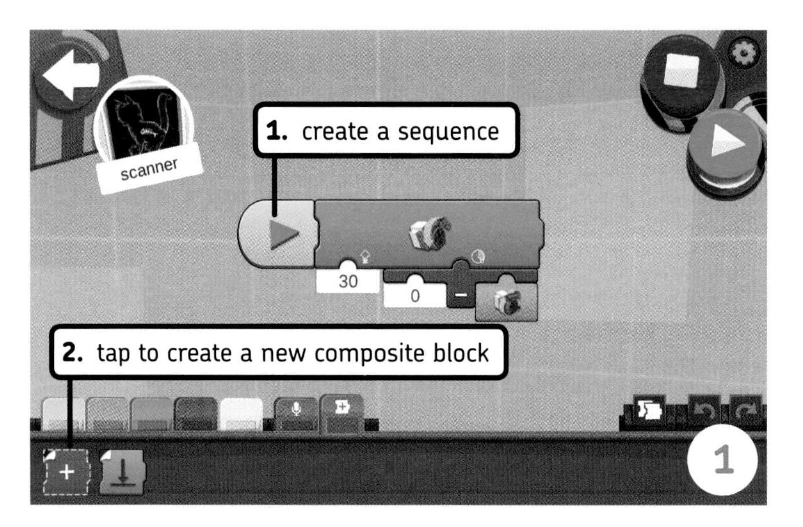

2: Drag your programming sequence into the c-block preview frame, and then tap the frame to edit the newly created c-block.

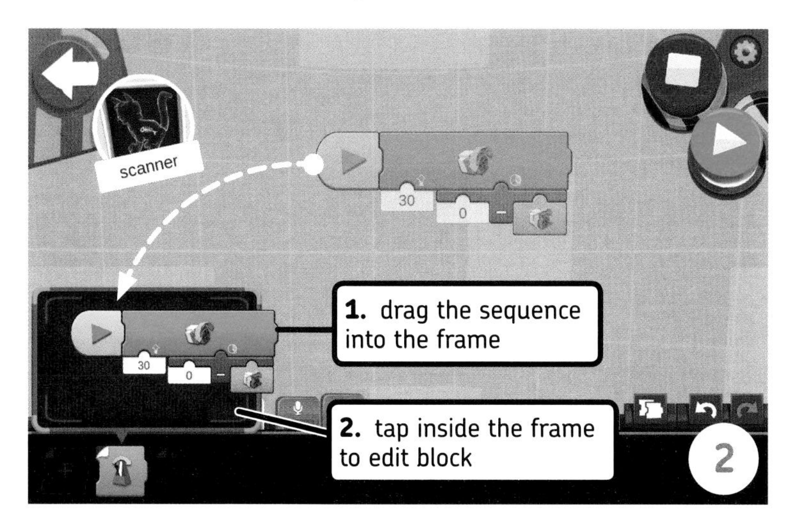

3: Change the block's icon to the external motor icon with the curved yellow arrow as shown ( ). Then drag **Numeric Input** block 1 ( ) and attach it to the Motor block's Speed parameter. Two Input blocks, both numbered 2, should appear as shown in the palette.

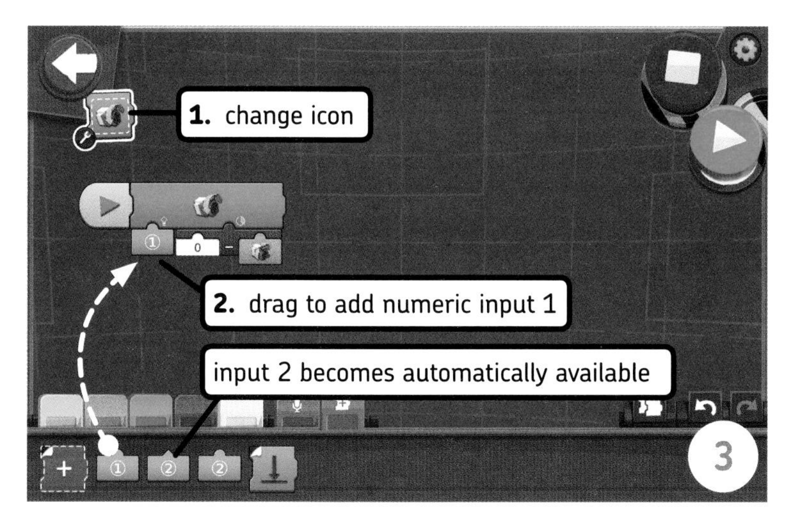

4: Drag **Numeric Input** block 2 (②) and attach it to the first input of the **Subtraction Operator** block as shown. Finally, tap the red back arrow to return to the main program.

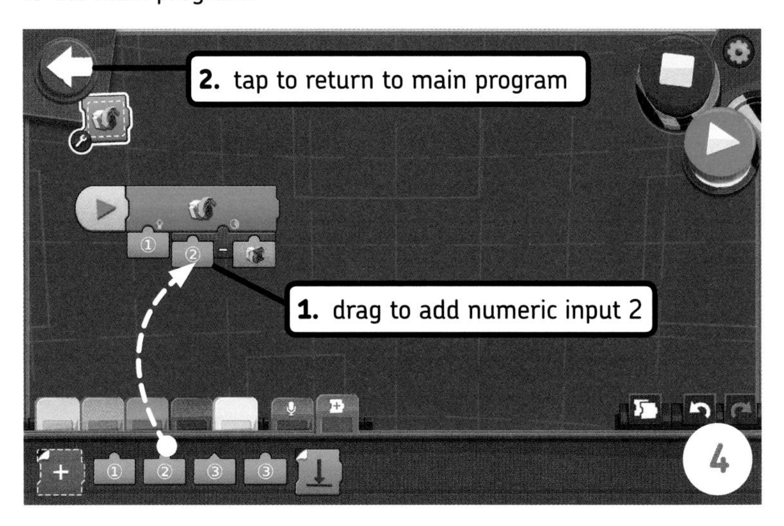

FIGURE 11-9 shows the final **MoveAbs** c-block. You will use this c-block later in the hand-following program.

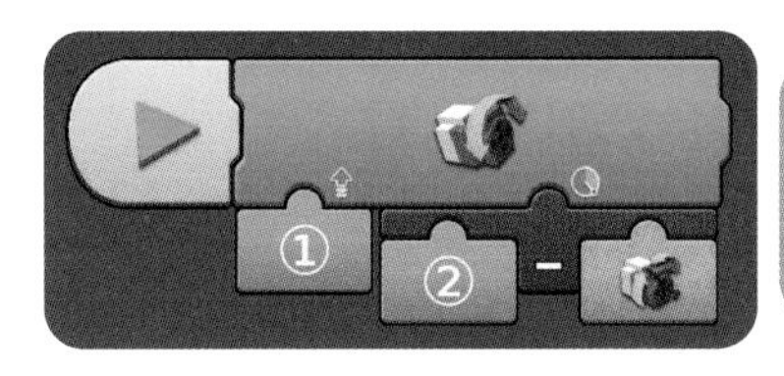

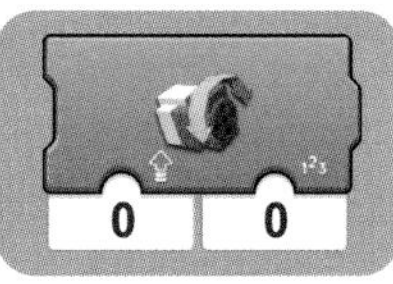

FIGURE 11-9 The MoveAbs composite block sequence and final appearance of the c-block

experiment 11-2

Use three **MoveAbs** c-blocks to make a sequence that works like the one in **FIGURE 11-3**. This time, make MARIO look 60 degrees to the right, 60 degrees to the left, and then straight ahead. Which values will you need for each angle parameter?

creating composite blocks from scratch

You can create a composite block from scratch even if you haven't already made the sequence that will go inside it. Tap the **+** icon (step 1) to create a new c-block. Then tap the empty preview screen (step 2). Once in the c-block–editing canvas, start creating the sequence as usual. If you tap the Back arrow without adding any programming blocks, the whole c-block will be automatically deleted.

editing and removing composite blocks

After you create a composite block, you can modify its code, as well as add, remove, or change its input parameter type (though *only* if that c-block is not used anywhere else in the project). To edit a c-block, go to the Composite blocks palette, tap a block, and tap the blue preview frame.

adding inputs

To add inputs to a composite block, simply drag them from the palette into the canvas. Each time you drop an Input block, two new Input blocks should appear (one for each data type, numerical and logical), as shown in **FIGURE 11-10**.

For example, if you don't use any inputs in your composite block, the palette should include only two Input blocks (Numeric and Logic), both labeled 1, since whichever one you drop into the canvas at this point will be the first Input block (**A**). If you drag and drop a **Numeric Input** block 1 onto the canvas, the two new Input blocks numbered 2 should appear in your palette (**B**). If you drag the **Logic Input** block 2 onto the canvas, two new Input blocks numbered 3 should appear (**C**).

Because each input can have only one data type, you will need to decide which to use before placing the Input block into the canvas. In (**B**) of **FIGURE 11-10**, for example, **Logic Input** block 1 has disappeared because you chose the numeric type for Input block 1.

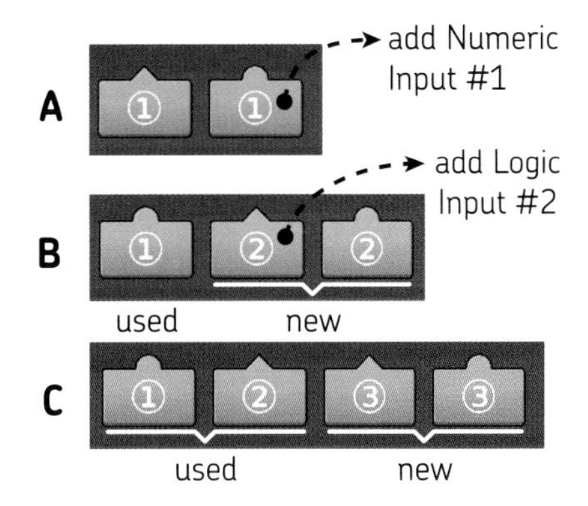

FIGURE 11-10 Adding inputs to a composite block

deleting inputs

To delete an input parameter, just drag all of its copies away from the sequence. You can attach the same Input block to more blocks in a sequence, but once the input is no longer used, the Input blocks in the palette should all decrease by one.

deleting a composite block

To delete a composite block from your project, first remove its instances from all sequences in your project, including the sequences inside any composite blocks. When you try to delete a composite block, you should see one of three icons, as shown in **FIGURE 11-11**.

The faded Trash Can icon in (**A**) shows that the block is used somewhere in the program and cannot be deleted. The icon in (**B**) tells you that the block is not used in the program and can be deleted. Tap the Trash Can icon to delete it; the icon should turn green, and ask for confirmation (**C**). To confirm deletion, tap the Trash Can icon again. To cancel deletion, tap anywhere else.

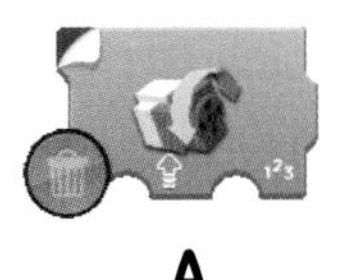

FIGURE 11-11 You'll see one of these when you try to delete a composite block.

experiment 11-3

Create a program that makes MARIO turn its head in random directions from −90 to 90 degrees in steps of 10 degrees (−90, −80, −70 . . . 0 . . . 10, 20 . . . 90) with a random pause between movements lasting from 0.1 to 1 seconds in steps of 0.1 seconds (0.1, 0.2, 0.3 . . . 1).

Hint: use the **Reset** and **MoveAbs** c-blocks.

hand following

In this section, you'll learn how to control MARIO's movement by having it follow your hand. We'll have MARIO scan for nearby objects and move toward an object it senses until it moves out of range.

With this program in place, you can make MARIO go forward by placing your hand in front of the sensor when it's looking straight and make it turn by showing your hand when the sensor is looking right or left.

This program repeats a sequence of code, the Follow procedure, four times (each time with different input values) in order to control the scanning direction and how the robot's steering will change when it detects an object. The pseudocode for this procedure looks like this:

```
Begin Follow procedure
   Turn head to target (input 1 = scanner angle)
   If distance read by sensor is less than 8, then
      Slowly move with steering set to (input 2 = steering)
      Wait until distance read by sensor is greater than 7
      Stop moving
   End If
   Wait 0.2 seconds
End procedure
```

The hand-following program uses this procedure four times in a loop:

```
Begin infinite loop
   Call Follow procedure with parameters: look right, steer right
   Call Follow procedure with parameters: look straight, move straight
   Call Follow procedure with parameters: look left, steer left
   Call Follow procedure with parameters: look straight, move straight
Go back to the start of the infinite loop
```

FIGURE 11-12 shows how to code the Follow procedure with a c-block with two inputs.

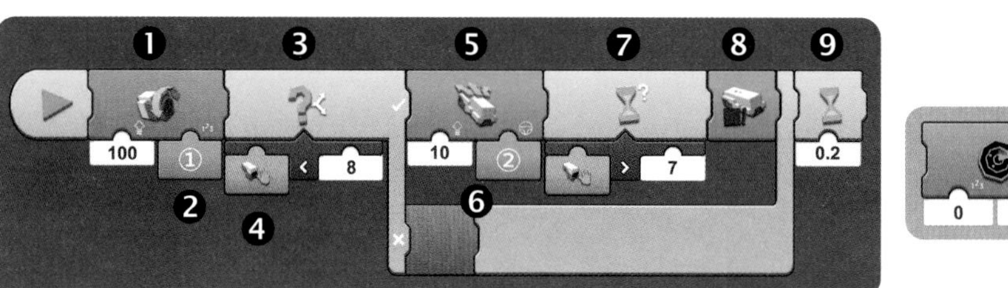

FIGURE 11-12 The Follow c-block sequence

In this sequence, the **MoveAbs** c-block ❶ first rotates the scanner at full speed to the angle specified by Numeric Input 1 ❷. Next, a **Switch** block ❸ checks whether the distance read by the **Sensor Distance Reporter** block ❹ is less than 8 (the range in which your hand is detected). If an object (your hand) is detected, the top sequence inside the **Switch** block will run, and a **Drivebase Move Steering Unlimited** block ❺ will move the robot at speed 10, setting the steering value with Numeric Input 2 ❻. The **Wait for True** block ❼ waits until the sensor measures a distance greater than 7, which keeps the robot moving until the sensor doesn't see your hand anymore, at which point the **Drivebase Stop** block ❽ stops the robot. The **Wait for Time** block ❾ after the **Switch** block pauses the scanner's rotation from one position to the next.

If the distance measured by the sensor is greater than or equal to 8, the **Switch** block executes the bottom sequence, which means nothing runs. The robot does not have to do anything when your hand is too far away.

As you can see in **FIGURE 11-13**, the complete hand-following program contains four copies of the **Follow** composite block. At the beginning of the program, before the infinite loops runs, the position of the scanner head is set by the **Reset** c-block. The sequence of **Follow** c-blocks makes the robot behave as described earlier.

FIGURE 11-13 The hand-following program

storing numbers with variables

The programs we've made so far don't remember any values because they use the numeric data from sensors as they receive it. Sometimes, however, you'll want your program to "remember" a value to be used later. (Note that your BOOST can only remember numbers.)

In order to store numbers in the robot's memory, you'll need to first assign a name to each stored number to avoid confusion. We'll store our numbers in variables, a kind of temporary, labeled container in the robot's memory. You can store a number in a variable and retrieve it later by referring to its variable name.

FIGURE 11-14 should help you to understand variables. The boxes represent variables, and the balls represent the data that we're storing in these variables.

Tweak the parameters of the **Follow** c-blocks to see how the hand-following behavior changes. For example, try changing the angle to 60 and -60 and the steering to 50 and -50.

FIGURE 11-14 Variables are like labeled boxes.

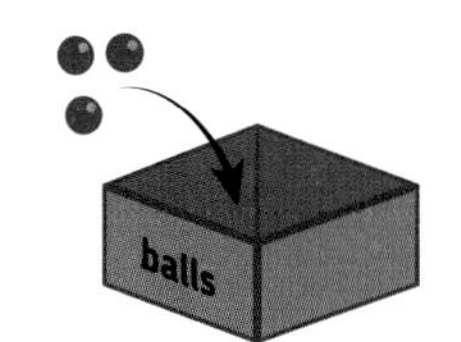

Writing a variable is like putting balls into an empty box.

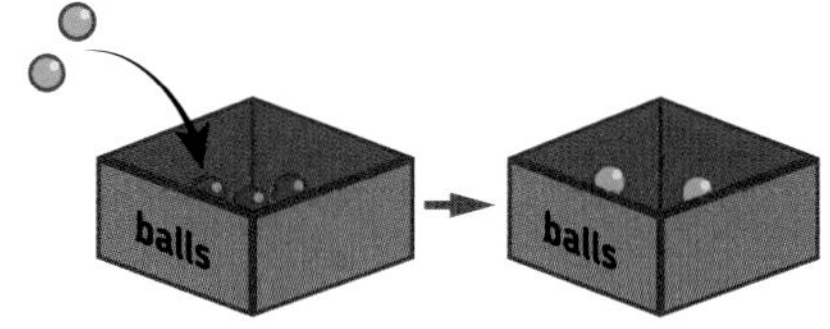

Writing a new number into a variable **replaces** the old value; it does not add to it.

Reading a variable is like looking into the box and counting the balls without removing them.

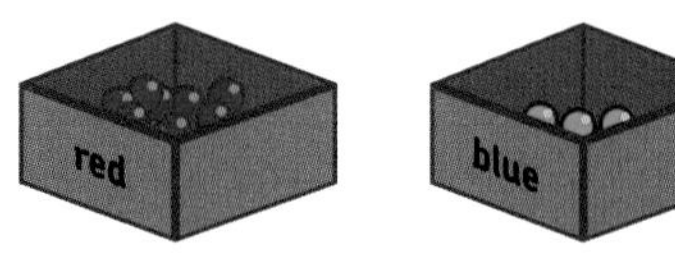

Using variables with **different names** allows you to store different numbers in separate boxes.

NOTE:

Select your variable name by tapping the input label.

The BOOST app includes a **Write Variable** block (**A**) and **Read Variable** block (**B**), as shown in **FIGURE 11-15**. Use these blocks to write a value into a variable or read a value from a variable. Labels in the figure show you where to find the variable name and its value.

FIGURE 11-15 The blocks to write (A) and read (B) variables

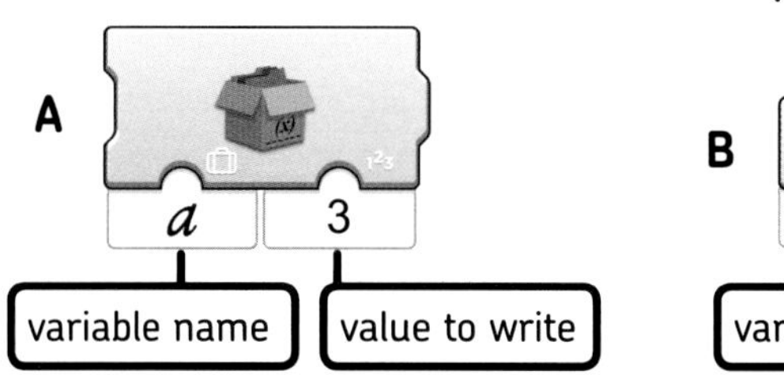

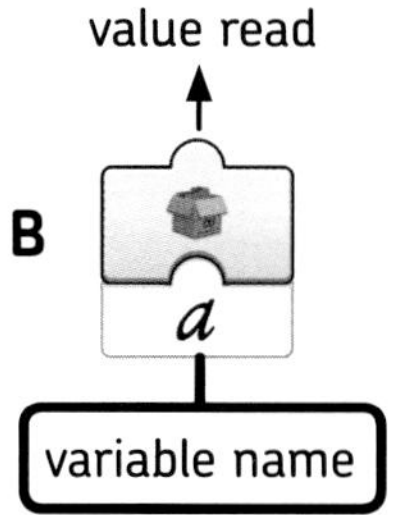

navigating around clutter

Until now, when MARIO is moving and sees an obstacle, we've made it turn in either a fixed or random direction. Now, we'll have MARIO scan both left and right, measure the distance of the nearest object in each direction, and steer towards the less cluttered direction, resulting in more efficient exploration. The pseudocode for this program looks like this:

```
Reset the scanner head
Begin infinite loop
    Go straight
    Wait for the sensor to measure a distance less than 8
    Stop moving
    Turn the scanner head 90 degrees to the right
```

```
        Store the distance read by the sensor in variable A
        Turn the scanner head 90 degrees to the left
        Store the distance read by the sensor in variable B
        Turn the scanner head straight
        Move back a bit
        If (the distance stored in A is greater than the
            distance stored in B), then
           Curve back to the left for a bit
        Else
           Curve back to the right for a bit
        End If
    Go back to the start of the infinite loop
```

As you can see in this pseudocode, we want MARIO to look right, store the distance reading in that direction into one variable, and then look left and store the distance reading in another variable. Next, we compare the two distance readings and turn in the direction of the greatest measured distance, where there are presumably fewer obstacles in its way.

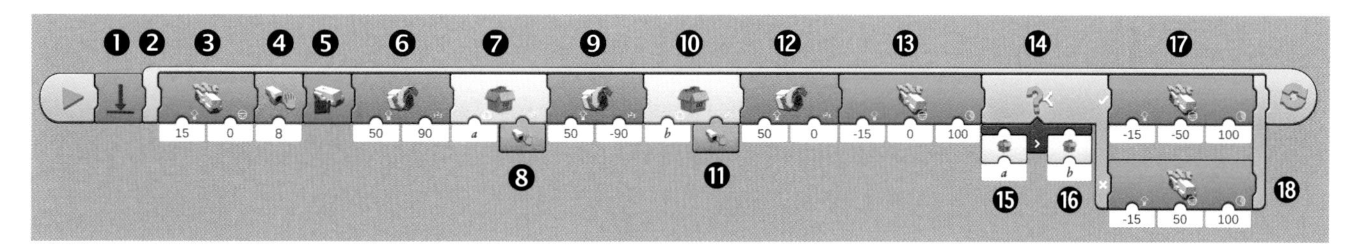

FIGURE 11-16 The *Go to Free Area* program

FIGURE 11-16 shows the finished BOOST code for this procedure. Copy the program *Go to Free Area* and test it.

At the beginning of this sequence, we use the **Reset** c-block ❶ to bring the scanner to the straight-ahead position. The rest of the sequence repeats forever with the **Infinite Loop** ❷. The **Drivebase Move Steering Unlimited** block ❸ makes MARIO go slowly forward. When it detects an obstacle, the **Wait for Distance** block ❹ lets the sequence continue, and the **Drivebase Stop** block ❺ halts MARIO.

The **MoveAbs** c-block ❻ rotates the scanner 90 degrees to the right. At this point, we use the **Write Variable** block ❼ to store the value read by the **Sensor Distance Reporter** block into ❽ variable *a*. The **MoveAbs** c-block ❾ rotates the scanner 90 degrees to the left (the minus sign means we tell the motor to rotate to the other direction with respect to before). Again, we use the **Write Variable** block ❿ to store the value read by the **Sensor Distance Reporter** block ⓫ in variable *b*. The **MoveAbs** c-block ⓬ brings the scanner to the straight-ahead position (the second input is 0).

Now, the **Drivebase Move Steering for Angle** block ⓭ makes MARIO go back for a bit. The **Compare Greater Than** block compares the value stored in variable a with the value stored in variable b. The **Read Variable** blocks ⓯ and ⓰ are used to return these values, which represent the distance reading at right and left, respectively. The result returned by the Compare block is the input of the **Switch** block ⓮. If the value of variable a is greater than the value of variable b, then the **Drivebase Move Steering for Angle** block ⓱ is executed and makes MARIO steer backward to the left (the heading changes to the right). Otherwise, the **Drivebase Move Steering for Angle** block ⓲ is executed and steers MARIO backward to the right (the heading changes to the left).

Copy the program *Go to Free Area* and test it.

what you've learned

In this chapter, you built a scanner head for MARIO and learned how to use the blocks that control single motors—as well as the sensor blocks that measure a motor's position and current speed. You also learned how to pack complex sequences into composite blocks and how to add input parameters to make your composite blocks more flexible. Finally, you learned how to store and retrieve numbers using variables. In Chapter 12, you'll make a dart shooter with a gunsight so MARIO can identify a target and fire a dart at it.

12

playing darts

In this chapter, you'll learn how to operate your robot via remote control from the LEGO BOOST app and build a dart shooter with a sight that MARIO can use to find its target, as shown below. You'll improve the remote control to make MARIO shoot on your command. Finally, you'll program MARIO to search for and shoot down targets on its own.

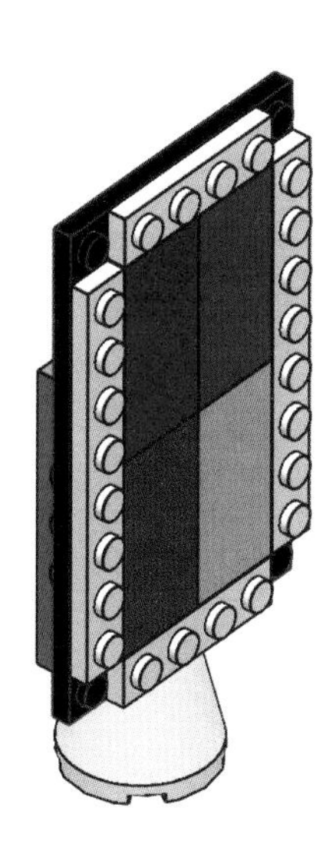

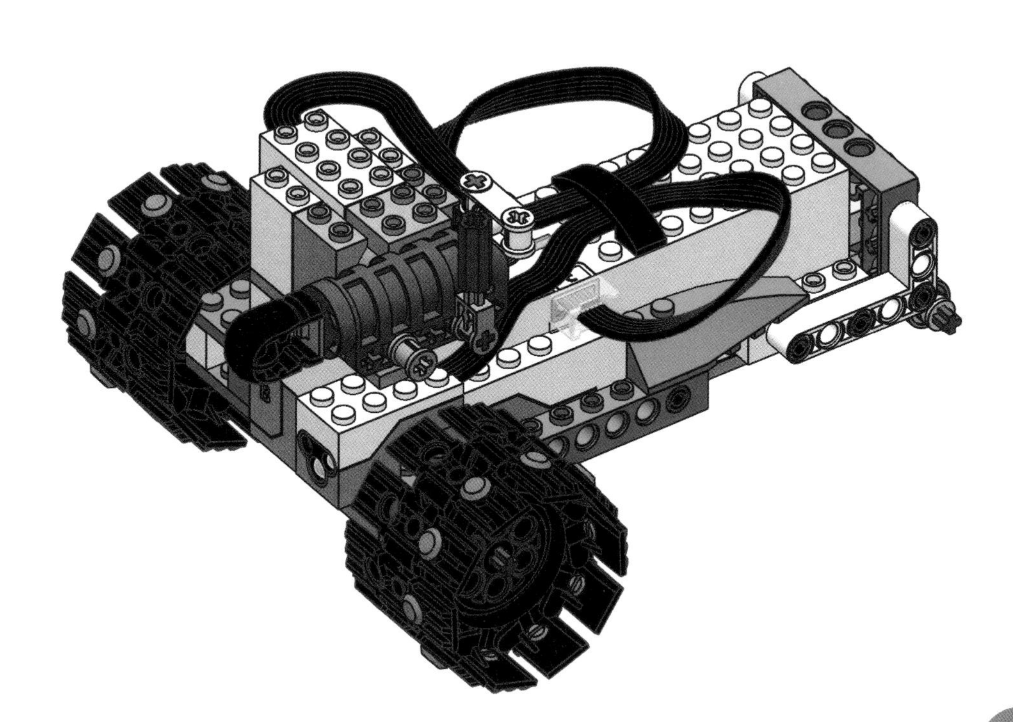

remote control blocks

The Sensor Blocks palette contains programming blocks that you can use to create a remote control for your robots, like a two-dimensional joystick, a button, a slider, and a numeric display, as shown in **FIGURE 12-1**. You can use these blocks to create the specific controller that you want.

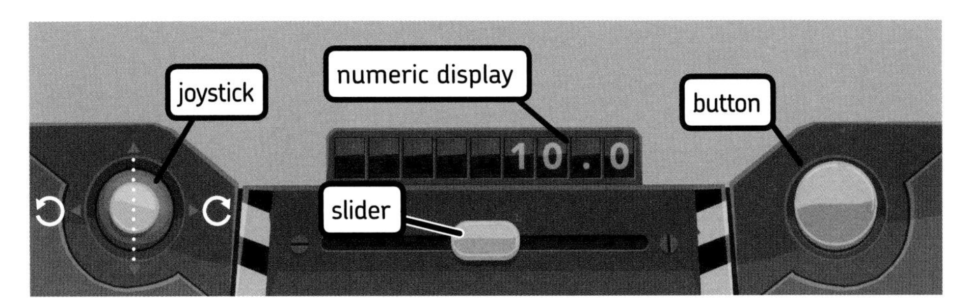

FIGURE 12-1 The remote-control interface includes a joystick, slider, button, and a numeric display.

You can show or hide each widget as shown at right. For example, you can show only the joystick, hiding all the other widgets. Here's a look at each in detail:

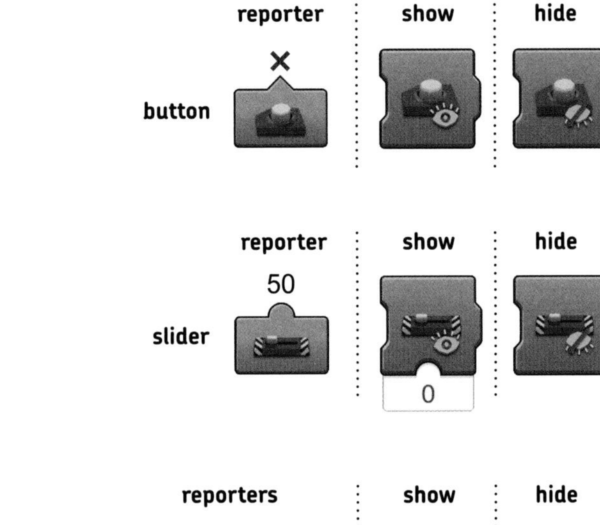

- The **Button State Reporter** block tells you the state of the button, returning true if the button is pressed and false otherwise. You can use the button to trigger an action, like shooting a dart. Show or hide the button with the **Show Button Widget** or **Hide Button Widget** blocks.
- The **Show Slider Widget** block has an input that lets you choose the position of the slider cursor. The **Slider Position Reporter** block returns the slider position as a number in the range from 0 to 100, where 0 represents the leftmost position and 100 represents the rightmost position. Show or hide the slider **Show Slider Widget** or **Hide Slider Widget** blocks, respectively.
- The BOOST app will use the joystick position to compute the Speed and Steering values that you can use as the inputs to a **Drivebase Move Steering Unlimited** block. The **Joystick Speed Reporter** block returns the Speed in a range from –100 to 100 (–100 when the joystick is all the way down and 100 when it's all the way up). The **Joystick Steering Reporter** block returns the Steering

value in a range from –100 to 100. (Negative numbers mean the joystick is in the left half of the circle, while positive numbers mean that it's in the right half, as indicated by the dashed line in **FIGURE 12-1**.) Show or hide the Joystick Widget with the **Show Joystick Widget** or **Hide Joystick Widget** blocks.

- The **Display Reporter** block returns the number displayed. Show or hide the Display Widget with the **Show Display Widget** or **Hide Display Widget** blocks. An input on the **Show Display Widget** block lets you set a number from 0 to 9999.9 to show on the display.

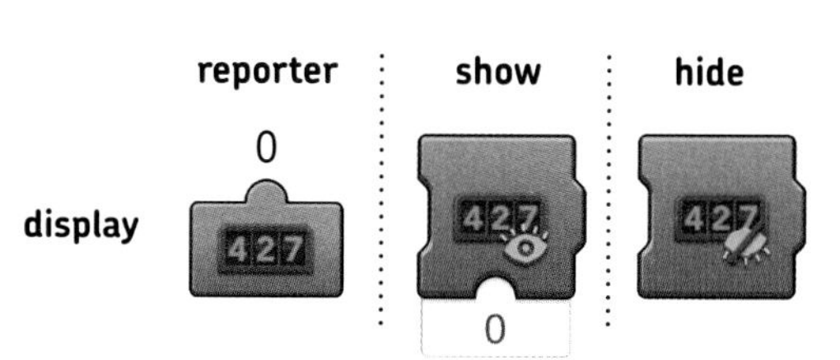

making a remote control for MARIO

Let's make a simple remote-control program that will allow us to drive MARIO around with the joystick. Create a project called `simpleRC` and then build the program shown in **FIGURE 12-2**. (You can use this program with any version of MARIO—the basic version of the robot that you built in Chapter 2 is fine.) If MARIO still has the scanner head mounted, disassemble it now.

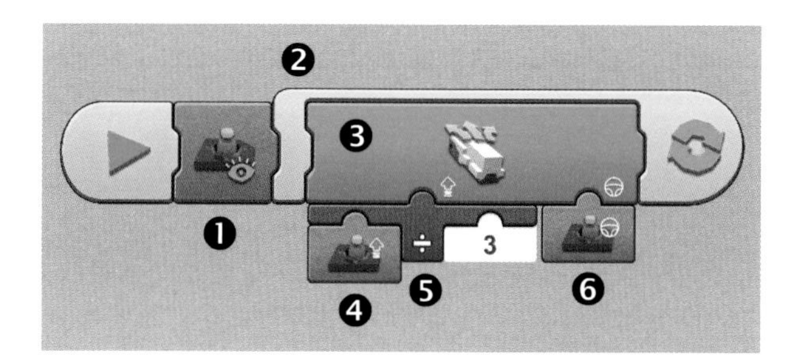

FIGURE 12-2 A basic remote-control program

The sequence starts with the **Show Joystick Widget** block ❶, which opens the remote-control interface with only the Joystick Widget visible. Next, the **Infinite Loop** block ❷ repeatedly executes a **Drivebase Move Steering Unlimited** block ❸, whose inputs come from the **Joystick Speed Reporter** ❹ and the **Joystick Steering Reporter** ❻ blocks. In order to make the robot easier to drive, we limit its maximum speed by dividing the value provided by the **Joystick Speed Reporter** block ❹ by 3. Thus, the maximum speed you can set for the robot is 100 divided by 3, or about 33. If we didn't use this **Division Operator** block ❺ to reduce the robot's speed, it would be very difficult to control because the wheels would move too fast and tend to slip.

tilt and drive!

There's another cool way to remote-control your robot: by tilting the device you're holding in your hands, as shown in **FIGURE 12-3**. Two Sensor blocks allow you to measure how much your device is tilted:

- When you tilt the device sideways, the **Hub Tilt X Reporter** returns a number from -100 to 100. When you hold the device with the long edge perfectly horizontal (flat on a table, for example), the block returns 0. It returns a positive number when you tilt the device to the right and a negative number when you tilt it to the left.
- When you tilt the device backward and forward, the **Hub Tilt Y Reporter** returns a number from -100 to 100. The value 0 is returned when the device screen is slightly tilted toward you, at an angle that is ideal to read the screen. You get positive values when you tilt the screen away from you and negative values when you tilt the screen farther toward you.

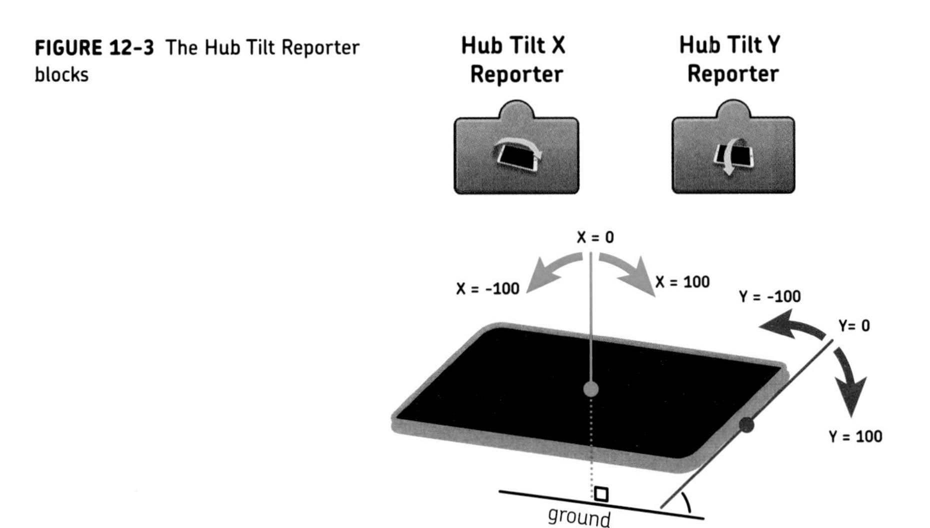

FIGURE 12-3 The Hub Tilt Reporter blocks

The program shown in **FIGURE 12-4** lets you control your robot by tilting the device that is running the LEGO BOOST app. (Notice that this program looks very similar to the one shown in **FIGURE 12-2**.) The **Hub Tilt Y Reporter** block is used to control the speed of the robot, and the **Hub Tilt X Reporter** block is used to control the steering of the robot.

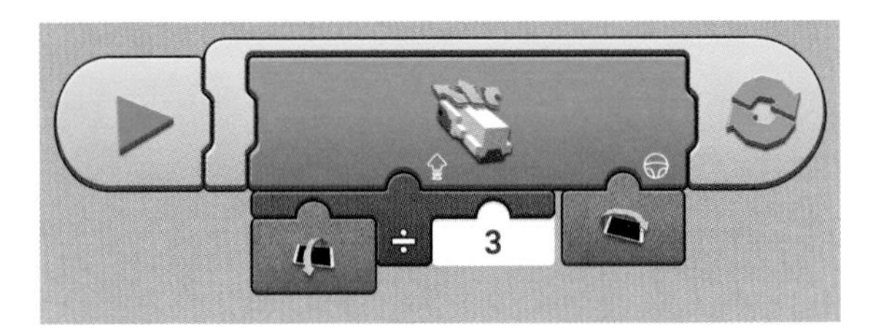

FIGURE 12-4 This program lets you remotely control your robot's movement by tilting the device that is running the LEGO BOOST app.

adding the Button Widget to the remote control

In this section, we'll improve our remote-control program by adding the Button Widget to the remote-control interface. Pressing the button will change the color of the Move Hub LED from green to red. **FIGURE 12-5** shows the new program with the newly added blocks marked with numbers.

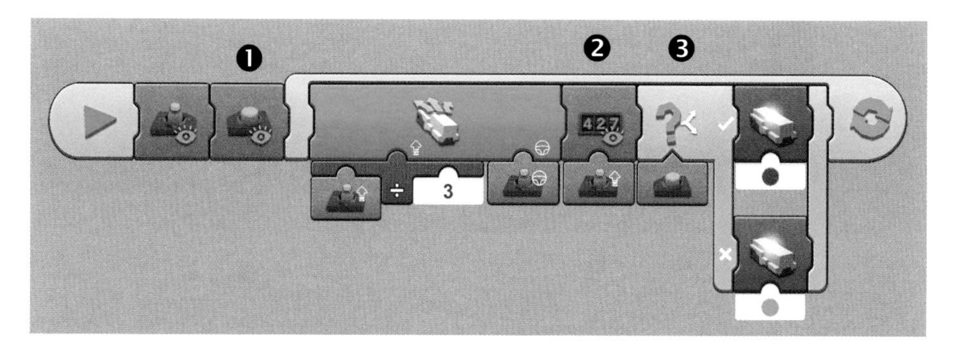

FIGURE 12-5 A remote-control program that lets you drive MARIO around and change the color of the light on the Move Hub

The **Show Button Widget** block ❶ shows the Button Widget on the remote-control interface together with the joystick. The **Show Display Widget** block ❷ displays the current Joystick Widget speed on the display. The **Switch** block ❸ checks whether the Button Widget is pressed and sets the color of the Move Hub light to red or green, respectively.

experiment 12-1

Make a program that lets you use the button as a toggle. If you press it once, the light should turn red and stay red when you release the button. When you press the button again, the light should turn green and remain green.

Hint: you need to make two sequences of blocks, and you need to wait for the button to be pressed and released.

experiment 12-2

Make a program for MARIO that plays a shooting sound with an echo effect when you press the button. You should be able to control the amount of echo with the slider.

building the shooter and the target

Beginning with the basic version of MARIO that we built in Chapter 2, build the shooter attachment and the target by following the instructions below. (If you haven't already disassembled the scanner head, do so now.).

1

1x

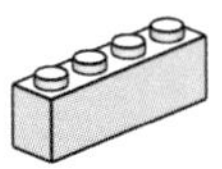

1x

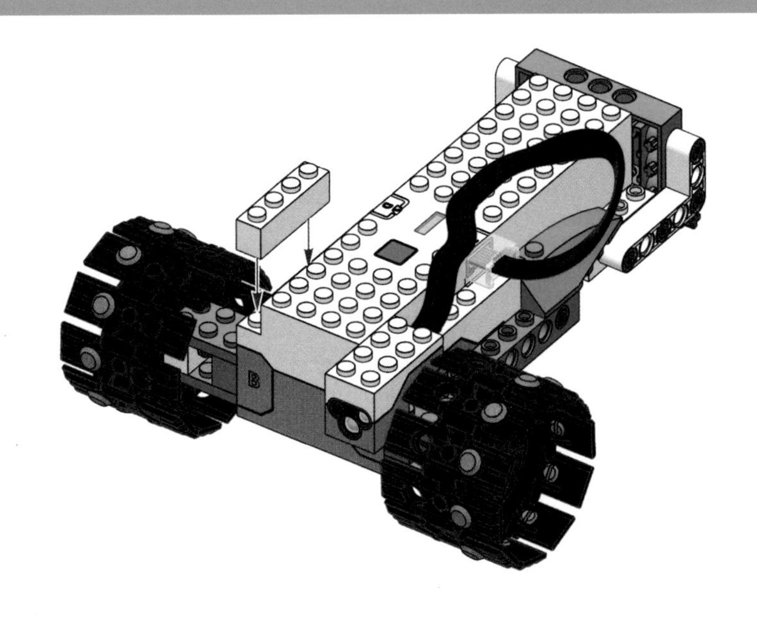

2

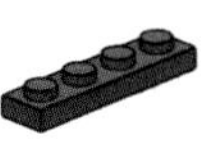

1x

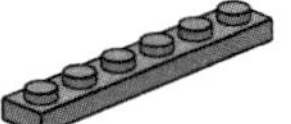

1x

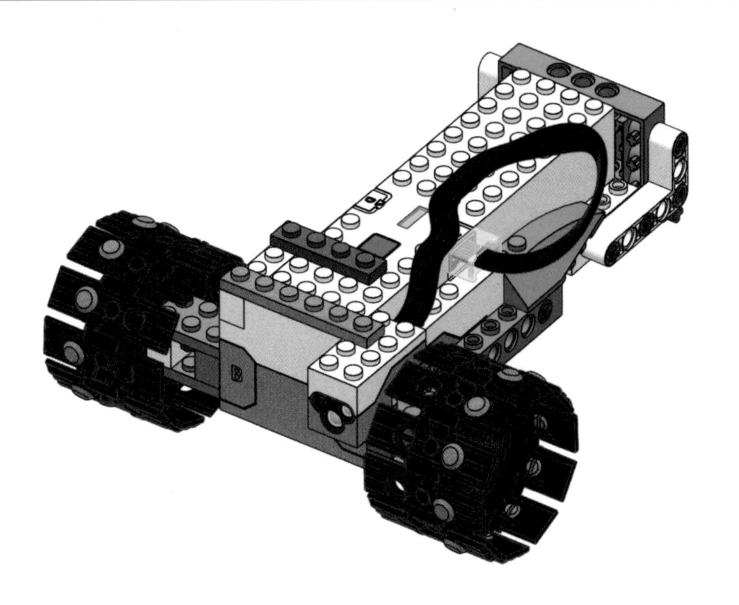

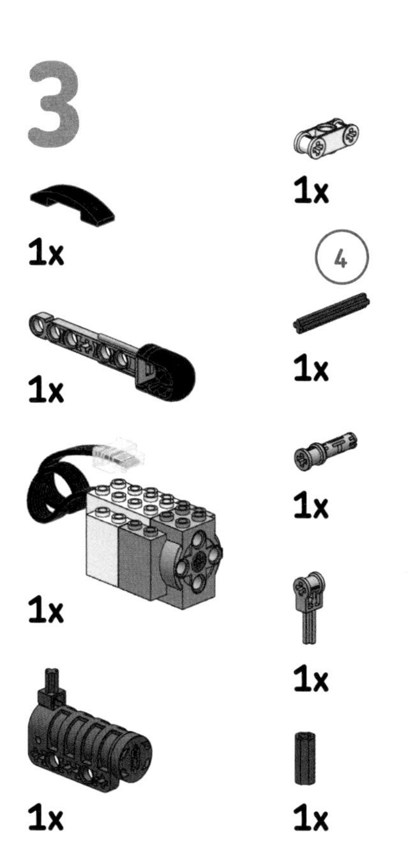
3
1x
1x
1x
1x
1x
4
1x
1x
1x
1x
1x

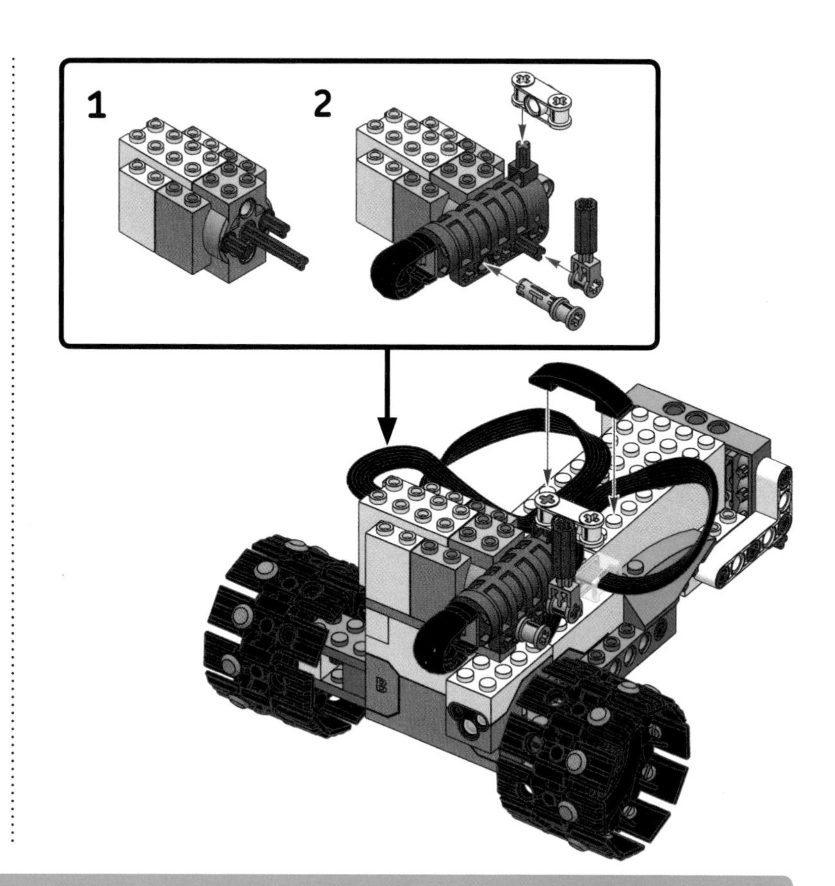
1
2

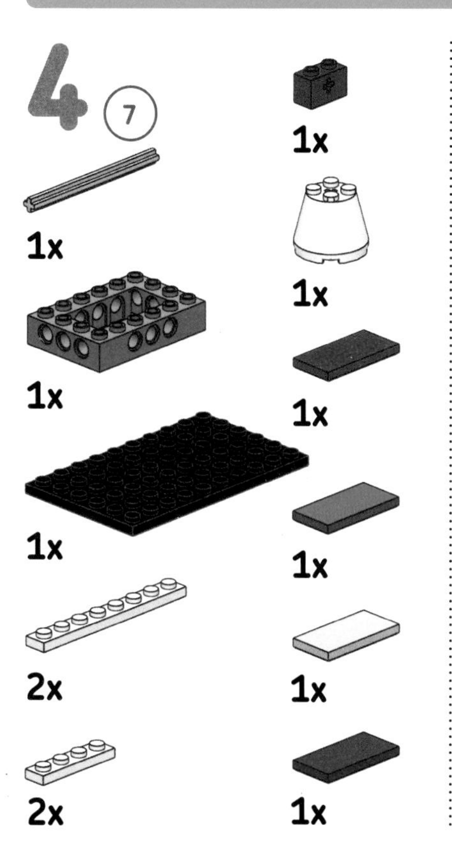
4
7
1x
1x
1x
2x
2x
1x
1x
1x
1x
1x
1x

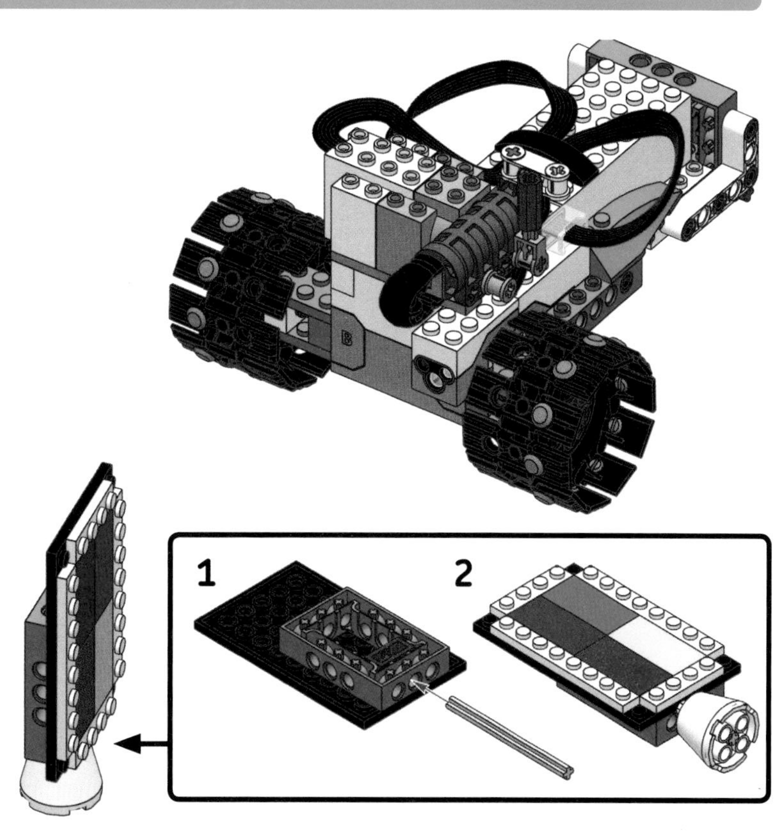
1
2

QuickDraw: a dart-shooting game

In this section, we'll program a "race against time" shooting game called *QuickDraw*. The basic setup is shown in **FIGURE 12-6**. When the game starts, you'll have 10 seconds to move MARIO to the target, take aim, and shoot using the remote control. If time runs out before you shoot, you lose. As long as you shoot before the time's up, the program assumes you win, even if you miss the target (because the app can't verify whether or not you hit the target). You can modify the setup by changing the starting point and the target position or by adding obstacles on the playmat.

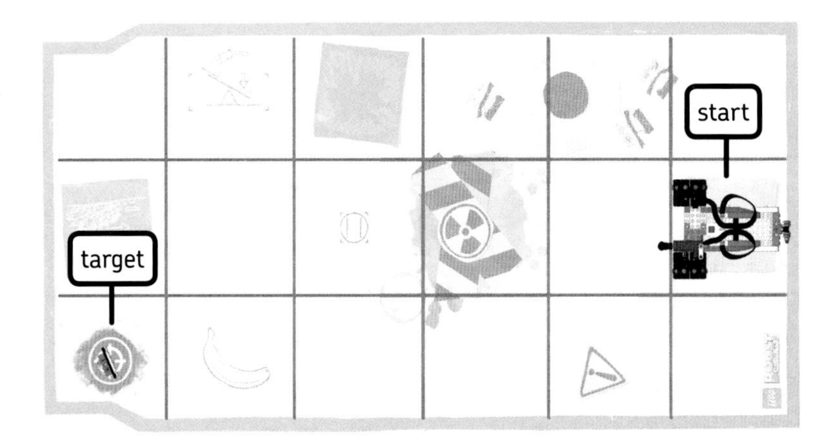

FIGURE 12-6 Place MARIO on the start cell and race against time to shoot down the target.

program description

The following pseudocode shows the steps needed to program this game. The lines marked with an asterisk (*) are procedures that need more than a basic block.

```
Main sequence:
Reset shooter trigger*
Start countdown sequence
Drive MARIO around the playmat with the joystick until the
    button is pressed*
Stop motors
Aim toward the target using the slider until the button is
    pressed*
Interrupt the countdown sequence
Shoot*
Play victory sound
```

The program includes a main sequence and a countdown sequence, as shown in **FIGURE 12-7**. The numbers above each block should help you match the blocks with the items in the description that follows.

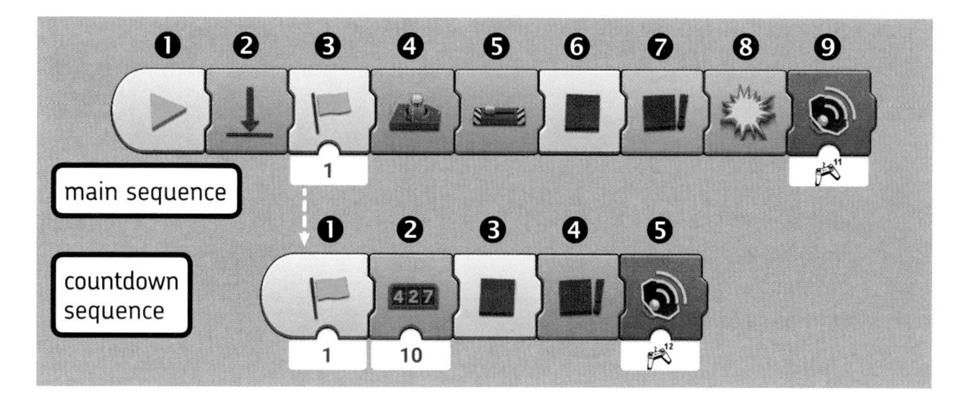

FIGURE 12-7
The *QuickDraw* program

main sequence

The main sequence controls the robot's actions and starts the execution of the countdown sequence.

- The main sequence begins with a **Start Sequence** block ❶. When you tap on the Play button, only the main sequence starts.
- The **Reset** c-block ❷ resets the trigger lever.
- The **Flag Trigger** block ❸ starts the countdown sequence attached to the **Start on Flag** block, as highlighted by the dashed arrow. (Notice that both blocks have the input set to the same value, 1.)
- After the clock starts ticking, the **Drive** c-block ❹ lets you control MARIO's movements with the joystick. When you press the button, the **Drive** c-block stops the motors and ends.
- The **Aim** c-block ❺ allows you to make the robot aim at the target. You'll control how it aims with the Slider Widget. When you press the button again, the block ends.
- The **Stop All Other Sequences** ❻ block interrupts the countdown sequence, while this main sequence continues to run.
- The **Stop** c-block ❼ stops the Move Hub motors and hides all the remote-control widgets.
- The **Shoot** c-block ❽ shoots the dart.
- The **Play Sound** block ❾ plays an orchestra hit (Game Sound 11) to let you know you won the game, and the sequence ends. The program ends at this point because this was the only sequence running. (The other one was interrupted before by the **Stop All Other Sequences** block ❻.)

countdown sequence

The countdown sequence in the pseudocode counts down from 10 to 0, showing how many seconds remain on the Display Widget. When the countdown reaches 0, the main sequence stops the robot, hides the remote control, and plays a "fail" sound.

- The countdown sequence begins with a **Start on Flag** block ❶ that's triggered by the **Flag Trigger** block in the main sequence. This sequence runs in parallel with the main sequence.
- The **Countdown** c-block ❷ shows a countdown on the display, starting from the number you specify as the input of this c-block and counting down a number every second until it reaches 0.
- Once the countdown reaches 0, which means MARIO wasn't able to shoot in time, the **Stop All Other Sequences** block ❸ stops the main sequence, preventing you from moving MARIO any longer. However, this sequence continues to run.
- The **Stop** c-block ❹ stops the Move Hub motors and hides all the remote-control widgets.
- The **Play Sound** block plays the classic muted trombone "wah wah waahh" sound (Game Sound 12) to indicate that you lost the game, and the sequence ends. Now, the whole program ends because this was the only sequence still running; the main sequence was interrupted earlier by the **Stop All Other Sequences** block labeled ❸.

the composite blocks

Let's take a closer look at the other c-blocks used in this program: **Reset**, **Countdown**, **Drive**, **Aim**, **Stop**, and **Shoot**. In the Creative Canvas lobby, create a project named `QuickDraw` and make the c-blocks using the figures in the following discussion as reference.

the Reset composite block

At the beginning of the program, the robot doesn't know the trigger's position. To determine its initial position, we'll create a **Reset** c-block similar to the one we made in Chapter 11 that reset MARIO's scanner head.

This c-block (see **FIGURE 12-8**) runs the external motor to bring the trigger lever down for half a second (enough time for it to touch the grey pin with bushing), and then brings it up again, almost touching the cannon trigger. Build the **Reset** c-block now.

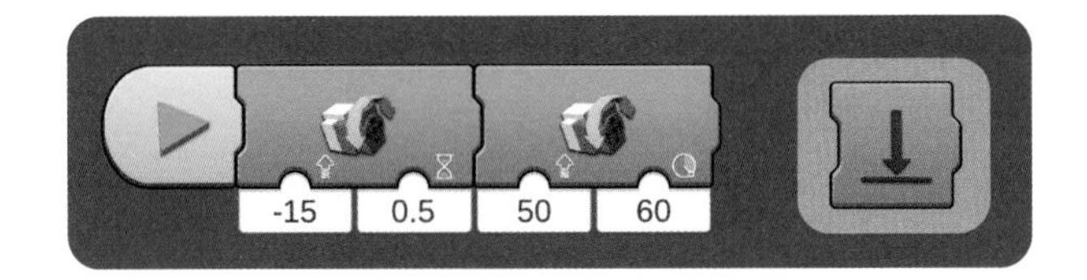

FIGURE 12-8 The Reset composite block resets the trigger to its zero position.

the Countdown composite block

The **Countdown** c-block is shown in **FIGURE 12-9**.

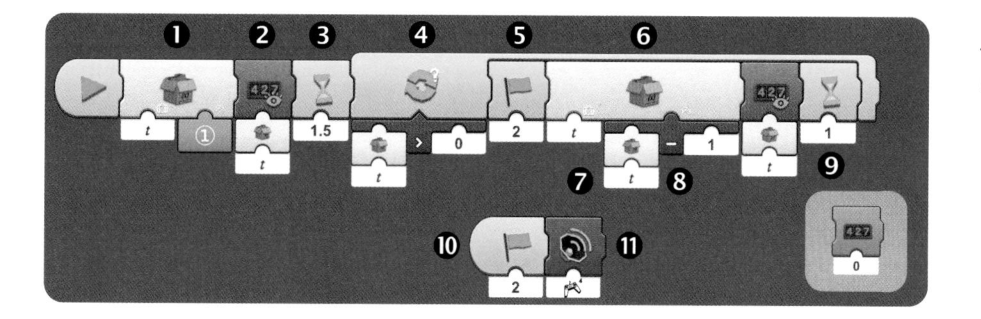

FIGURE 12-9 The Countdown composite block

The variable *t* is where we store the number of seconds specified in the c-block Numeric Input 1, the number of seconds in the countdown sequence (described on page 129). The number is stored in variable *t* by the **Write Variable** block ❶ and shown on the display by the **Show Display Widget** block ❷. The **Wait for Time** block ❸ pauses the countdown for 1.5 seconds to give the player time to get ready.

The **Loop While True** block ❹ runs the main sequence as long as *t* is greater than 0. Inside the loop, we use a **Subtraction Operator** block ❽ to decrease the value of *t* by 1 every second; we subtract 1 from the old value of *t* (retrieved by the **Read Variable** block ❼) using a **Subtraction Operator** block ❽) and feed the result to the **Write Variable** block ❻ input. Now, the **Wait for Time** block ❾ pauses the loop for 1 second.

The **Flag Trigger** block ❺ triggers another sequence, starting with a **Start on Flag** block ❿, that plays a "tick" sound (Game Sound 4) with a **Play Sound** block ⓫. Placing the **Play Sound** block directly inside the loop would slow down the loop because the program would wait for the **Play Sound** block to complete before it could continue. By playing the sound in a separate sequence, the sound can play without interfering with the countdown timing. The loop ends when the value of *t* reaches 0.

the Drive composite block

The **Drive** c-block shown in **FIGURE 12-10** lets you use a joystick to drive MARIO on the playmat.

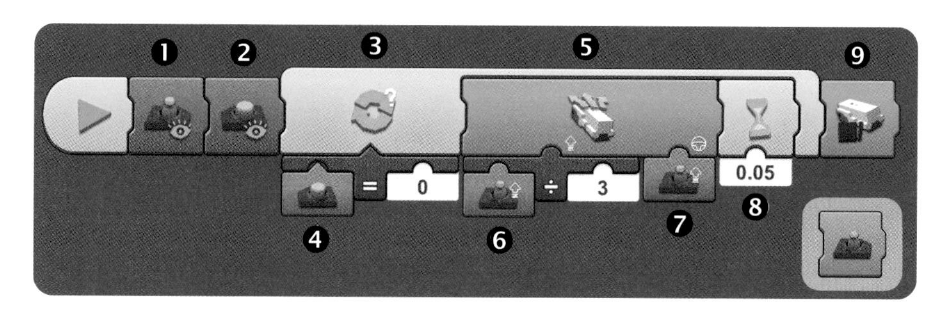

FIGURE 12-10 The Drive composite block sequence

The first two blocks ❶ and ❷ display the Button and the Joystick Widgets on the remote-control interface. The **Loop While True** block ❸ runs while the button is not pressed and ends when you press the button, whose status is read by the block ❹. Inside the loop, a **Drivebase Move Steering Unlimited** block ❺ gets the values for its inputs from the joystick's Speed and Steering commands.

To do this, we use the **Joystick Speed Reporter** ❻ and **Joystick Steering Reporter** ❼ blocks, and scale the Speed down by a factor of 3 to prevent the robot from moving too fast. The **Wait for Time** block ❽ is set to pause the loop for 0.05 seconds to avoid overwhelming the robot with too many commands. After the Loop ends, the **External Motor Stop** block ❾ stops the robot.

the Aim composite block

The **Aim** c-block shown in **FIGURE 12-11** plays Game Sound 9 ( ) in a separate sequence to avoid pausing the main program, and then it shows the Slider Widget with the cursor in the middle (input is set to 50). The Button Widget is shown, while the joystick is hidden. (From now on, you can just control MARIO's orientation with the slider.)

The **Preset Drivebase Angle** block ❶ resets the rotation sensor values to 0, making MARIO spin in place. The **Loop While True** block ❷ runs again until the button is pressed, and a **Drivebase Move Steering for Angle** block ❸ in the loop makes MARIO spin in place by a certain number of degrees relative to the last rotation sensor reset. We compute the Degrees value like this.

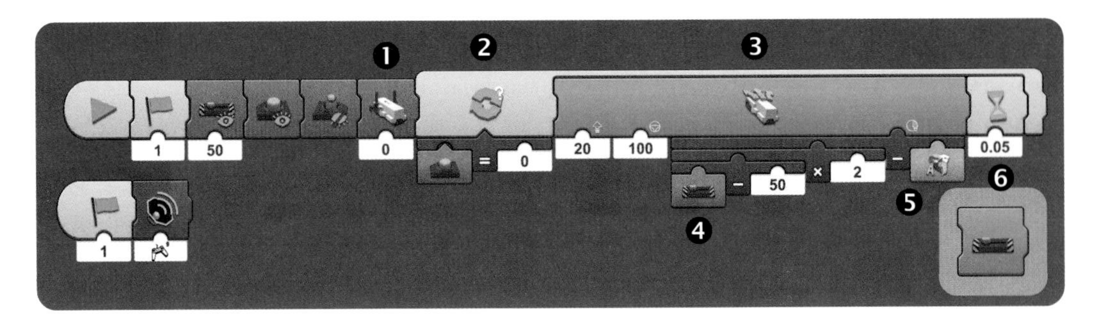

FIGURE 12-11 The Aim composite block sequence

1: Subtract 50 from the value returned by the **Slider Position Reporter** block ❹ (ranging from 0 to 100), which gives a number between –50 and 50.

2: Multiply the result from step 1 by 2 to get a number from –100 to 100.

3: Recall from the "moving relative to a zero position" on page 107 that, in order to rotate a motor a specific amount relative to a given position, we subtract the current value of the angle from our goal value. In this case, we subtract the current angle of motor A (reported by block ❺) from the number we got in step 2 to make MARIO spin from about –45 degrees (on the left) to about 45 degrees (on the right).

Finally, we use the **Wait for Time** block ❻ to wait for 0.05 seconds to avoid overwhelming the robot with too many commands.

the Stop composite block

The *Stop* c-block, shown in **FIGURE 12-13**, simply calls the **Drivebase Stop** block and then calls the blocks that hide all the remote-control widgets.

FIGURE 12-13 The Stop composite block sequence and final look.

the Shoot composite block

Next we'll create a composite block to control the shooting mechanism. The *Shoot* c-block runs the external motor to trigger the shooter, as you can see in **FIGURE 12-14**.

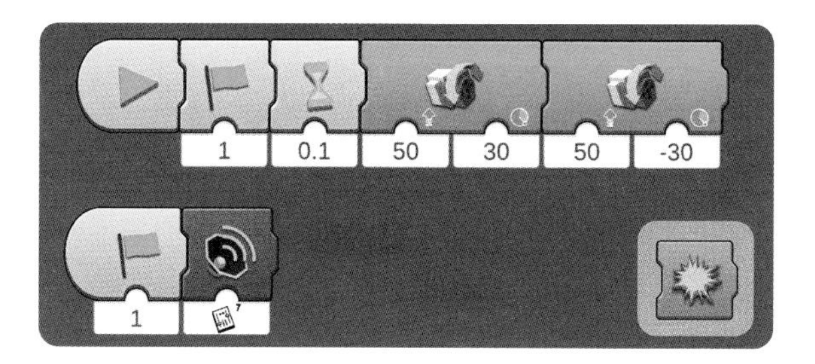

FIGURE 12-14 The Shoot composite block aims and shoots the dart while playing a sound.

To play a shooting sound effect in sync with the action, the main sequence runs a **Flag Trigger** block that starts the parallel sequence attached to the **Start on Flag** block. This sequence runs a **Play Sound** block playing the Sound 7 from the *Shoots and Hits* category (7). We need the **Wait for Time** block in the main sequence to wait 0.1 seconds after starting the sequence that plays the sound; otherwise it won't be perfectly in sync with the shooting.

making the main program

Now you're ready to reproduce the program shown in **FIGURE 12-15**. At the end of the main sequence, place a **Play Sound** block that plays an orchestra hit (Game Sound 11). At the end of the countdown sequence, place a **Play Sound** block that plays the classic muted trombone "wah wah waahh" sound (Game Sound 12).

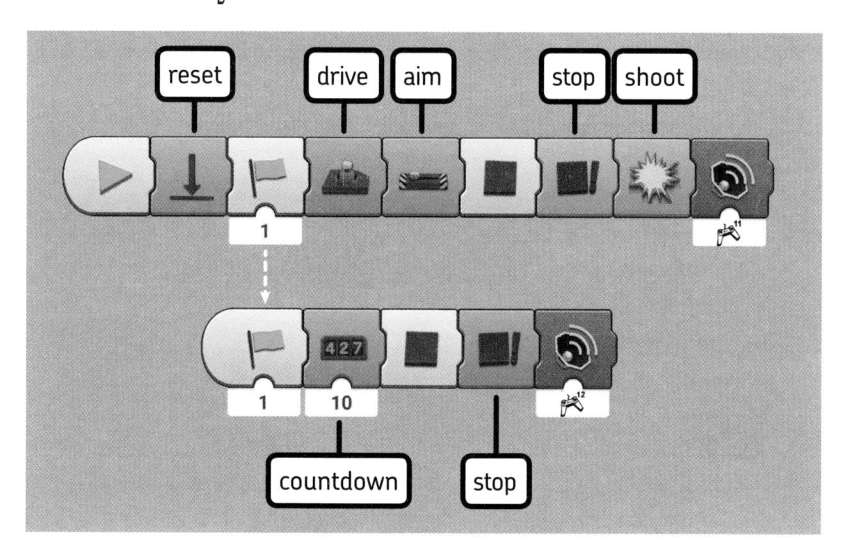

FIGURE 12-15 The *QuickDraw* program with the c-blocks labeled

using the remote control

On the remote-control interface, you should see the countdown on the display, the joystick, and the button. Move MARIO toward the target with the joystick. When you're close enough to the target, press the button to switch to aiming mode so that the joystick disappears and the slider appears. Now, drag the slider to aim and press the button again to shoot. To win the game, shoot down the target before the countdown ends!

automatic shooting

Let's program MARIO to play darts automatically by scanning for any targets within the sensor range (about 20 cm or 8 inches) and shooting once a target is detected. The pseudocode for this program looks like this:

```
Reset shooter trigger*
Begin Infinite Loop
   Wait for the sensor to measure a distance greater than 3
   Change the sensor light color to red
   Start the motors to slowly spin in place clockwise
      (searching for a target)
   Wait for the sensor to measure a distance less than 9
   Adjust the heading and shoot*
   Wait for the user to reload the dart*
Go back to the start of the infinite loop
```

The lines above marked with an asterisk (*) are complex operations that will need the composite blocks shown in **FIGURE 12-16**.

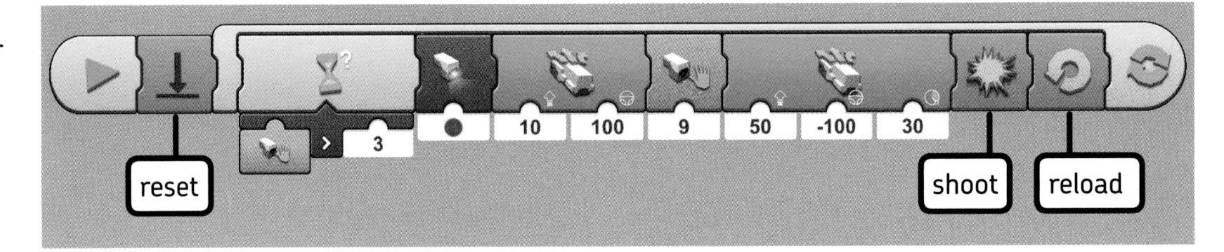

FIGURE 12-16 The program to search for a target and shoot it with a dart

Since you've already made the **Reset** and **Shoot** c-blocks, reuse them by duplicating the **QuickDraw** project from the Creative Canvas lobby and renaming the copied project **darts**. Edit the copied project and start making the **Reload** c-block.

the Reload composite block

The **Reload** c-block, shown in **FIGURE 12-17**, changes the Move Hub light to green and waits for you to come close to the robot to reload the dart. A **Loop**

While True block repeats a **Play Sound** block that plays Game Sound 5 (🎮) while you're close to the robot. When you move away, the Hub light turns blue again, and Game Sound 9 is played (🎮). After a half-second pause, the c-block sequence ends.

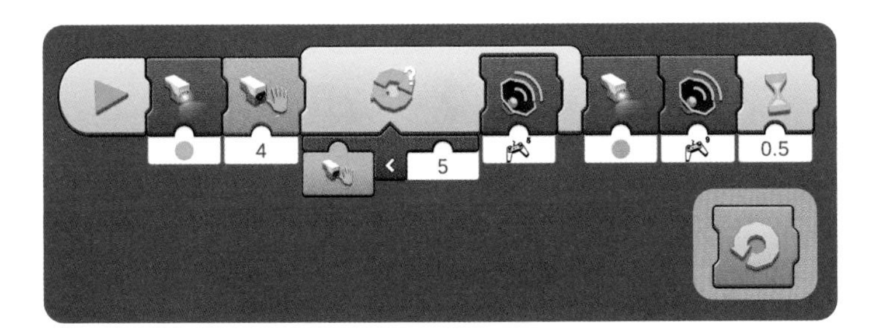

FIGURE 12-17 The Reload composite block waits for you to reload the dart in the cannon.

how the program works

Once you have all the needed c-blocks, complete the program shown in **FIGURE 12-18**.

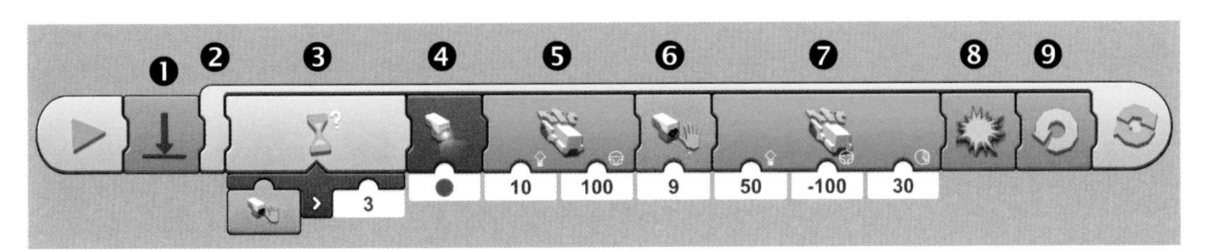

FIGURE 12-18 The program that allows MARIO to search for and shoot down a target

Let's analyze the program in **FIGURE 12-18** block by block:

- The **Reset** c-block ❶ resets the shooter mechanism.
- The searching and shooting sequence is repeated forever inside an **Infinite Loop** block ❷.
- The **Wait for True** block ❸ waits for the distance read by the sensor to be greater than 3. In other words, it waits for you to load the dart into the shooter and get away.
- The **Set Sensor LED Color** block ❹ changes the color to red to indicate that the robot is armed and ready.
- The **Drivebase Move Steering Unlimited** block ❺ makes the robot slowly spin around.
- The **Wait for Distance** block ❻ waits for the sensor to detect the target.
- Once the target is detected, this **Drivebase Move Steering for Angle** block ❼ makes MARIO spin back by a few degrees to aim better.
- The **Shoot** c-block ❽ shoots the dart and plays a sound.
- The **Reload** c-block ❾ allows you to get near the robot to reload the dart.

experiment 12-3

Make a program that allows you to direct MARIO toward the target by remote control. When you press the button, MARIO should start the automatic scanning and aiming procedure. It should then shoot the target when it finds it.

Hint: you could reuse the **Reset**, **Drive**, and **Shoot** c-blocks and part of the **darts** program shown in **FIGURE 12-18**.

experiment 12-4

Configure MARIO in line-following mode as you did in Chapter 8, using **FIGURE 8-4** as reference. Make a program to play the following game on the BOOST playmat. Before the countdown ends, use the remote control to move MARIO to the blue area (to collect water) and then move to the red area (to extinguish the fire).

The robot must move in this order, from the blue area to the red area. If MARIO reaches the fire before collecting water, you lose the game. If you drive it across areas of different colors by mistake (for example, the banana or the radioactive area), you lose the game. (This can be quite tricky, so write the pseudocode first and be patient with yourself!)

Hints: Reuse the main sequence of the `QuickDraw` program you just made. Make a new c-block that lets you control MARIO with the joystick until it sees the color specified by the c-block Numeric Input 1. Place two copies of this block in the main sequence: one configured to run until the sensor sees blue, the other to run until the sensor sees red. When you're ready to check your answer, turn to page 246 in the appendix, where you'll find the solution.

what you've learned

In this chapter, you built a dart shooter with a gunsight for MARIO. After learning how to build a modular remote-control interface, you programmed some simple remote-control applications and created a game that makes MARIO race against time to complete a remote-controlled mission on the BOOST playmat. You also made a program to let the robot search and shoot down a target autonomously.

This chapter concludes the first part of the book, which has covered programming from the basics to some more advanced topics. At this point, you've explored all of the LEGO BOOST app programming blocks available in the intermediate level. In Chapter 13, we'll review some LEGO building techniques, beginning with the basics of LEGO geometry and moving on to more advanced techniques to build models that are both sturdy and good looking. Then, you'll learn how to use gears and how to transform the motion of the motors to make arms swing and legs walk.

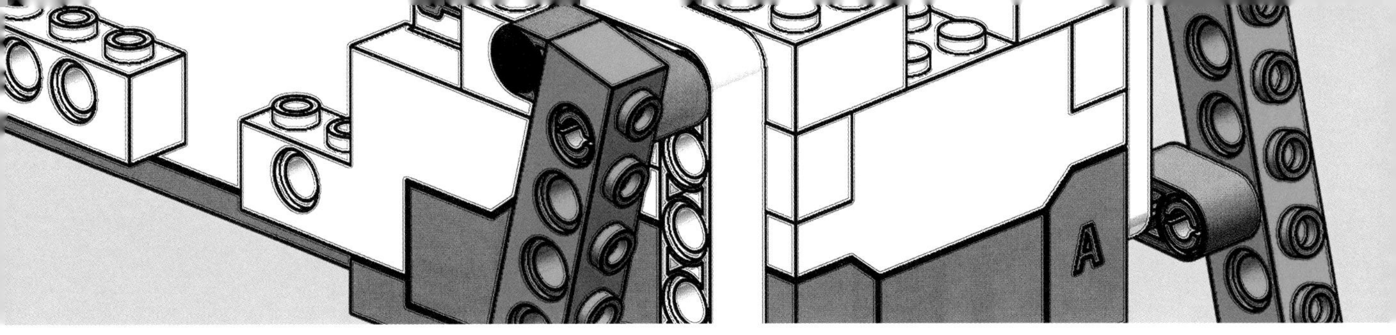

13

building techniques

Let's explore some building techniques so you can start designing your very own robots as a master builder. We'll start by reviewing the basics of LEGO geometry. Then, you'll learn how to build sturdy structures, create functional gear systems that transmit motion, and make mechanisms that transform motion.

LEGO geometry

The carefully designed LEGO building system comes with some precise rules. **FIGURE 13-1** shows the relationships between the dimensions of typical LEGO parts. *M* stands for *module*, or 1 stud, the standard LEGO unit of measurement.

- The height of a plate is one-third of the height of a brick, so three stacked plates are as tall as one brick (**A**), and five stacked plates are 2M tall (**B**).
- Five stacked bricks are 6M long and 6M tall (**C**). Thus, a LEGO brick is 6/5 = 1.2 LEGO units tall.
- To brace two Technic bricks with a vertical beam (or a Technic brick), you need to use two plates between the Technic bricks as spacers (**D**). When the bricks are stacked this way, their holes are 2M apart.

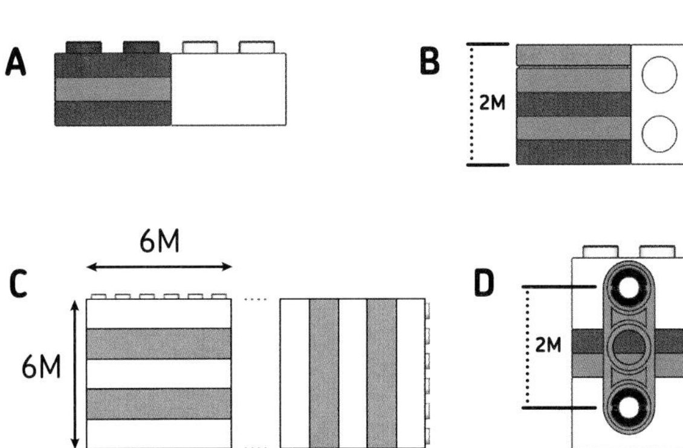

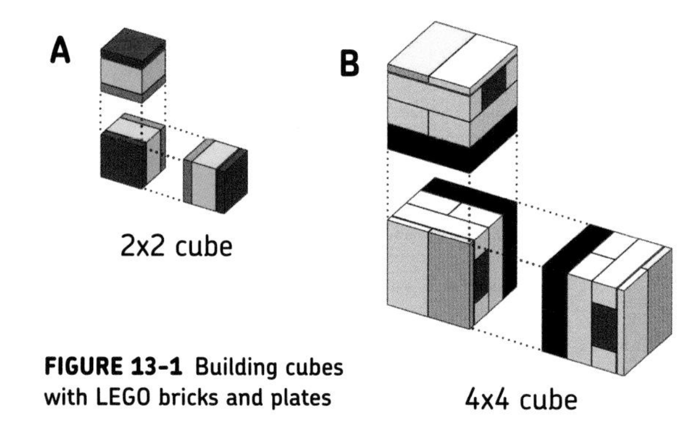

FIGURE 13-1 Building cubes with LEGO bricks and plates

FIGURE 13-1 shows some 3D relationships.

- One brick and two plates are 2M tall (**A**).
- Three bricks and one plate are 4M tall (**B**).

SNOT building

SNOT is an acronym coined by the online LEGO community that stands for **S**tuds **N**ot **O**n **T**op. Every time you add pieces sideways or upside down, you're using the SNOT technique.

FIGURE 13-2 shows some assemblies that demonstrate how the SNOT elements included in the LEGO BOOST set fit within the classic LEGO building system:

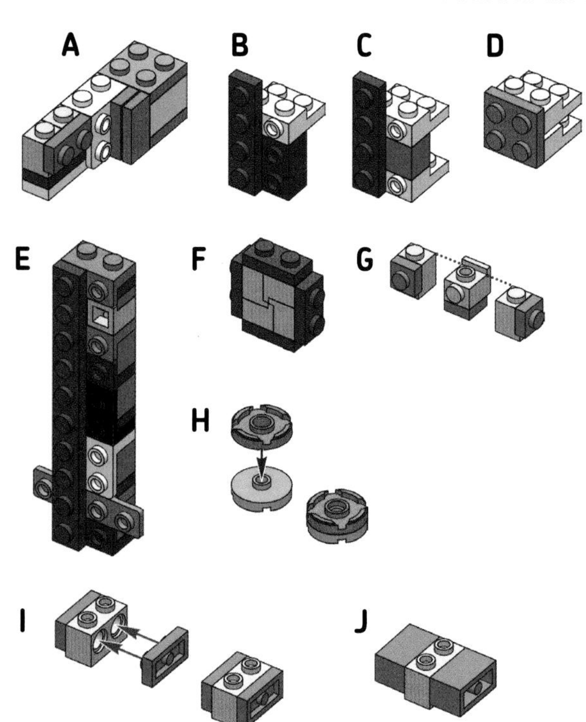

FIGURE 13-2 Various examples of the SNOT building technique

- In assembly **A**, attaching two plates to the white bracket makes the assembly exactly 2M wide. Attaching one plate to the yellow headlight brick makes the assembly as wide as the white bracket.
- Assemblies **B** and **C** show two ways of stacking the SNOT elements correctly.
- Assembly **D** is wrong because the two white SNOT plates are not attached together, and the space left between them is not one brick or one plate high.
- Assembly **E** shows how brackets can be used to brace the dark azure bricks and lock them together with a grey plate. Notice how the yellow headlight brick fits within the assembly.
- **F** is a clever example of SNOT assembly using headlight bricks in a spiral.
- **G** shows the proportions of the headlight brick.
- Assemblies **H**, **I**, and **J** show how to invert the orientation of the studs by 180 degrees, allowing you to build upside down. In **I** and **J**, notice the orientation of the hollow side of the dark azure pieces.

making your robots strong and sturdy

If a classic LEGO model made with bricks and plates falls to the ground, it breaks into smithereens. But LEGO Technic building techniques are sturdier since they have to endure the wear and tear caused by motors, gears, and levers.

using Technic connections

Let's take a closer look at how Technic connections can make a sturdier robot. For example, if you wanted to extend a beam, you could build the assembly shown in **A** of **FIGURE 13-3**. But if this assembly fell or got hit, it would probably break into pieces. Instead, you could use pegs to extend Technic bricks, as shown in **B**. This assembly will resist bending better than **A**, but it will come apart when you pull the bricks sideways.

To make your assembly (virtually) indestructible, you could add some plates to *brace* the bricks, as in assembly **C**; this combination of pegs and plates incorporates the advantages of both **A** and **B**.

You can extend Technic beams with pegs only, as in assembly **D**, because beams don't have studs. To make the assembly resistant to lateral tension and bending, use two cross blocks and a 5M beam (azure) to brace the beams, as shown in assembly **E**.

You can follow the instructions in **FIGURE 13-4** to build assembly **E**.

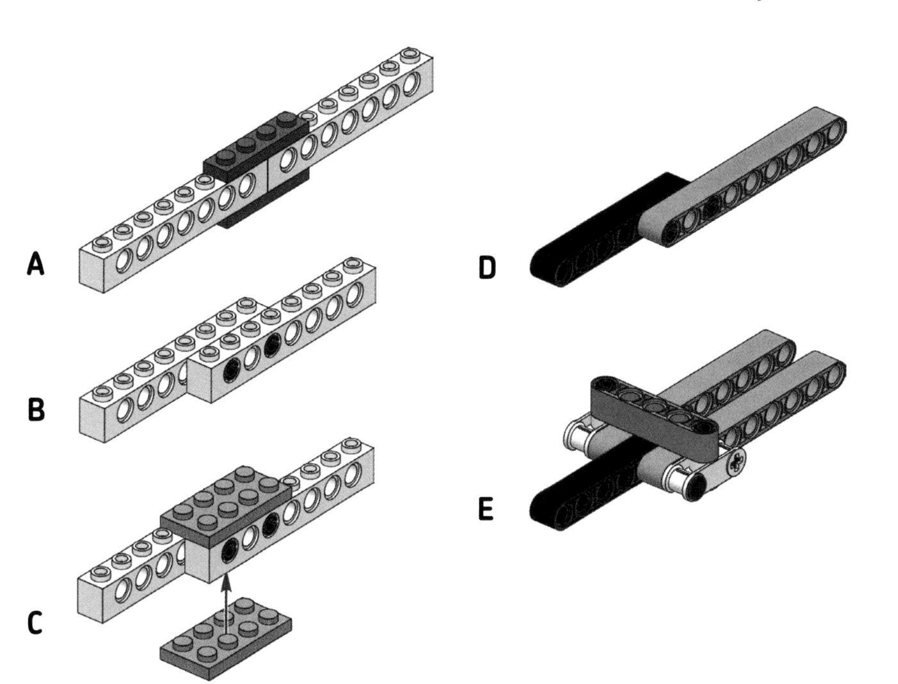

FIGURE 13-3 Two methods of extending bricks and beams

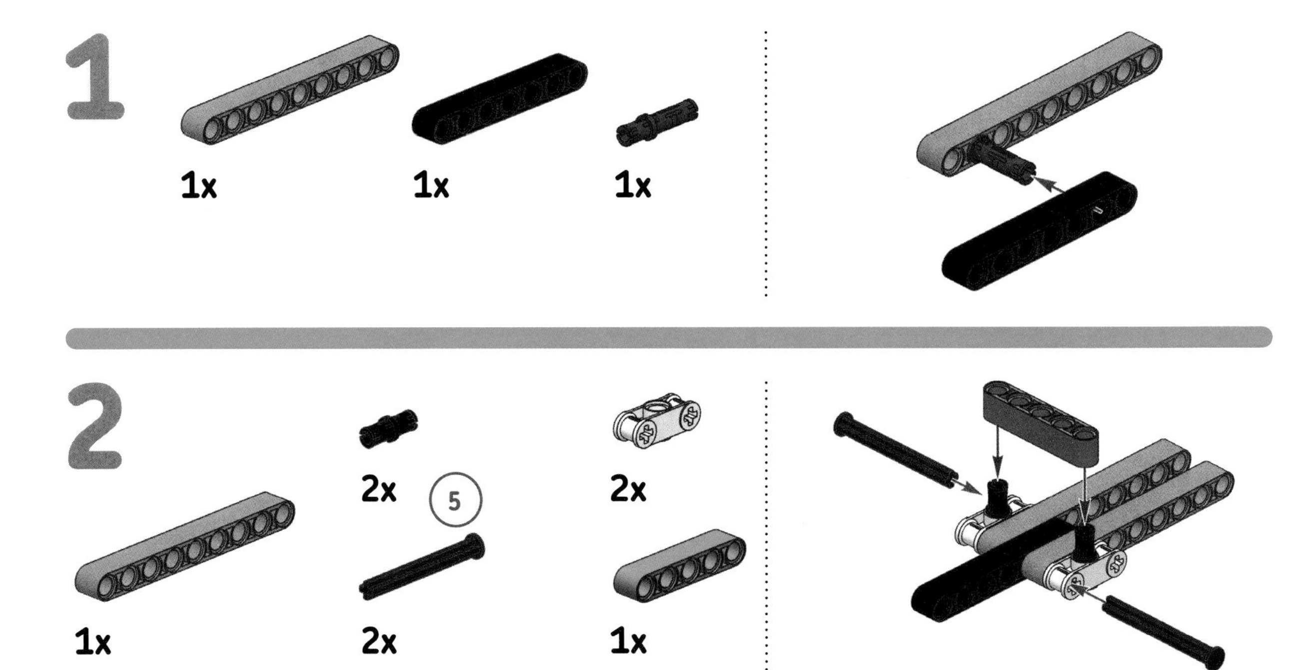

FIGURE 13-4 Building instructions for assembly E of **FIGURE 13-3**

bracing techniques

FIGURE 13-5 shows four ways to brace bricks using vertical beams or bricks.

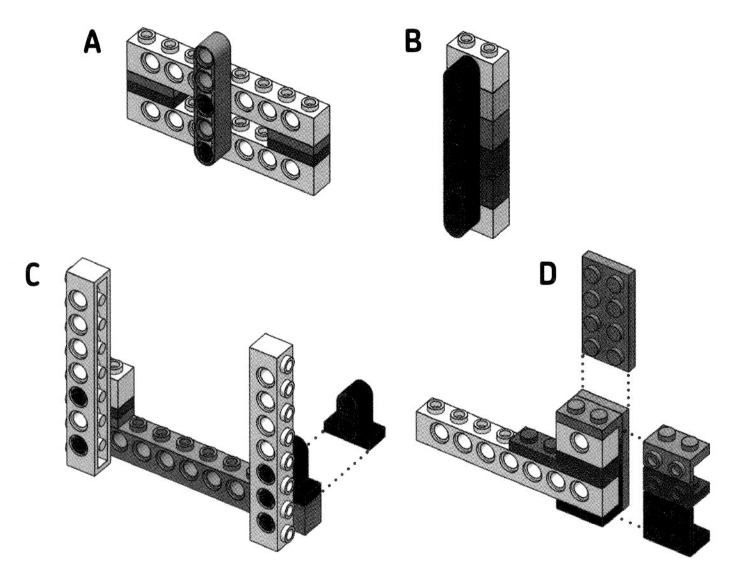

FIGURE 13-5 Bracing bricks with bricks and beams connected vertically and at right angles

- Assembly **A** exploits the essential property of Technic bricks shown in **C** on page 137 by using two plates as spacers between Technic bricks. Using this technique, you won't be able to pull away the white bricks without first removing the bracing beam.
- Assembly **B** shows a 7M beam bracing two bricks that are four bricks apart.
- You can use Technic bricks at right angles to brace just as easily, as shown in assembly **C**. Instead of two plates and one brick, you can also use the special plate with two holes (the black element).
- In **D**, you can see how brackets and plates can brace bricks.

Bracing is essential to building sturdy models. For more bracing ideas, check out the official LEGO models, which are an endless source of inspiration. For example, in **FIGURE 13-6**, you can see how the bracing technique is used to attach the motor firmly to the Move Hub in Frankie the cat.

The 16M brick forms the cat's leg and braces many stacked bricks. Without the plates attached to the brackets, the external motor could be pulled away from the Move Hub.

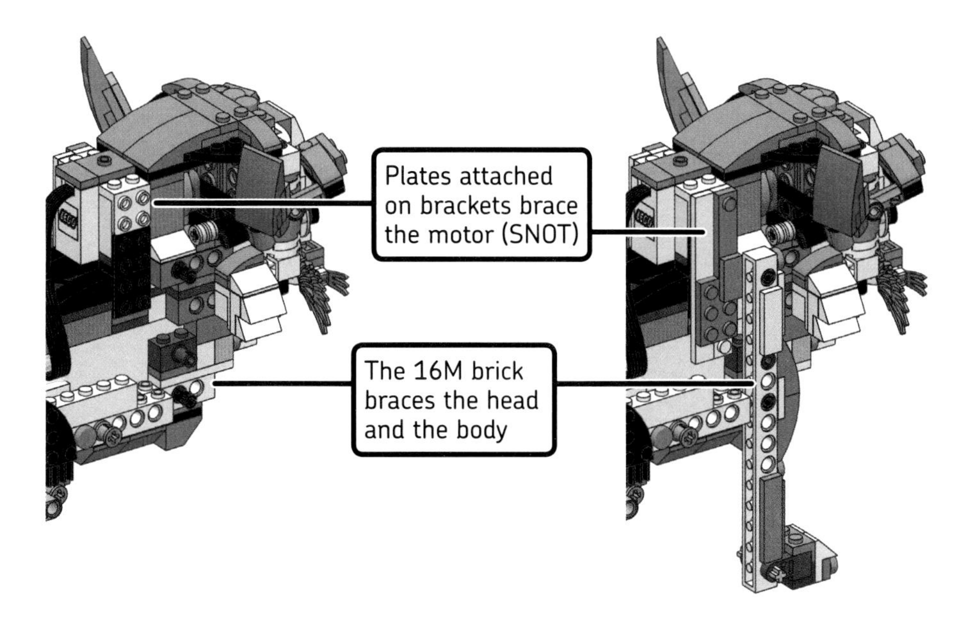

FIGURE 13-6 You can observe the bracing technique in the LEGO BOOST official models, as in Frankie the cat, for example.

understanding the angular beams

Every LEGO piece is designed to fit on a perfect grid of equally spaced holes, and the bent beams are no exception. But their geometry isn't always simple to understand. The 3x5 angular beam and the T beam are easy enough because they have right angles (90 degrees). But what about the 4x4 angular beams, which are bent at an odd angle?

FIGURE 13-7 shows an assembly that includes a 4x4 bent beam. The triangle overlaying the beam has a right angle (90 degrees) at its base, making it a *right triangle*. Its sides measure 3M, 4M, and 5M in LEGO units. Even though there are six holes on the longest side, it's actually 5M because we're measuring from hole to hole, subtracting half a unit from each end.

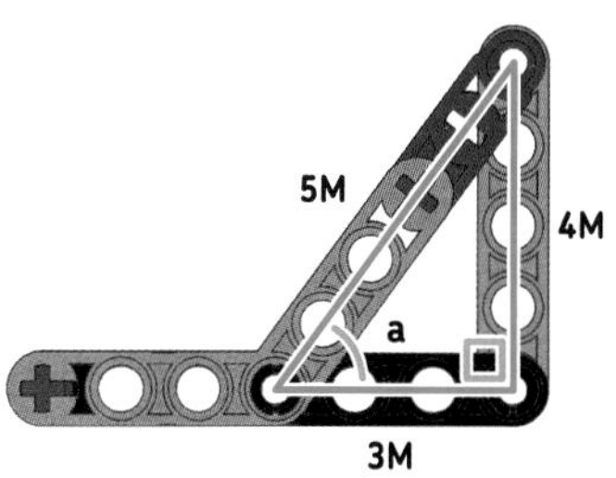

FIGURE 13-7 Geometry of the LEGO bent beam

The angle at the base of the triangle, *a*, results from the geometry of the LEGO Technic system.

You can *double* the dimensions of this right triangle to make a triangle whose sides are 6 (3×2), 8 (4×2), and 10 (5×2) LEGO units, as you can see in **FIGURE 13-8**.

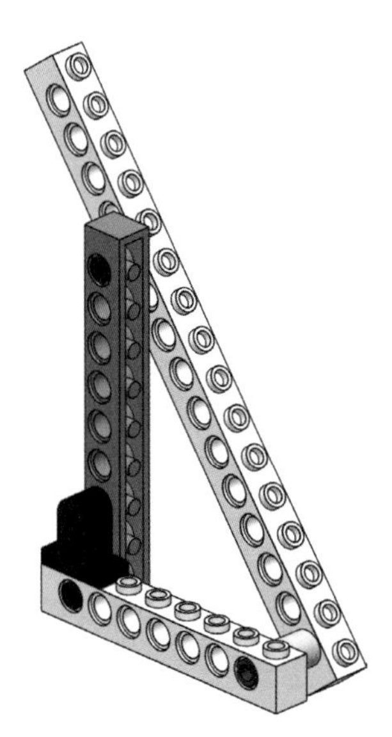

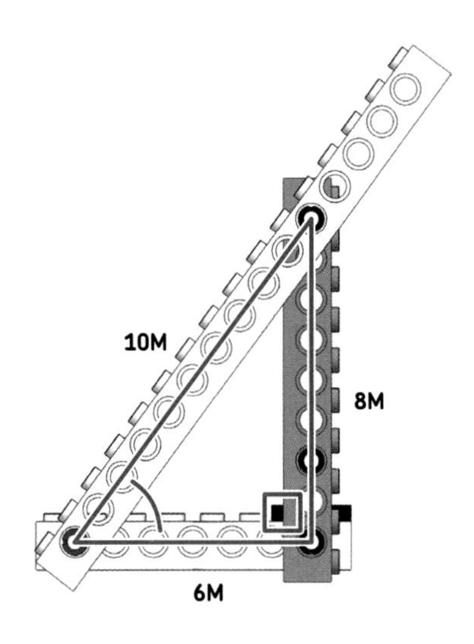

FIGURE 13-8 A larger right triangle built with LEGO Technic bricks. Its sides measure 6M, 8M, and 10M in LEGO units.

NOTE:

The 3×7 and 4×6 angular beams (not included in the BOOST set) feature the same angle as the 4×4 angular beam.

working with gears

Gears are toothed wheels that mesh with other gears to transmit rotation, for example, from a motor to a wheel.

To better understand how gears can be used to control the speed of your robot's movements, we'll build a gear train (steps 1 to 4). A gear train is a system of gears that transmit motion from one axle to another. The one you are going to build is composed of a 12-tooth (12z) double-bevel gear meshing with a 36-tooth (36z) double-bevel gear.

When you rotate the small gear in the gear train three times, the bigger gear will rotate once. The smaller gear is called the *input gear* (the driving gear), and both the number of rotations and the rotational speed of the larger *output gear* (the driven gear) are less than those of the input gear.

The relationship between input and output gears is expressed in terms of the ratio between the numbers of their teeth, which we call the *gear ratio*.

```
Gear ratio = number of teeth of output gear / number of teeth of input gear
```

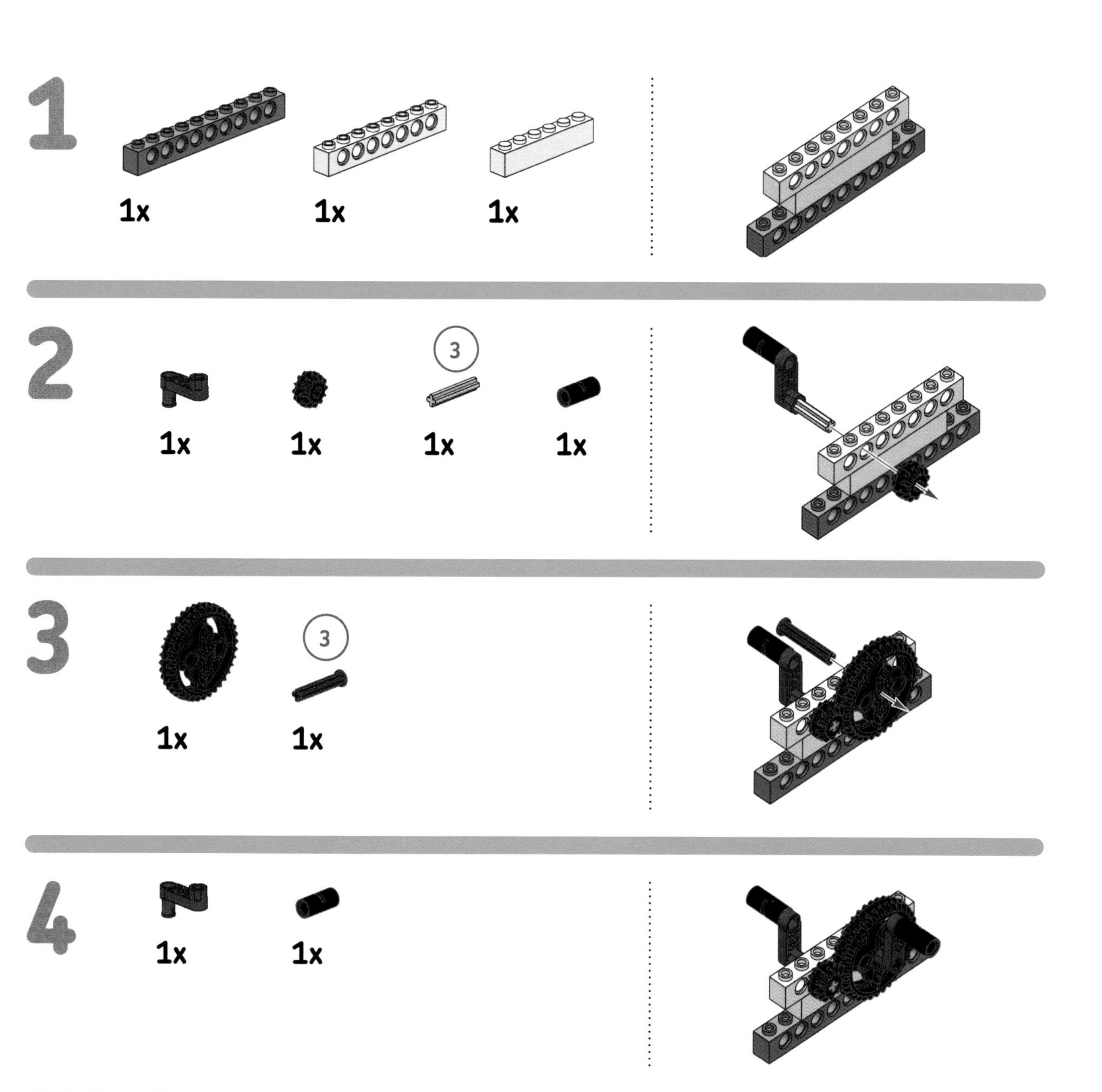

The gear ratio is 36/12 = 3. That means it takes three turns of the input gear to make the output gear turn once. The axles attached to the gears rotate in *opposite* directions.

On the other hand, if you rotate the crank attached to the bigger gear by one turn, the smaller gear will make three turns. The gear ratio is now 1:3 instead.

Now, change the assembly by undoing step 4 and placing a load on the end of the brick, as shown in step 5.

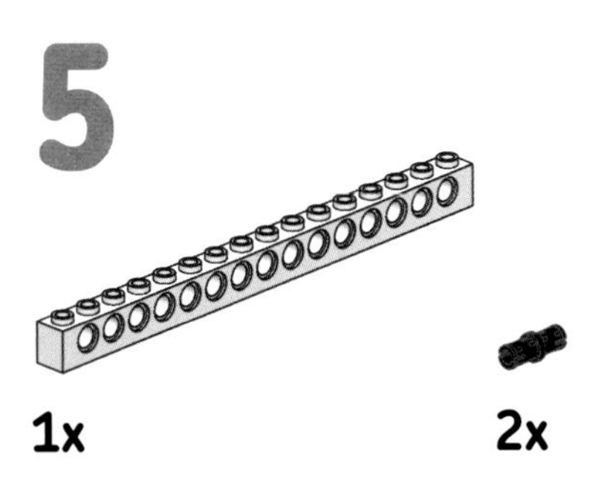

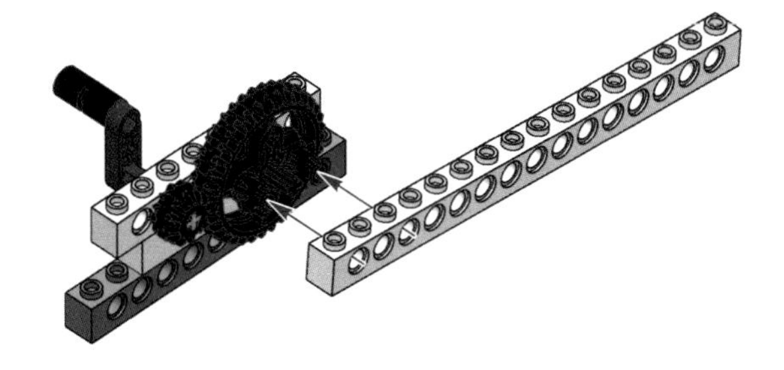

Place a load on the end of the brick and try to lift it using the crank, as shown in **FIGURE 13-9**.

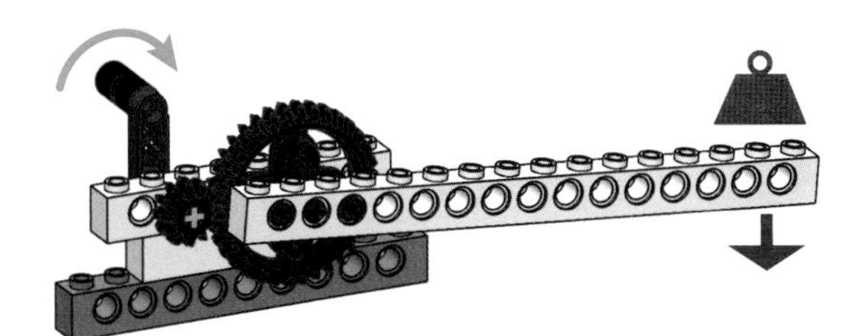

FIGURE 13-9 You can use gears to increase the torque of the output gear, making it possible to lift a load with little effort.

When you turn the 12z input gear, the 36z output gear will have three times more torque than the input gear. *Torque* is a twisting force that, when applied to an object, makes it rotate. This relatively high level of torque allows you to lift the load with *three times less effort* than you would have to use if you were lifting to lift the load by turning the axle directly.

when to use gears

Gears are useful when you need to transfer the rotation of the motors to an axle that is *far away* from the motor shaft or oriented in a different way, but you should use gears sparingly. Gears add *friction* to your mechanism, which will cause the rotation to slow down. To reduce this friction, place any gears loosely on your axles, as shown in **FIGURE 13-10**.

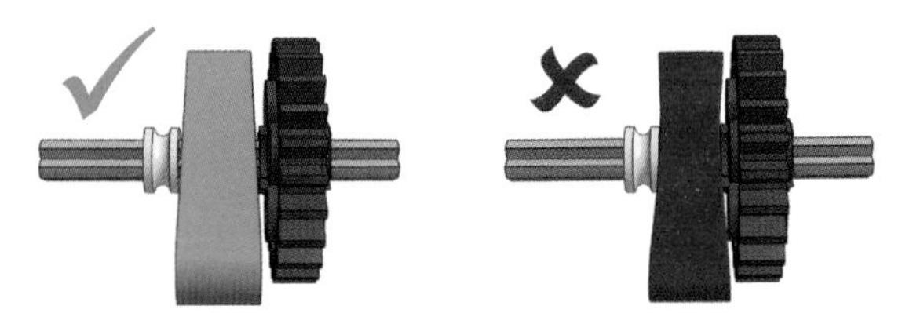

FIGURE 13-10 To avoid friction, place bushings and gears loosely on axles.

Gears also add *backlash*, which refers to the amount of wiggle room in the mechanism. To see for yourself, block the large gear in the assembly you built on page 143, and you'll see that you can still move the crank attached to the smaller gear by a little bit. Backlash occurs because there are little gaps between the meshing teeth. The more gears in your gear train, the more backlash you'll have. Backlash makes the end shaft of a gear train shake a little bit even if the motor is still. You cannot control for this wiggling from the program because the motor rotation sensor won't detect it. For example, this wiggling could affect the position of the tip of a robot arm or could cause inaccuracies in your robots' movements.

getting gears to mesh well

In this section, you'll learn how to make two gears mesh well. **TABLE 13-1** lists the radius of each gear in LEGO units. To verify these values, measure the radius of gear wheels using a beam as a reference.

TABLE 13-1 the radius of each gear expressed in LEGO units

CATEGORY	GEAR	TEETH	RADIUS (IN LEGO UNITS)	CATEGORY	GEAR	TEETH	RADIUS (IN LEGO UNITS)
spur		8	0.5M	double-bevel	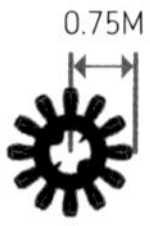	12	0.75M
	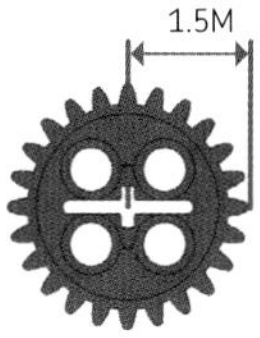	24	1.5M		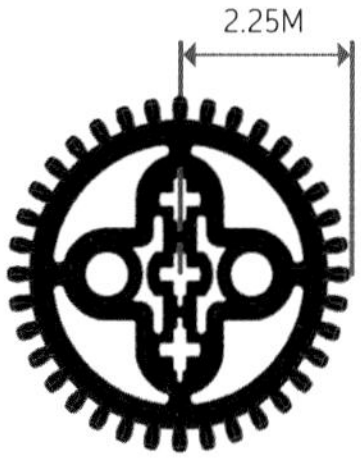	36	2.25M
bevel		12	n/a			28	1.75M
	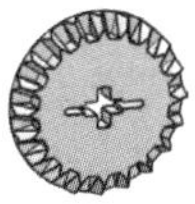	20	n/a				

perfect and imperfect gear combinations

There are two kinds of gear combinations: perfect and imperfect. A *perfect gear combination* is when the radii of the gears add up to a *whole number* in LEGO units. In this case, the gears can be mounted on axles inserted on a Technic brick or a beam. An *imperfect gear combination* is when the radii of the gears add up to a decimal number in LEGO units. In this case, the gears cannot be directly mounted on axles inserted in bricks or beam holes.

Imperfect gear combinations can be very useful, but when you use them, keep in mind that LEGO element designers didn't plan for them. The means that the teeth may mesh a bit loosely, or you may find it hard to build a frame to hold the gears correctly. (You'll see examples of imperfect gear combinations in the next section.)

meshing gears on parallel axles

This section is a sort of handbook where you can find many examples of gear trains to add to your robots. **FIGURE 13-11** shows some examples of how to mesh gears mounted on parallel axles.

Each assembly is labeled with the gear ratio in bold, and the distance (in LEGO units) between the gear centers in red. For example, assembly **F** has the same gear ratio as **D**, but the addition of a 3M beam bracing the axles makes it impossible for the gears to disengage.

Assemblies **B**, **H**, and **I** feature imperfect gear meshing but work very well.

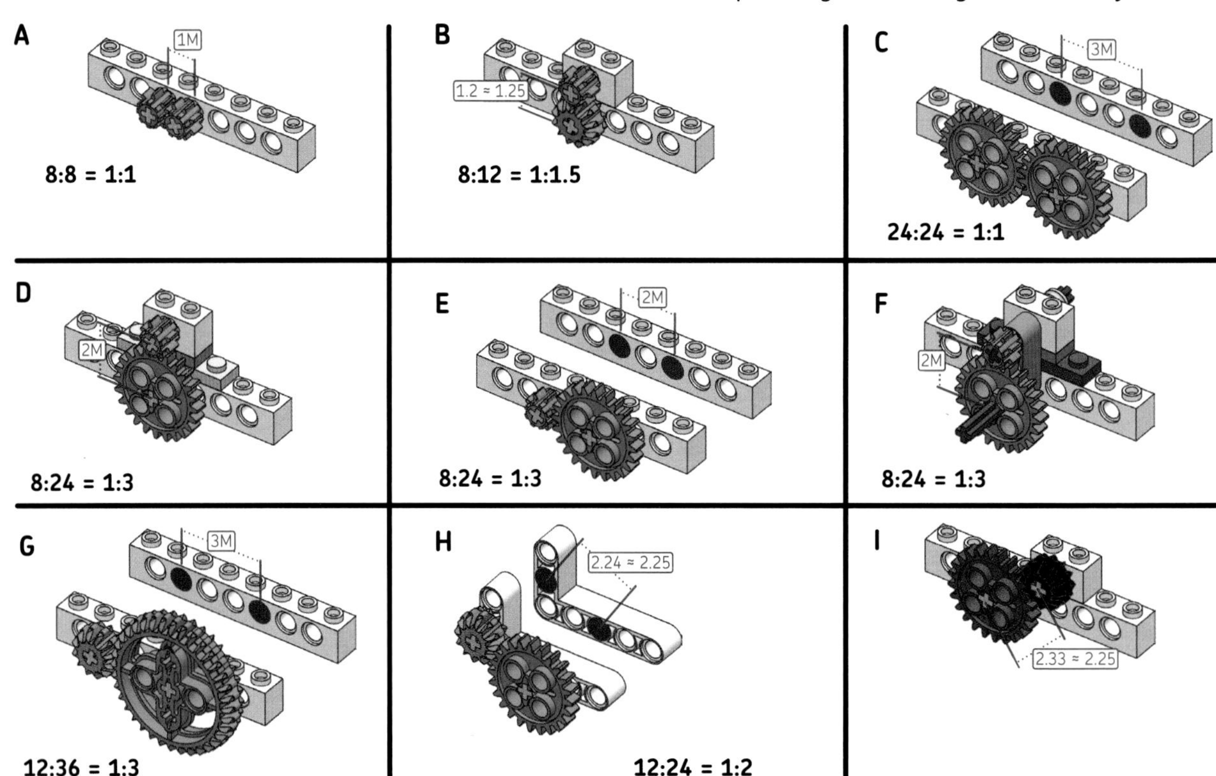

FIGURE 13-11 Gears mounted on parallel axles. The red numbers indicate the distance between the axles in LEGO units.

meshing gears at right angles

FIGURE 13-12 shows some examples of how to mesh gears mounted at right angles to each other. Notice that some assemblies use a thin bushing or a 1x2 Technic brick with two holes to add a half-module offset that'll allow the gears to mesh.

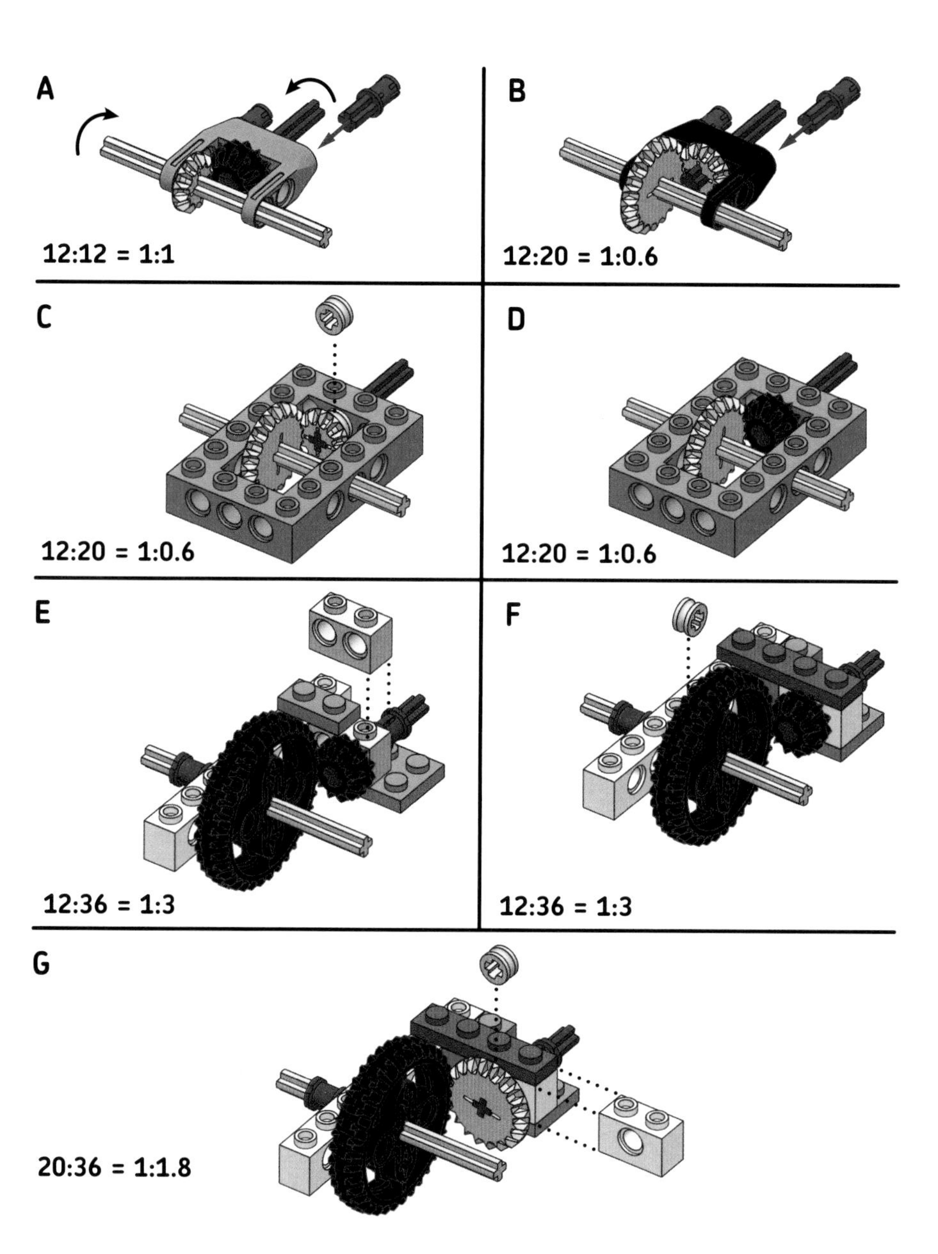

FIGURE 13-12 Gears coupled at right angles

driving the turntable

FIGURE 13-13 shows how to drive the 28z turntable included in the BOOST set with a 12z double-bevel gear and an 8z gear. By using the 12z gear, the driving axle is perpendicular to the rotation axis of the turntable. By using the 8z gear, the driving axle is parallel to the turntable's rotation axis.

Follow the steps below to build assembly **A** of **FIGURE 13-13**. Follow the steps on page 149 to build assembly **B** of **FIGURE 13-13**. You can pass an axle through the turntable center to drive a mechanism across the turntable itself (as you will see in the next chapter).

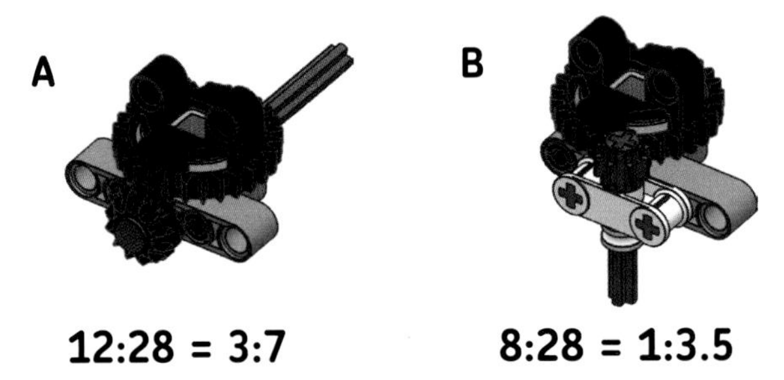

FIGURE 13-13 How to drive the 28z turntable

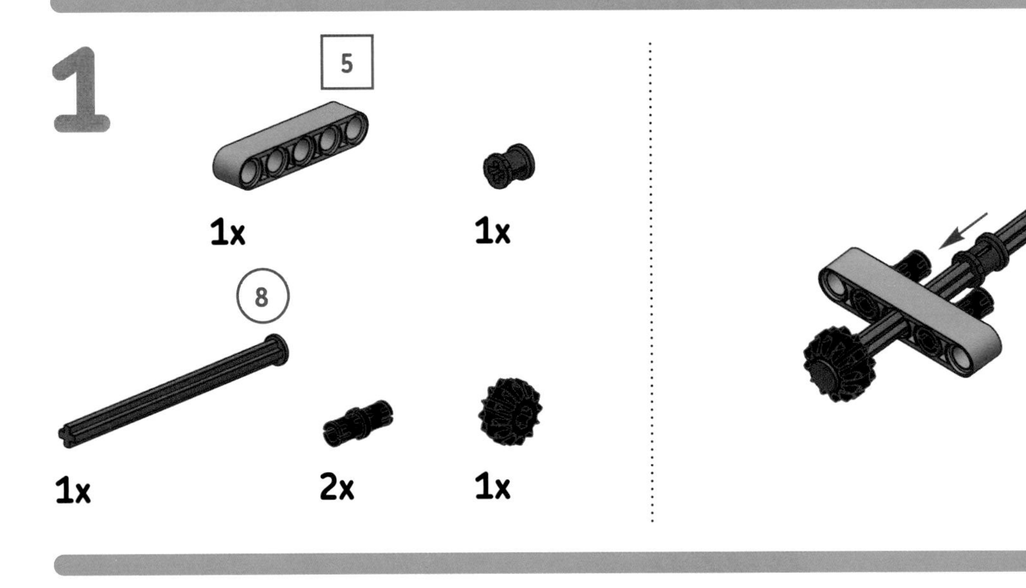

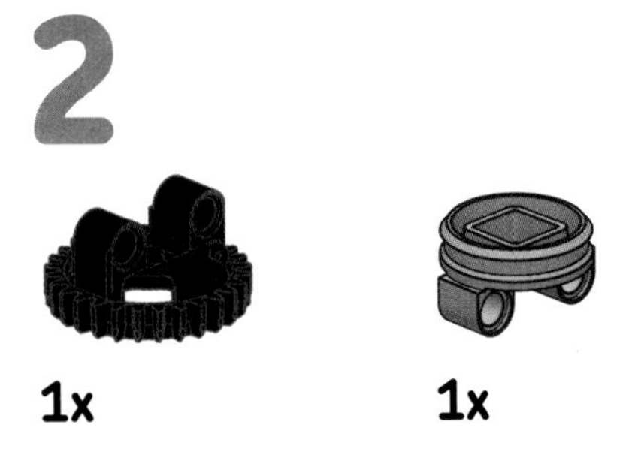

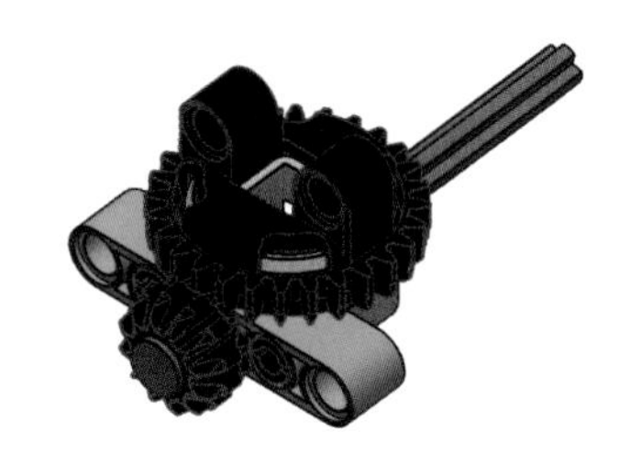

1

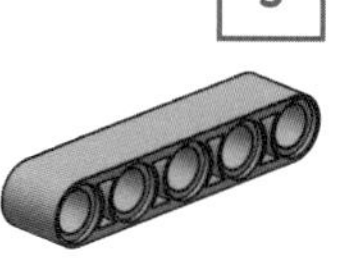

1x 2x 2x

2

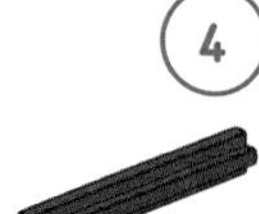

1x 1x

1x 1x

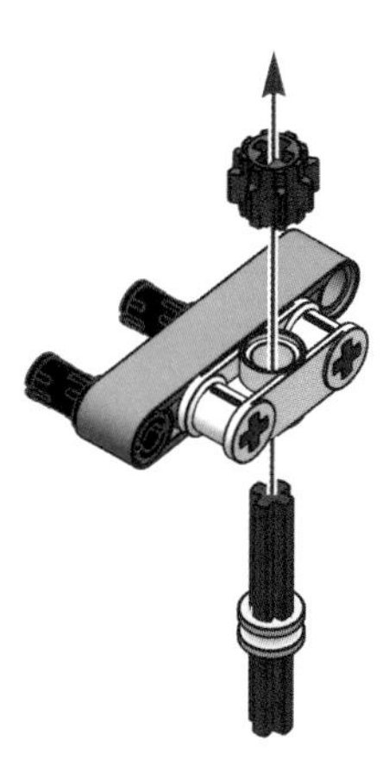

3

1x 1x

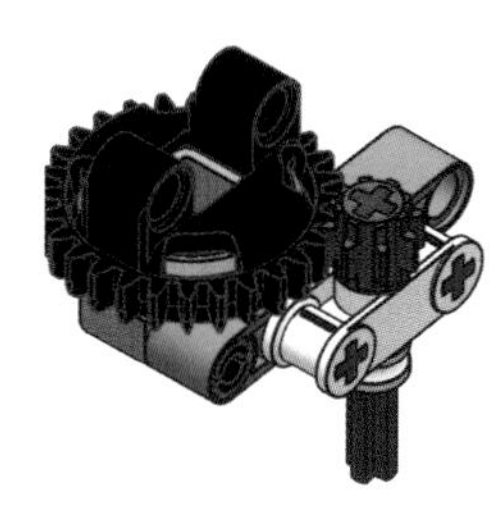

gear racks

Assembly A shows how you might build a gear rack, a kind of "unrolled gear" that converts rotation into linear motion. If you attach a gear rack to a brick or a plate, you can make it slide from side to side by turning an axle.

Follow these instructions to build assembly **A**.

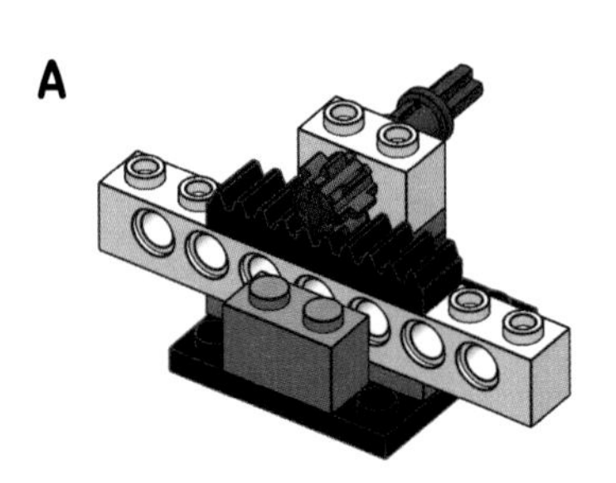

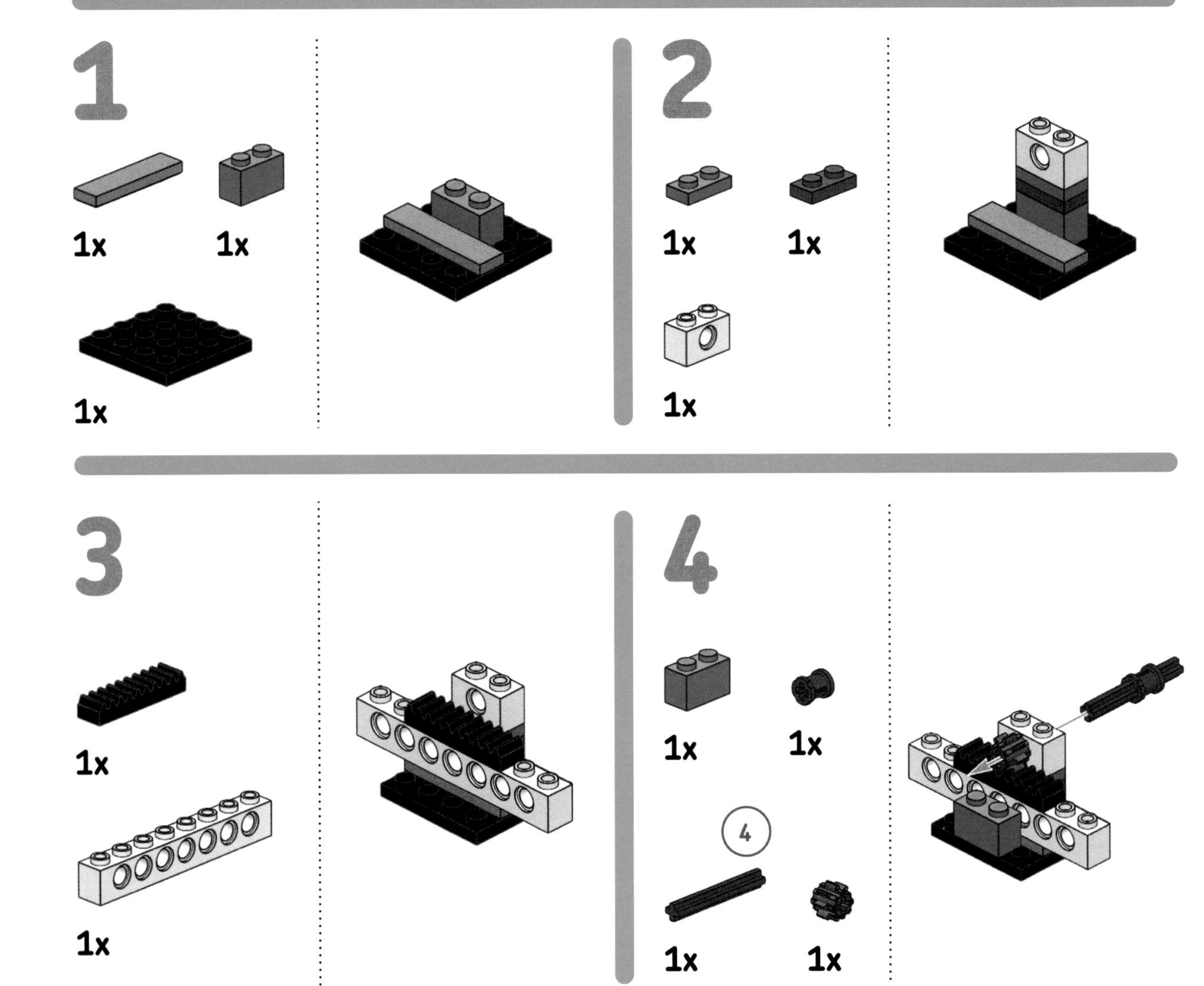

Follow these instructions to build assembly **B**. This assembly is more compact than assembly **A** and does not fall apart under stress.

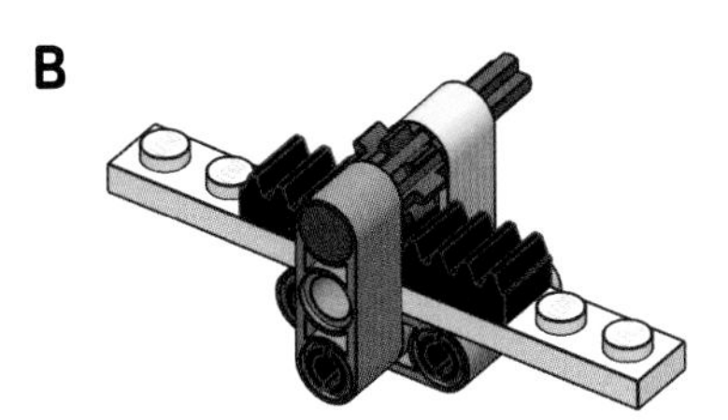

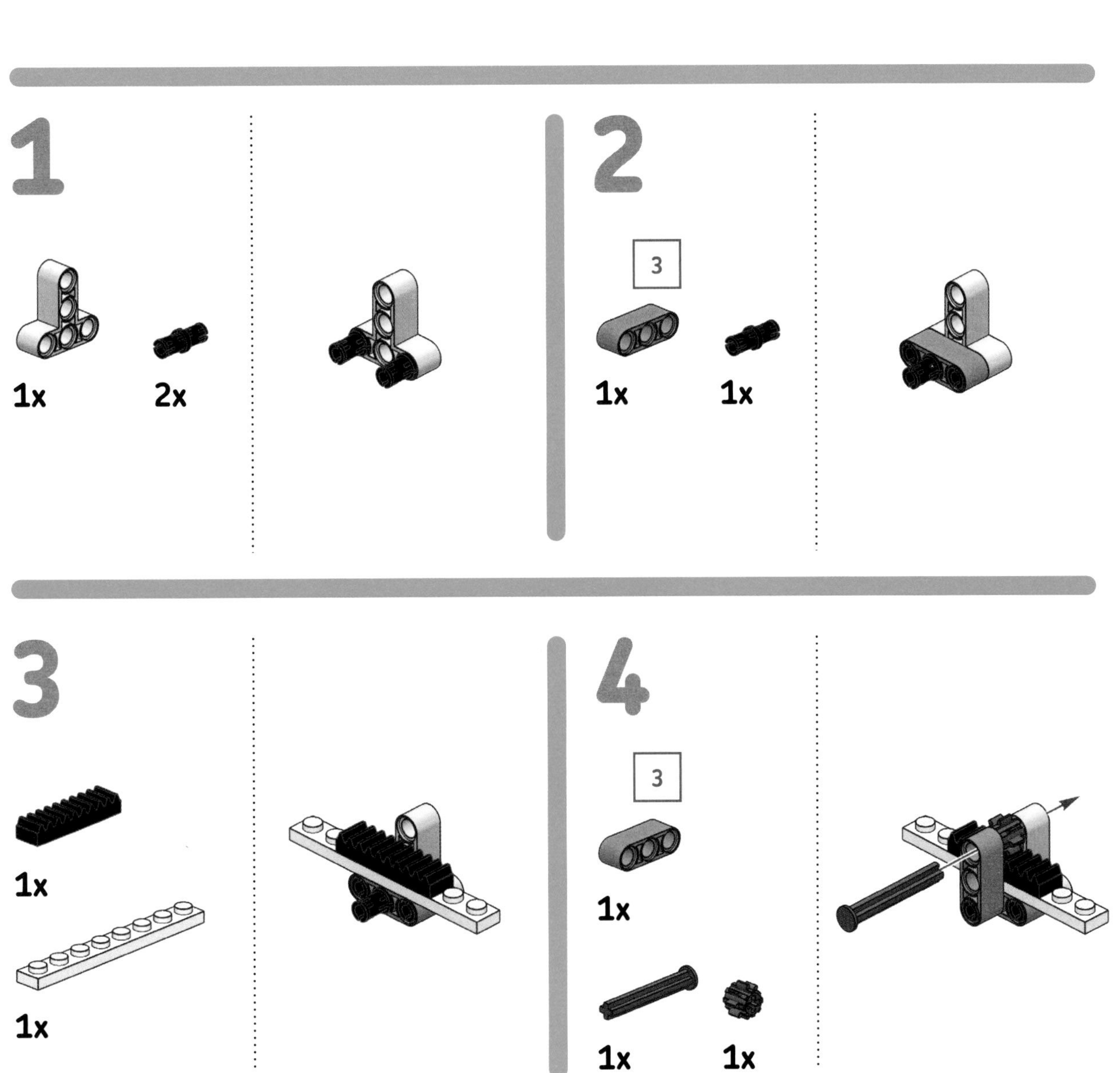

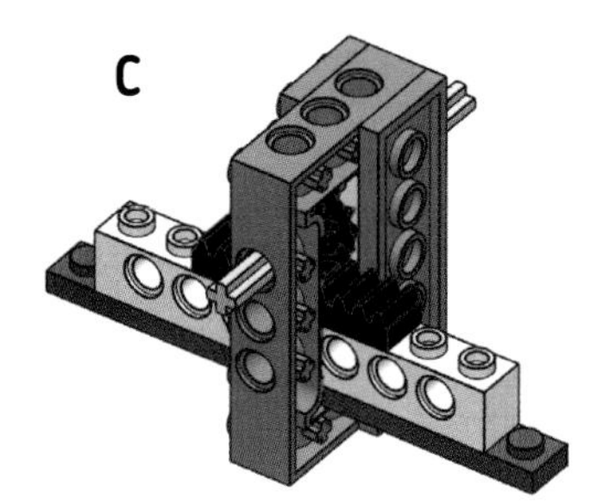

Follow the next set of instructions to build assembly **C**. This assembly is an excerpt of the assembly arm of LEGO BOOST Auto Builder model. It uses the Technic frame to embrace the sliding part.

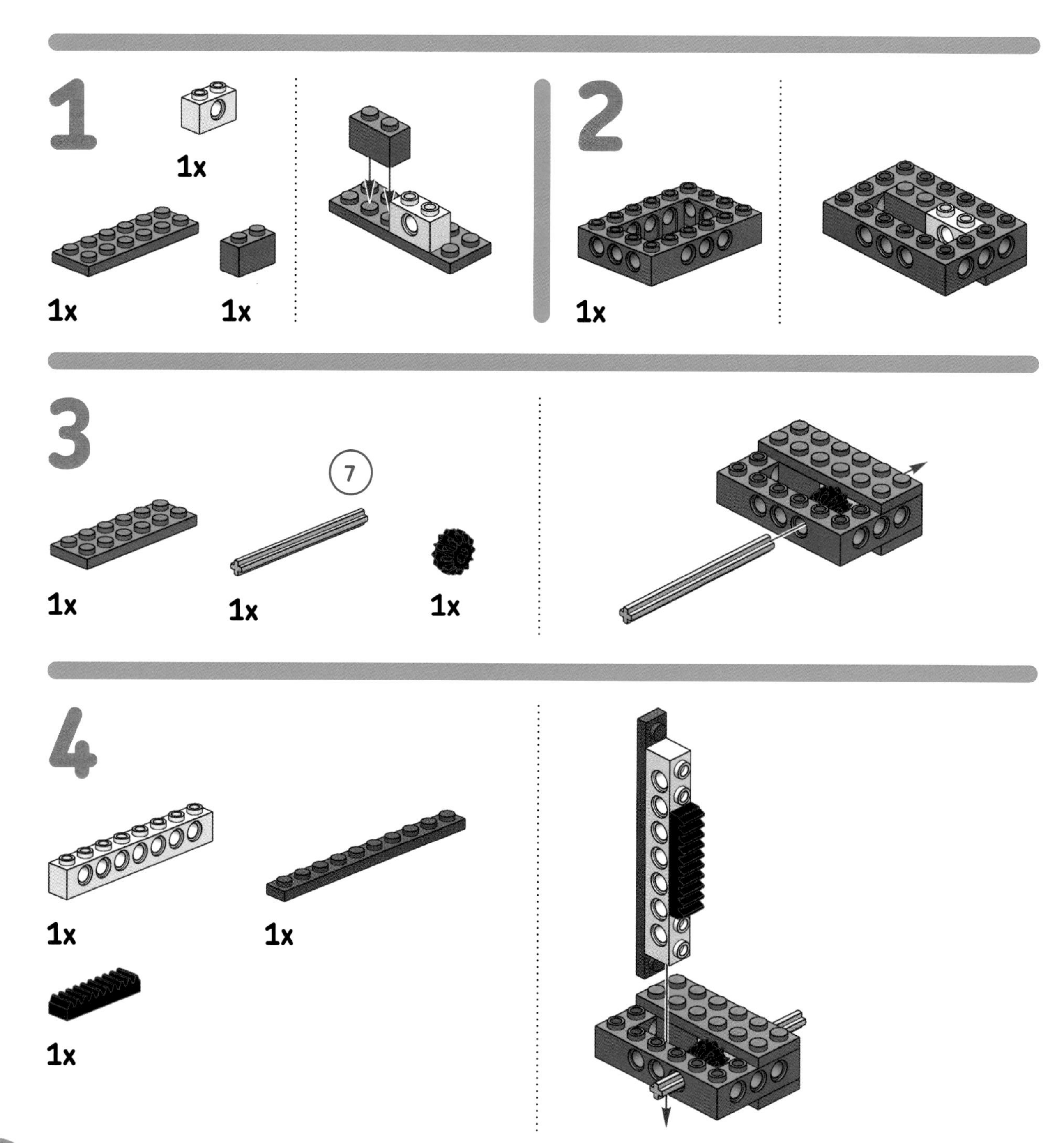

longer gear trains

You can combine gears to make longer gear trains. For example, **FIGURE 13-14** shows a gear train with three gears. The 8z gear in the middle is called an *idler gear*; it changes the direction of rotation from the input to the output gear without affecting the gear ratio. When using an idler gear, our output gear turns in the same direction as the input gear.

To get higher gear ratios, you can combine more gears, as shown in **FIGURE 13-15**. For example, on assembly **A**, the orange 24z gear is inserted on the same axle of the second 8z gear. (These gears are not idler gears because they affect the overall gear ratio.)

To compute the gear ratio of such a compound gear train, multiply the gear ratios of each pair of gears. For example, in assembly **A**, the gear ratio of each pair of gears is 1:3 (8:24 reduced to lowest terms). We multiply 1:3 and 1:3 to get 1:9. This means that to make the yellow axle rotate one turn, the red axle must perform nine full turns.

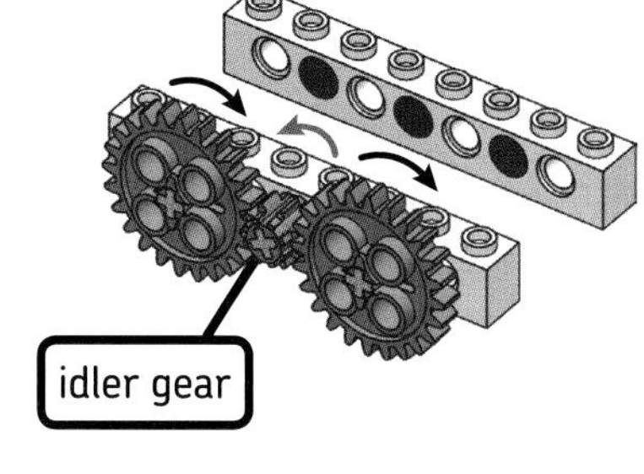

(24:8) x (8:24) = 1:1

FIGURE 13-14 A gear train with idler gear

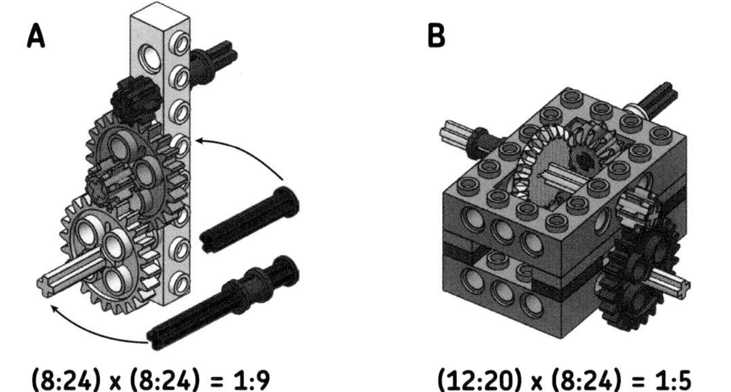

(8:24) x (8:24) = 1:9

(12:20) x (8:24) = 1:5

FIGURE 13-15 Gear trains achieve higher gear ratios.

The following steps show you how to build assembly **B**. Notice in assembly **B** that the gear ratio is 1:5, the result of multiplying 3:5 and 1:3. This tells us that in order to make the red 24z gear rotate one turn, the red axle that drives the 12z gear must rotate five full turns. Notice that the azure Technic frames are spaced by two layers of plates.

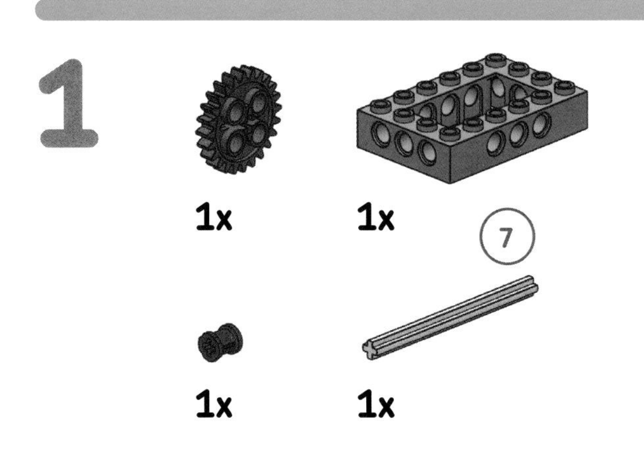

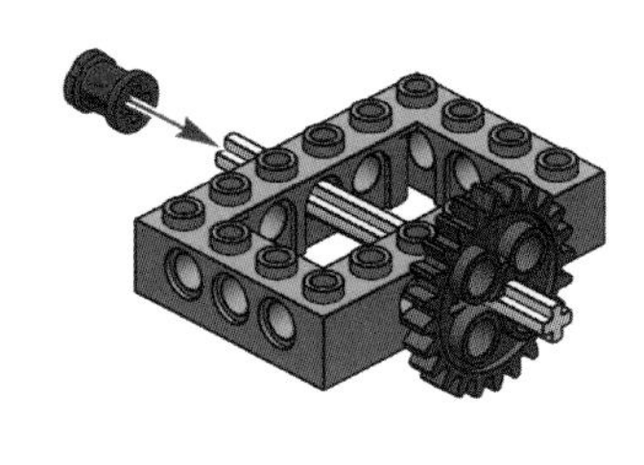

2

4x

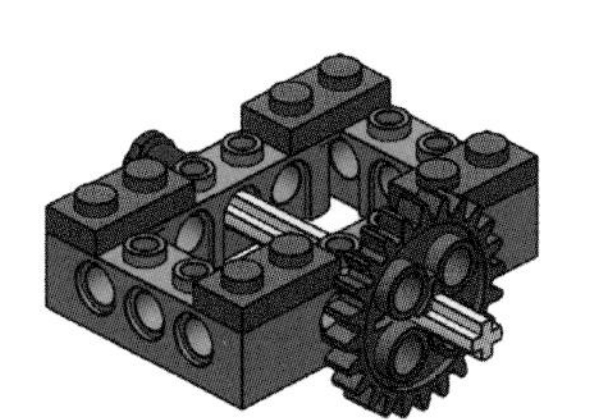

3

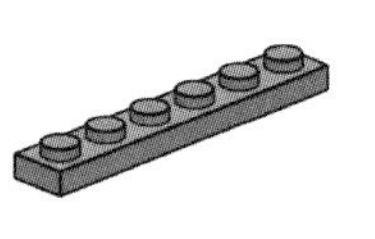

2x

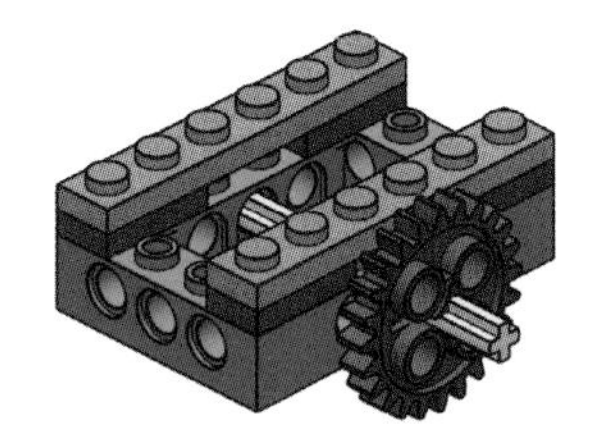

4

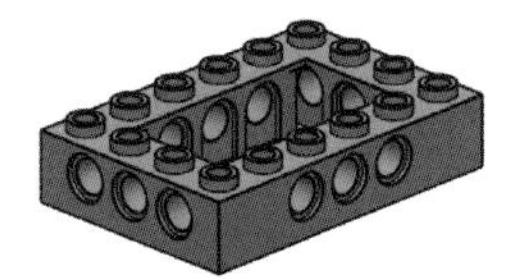

1x

4

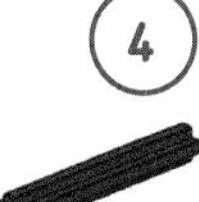

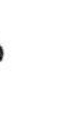

1x 1x 1x

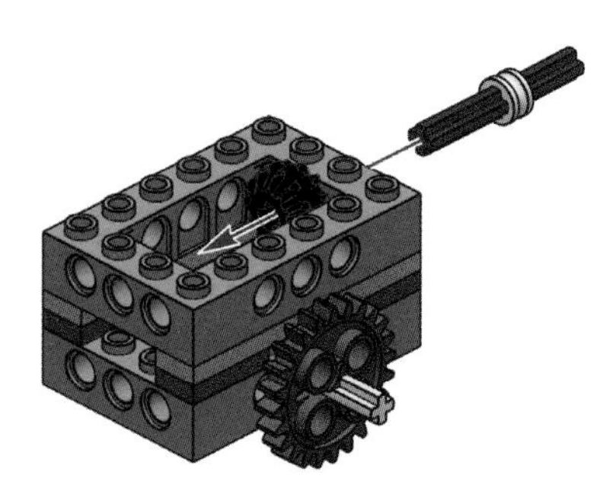

5

7

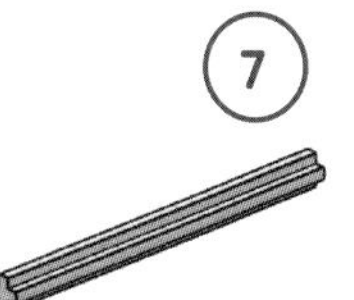

1x

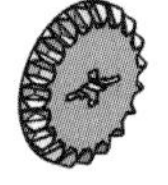

1x 1x 1x

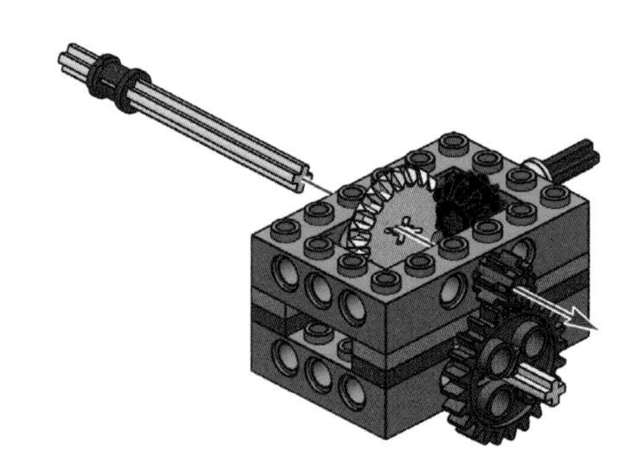

transforming motion

FIGURE 13-16 shows some examples of how we might transform rotation into different kinds of motion, like pushing or swinging. All of these mechanisms use a 2M beam with an axle hole as a crank. Assembly **A** works like a windshield wiper, swinging back and forth. Assembly **B** transforms rotation into a back-and-forth motion, similar to a piston in a car engine. Follow the instructions below to make Assembly **B**.

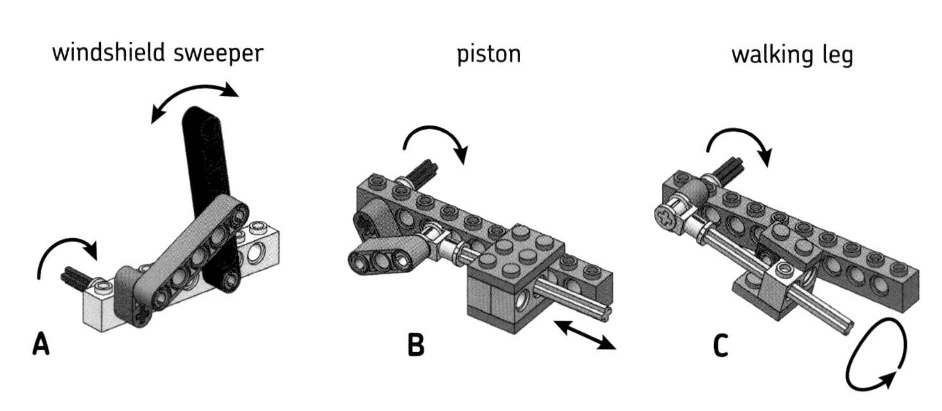

FIGURE 13-16 Examples of mechanisms that transform rotational motion into linear or reciprocating motion

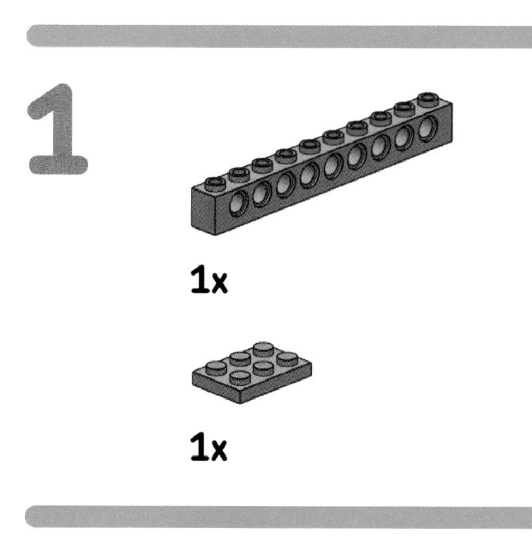

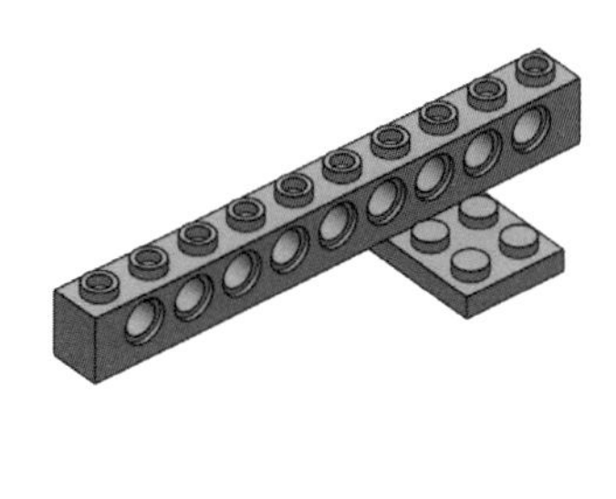

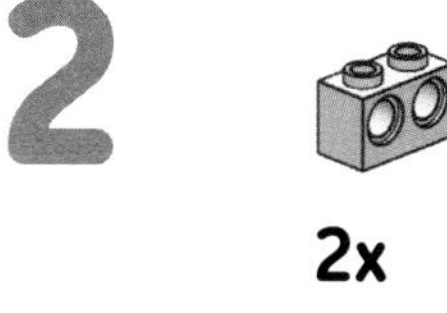

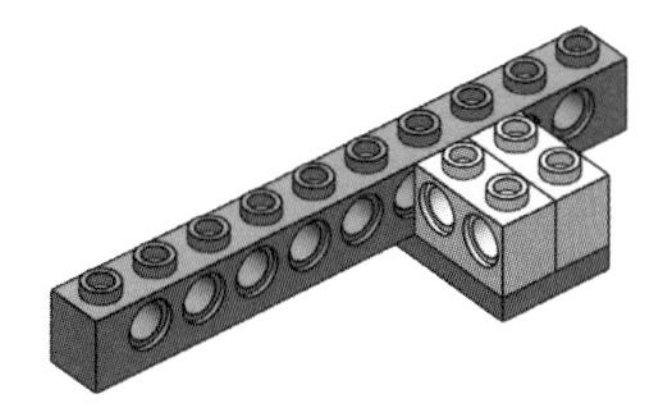

3

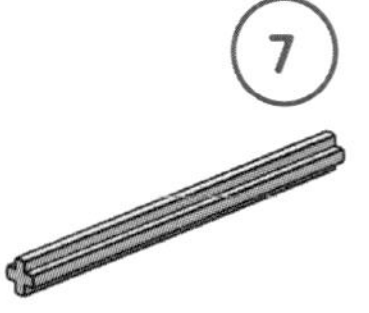

1x

1x

1x

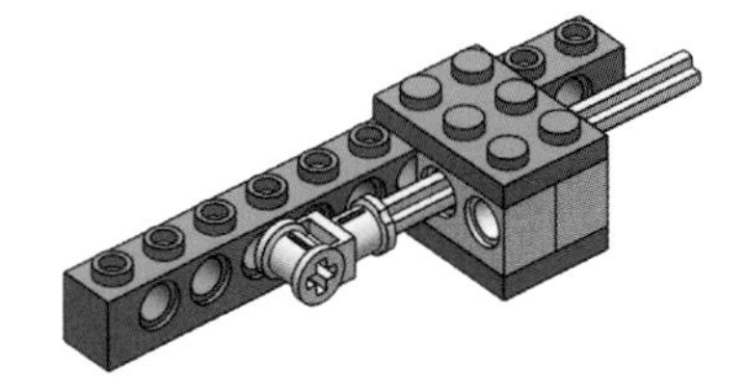

4

1x

1x

1x

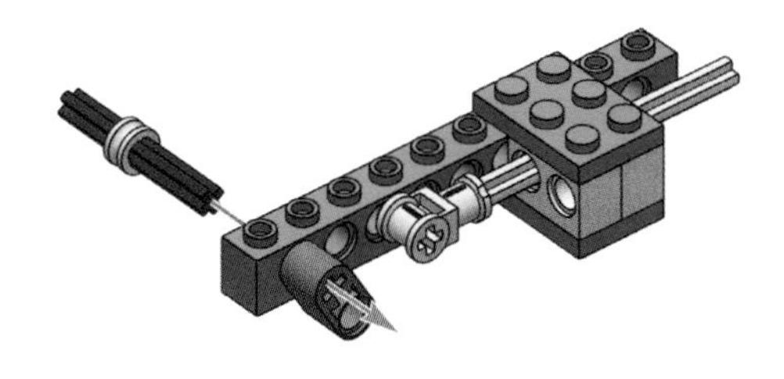

5

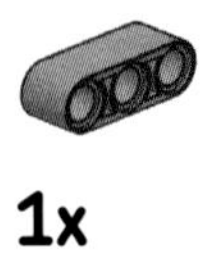

1x

1x

1x

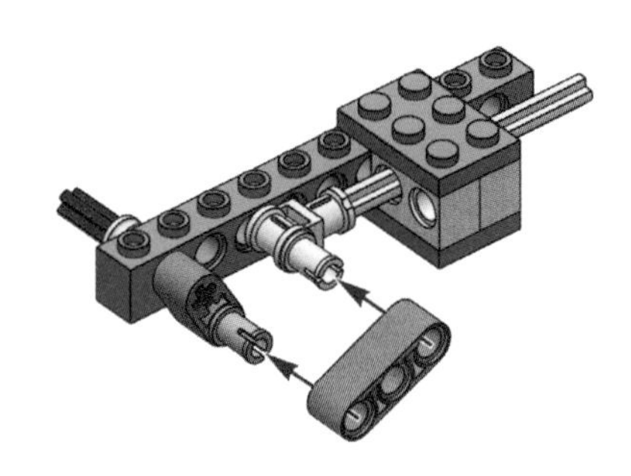

With a bit of modification, as shown below, we can turn assembly **C** into a functional leg.

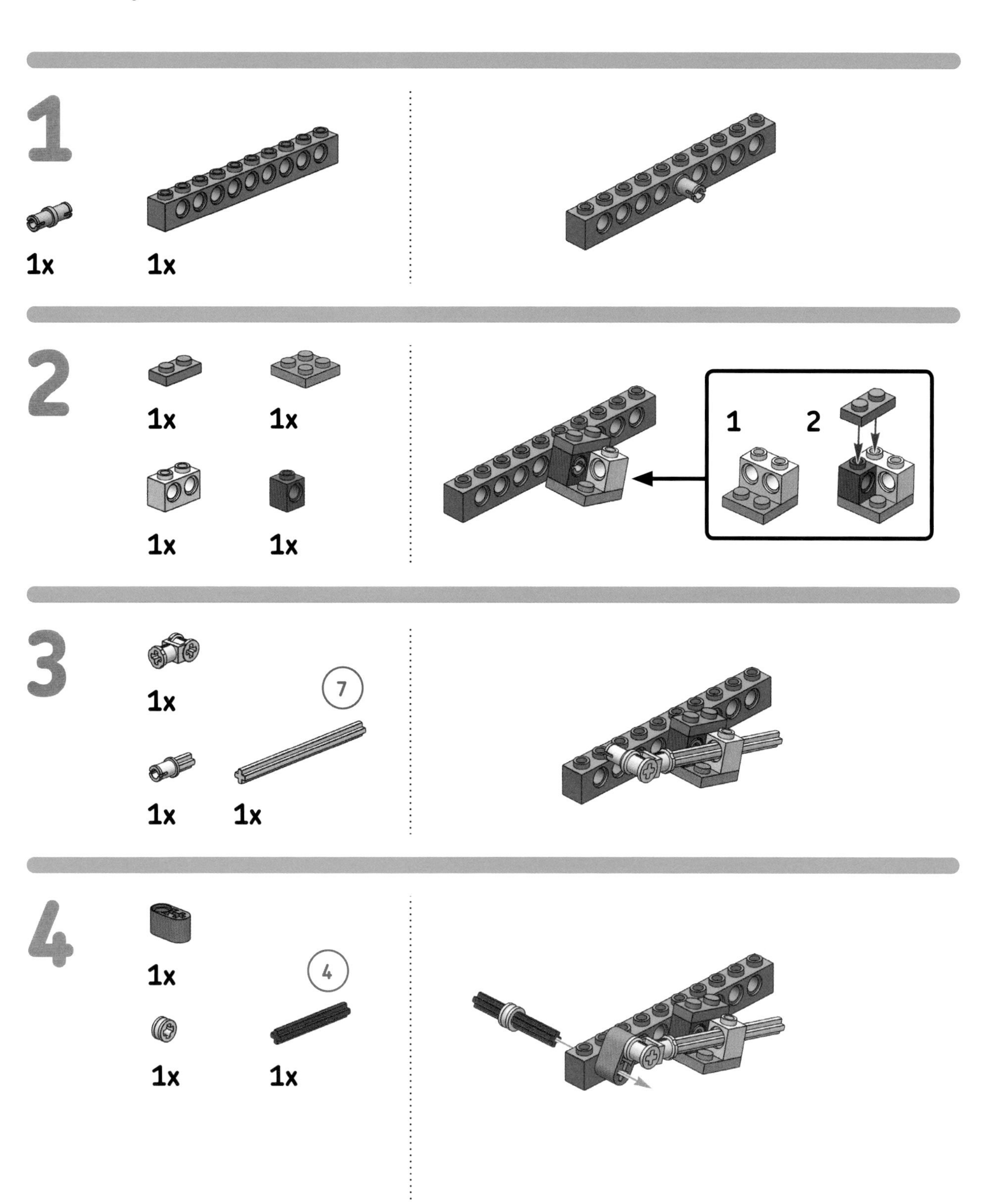

motor assemblies

Motors power every movement in your LEGO BOOST creations. For example, the assemblies below are examples of how to attach gears or frames to the BOOST external motor or Move Hub.

- Assembly **A** shows how to brace the external motor with vertical bricks. If you need to add gears, you can use any of the assemblies of **FIGURE 13-11** by attaching the brick to the motor using black pegs.
- Assemblies **B** and **C** show how to drive an axle perpendicular to the motor shaft (horizontally and vertically, respectively). You can attach assemblies **C** and **D** of **FIGURE 13-12** to the motor to obtain the same gearing.
- Assemblies **D** and **E** show how to gear down (or up if you swap gears) the rotation of the Move Hub motors. In **E**, the black beam braces the Move Hub.

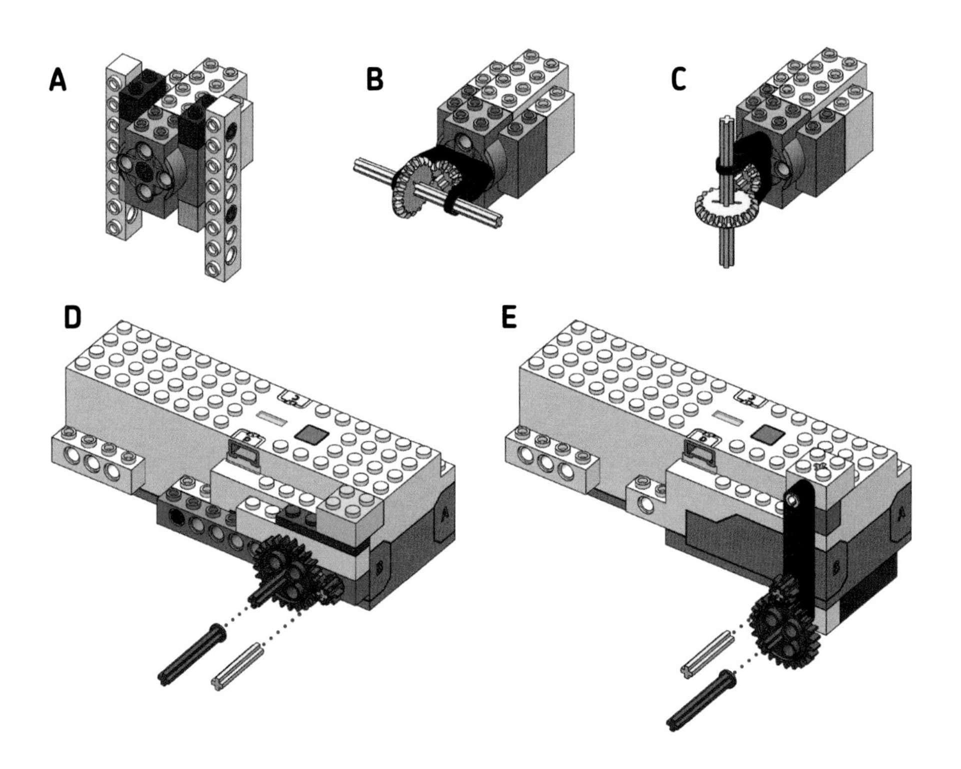

FIGURE 13-17 shows the base assembly for a walking robot. Here, the 2M beam acts as a crank, transforming the rotation of the motor into an alternating motion for the legs to mimic walking. Start from this base design to make your own walking robot!

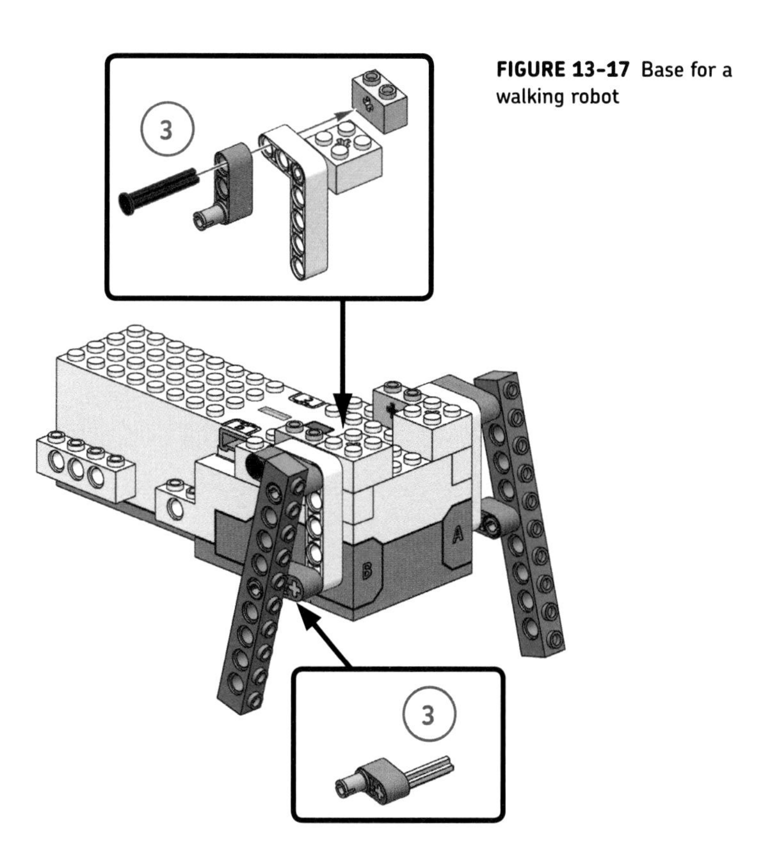

FIGURE 13-17 Base for a walking robot

what you've learned

I hope you've found this chapter a useful cookbook of sorts. You gained some basic knowledge about LEGO geometry and learned how to build sturdy structures and functional gear trains. You've seen some ideas for building modules that transmit motion and transform motion, as well as some sample motor assemblies you can use in your amazing BOOST creations!

PART III

BrickPecker

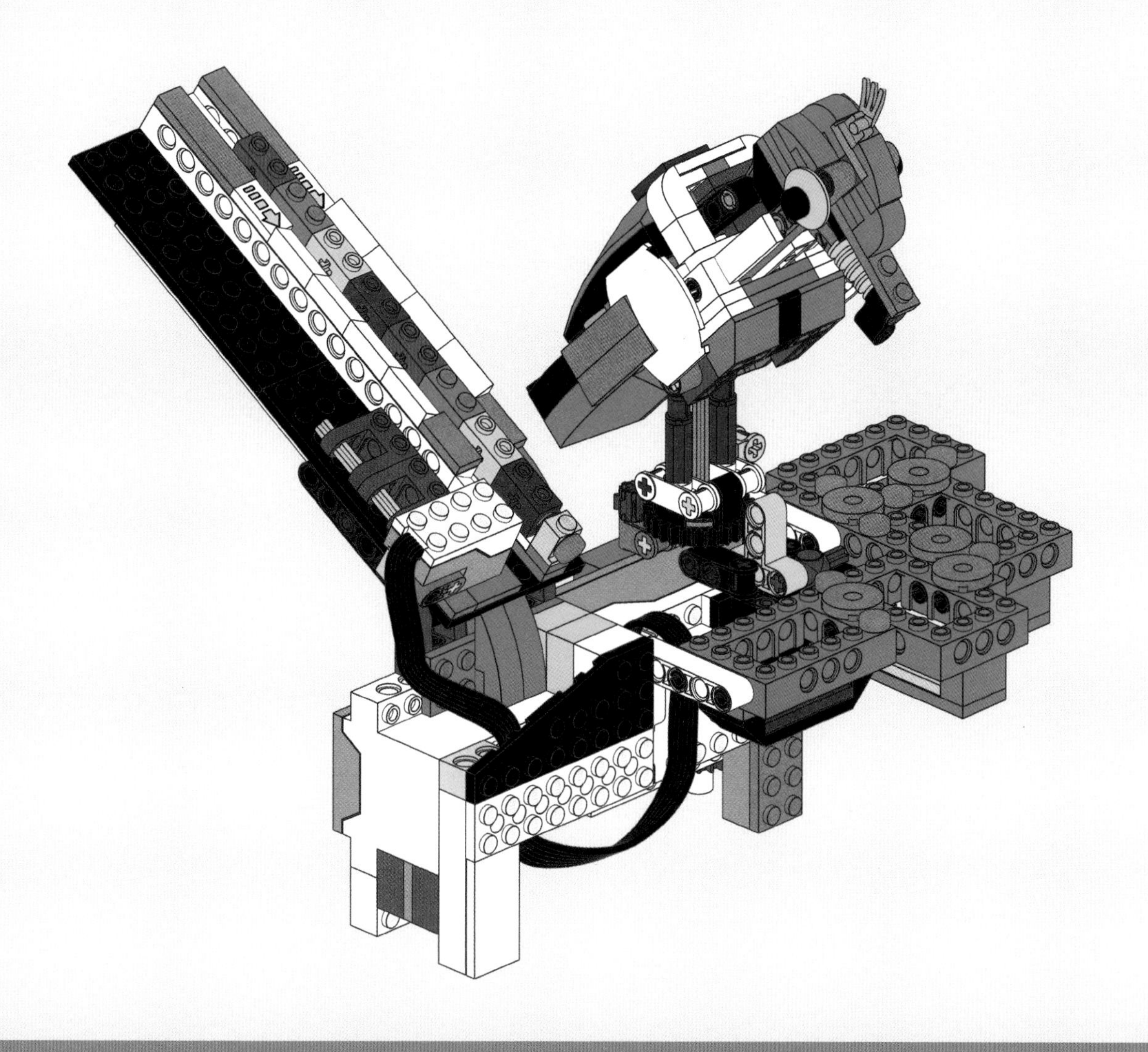

14

BrickPecker, a Brick-Sorting Bird

In this chapter, you will find detailed building instructions for BrickPecker (**FIGURE 14-1**), a bird that can sort bricks in its nest by color. You can feed BrickPecker colored "seeds" by sliding them into the feeder, and the robot will carefully pick them up with its beak and sort them into the various bins.

For each step, you'll find a list of the parts you'll need to complete that step.

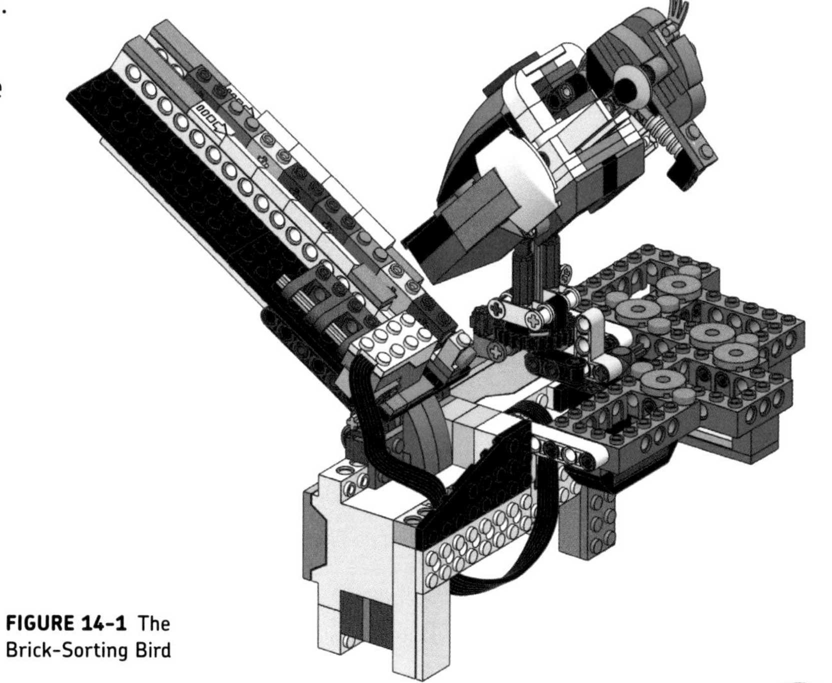

FIGURE 14-1 The Brick-Sorting Bird

1

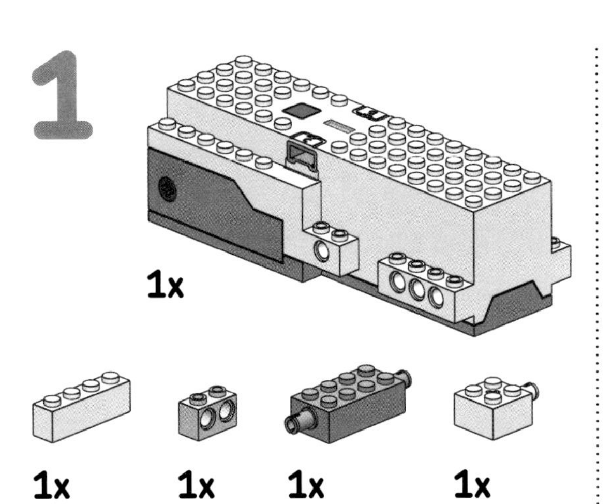

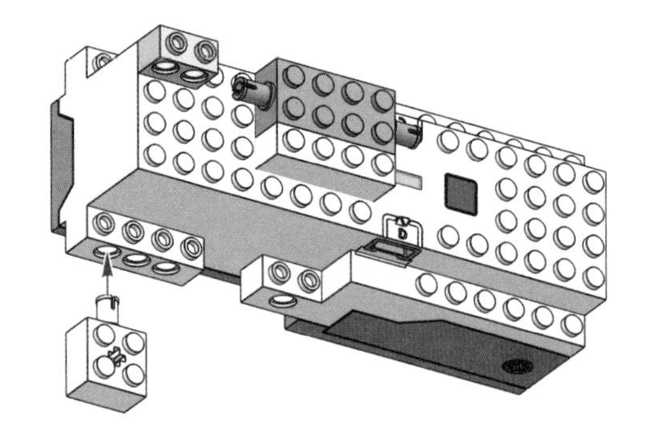

2

2x

1x

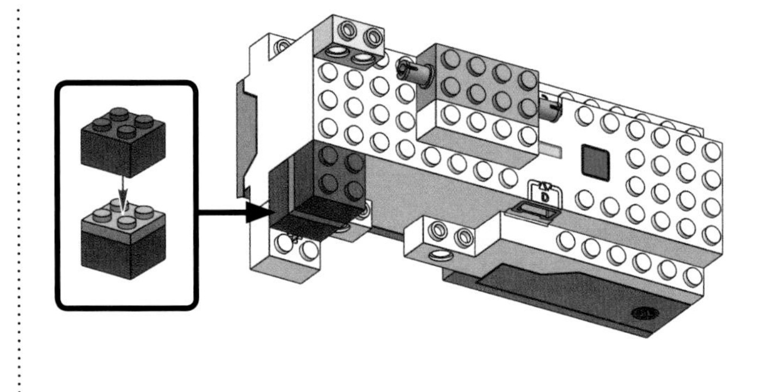

3

2x

1x

1x

2x

2x

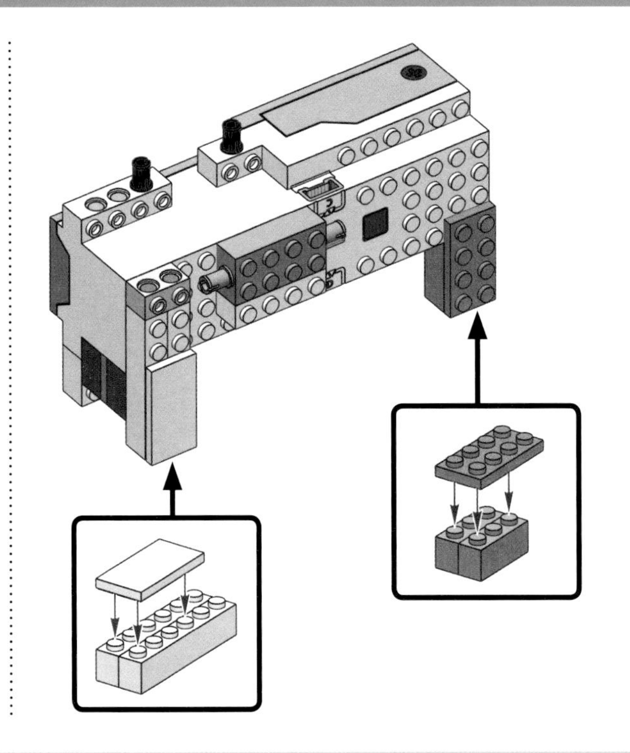

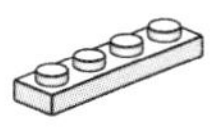 

1x 1x

1x 1x

1x 2x

2x 1x

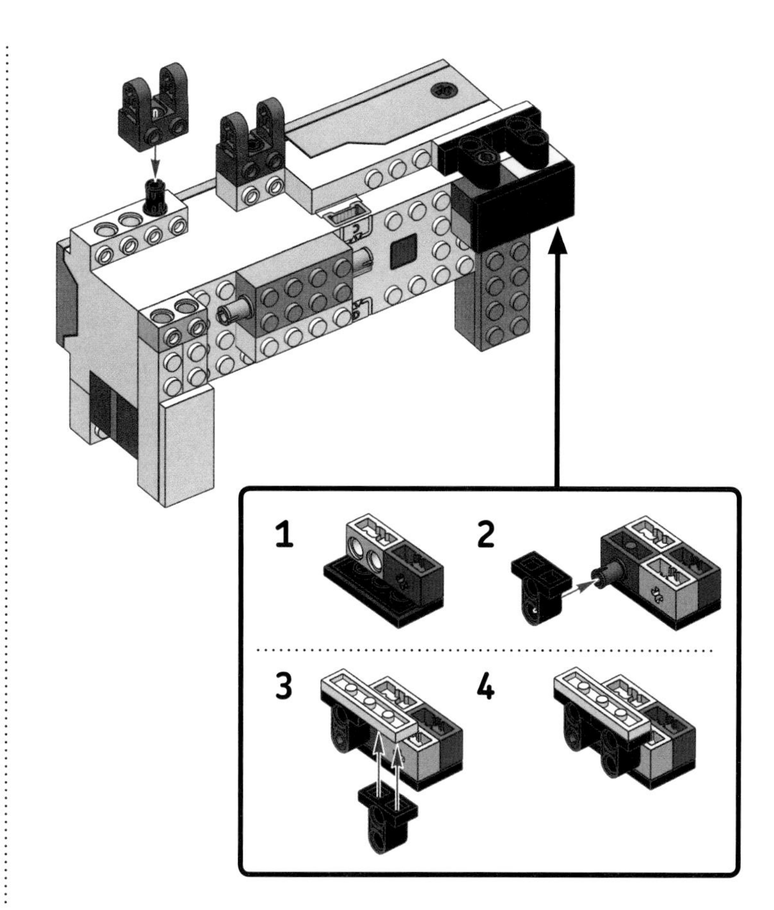

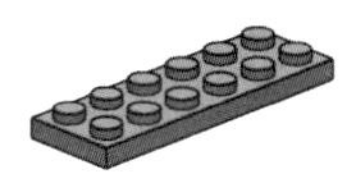 

1x 1x

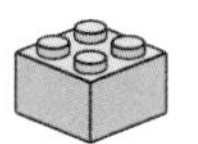 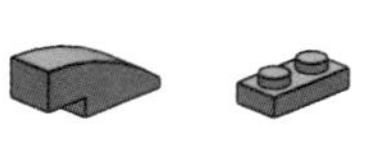

2x 2x 1x

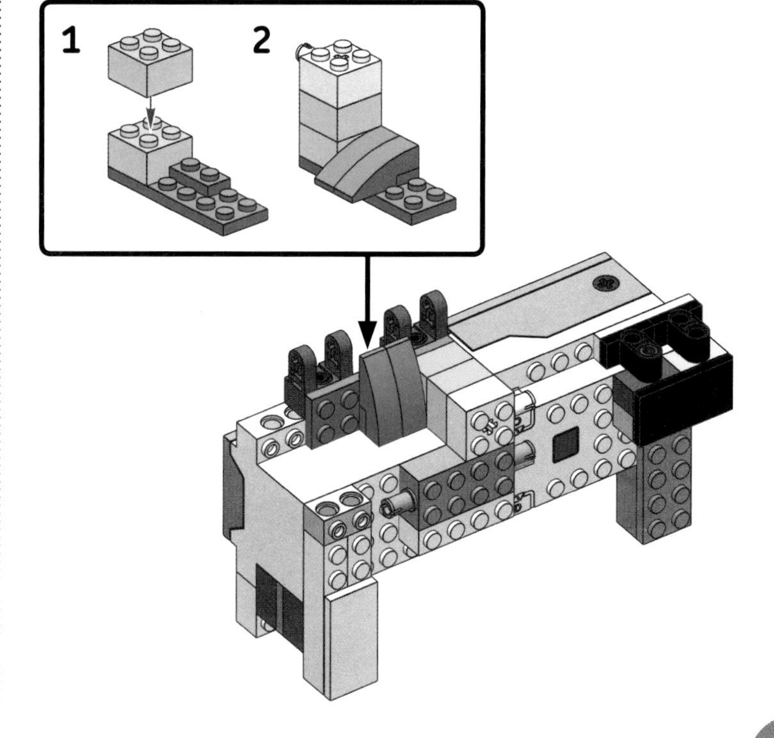

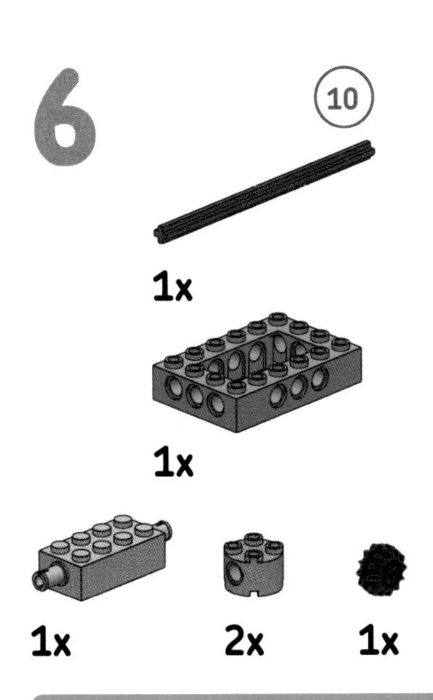

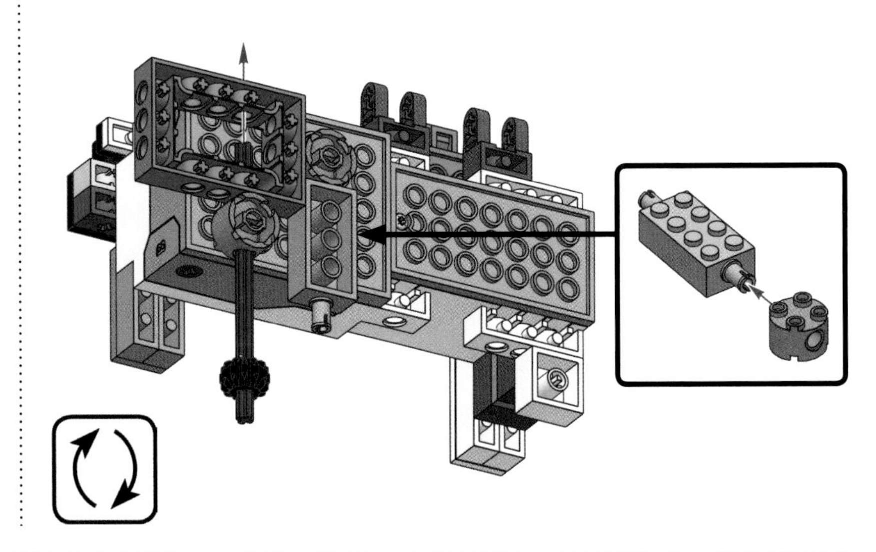

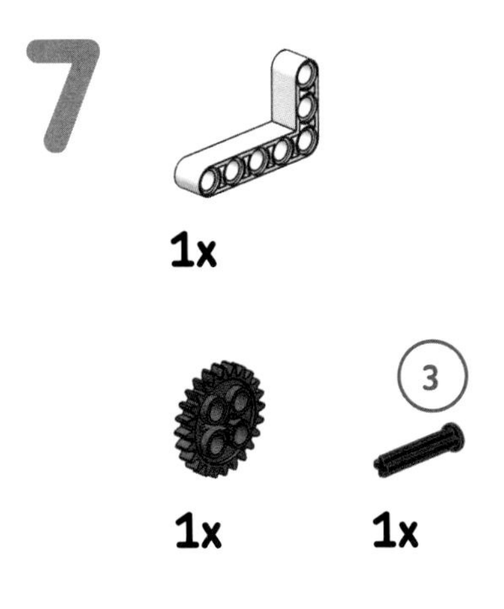

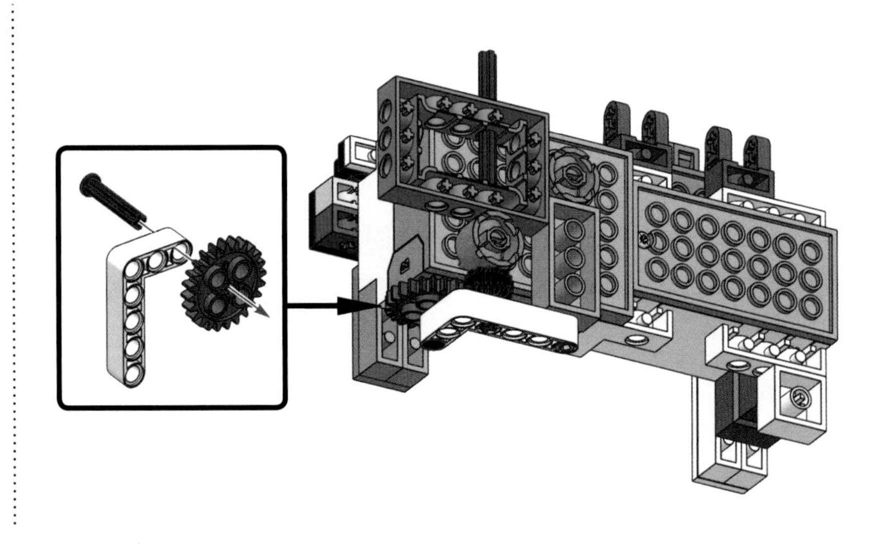

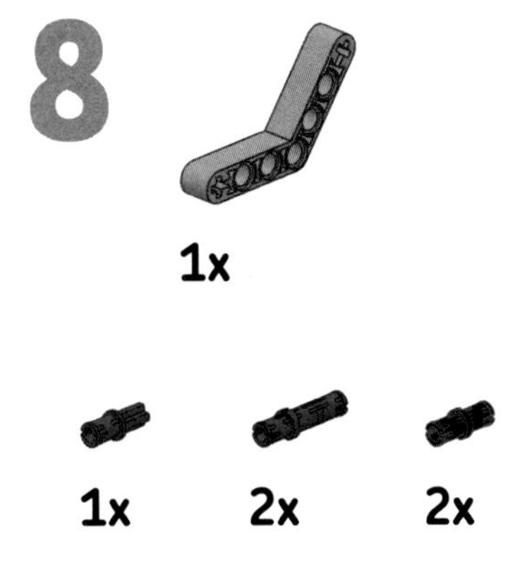

Building the brick feeder.

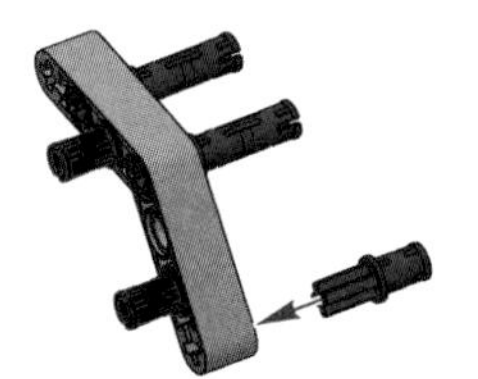

9

10

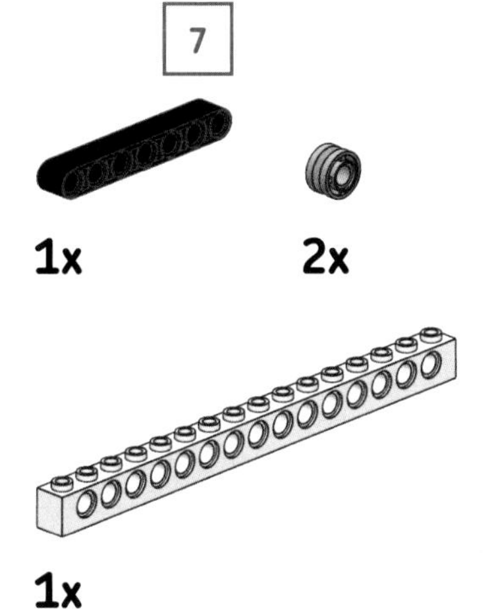

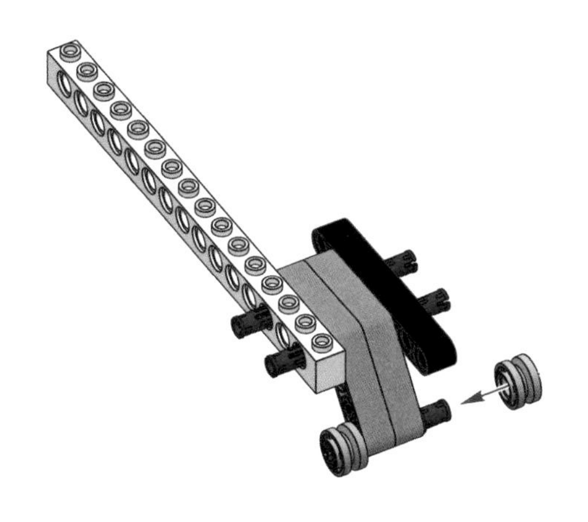

11

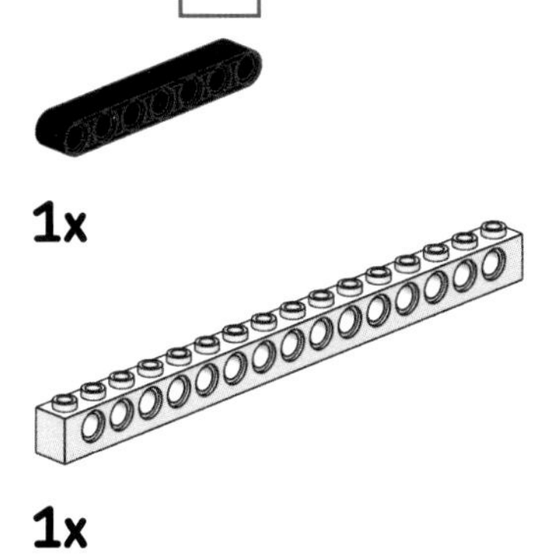

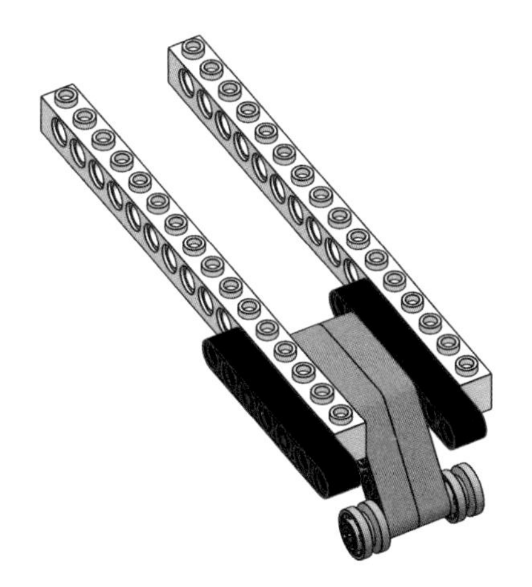

12

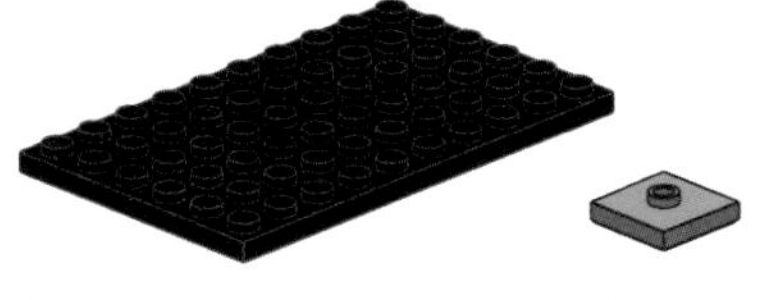

2x

1x

1x

2x

1x

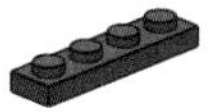

1x

1x

1x

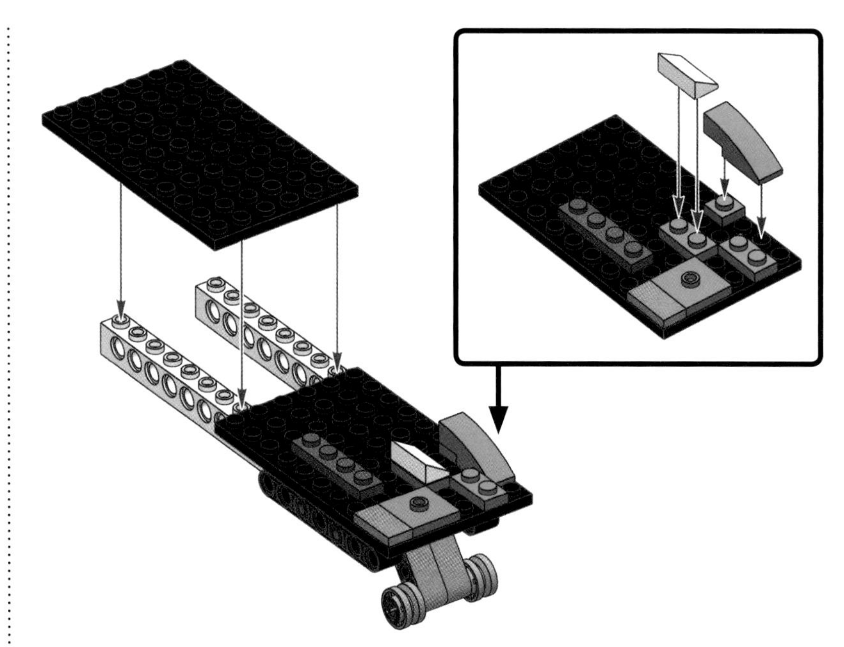

13

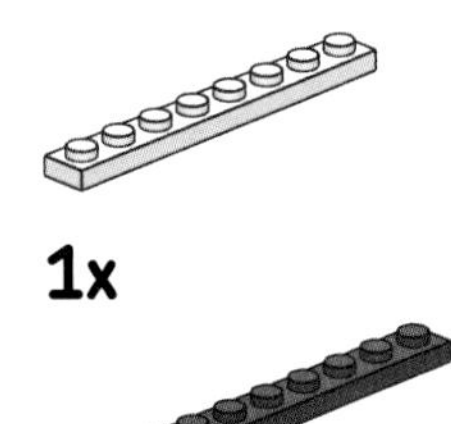

1x

1x

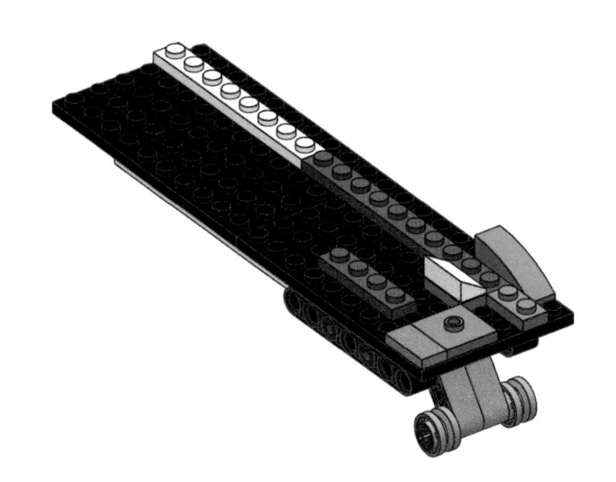

14

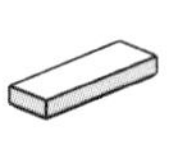

1x

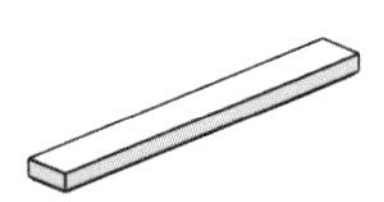

2x

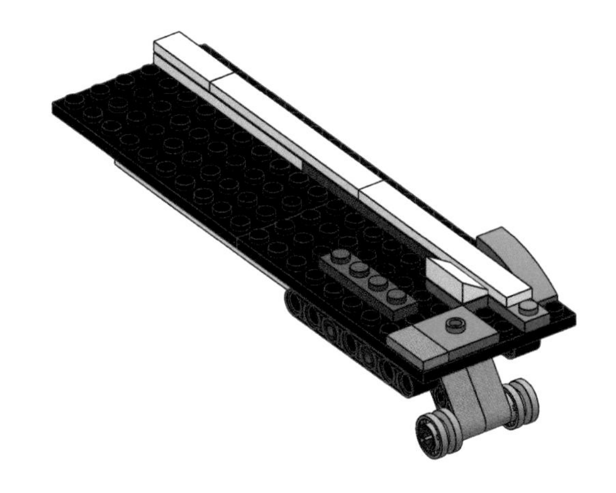

15

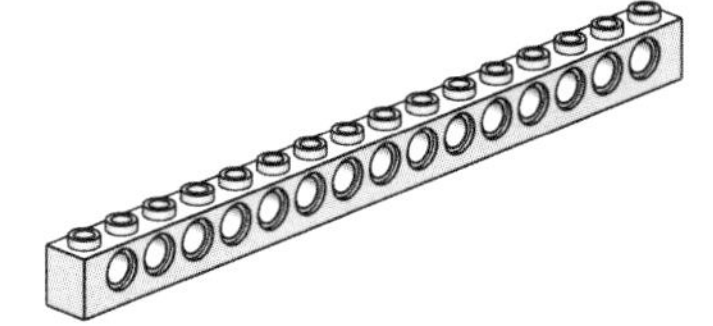

2x

2x 2x

2x 8x

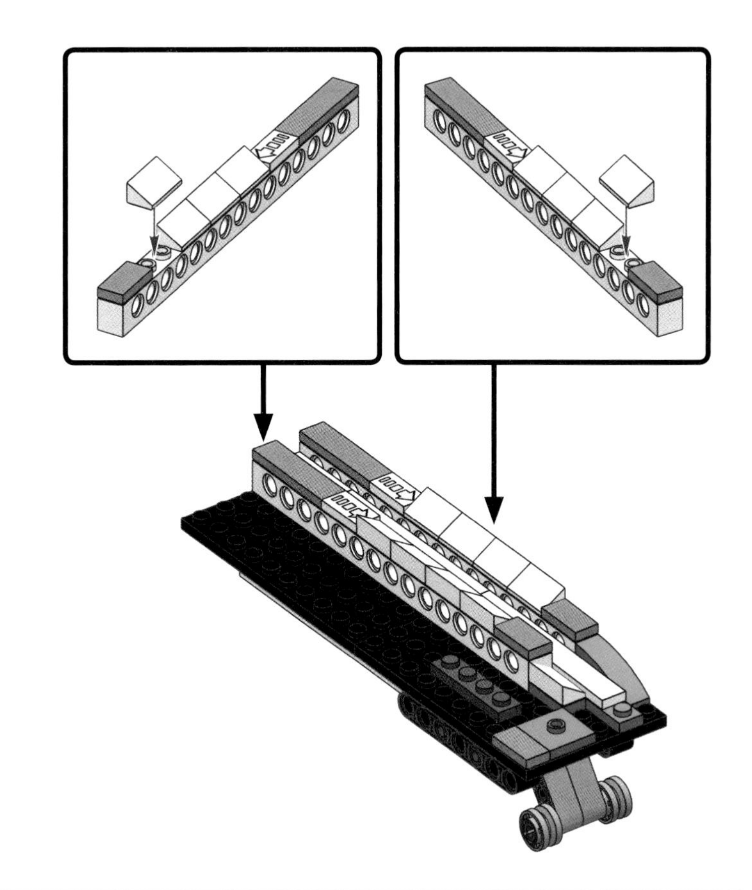

16

2x 1x 1x 1x

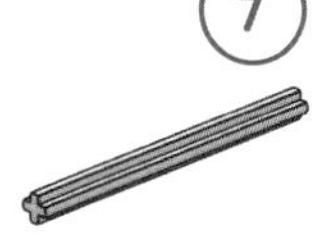

7

1x 1x 1x

1x 1x 1x

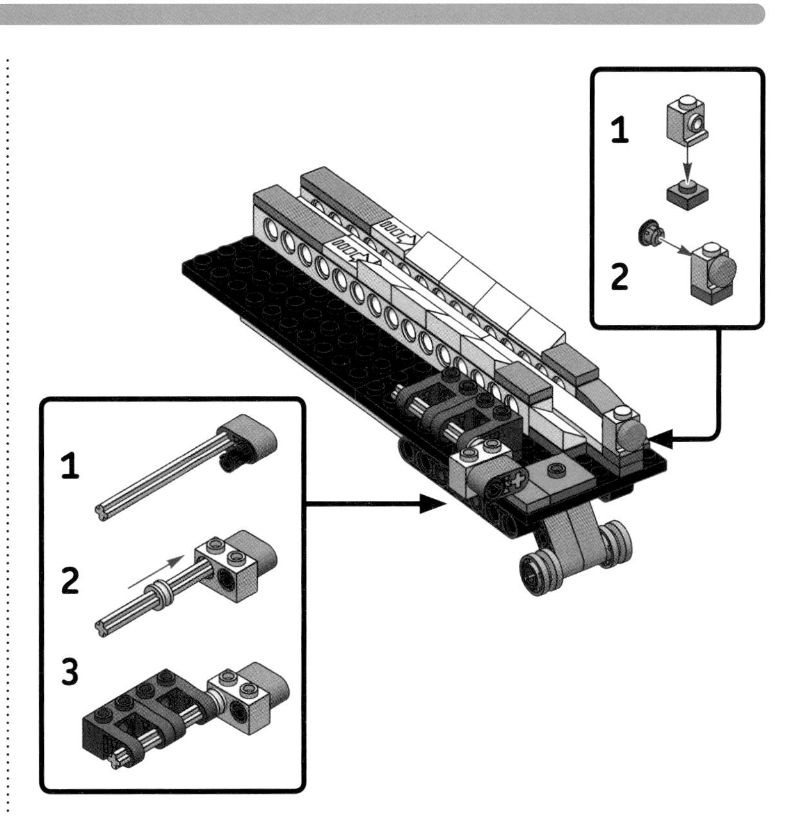

17

1x

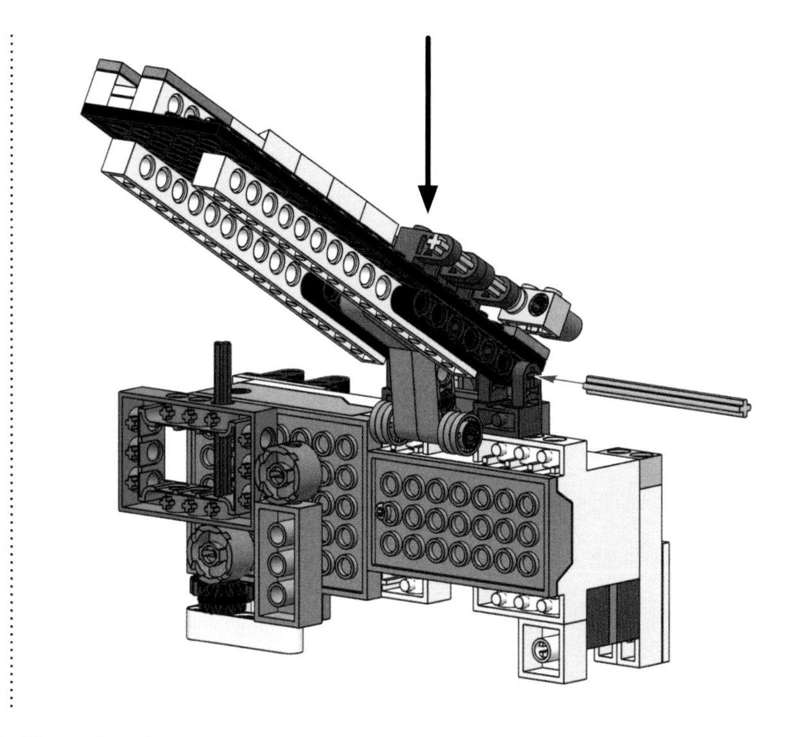

18

1x

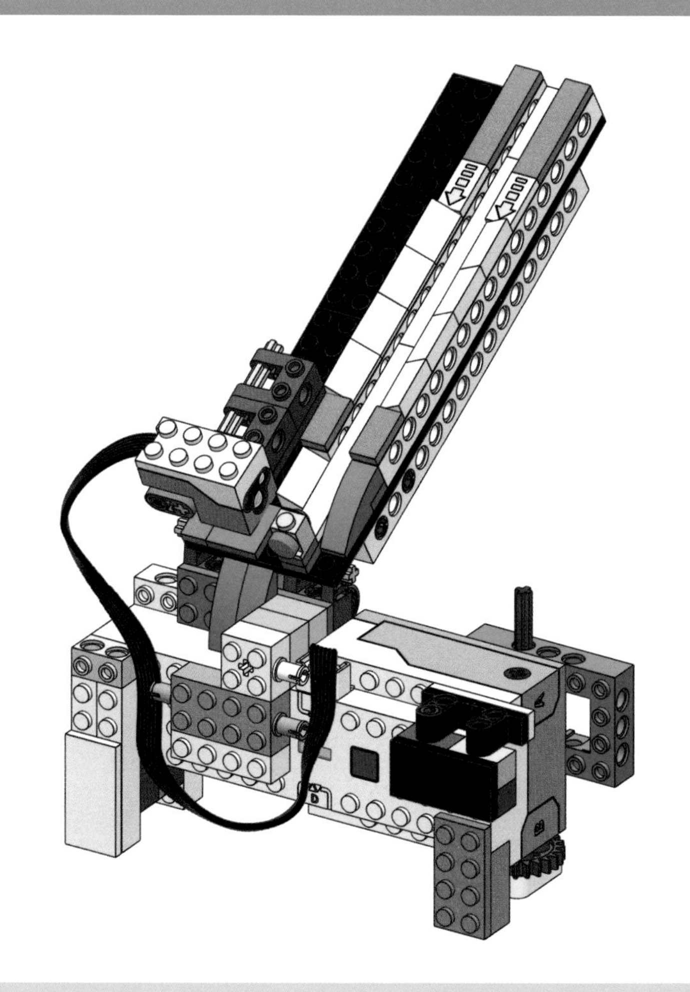

19

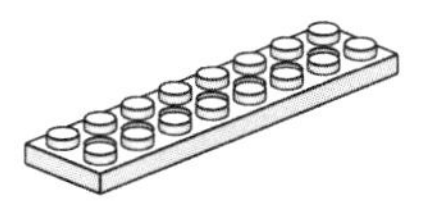

1x

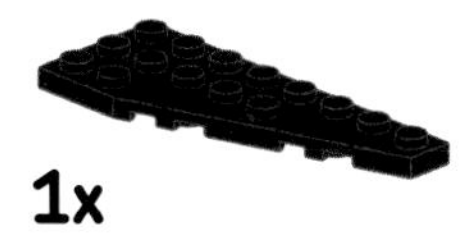

1x

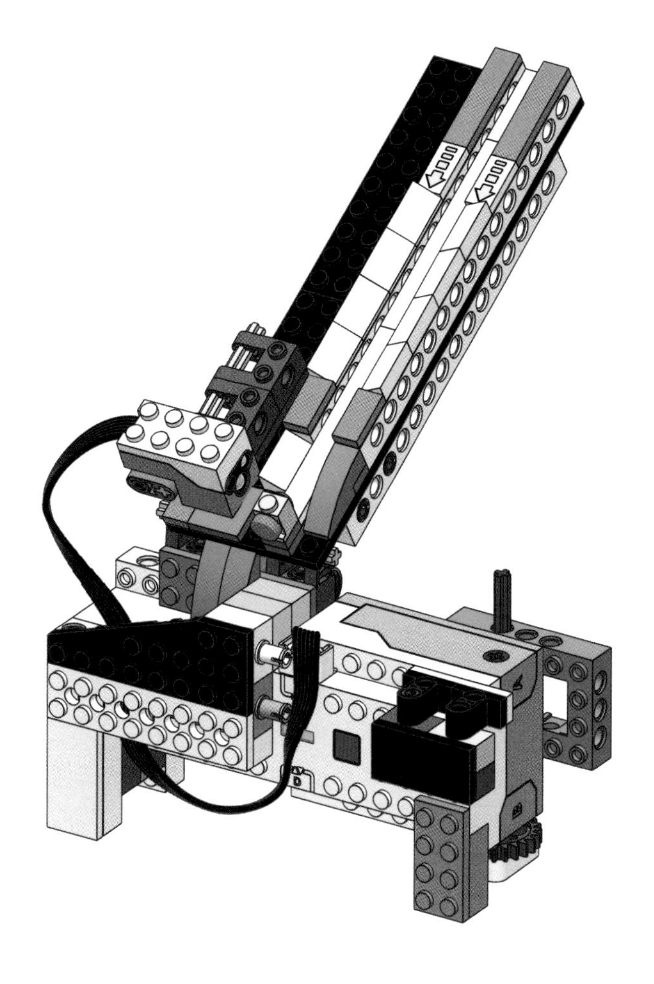

20

1x 1x

Building the turntable assembly.

21

1x

1x

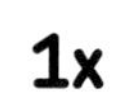

1x

1x

22

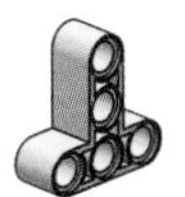

1x

1x

1x

23

1x

1x

2x

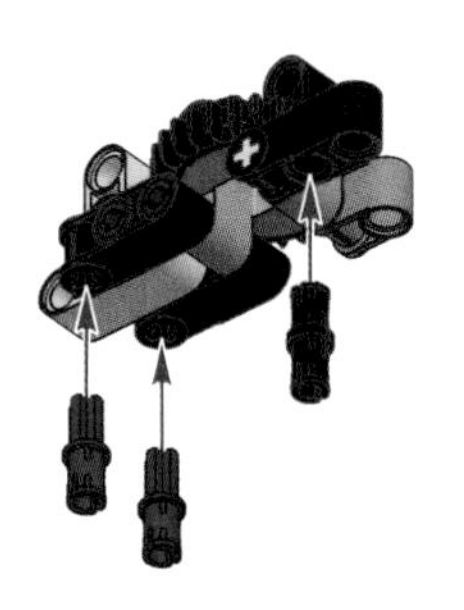

24

1x

4

3

1x

1x

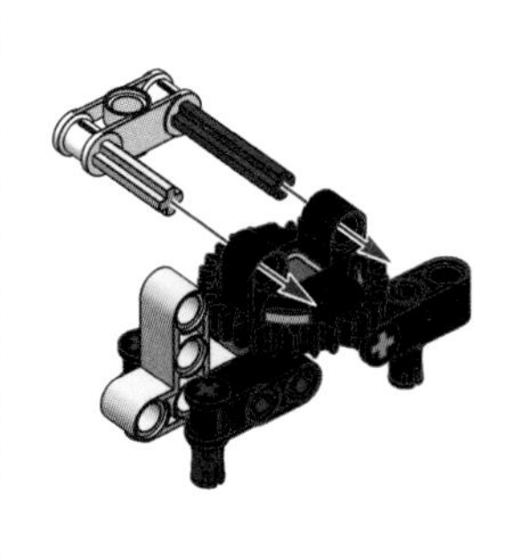

25

1x

1x

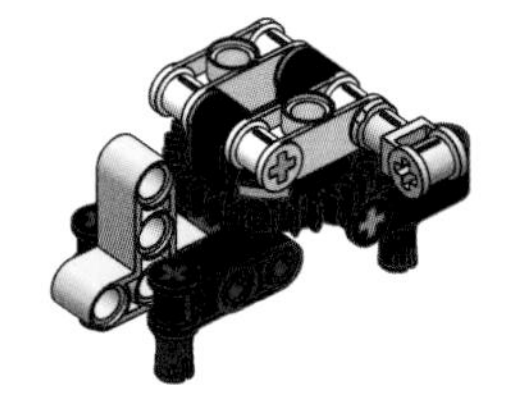

26

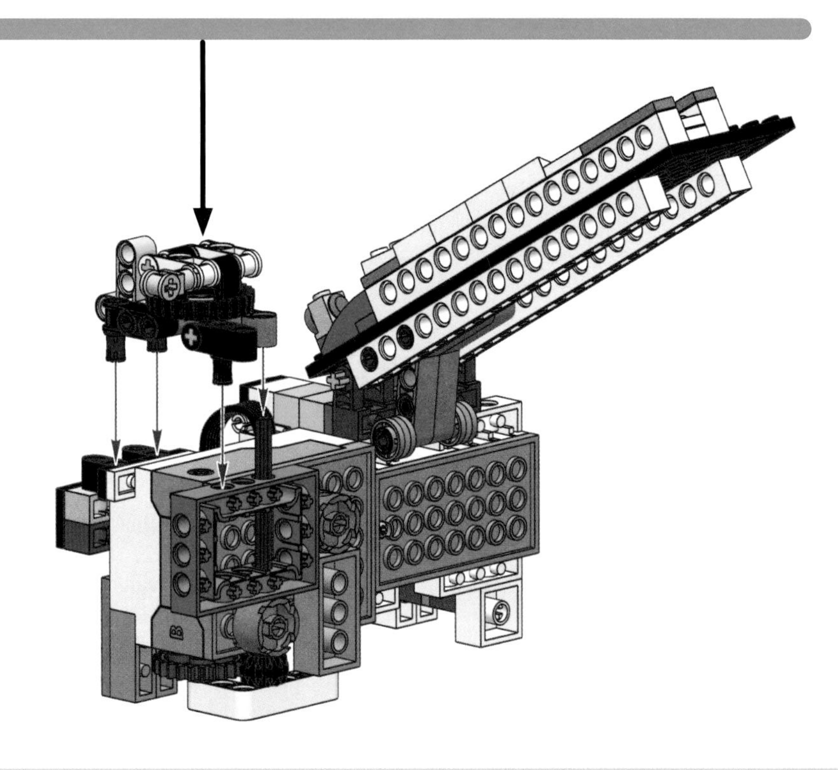

27

1x

1x 1x

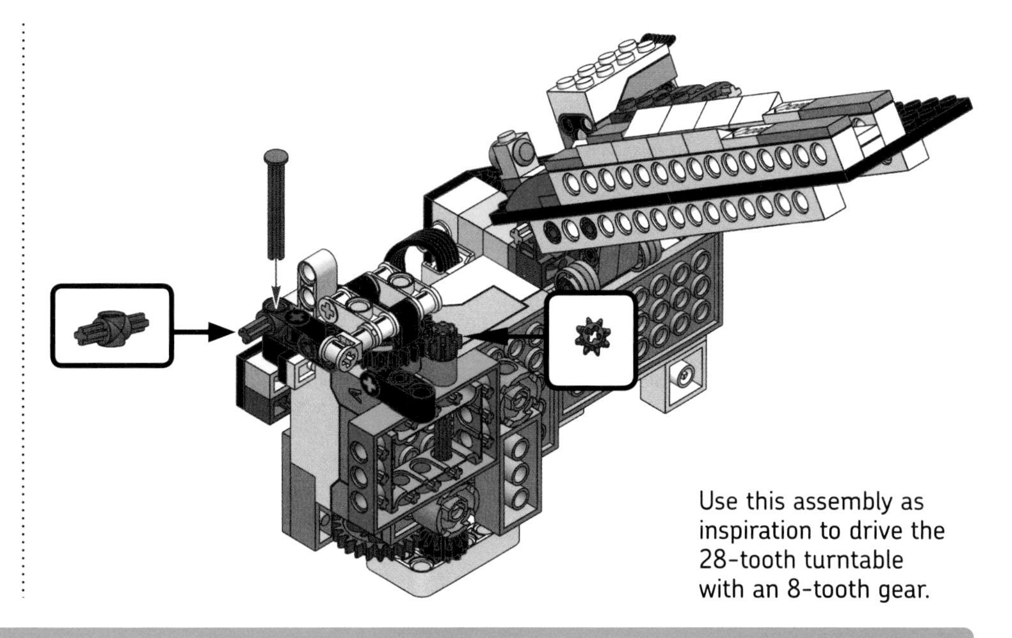

Use this assembly as inspiration to drive the 28-tooth turntable with an 8-tooth gear.

28

3x

1x

Building the bird's nest.

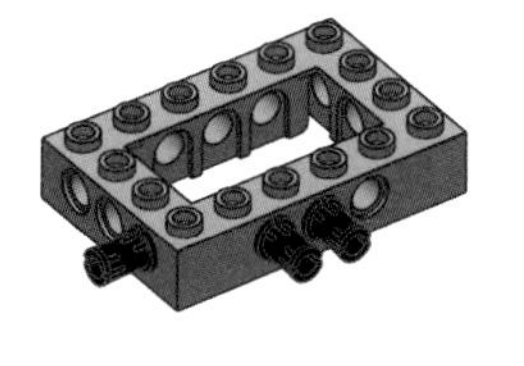

29

1x

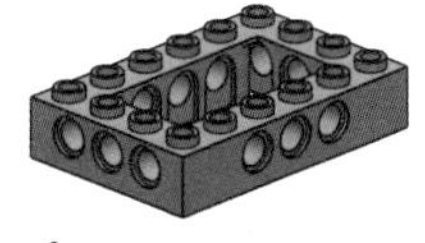

1x

30

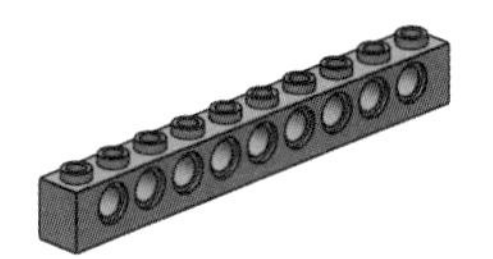

1x

4x

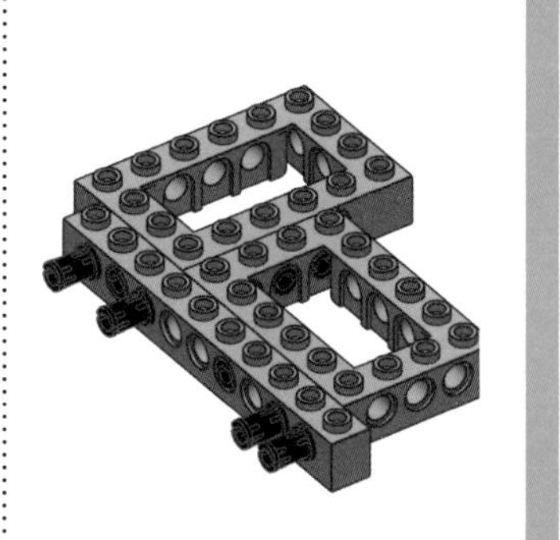

31

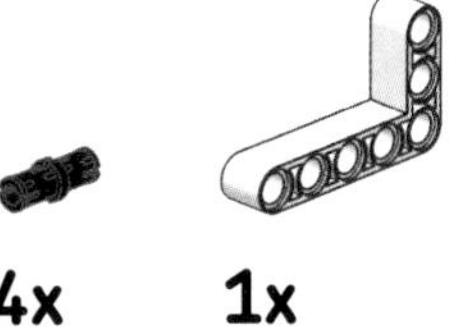

4x 1x

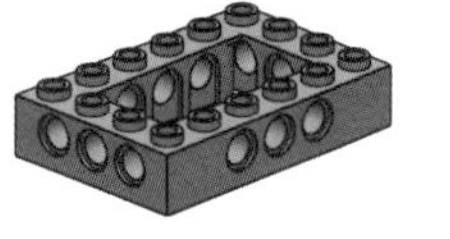

1x

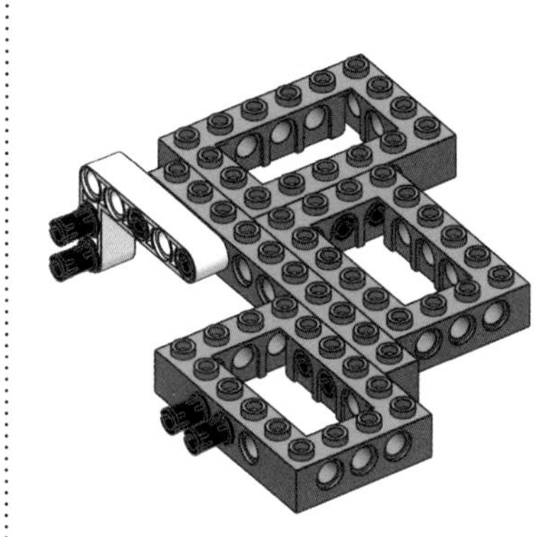

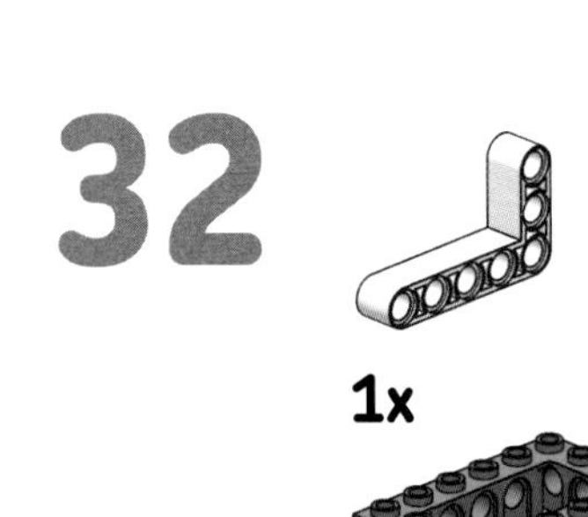

32

1x

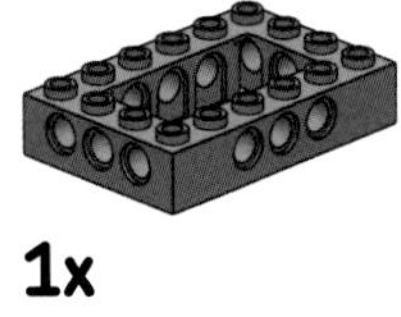

1x

2x

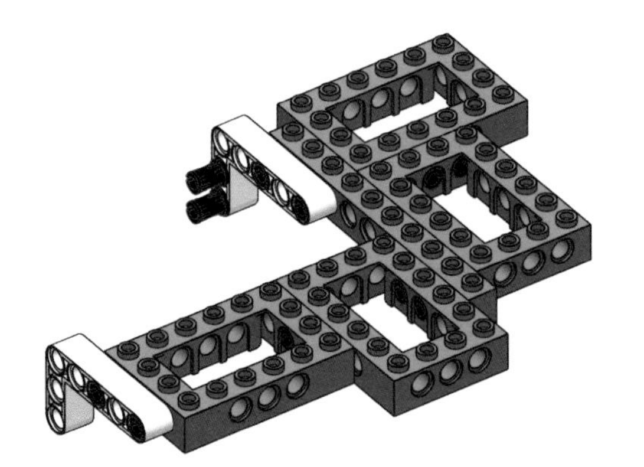

33

5x

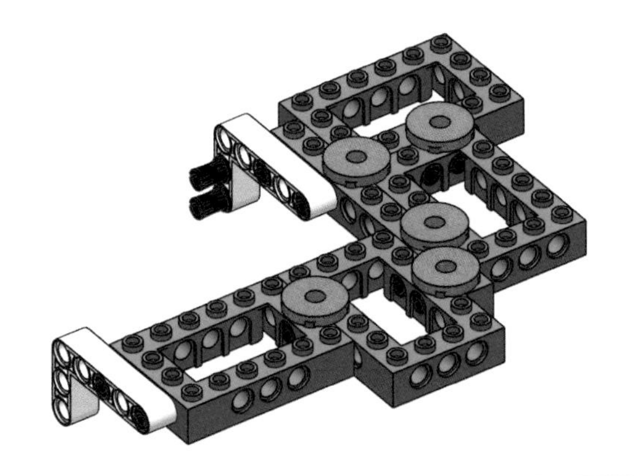

34

7x

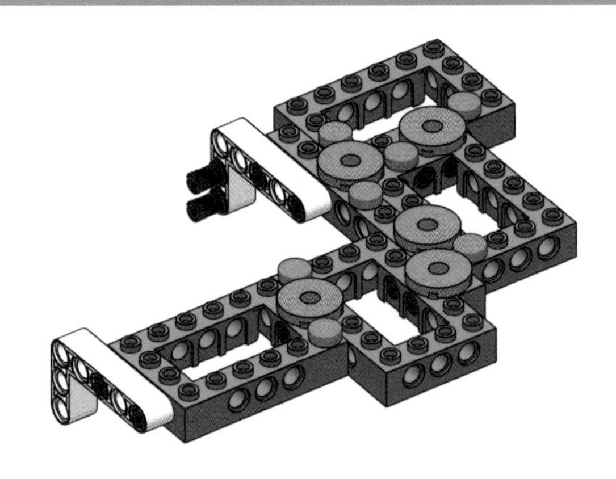

35

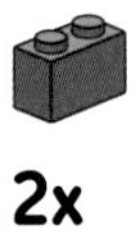

2x

2x

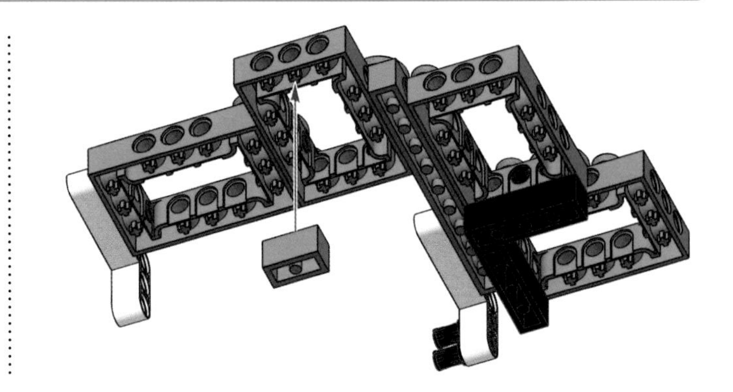

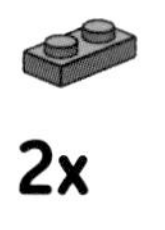
2x

1x

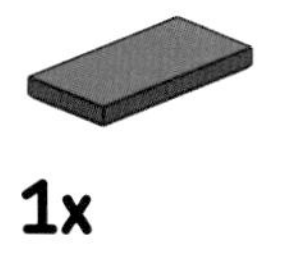
1x

1x

1x

1x

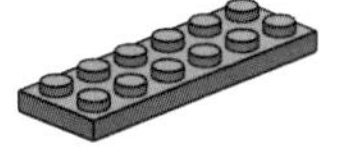
3x

3x

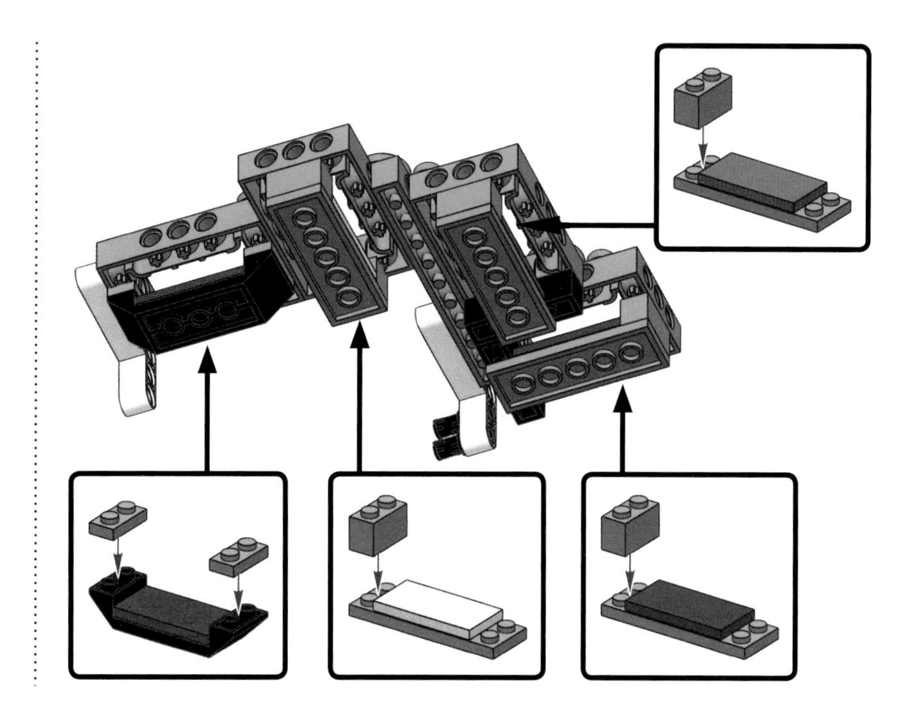

37

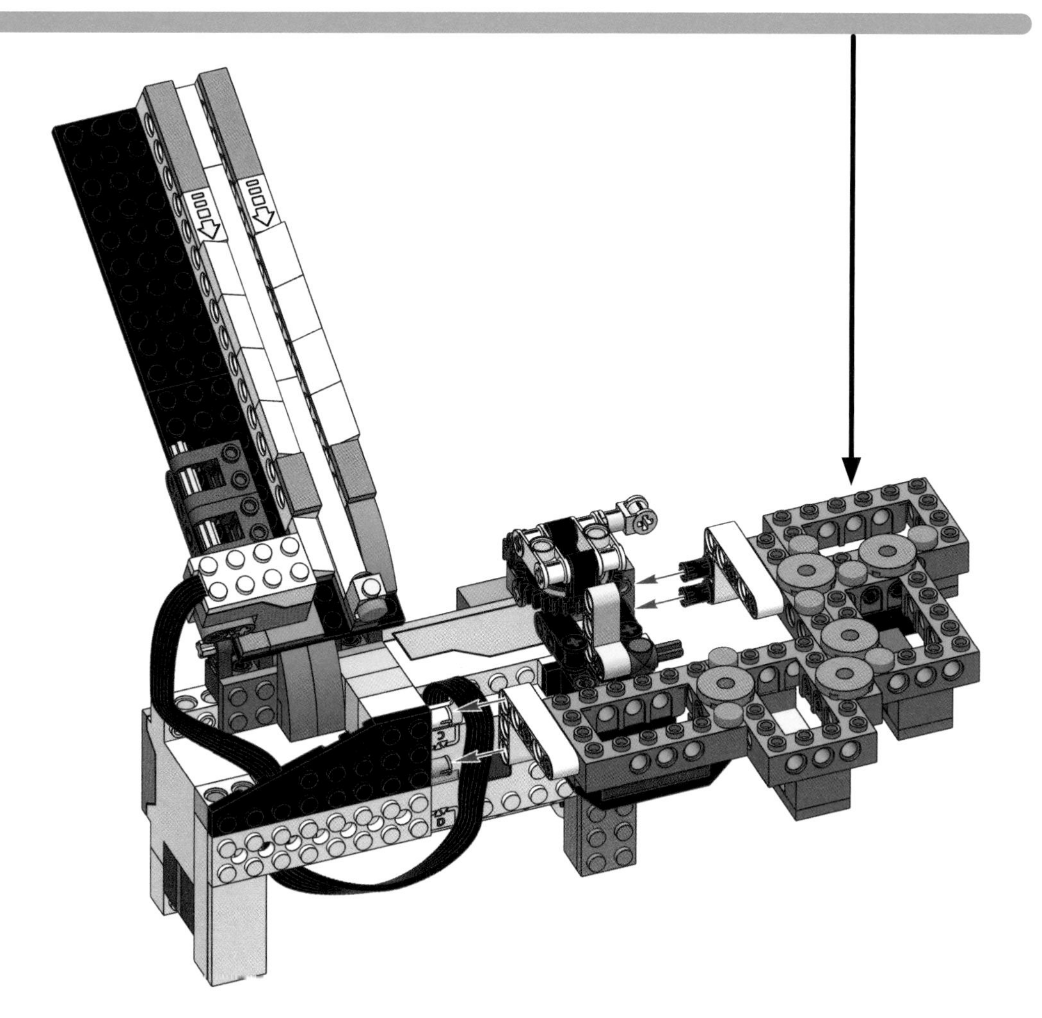

38

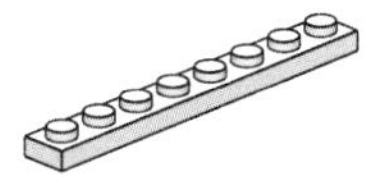

1x

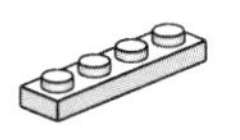

1x

Building the bird's body.

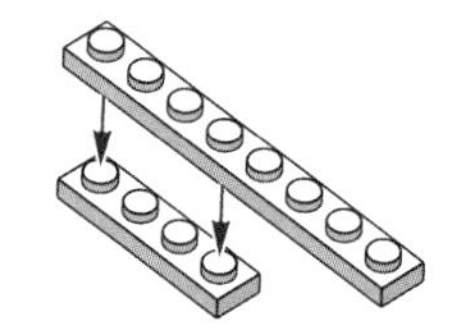

39

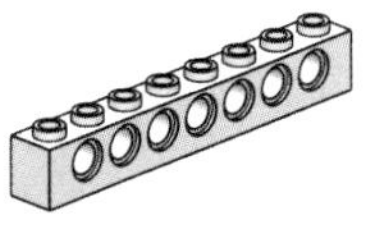

1x

3x 1x

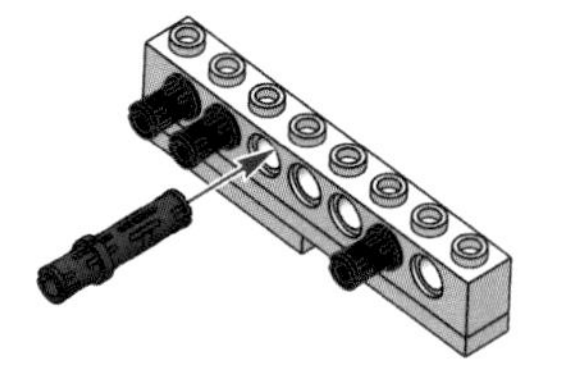

40

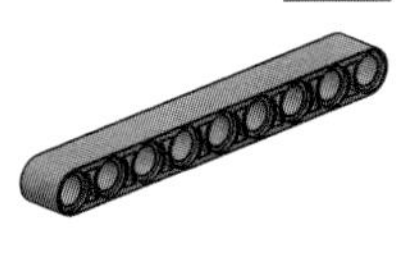

1x

1x

1x

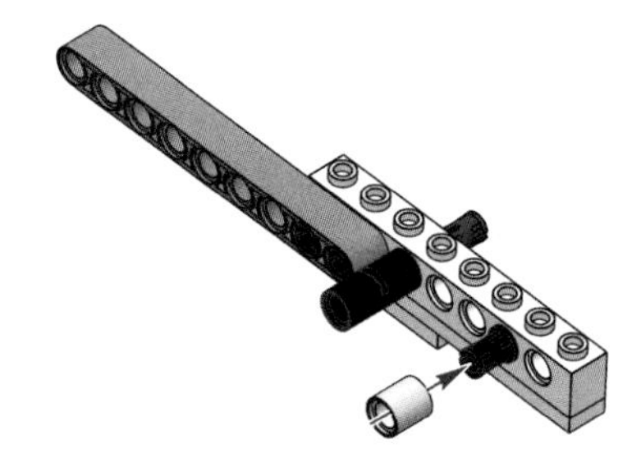

41

3x

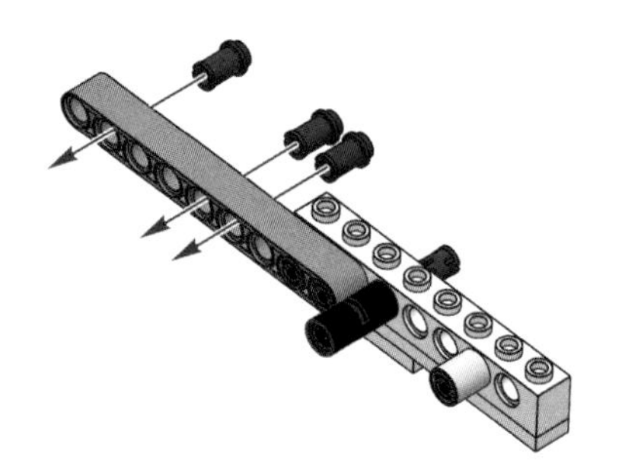

42

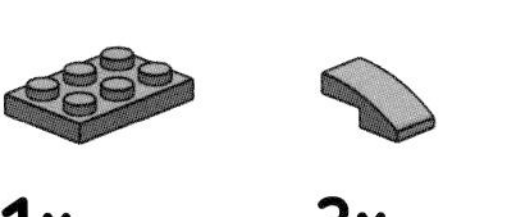

1x 3x

1x 1x 1x

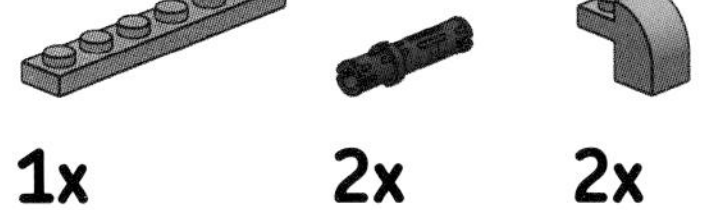

1x 2x 2x

1x 6x 1x

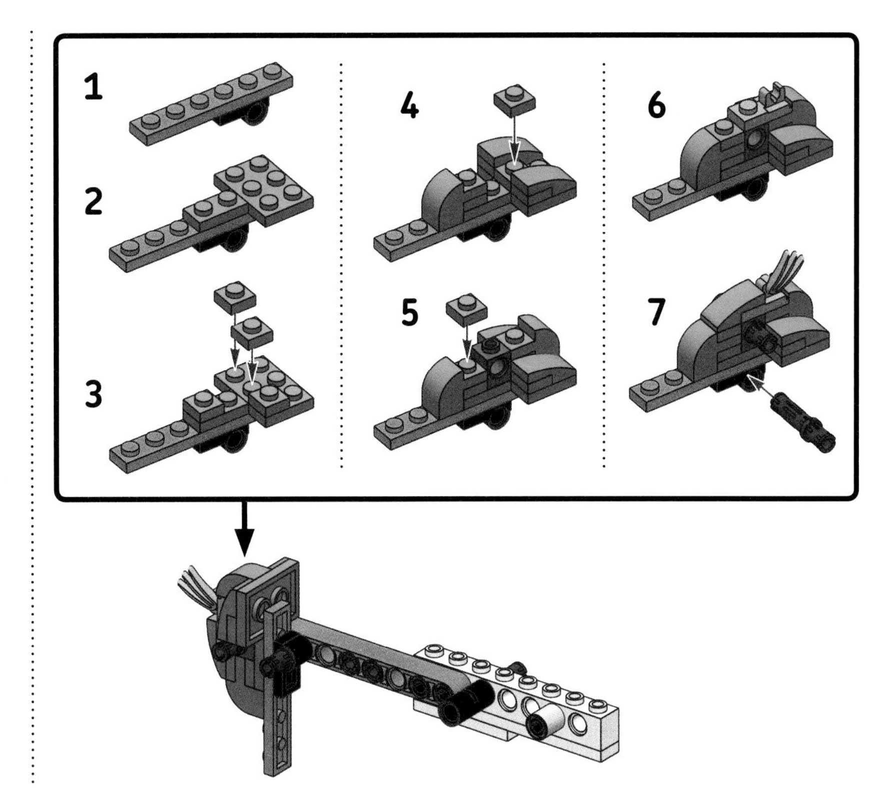

43

#2

1x 2x 1x

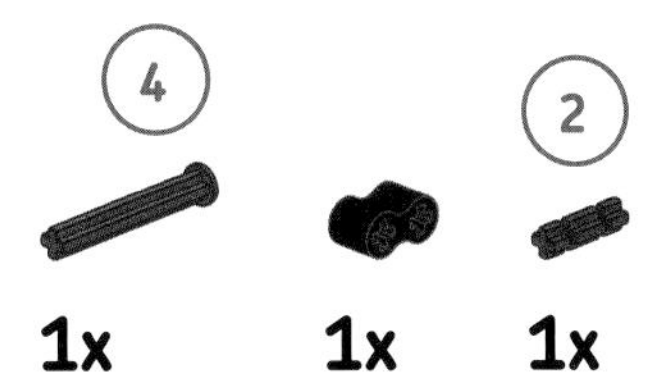

1x 1x 1x

1x

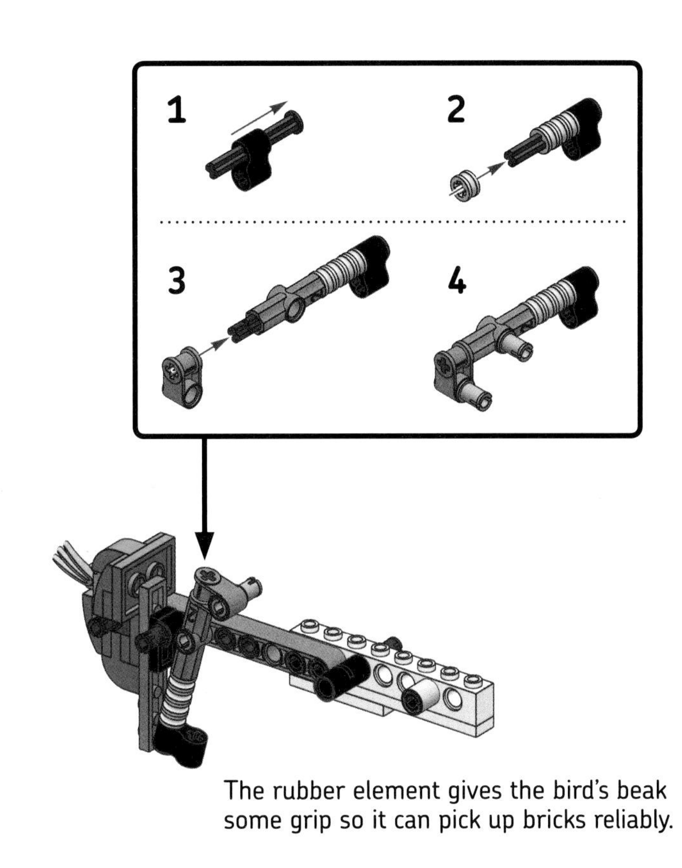

The rubber element gives the bird's beak some grip so it can pick up bricks reliably.

44

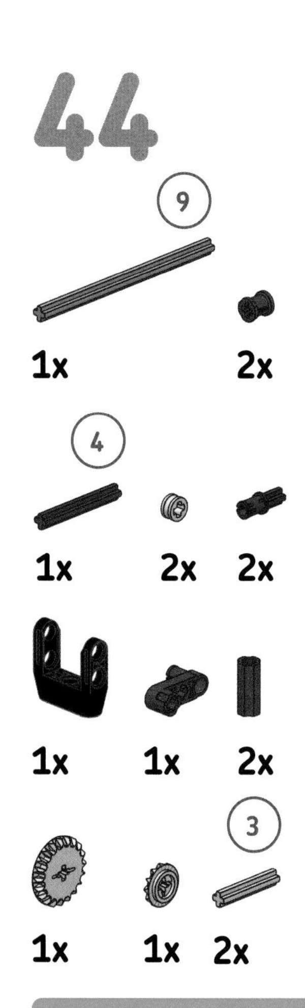

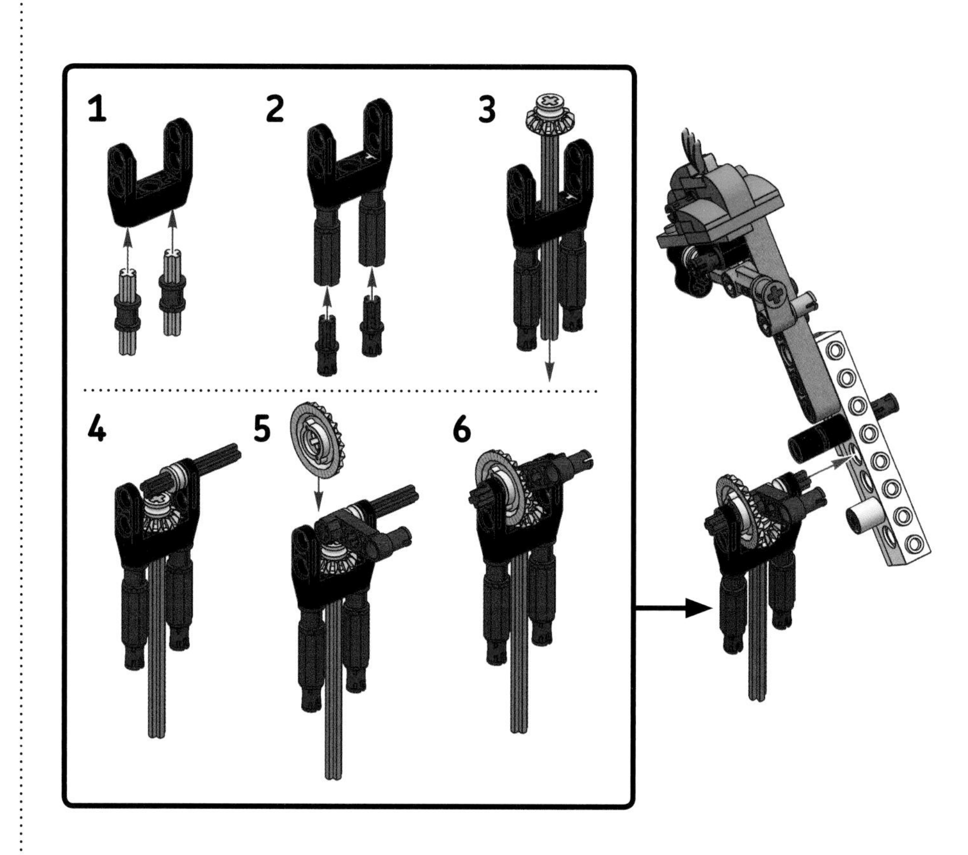

45

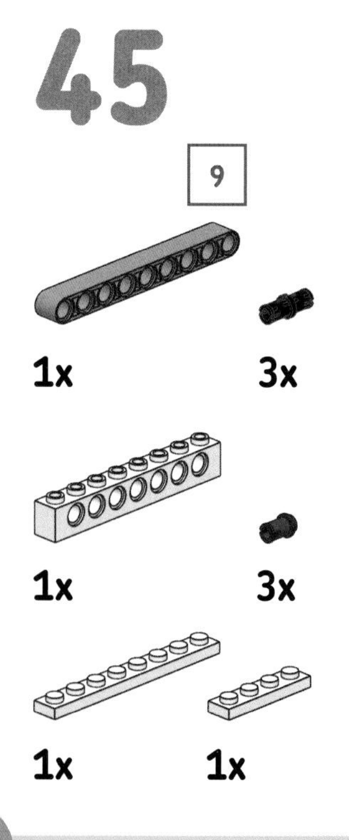

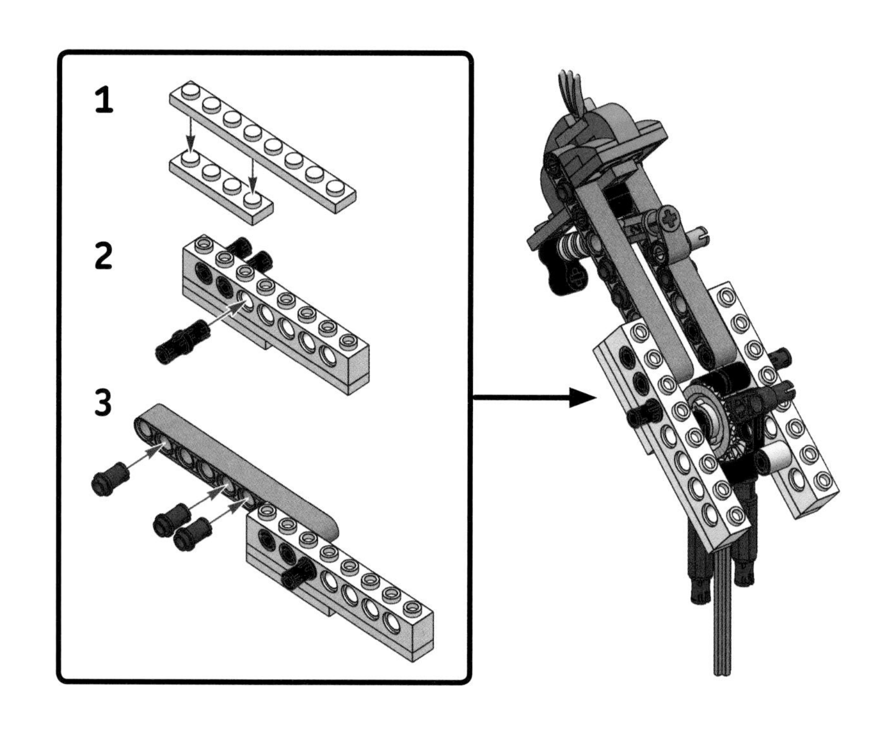

46

2x

2x

2x

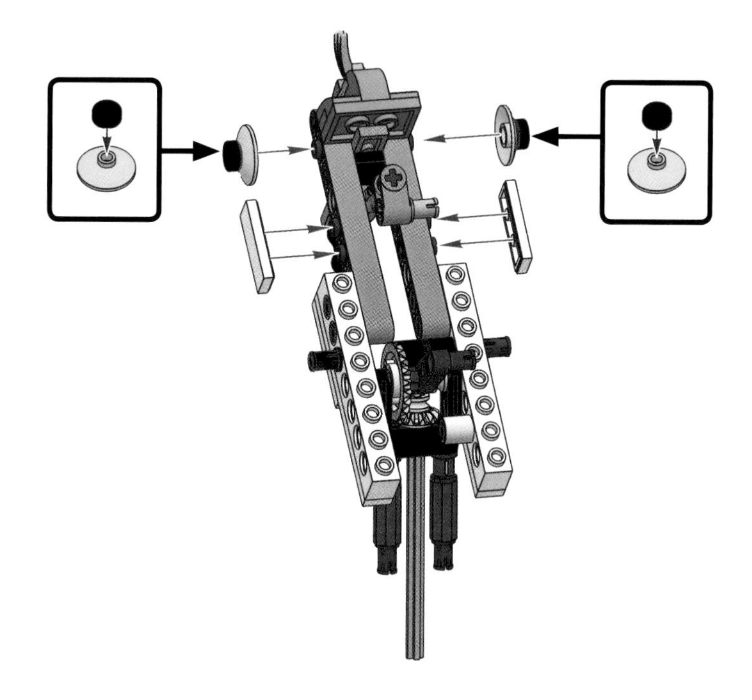

47

2x

4x

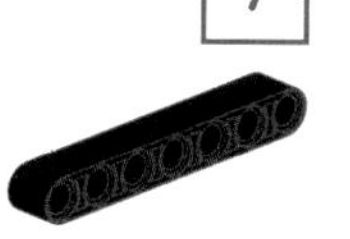

1x

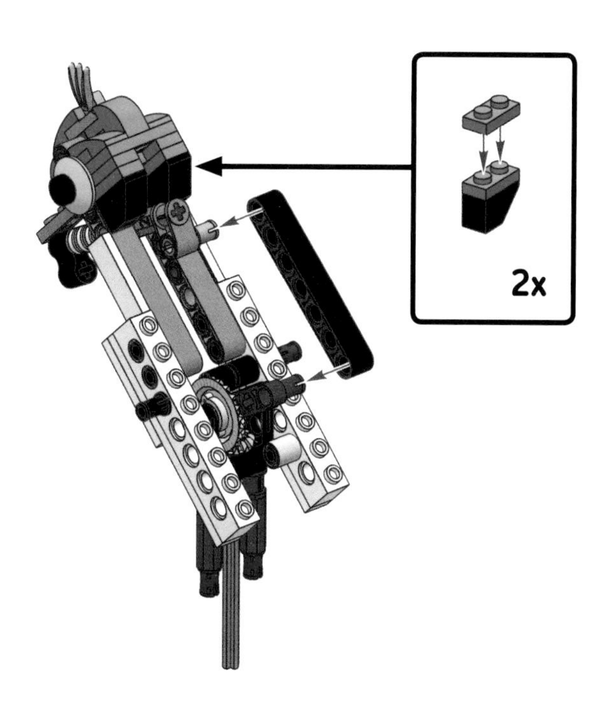

48

1x 2x

2x 1x

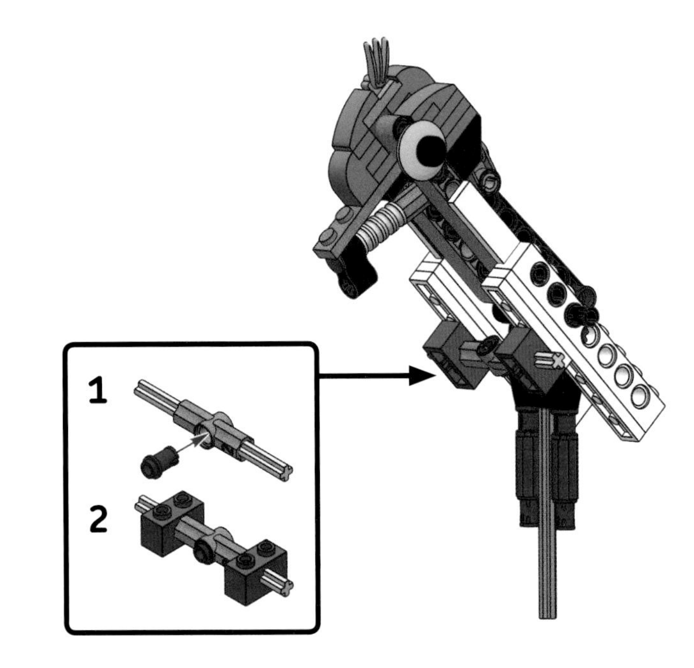

Attach the assembly so that the peg stud is facing the black gearbox.

49

2x 1x

1x 1x

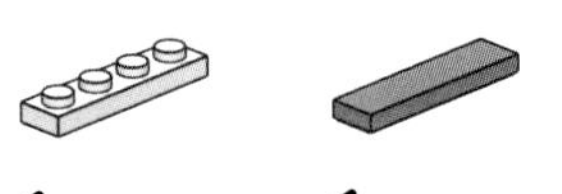

2x 1x

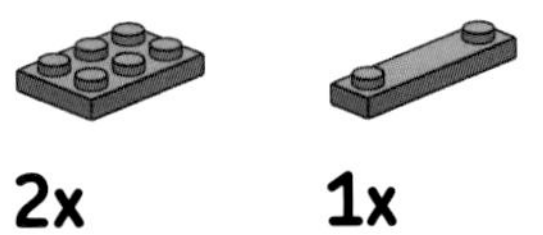

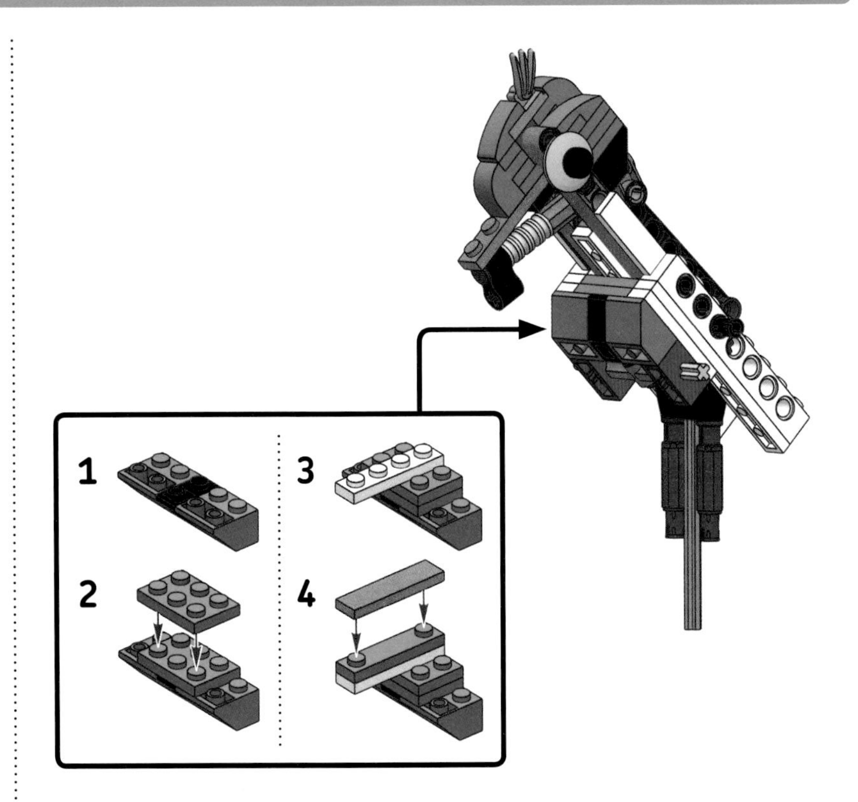

50

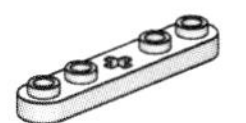
2x

2x

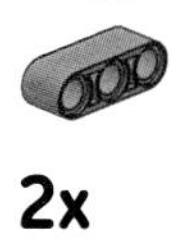

2x

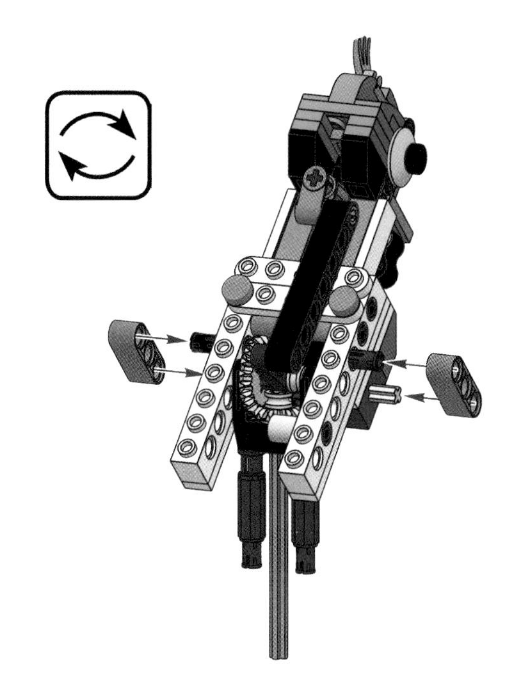

51

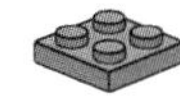
2x

2x

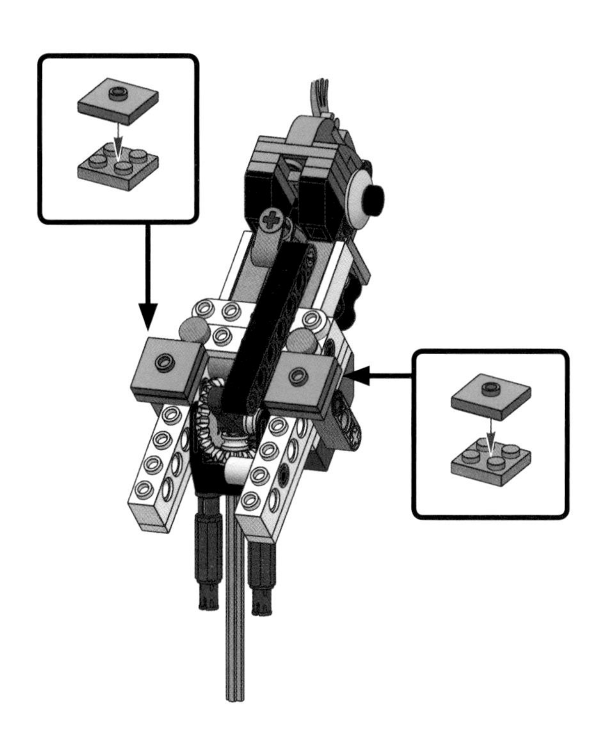

52

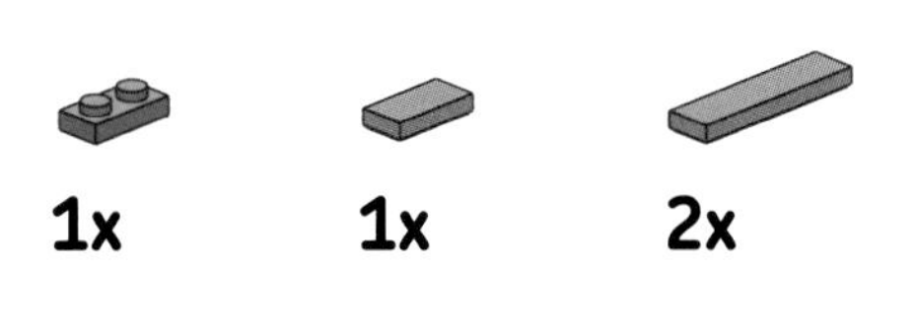

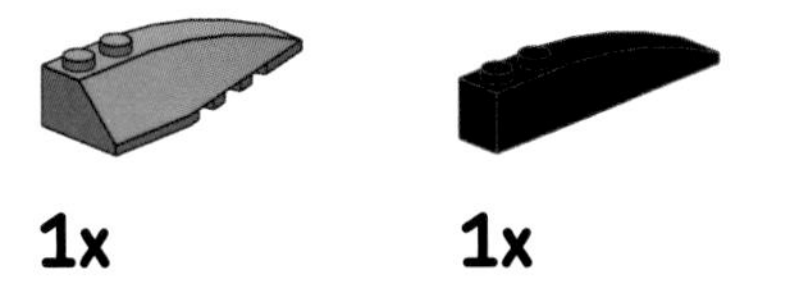

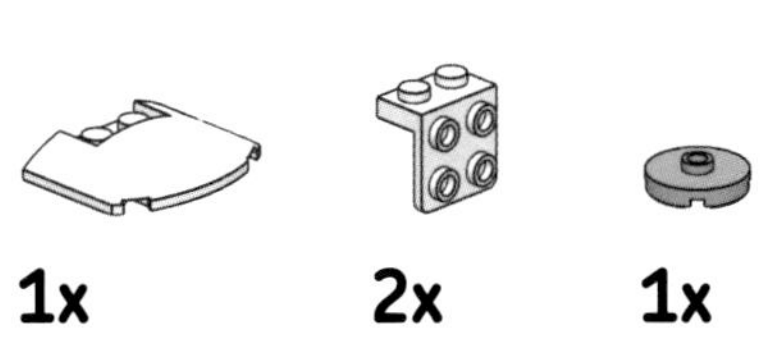

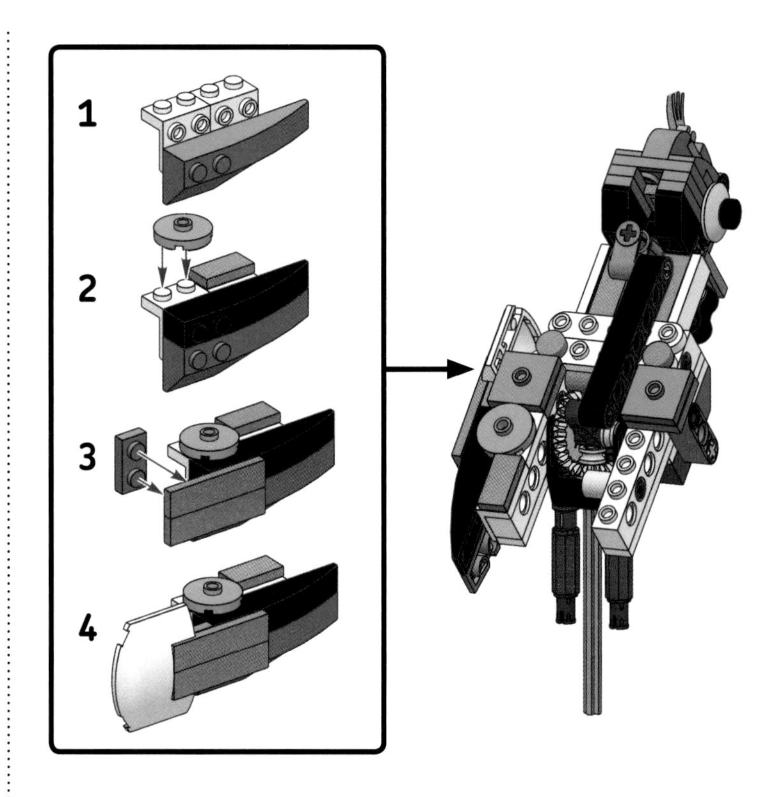

53

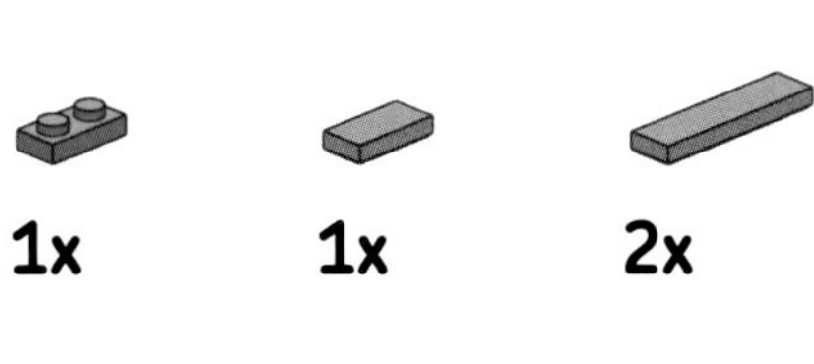

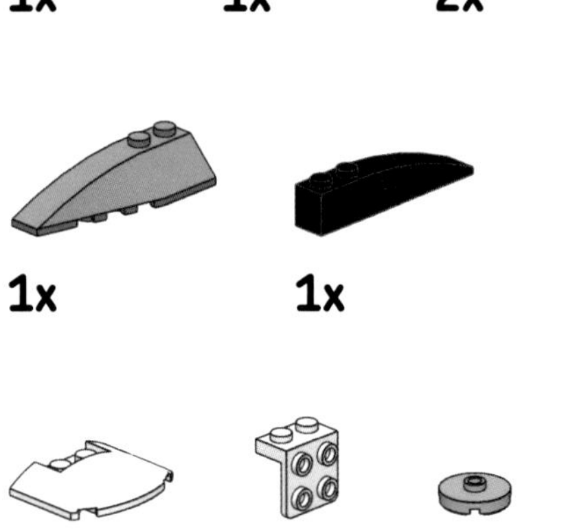

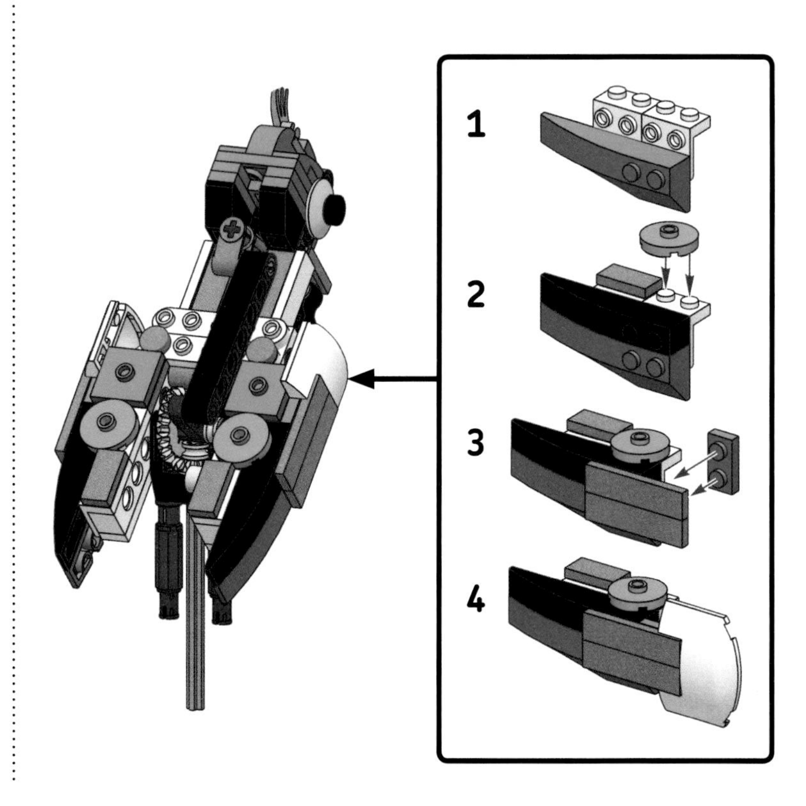

54

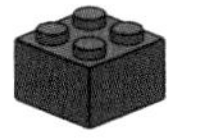
1x

1x

2x

1x

1x

1x

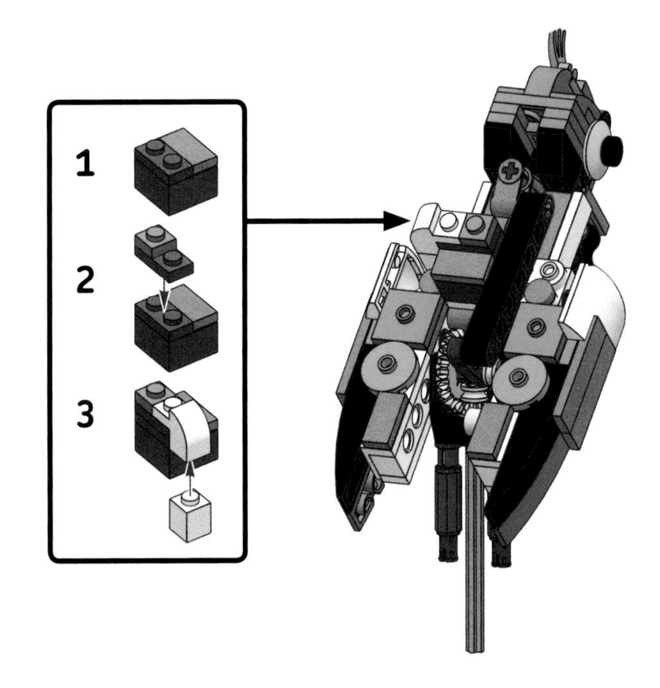

55

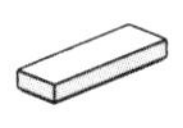
1x

1x

1x

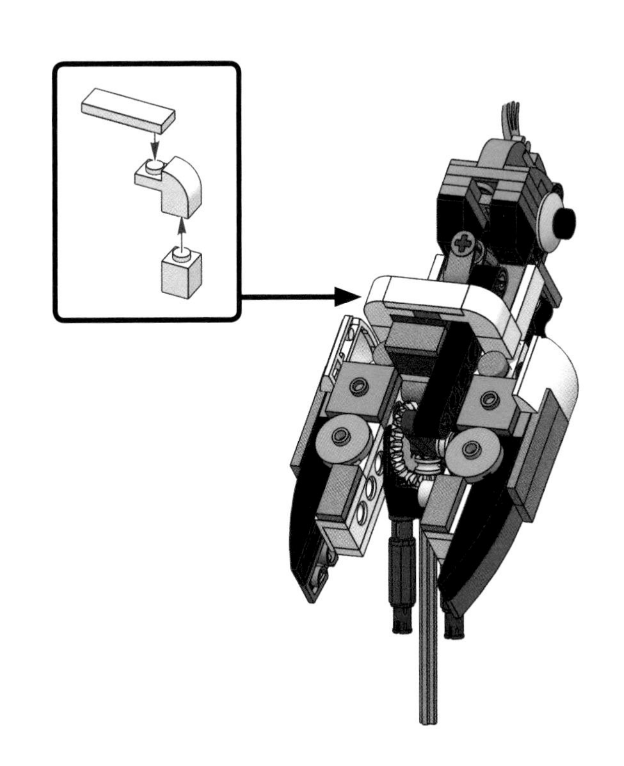

56

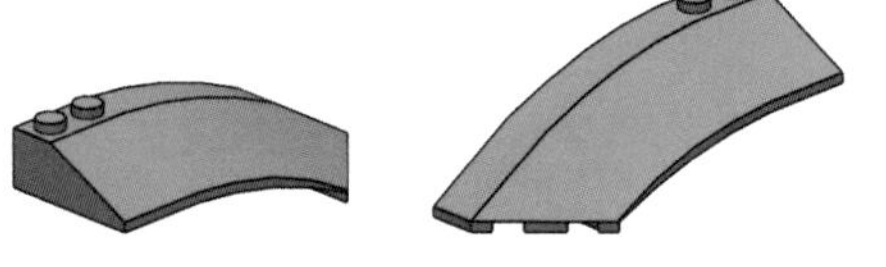

1x

1x

2x

1x

1x

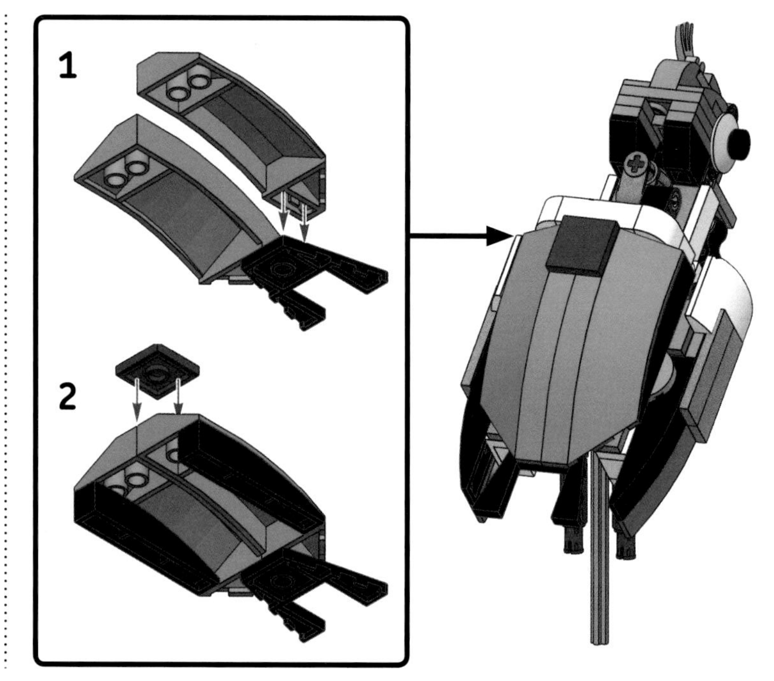

57

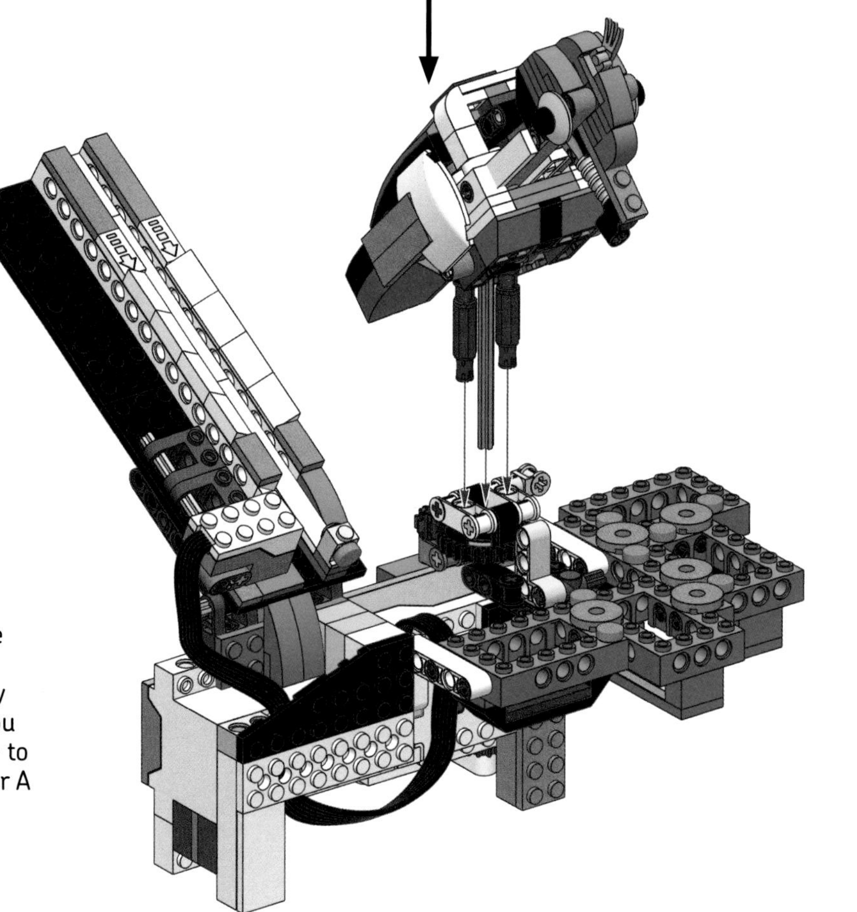

Before attaching the bird to the main assembly, hold it by its legs and test the mechanism by twisting the grey axle. When you push the axle down, make sure to insert it correctly into the motor A shaft hub.

58

2x

2x

2x

2x

The colored bricks are the seeds for BrickPecker to sort.

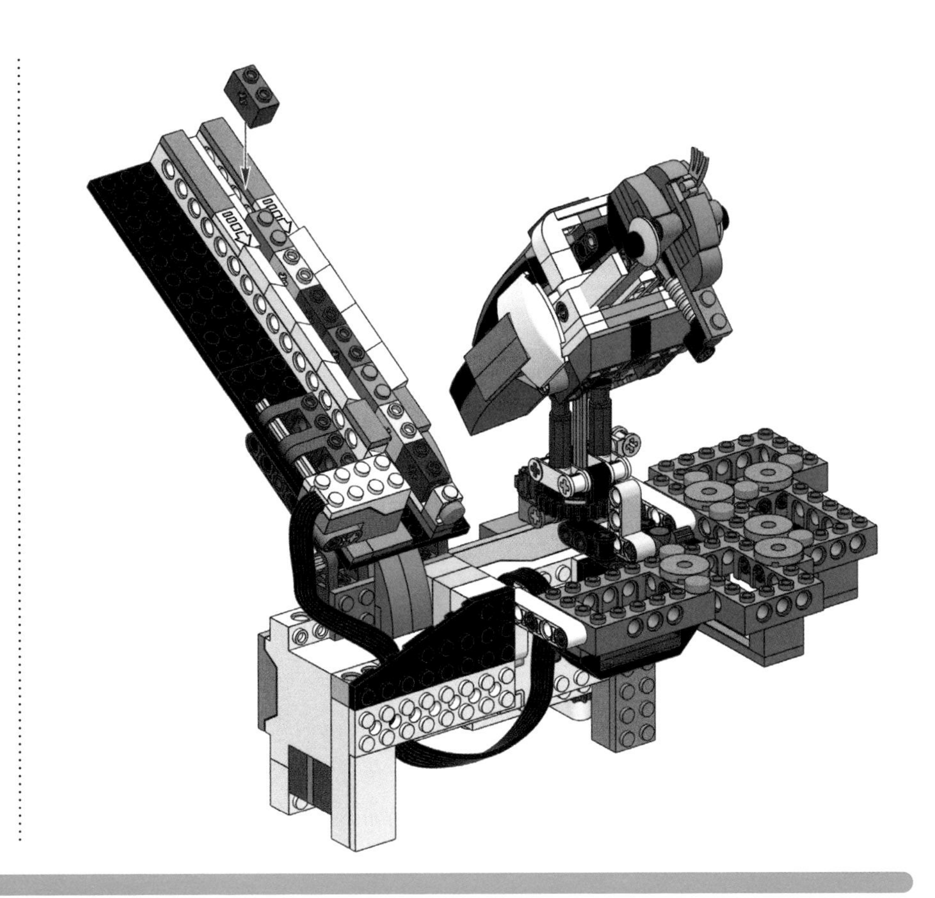

59

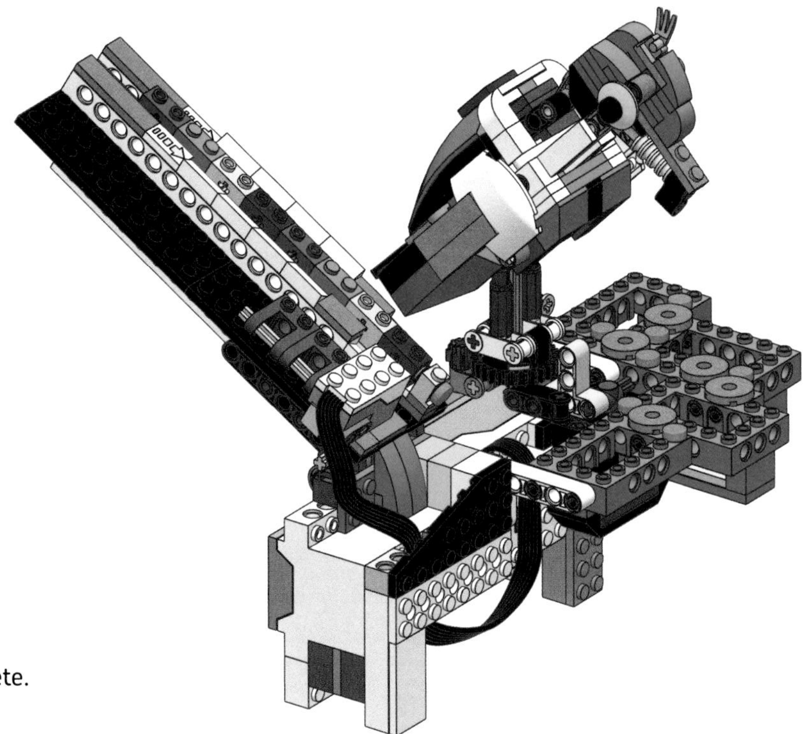

BrickPecker is complete.

one motor for two movements

A mechanism inside BrickPecker's body allows a single motor (Move Hub motor A) to move the beak and tilt the whole body. When the motor turns one way, it closes the beak and lifts the body. When the motor turns the other way, it lowers the body and opens the beak.

FIGURE 14-2 shows the basic mechanism inside the bird. At ❶, the body is tilted down, and the beak is open. When the grey axle is turned, the red lever pulls the black beam, and the beak closes while the body remains down because closing the beak requires less effort than lifting the whole body. When the beak is fully closed ❷, the red lever pulls the black beam and lifts up on the bird's body ❸, which shares a pivot (the red axle) with the bird's body. When the grey axle turns the other way, the movements are reversed, with the body tilting down and the beak opening.

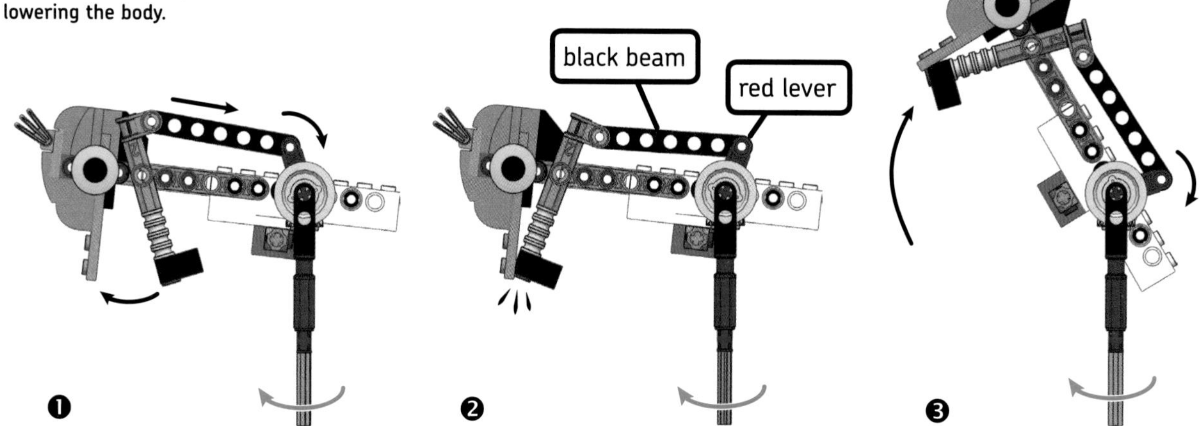

FIGURE 14-2 This mechanism allows a single motor to control multiple movements, such as opening and closing the beak, and raising and lowering the body.

what you've learned

In this chapter, you built a neat bird that can spin, tilt up and down, and open and close its beak. While building BrickPecker, you learned how to make a mechanism driven by a single motor that can control two movements. You can reuse a similar mechanism to build your own creations, like a robot arm that picks and places bricks, or a crane. In Chapter 15, you will learn how to program the BrickPecker to sort bricks by color.

15

programming BrickPecker

In this chapter, you'll learn how to program BrickPecker to pick up a brick from the feeder ramp and drop it into the nest that matches the color of the brick. As usual, before making the main program, you will build the composite blocks you'll need.

But even before explaining and making the c-blocks, let's review the peculiar gearing of the bird, which you'll need to know in order to understand how the composite blocks in this project work.

understanding the gear train

The axle that drives the bird's body up and down passes through the turntable's center, as shown in **FIGURE 15-1**. We want the green tilt-driving axle to rotate at the same speed as the turntable to maintain the bird's body at the same angle while the bird is rotating.

The gear ratio between motor B and the turntable to which the bird is attached is 28/8 × 12/24 = 3.5 × 0.5 = 7/4 = 1.75. This means that for the turntable to make one turn, motor B must make 1.75 turns. This in turn tells us that in order to make the tilt-driving axle turn at the same speed as the turntable, the speed of motor A must be 1.75 times slower than the speed of motor B.

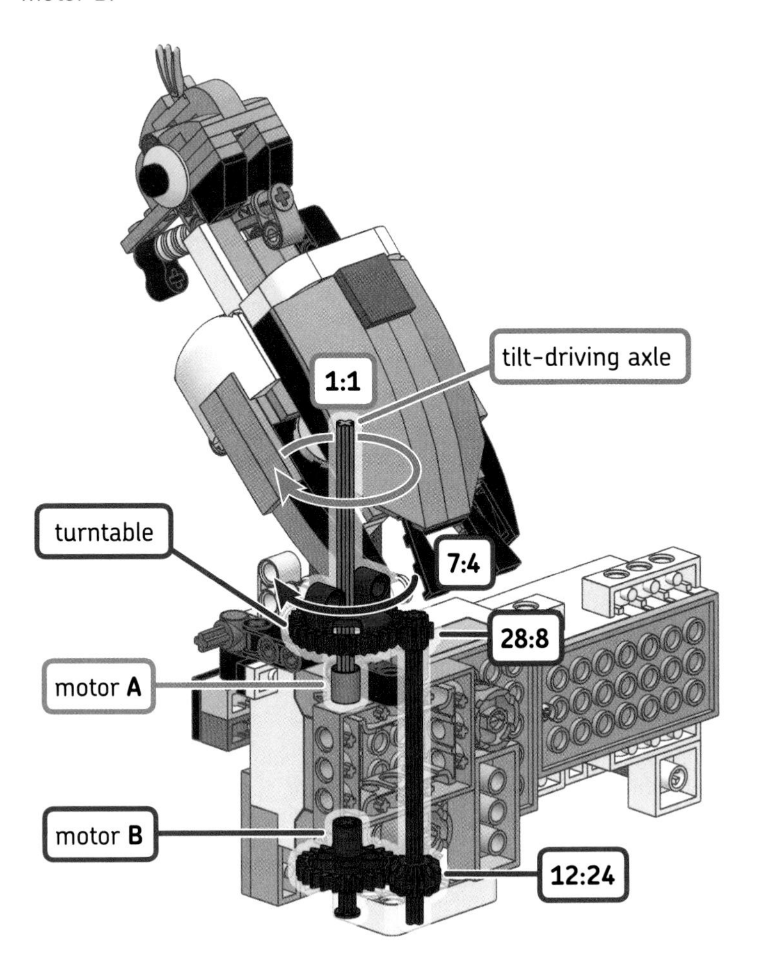

FIGURE 15-1 The bird's gear train

In order to rotate the bird from the feeder to the colored bins, you tell motor B to turn by an exact number of degrees. For example, to have both the turntable and the tilt-driving axle turn by 100 degrees, you set motor A to rotate by 100 degrees and motor B, which drives the turntable via the gear train, to rotate 175 degrees (the result of multiplying 100 by the gear ratio of 1.75).

the Reset composite block

When the LEGO BOOST Move Hub is powered up, the motor's position is unknown. The **Reset** c-block brings all of the robot's moving parts to the zero position (see **FIGURE 15-2**). In the case of the tilt movement, the zero position is when the bird is standing straight up with its beak closed. The zero position for the spinning movement is when the bird is at a right angle to the feeder, ready to pick up a brick.

We place the **Reset** c-block at the beginning of every program you create for BrickPecker so that it will always start from a known initial position. You can see the sequence in **FIGURE 15-2**.

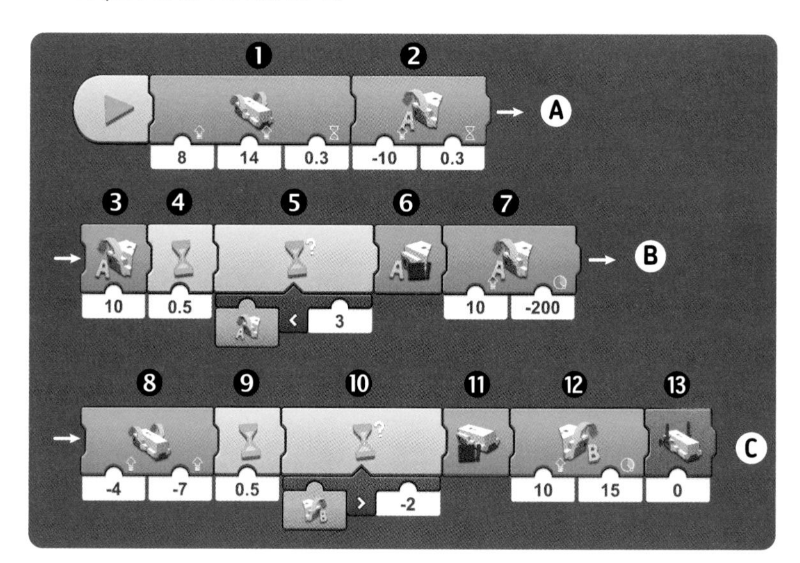

FIGURE 15-2 The Reset composite block sequence and what it looks like in the main program (shown below)

The sequence of the c-block shown in **FIGURE 15-2** is split into three parts labeled A, B, and C so you can better follow its description below. You must attach all these parts together in a single sequence for this c-block to work.

Part A: In this part of the programming sequence, BrickPecker spins away from the feeder, then closes its beak and tilts its body up.

Block 1: To spin the bird away from the feeder, we rotate motors A and B for 0.3 seconds. Notice that the speed of motor B (14) is equal to the speed of motor A (8) times 1.75, which is the gear ratio we calculated earlier. We set the motors' speeds according to this ratio to make sure that the bird's body remains still while rotating away from the ramp.

Block 2: We rotate motor A for 0.3 seconds at low negative speed (–10) to lift the bird up a bit.

Part B: In this part, the bird goes all the way down, then closes its beak and goes up to reach the tilting zero position.

Block 3: Start motor A at a slow speed (10) to lower the bird's body.

Block 4: Wait 0.5 seconds to allow the motor to gain speed.

Block 5: Wait until the reported speed of motor A is below 3, the point at which the bird has reached the lower limit of movement.

Block 6: Stop motor A.

Block 7: Rotate motor A by –200 degrees to lift the bird's body so that the beak closes and the body rises.

Part C: In this part, the bird spins toward the feeder until it reaches the spinning zero position.

Block 8: To spin the bird toward the feeder, we start motors A and B in reverse. Notice that the speed of motor B (–7) is equal to the speed of motor A (–4) times 1.75, which is the calculated gear ratio again. The speed of each motor is set so that the bird's body remains still while spinning clockwise.

Block 9: Wait 0.5 seconds to allow the motors to gain speed.

Block 10: Wait until the reported speed of motor B is above –2. (The motor is running at negative speed to make the bird spin clockwise.) When the yellow connector hits the yellow T-beam, the bird has reached the limit of movement and is at a right angle with respect to the ramp.

Block 11: Stop motors A and B.

Block 12: Rotate motor B by 15 degrees to spin the bird a bit away from the ramp. This relaxes the gear train that was stressed after reaching its limit of rotation.

Block 13: The **Preset Drivebase Angle** block resets the motor A and B rotation sensors.

the Spinning composite block

The **Spinning** c-block controls the movement of both motors A and B, allowing the bird to spin while keeping its body tilted at a constant angle. **FIGURE 15-3** shows the sequence of the **Spinning** c-block.

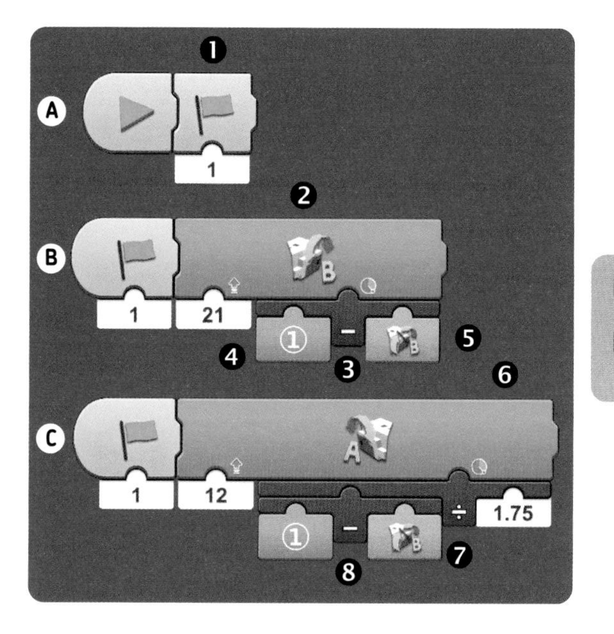

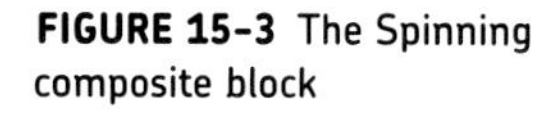

FIGURE 15-3 The Spinning composite block

The **Flag Trigger** block ❶ in sequence A starts sequences B and C at the same time, which will run in parallel, controlling each motor separately. Sequence B controls Motor B. As you can see, the **Motor B Run for Angle** block ❷ makes motor B rotate by an angle relative to the motor's zero position. Because motor B's rotation sensor was reset when the bird's body was at a right angle to the feeder, the **Motor B Angle Reporter** block ❺ returns the new angle of the bird along its vertical axis relative to the zero position. The value in the Degrees input to the **Motor B Run for Angle** is based on the **Subtraction Operator** block ❸, which computes the difference between the angle set in the c-block Numeric Input 1 ❹ and Motor B's current shaft angle read by **Motor B Angle Reporter** block ❺. The speed of the motor is set to 21.

Sequence C uses a **Motor A Run for Angle** block ❻ to control Motor A, which must rotate at the same speed as the turntable to keep the bird tilted at the same angle while the turntable spins. To achieve this, we've set the Motor A's speed to 12, (21 divided by 1.75). Once the bird reaches its destination, we want the tilt to be the same as it was before the bird started spinning. To accomplish this, we rotate Motor A by an angle that is 1.75 times smaller than the angle that motor B turns, using a **Division Operator** block ❼ to scale down the result of the **Subtraction Operator** block ❽.

the PickAndPlace composite block

The **PickAndPlace** c-block, shown in **FIGURE 15-4**, executes a series of movements that lets your bird pick up a brick from the feeder and drop it into a bin. Input 1 of the c-block sets how many degrees the bird should spin. This way, we can control how much the bird should spin before dropping the brick.

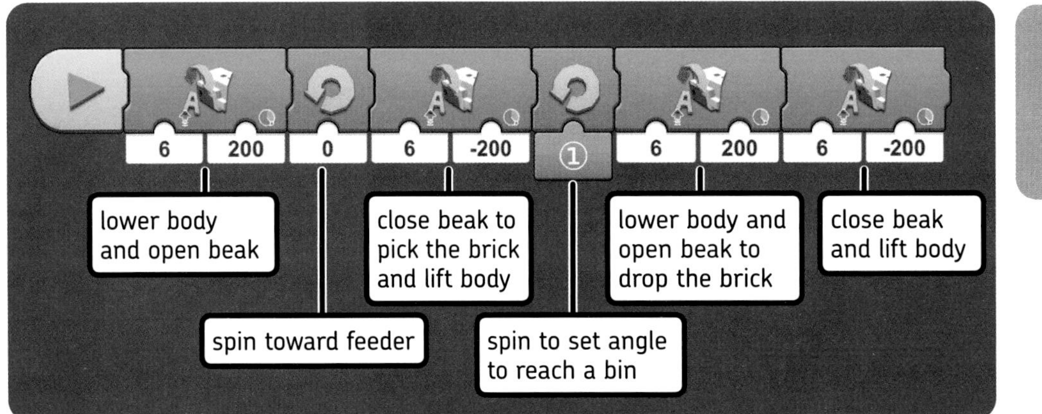

FIGURE 15-4
The PickAndPlace composite block

the Brick-Sorting Bird program

Now that you have all the c-blocks you need, let's put them together to make BrickPecker's main program. You can see what the final program looks like in **FIGURE 15-5**.

At the beginning of the program, we use a **Reset** c-block to move the bird to its zero position. Next, we change the Hub LED color to violet and use the **Spinning** c-block to turn the bird away from the feeder. Later, the **PickAndPlace** c-block will make the bird turn toward the feeder with its body tilted down and beak already open, ready to pick up that block. Once the bird has turned away from the feeder, we use the **Wait for True** block to wait until a brick other than black is detected at the end of the feeder ramp. Once a colored brick is detected, the program can continue.

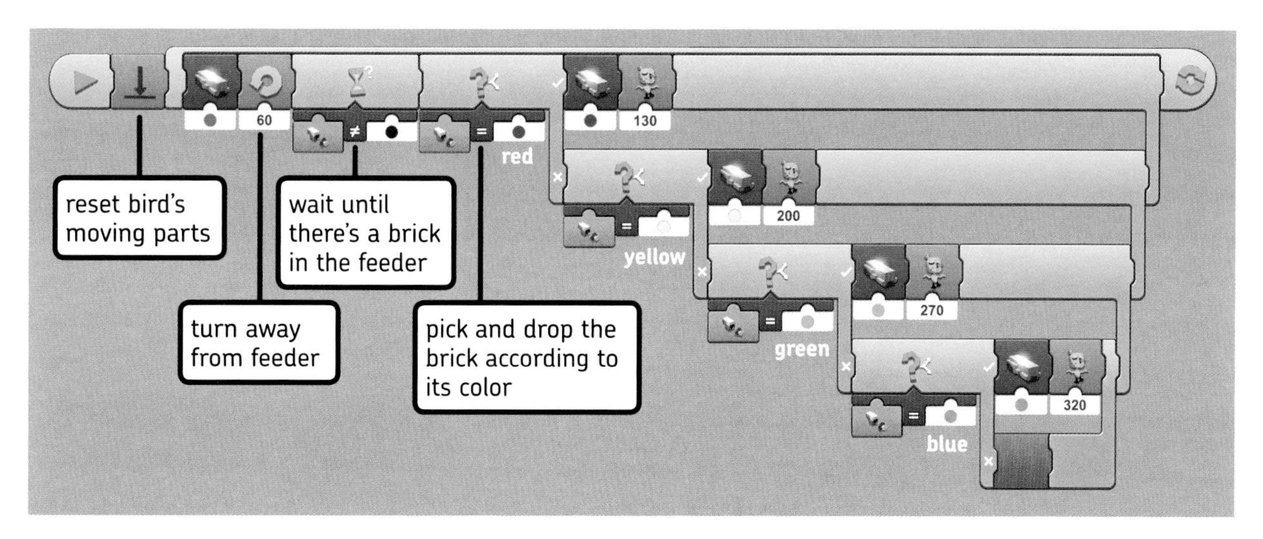

FIGURE 15-5 The program for the Brick-Sorting Bird uses Switch blocks to decide where the bird will put the brick, according to its color.

Switch blocks determine which bin the bird will spin to before dropping the brick. The bottom of each bin is marked with a color that matches the color of the bricks it should contain.

As you can see in **FIGURE 15-6**, there are four nested **Switch** block sequences in the program. Each **Switch** sequence has two sequences: the top one executes if the color detected matches the color in the **Compare Equal** block, and the bottom executes if the color doesn't match. **FIGURE 15-6** shows how the program operates when it detects a green brick.

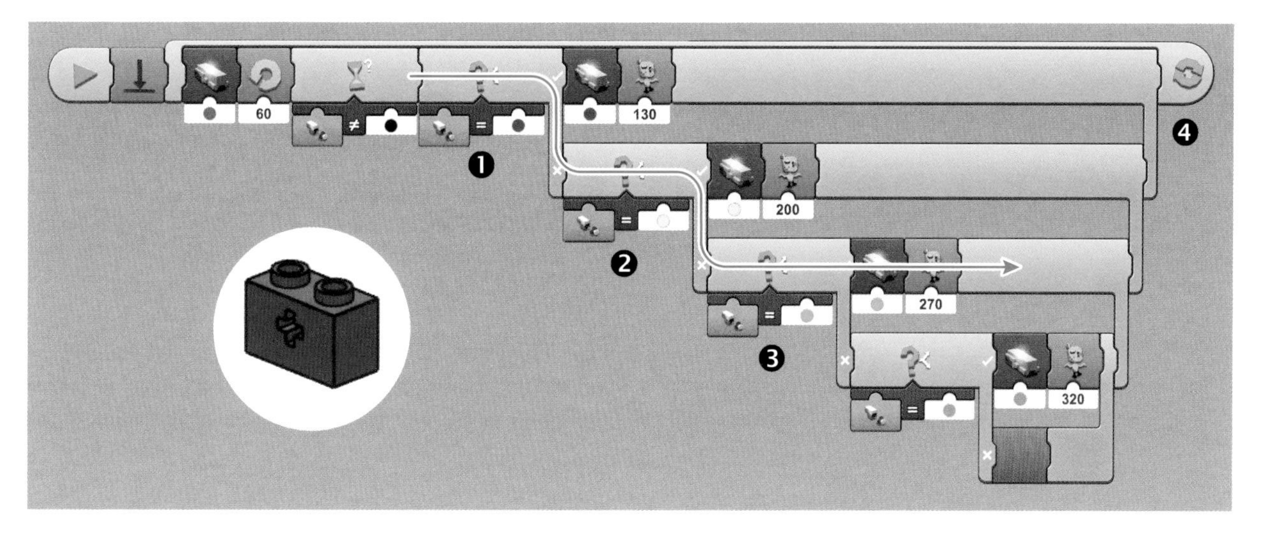

FIGURE 15-6 The program flow when a green brick is detected

Let's go over the program flow step by step.

1: A **Switch** block checks to see whether the sensor has detected a red brick. Because our brick is green, the condition is false, so the bottom sequence is executed.

2: A second **Switch** block checks to see if the sensor is detecting yellow. This condition is false again, so the program executes the bottom sequence of this **Switch** block.

3: Now a third **Switch** block checks to see if the sensor is detecting green. The condition is true. The top sequence of the third **Switch** block then runs, the program changes the Hub light color to green, and it executes the PickAndPlace c-block with the input set to the value that spins the bird to the correct colored bin.

4: The program continues running from the beginning of the sequence included in the **Infinite Loop** block, and the bird is ready to pick the next brick and place it in its bin.

what you've learned

I hope you enjoyed programming and feeding BrickPecker, a brick-sorting bird. In Chapter 16, we'll build and program CYBOT, a cool humanoid robot that can walk, talk, shoot targets, and react to voice commands.

experiment 15-1

Add a **Play Sound** block to make the bird cheerfully chirp before picking up a yellow brick. It should not chirp for other colors.

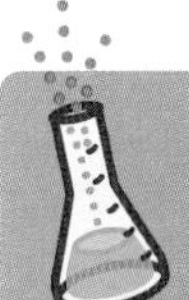

experiment 15-2

Make the bird dance and chirp when it hears a loud sound. Hint: try to make motor B rotate alone (without using the **Spinning** c-block) so the bird will tilt up and down while spinning.

experiment 15-3

Detach the BOOST sensor from the ramp and attach it to the nest on the edge of the red bin so that it's facing you. Design a program that makes the bird greet you with a chirp when you approach and then peck your fingers until you remove your hand.

PART IV

CYBOT

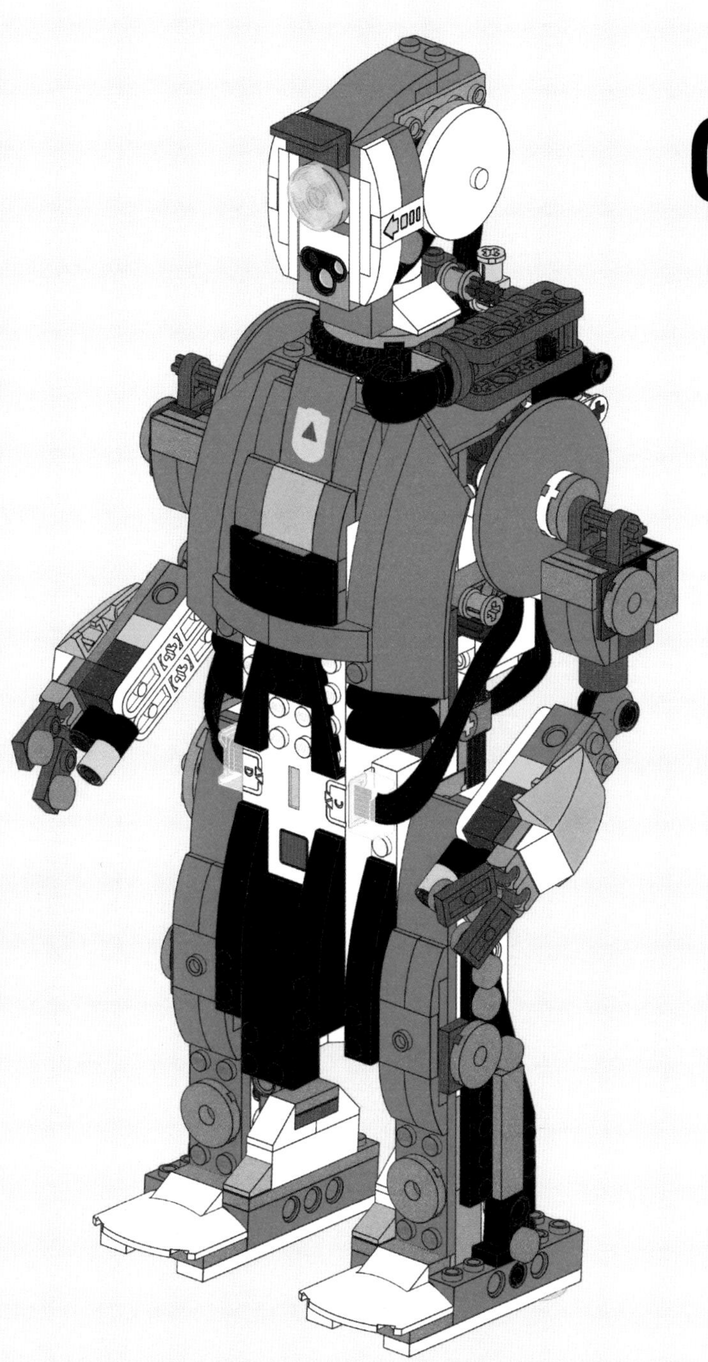

16

building CYBOT

In this chapter, you will find detailed instructions for building a humanoid walking robot named CYBOT. The robot can walk and turn, move its arms, turn its head, and even shoot!

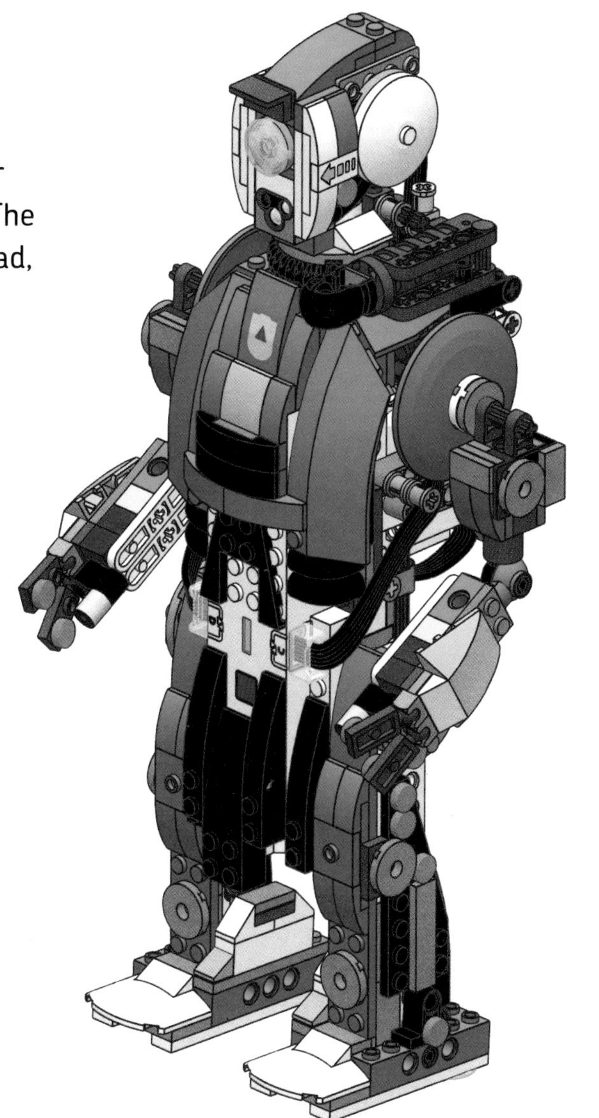

1

2x

1x

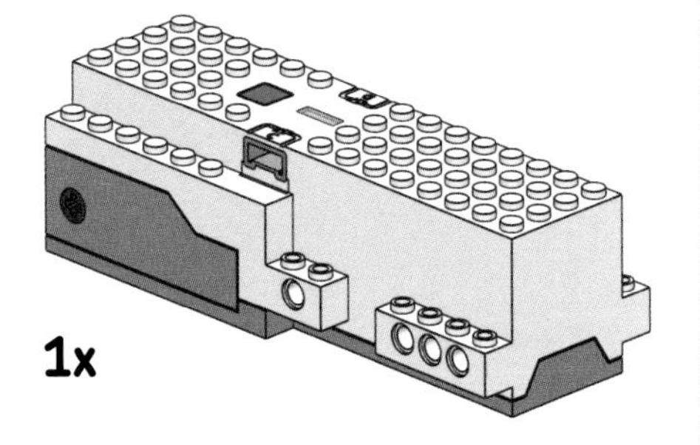

1x

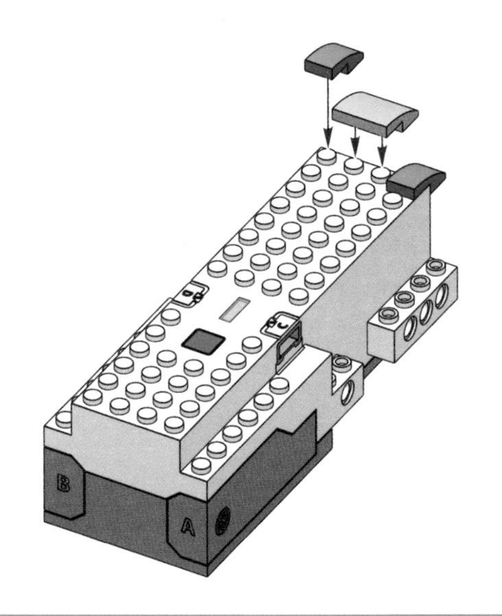

2

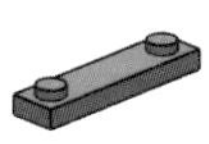

2x

1x

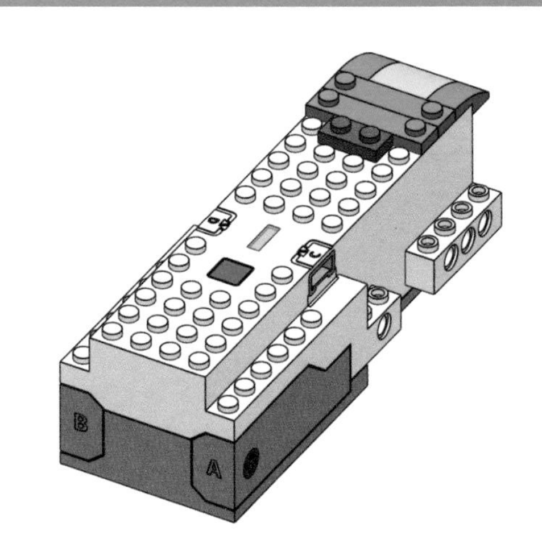

3

2x

2

2x

2x

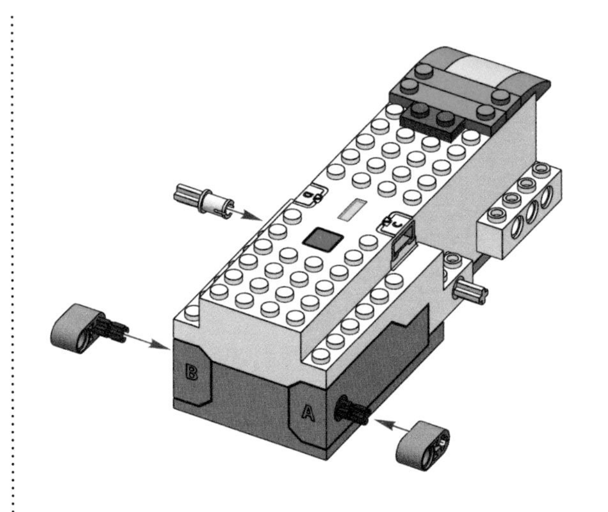

4

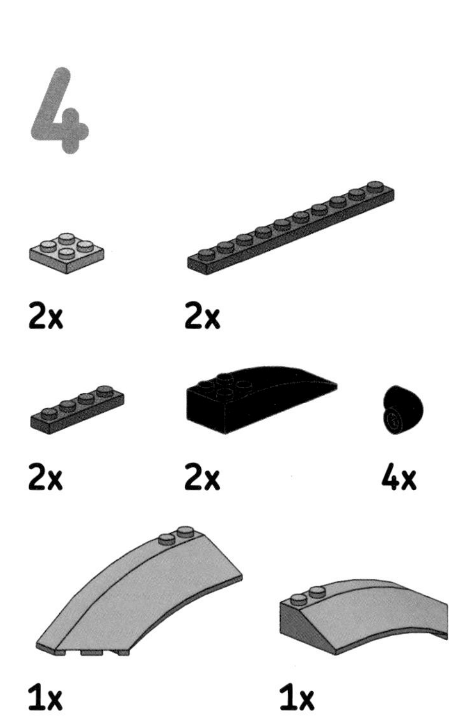

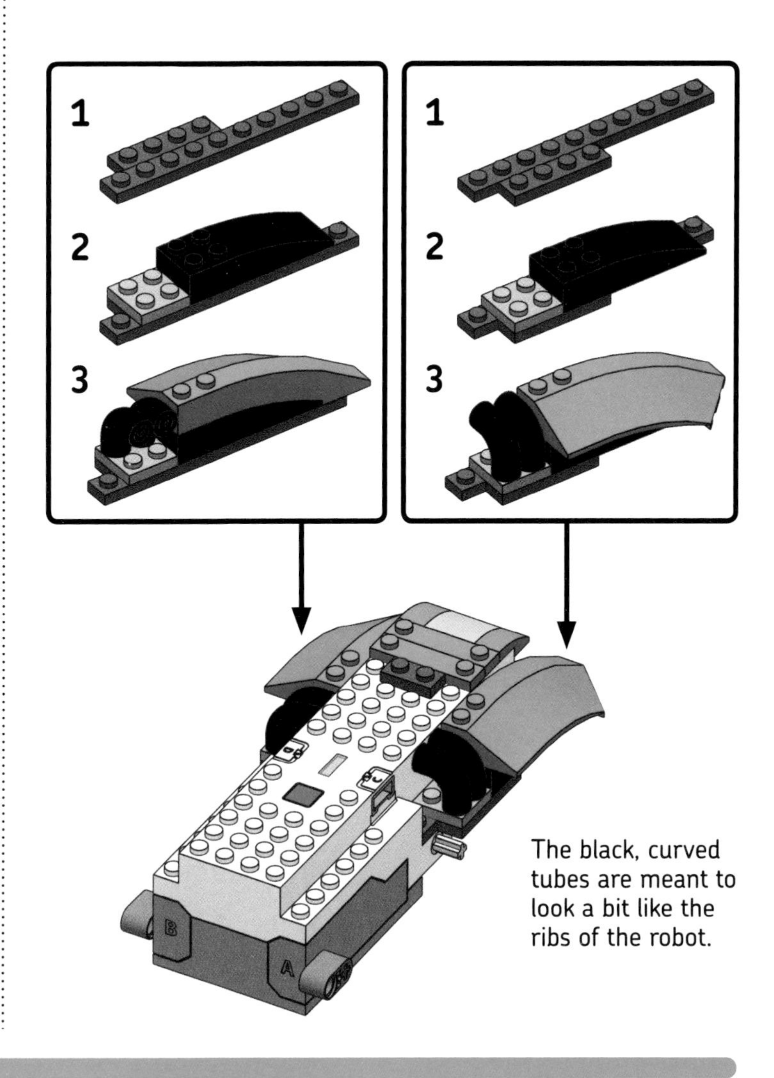

The black, curved tubes are meant to look a bit like the ribs of the robot.

5

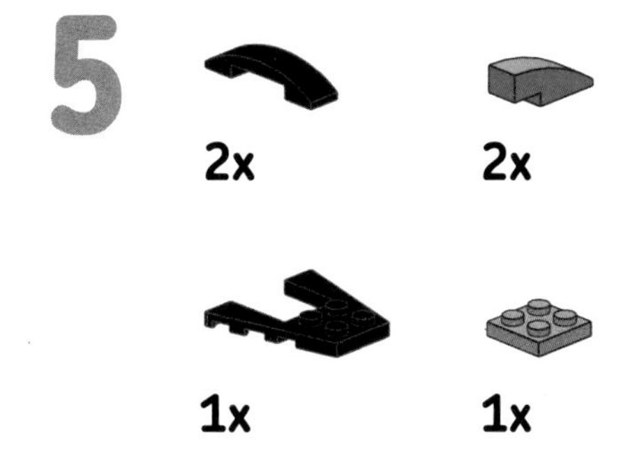

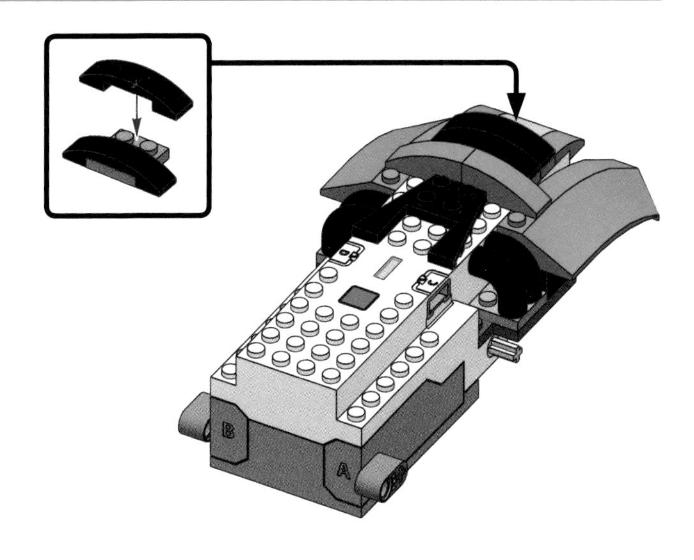

6

2x 1x

2x 2x 2x

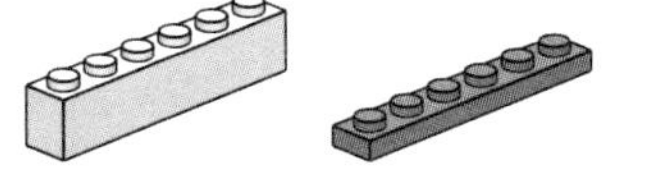

1x 1x

1x 2x 1x 2x

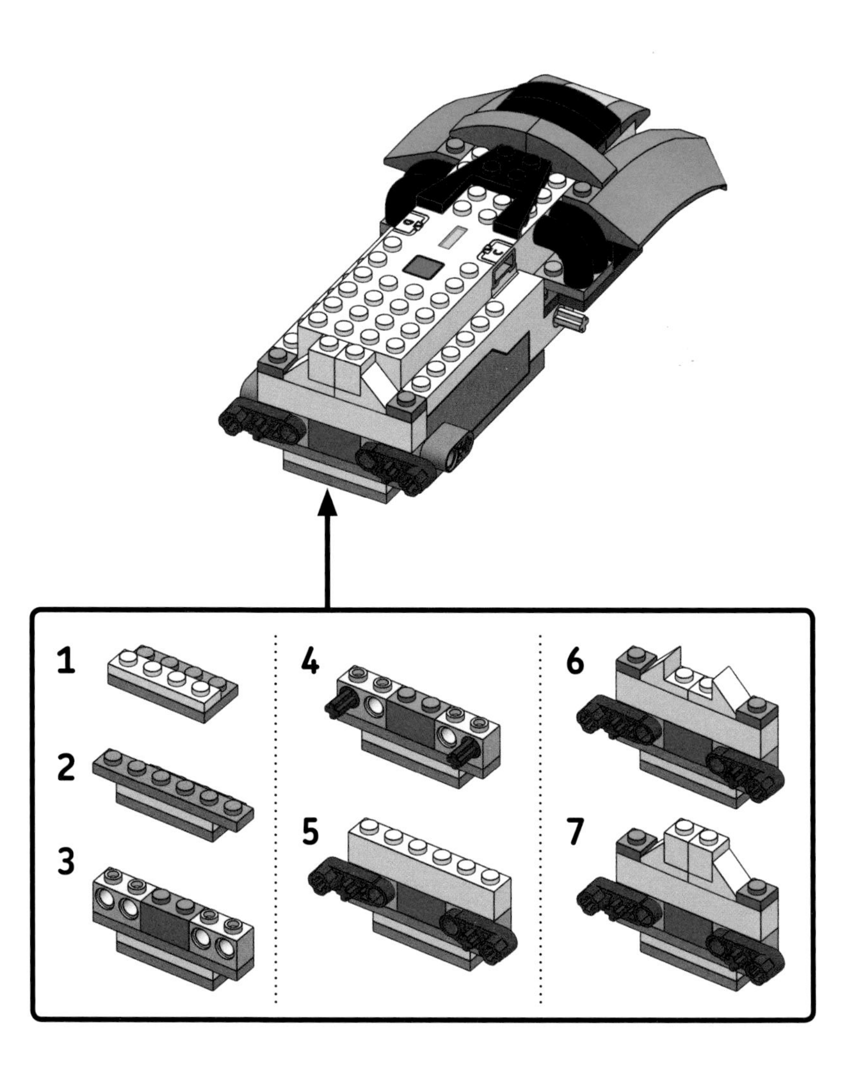

7

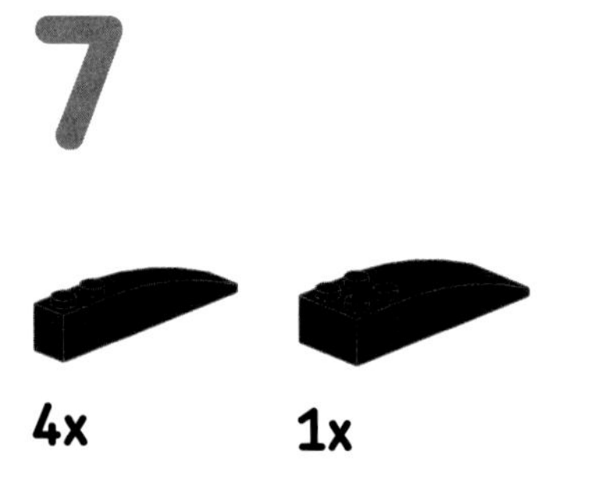

4x 1x

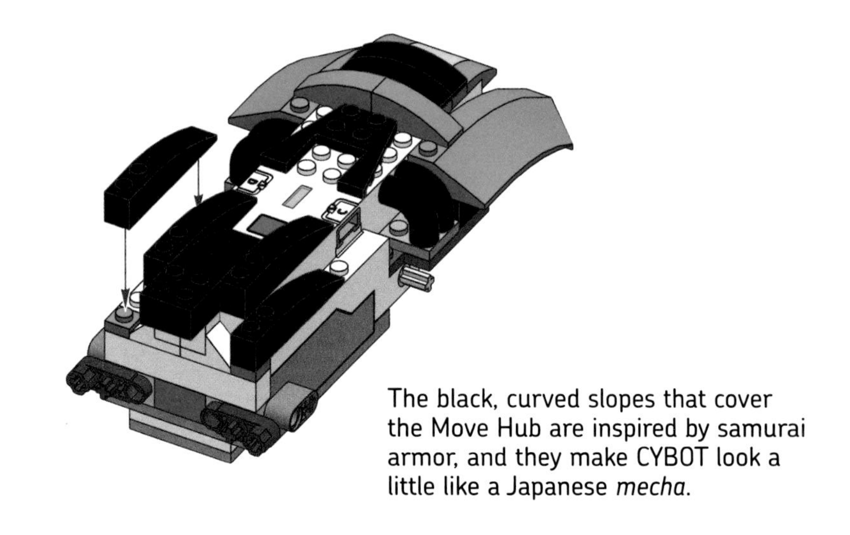

The black, curved slopes that cover the Move Hub are inspired by samurai armor, and they make CYBOT look a little like a Japanese *mecha*.

8

1x

3x 1x 3x

Building the left leg.

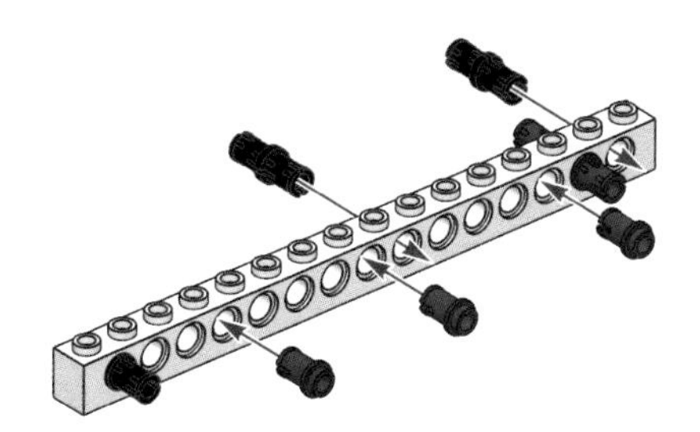

9

1x

5

1x

1x

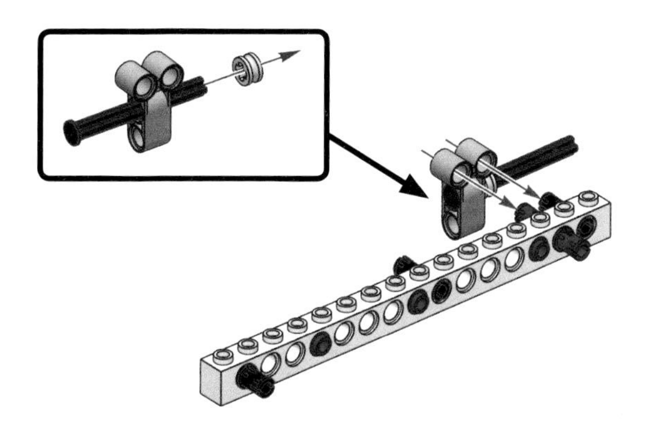

10

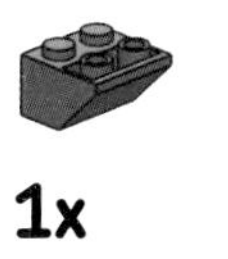

1x

1x

2x

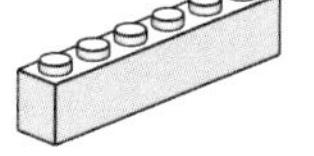

1x

2x

1x

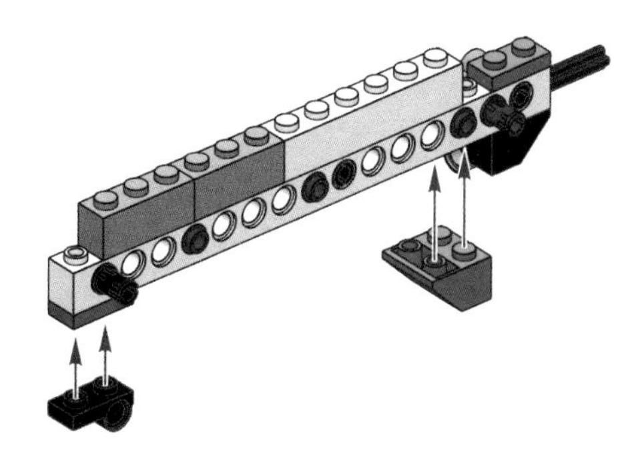

11

1x

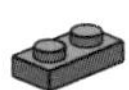

1x

1x

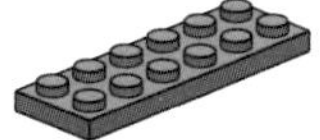

1x

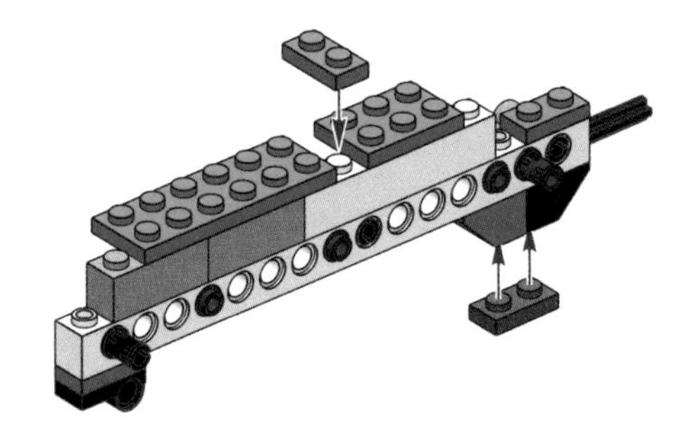

12

1x

1x

1x

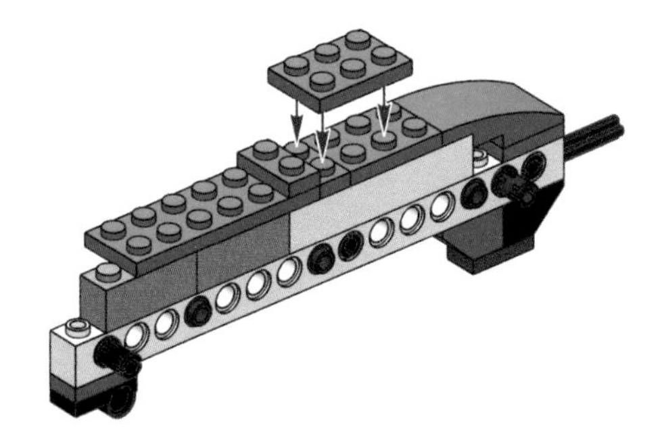

13

1x

1x

4x

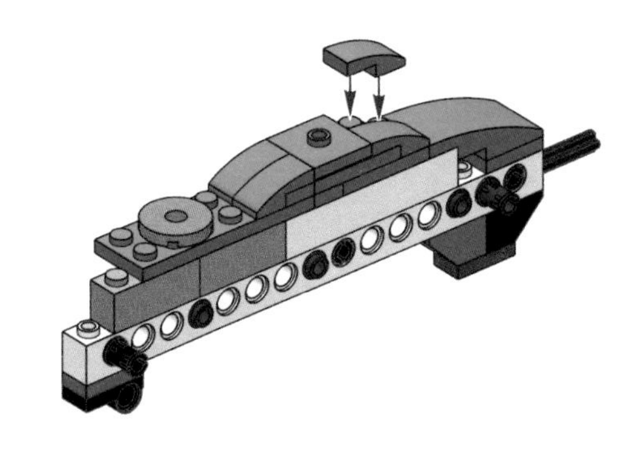

14

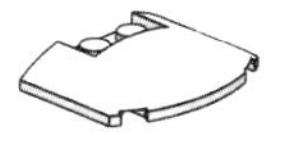

1x

1x

1x

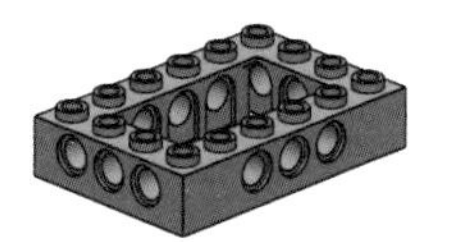

1x

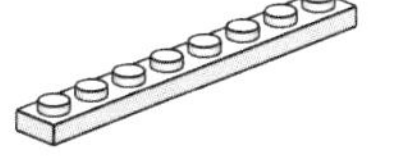

1x

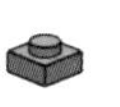

1x

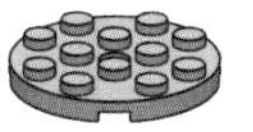

1x

1x

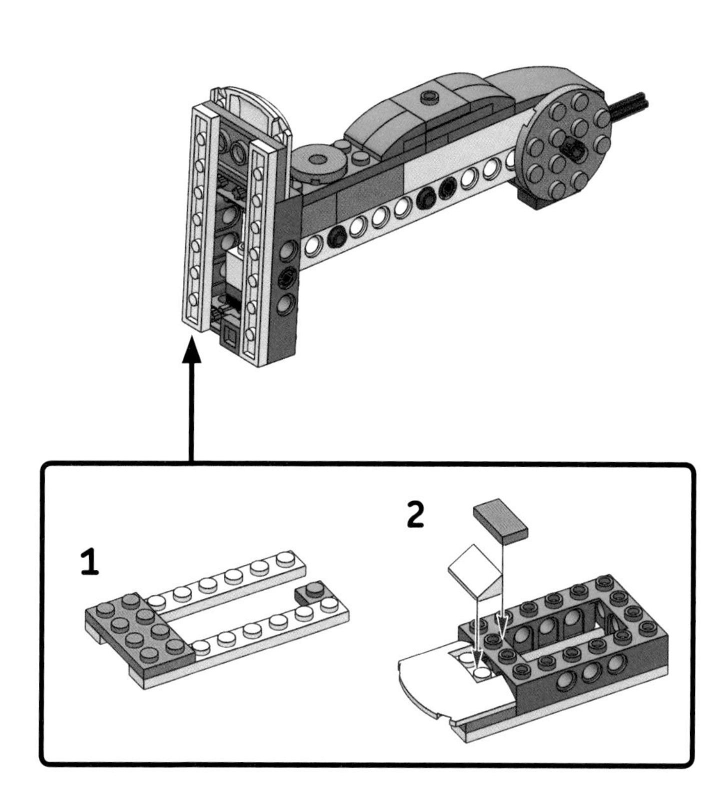

Make sure to attach the foot so that the leg is leaning slightly forward when the foot is on the ground. This forward angle will help the robot balance.

15

1x

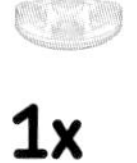

1x

2x

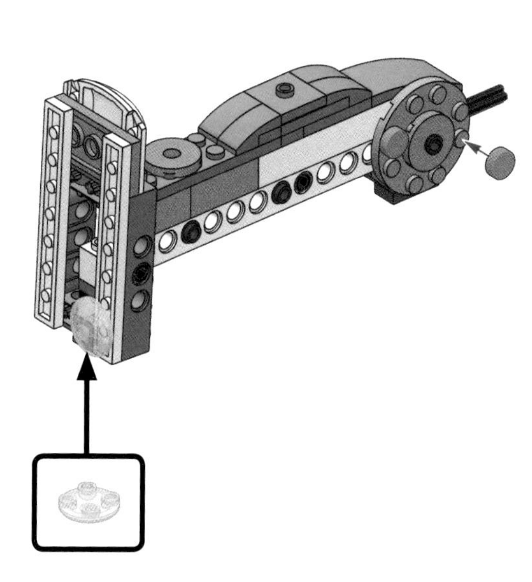

16

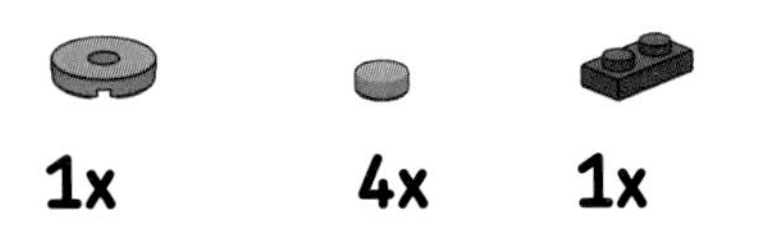

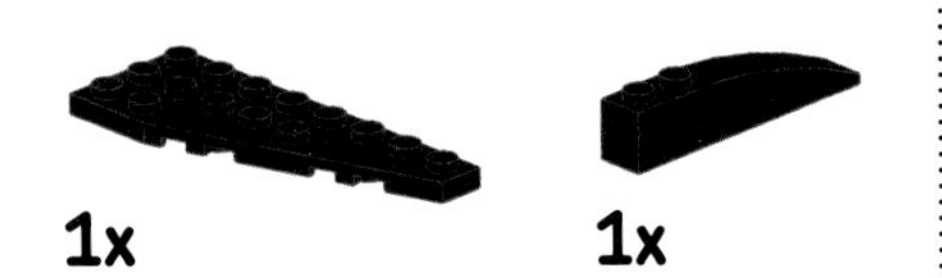

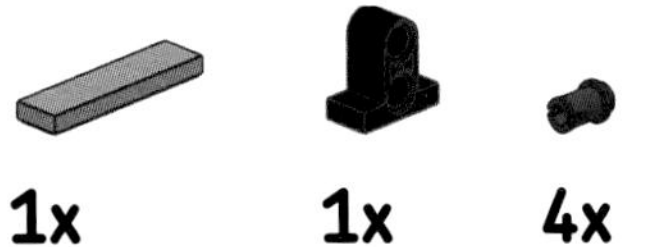

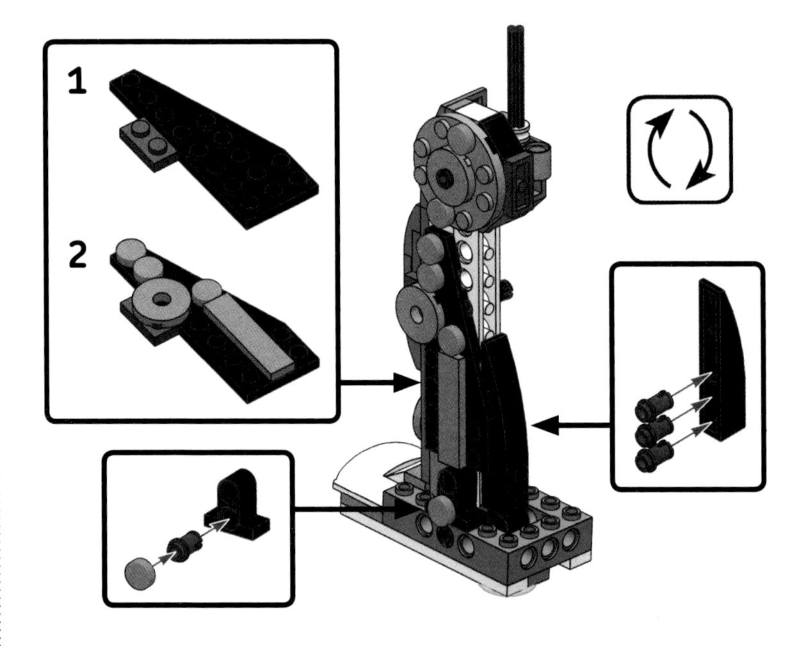

Notice the various examples of the SNOT technique in this step.

17

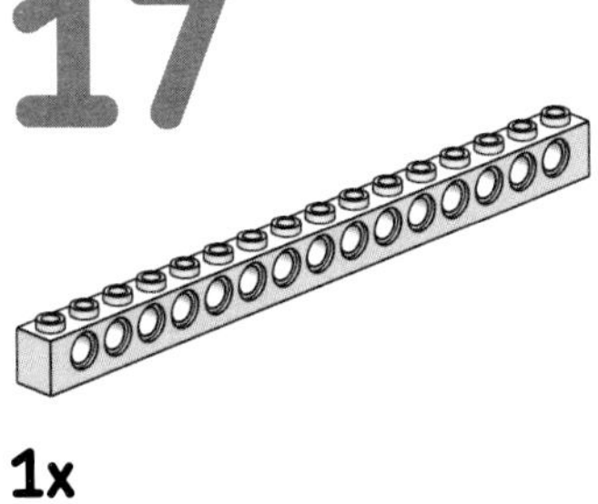

Building the right leg.

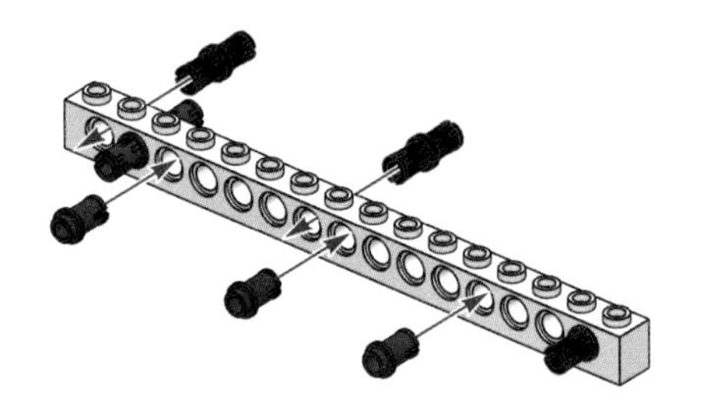

18

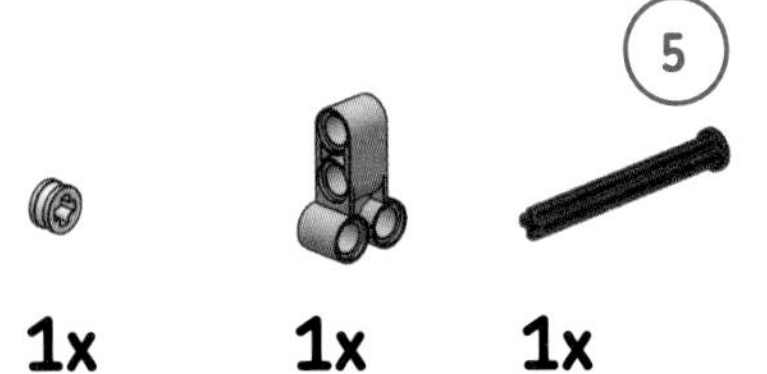

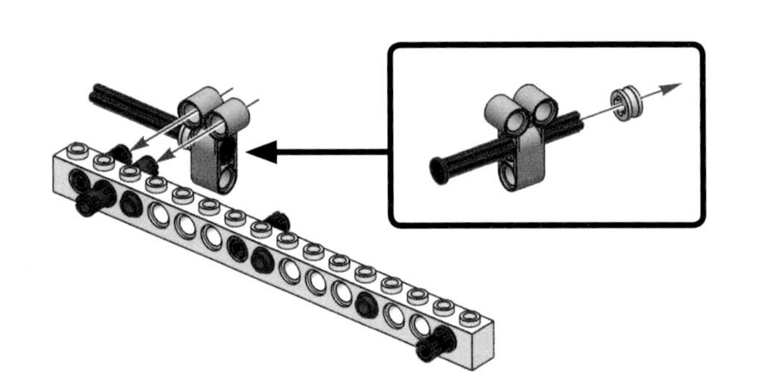

19

1x 1x 2x

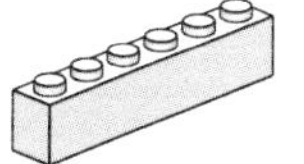  

1x 2x 1x

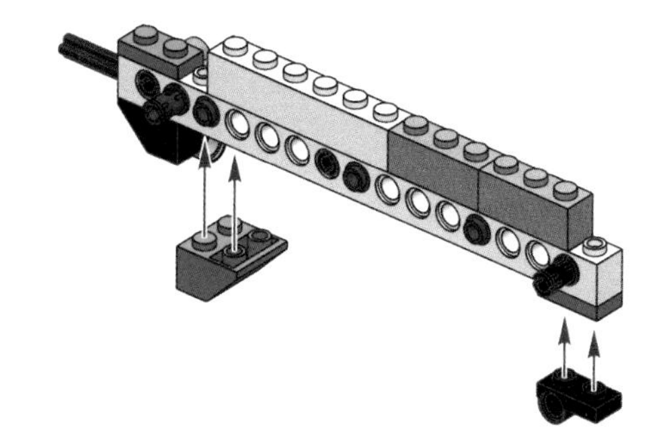

20

2x 1x

1x 1x

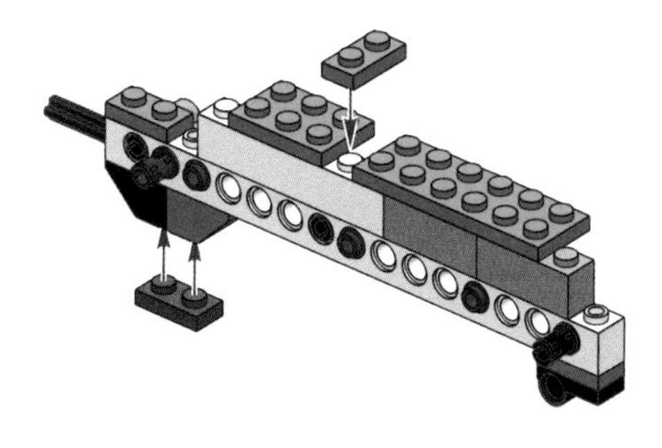

21

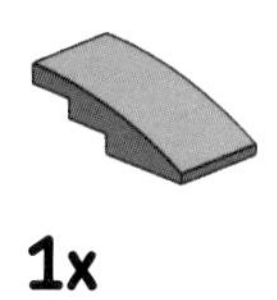    

1x 1x 1x

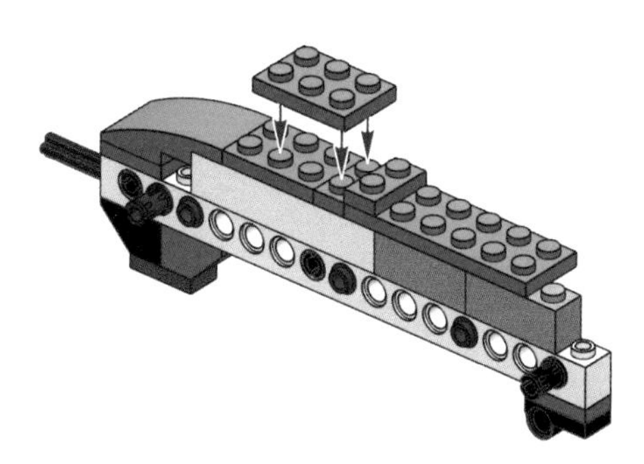

22

1x

1x

4x

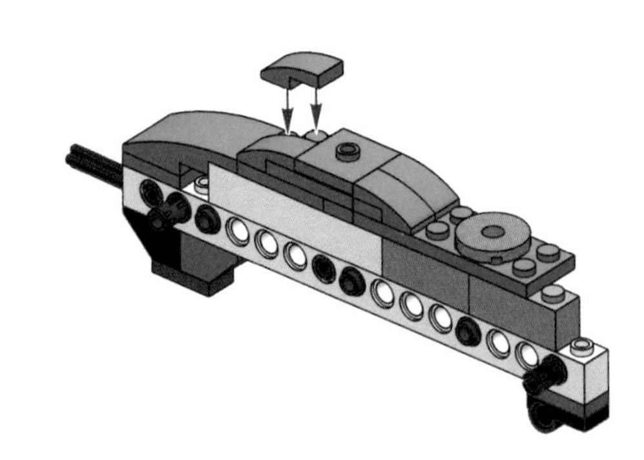

23

1x

1x

1x

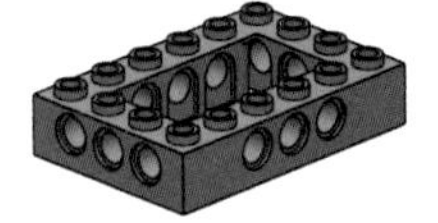
1x

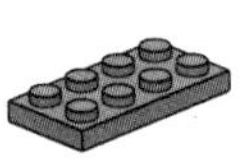
1x

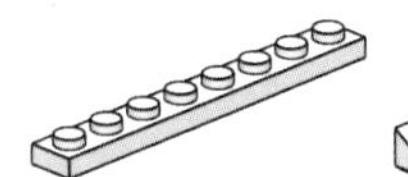
2x

1x

1x

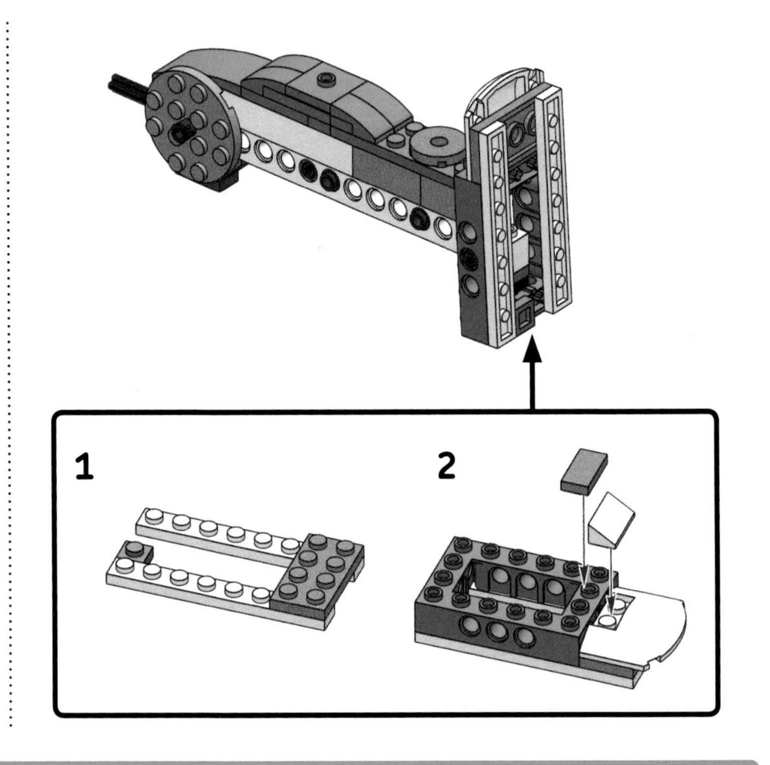

24

1x

1x

2x

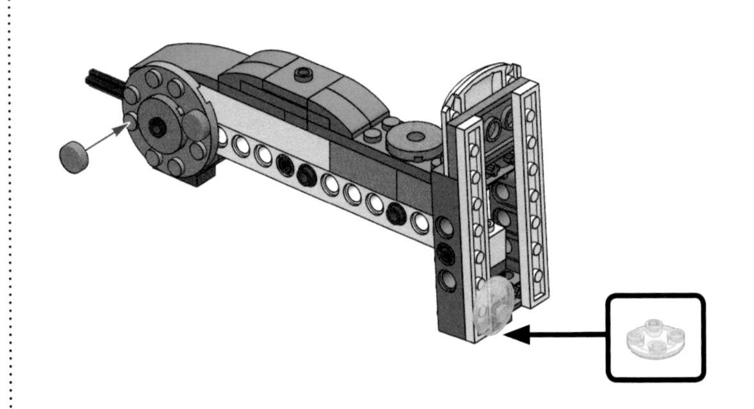

25

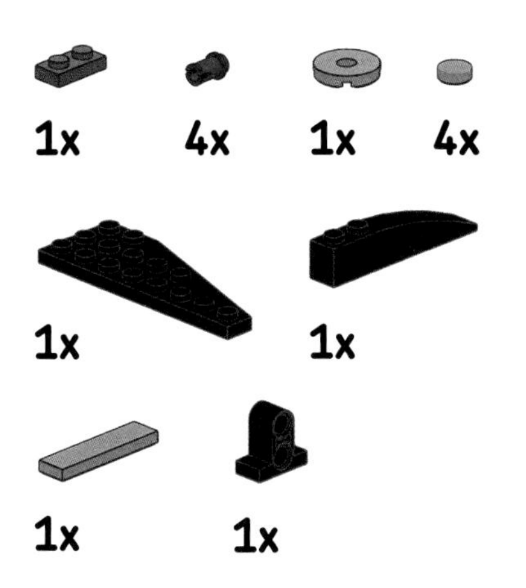

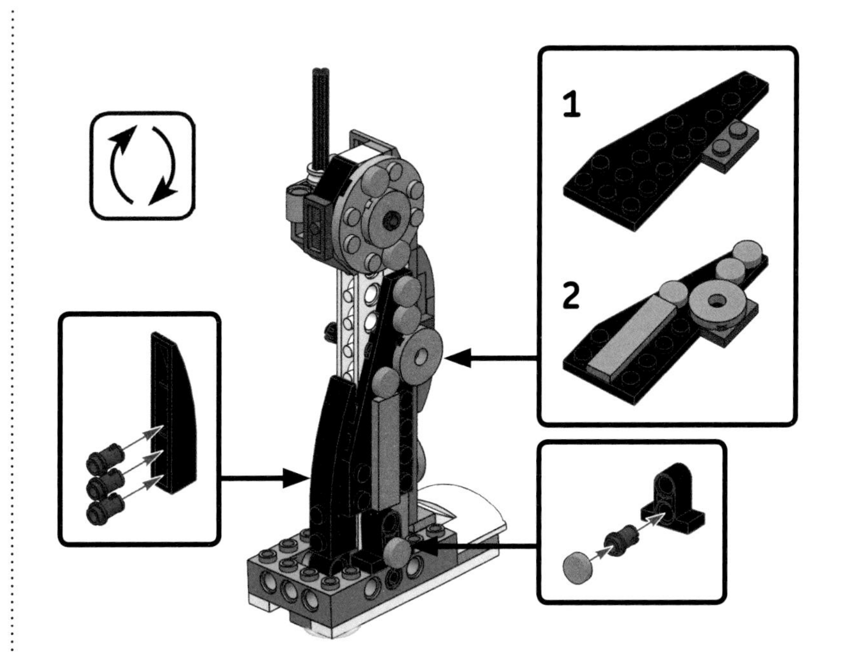

26

2x

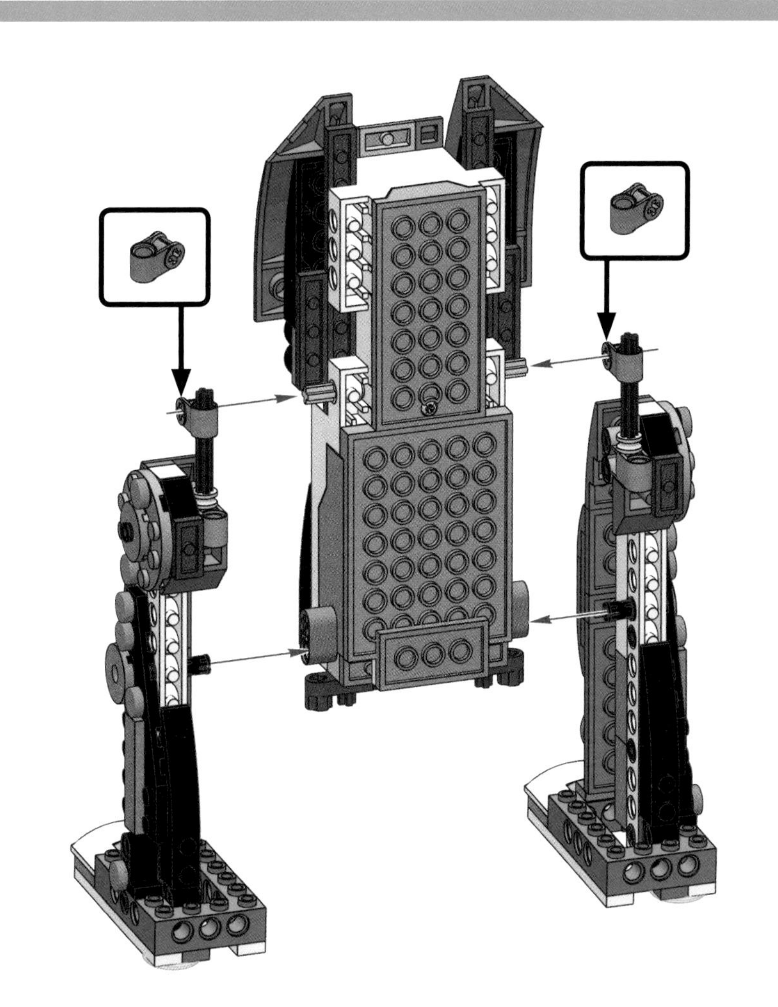

27

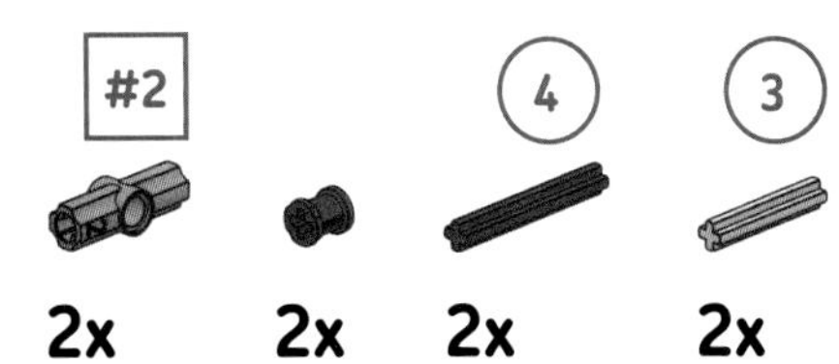

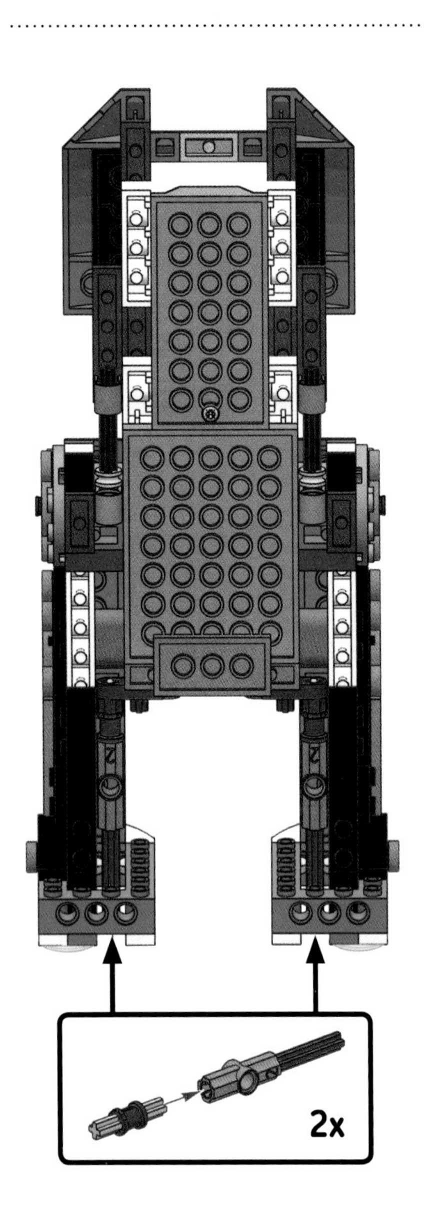

28

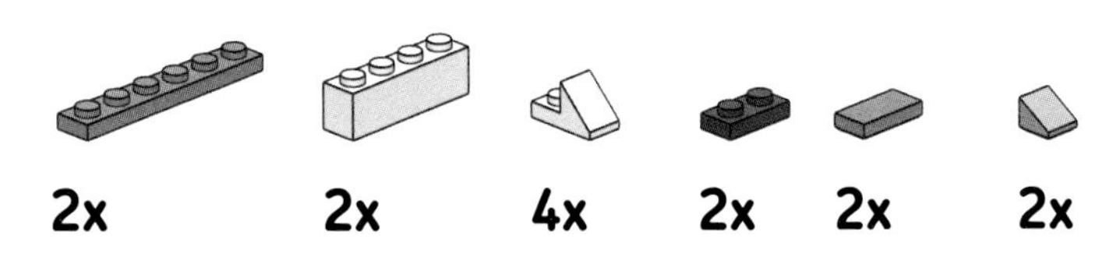

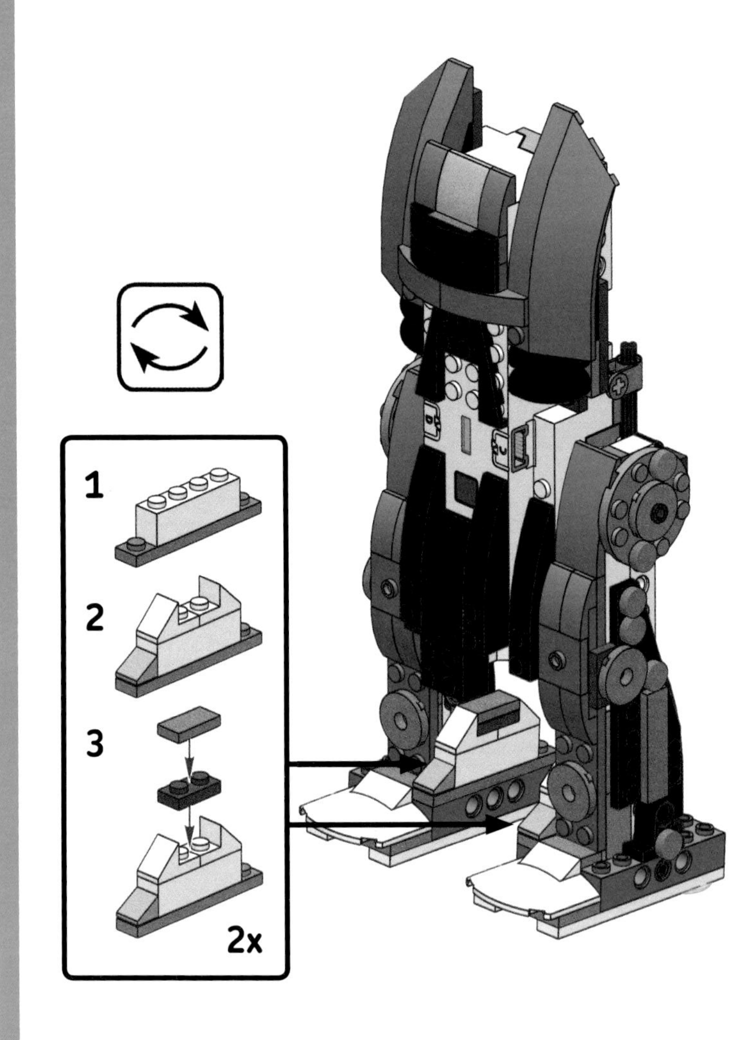

29

1x

4x

Building the torso.

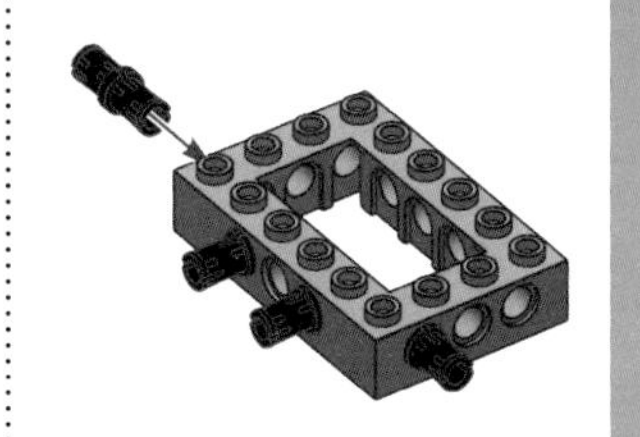

30

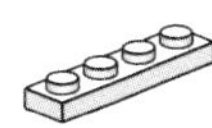

2x 1x

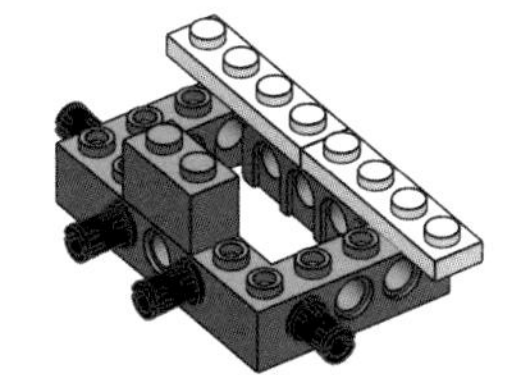

31

2x 1x 1x

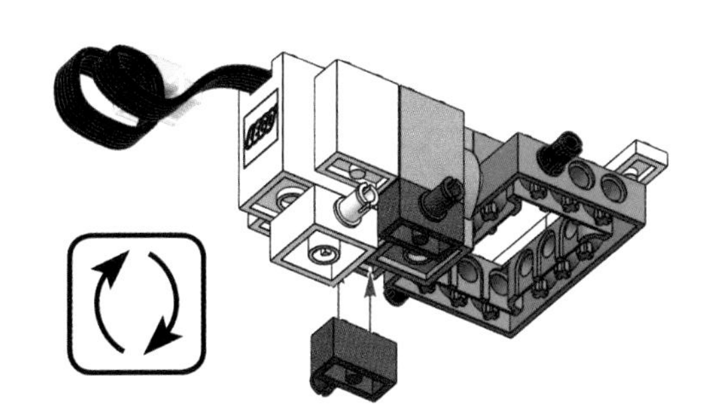

32

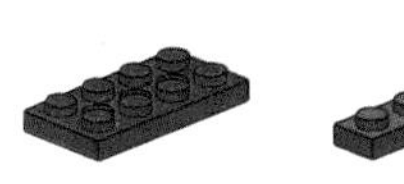

1x 1x 1x

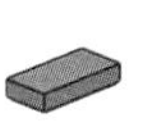

1x 1x 1x 2x

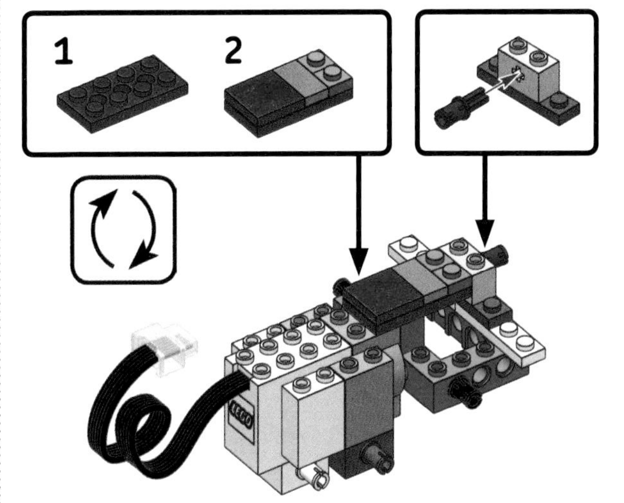

33

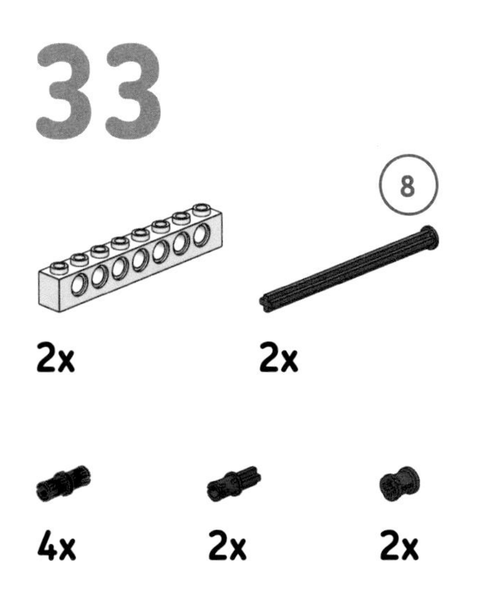

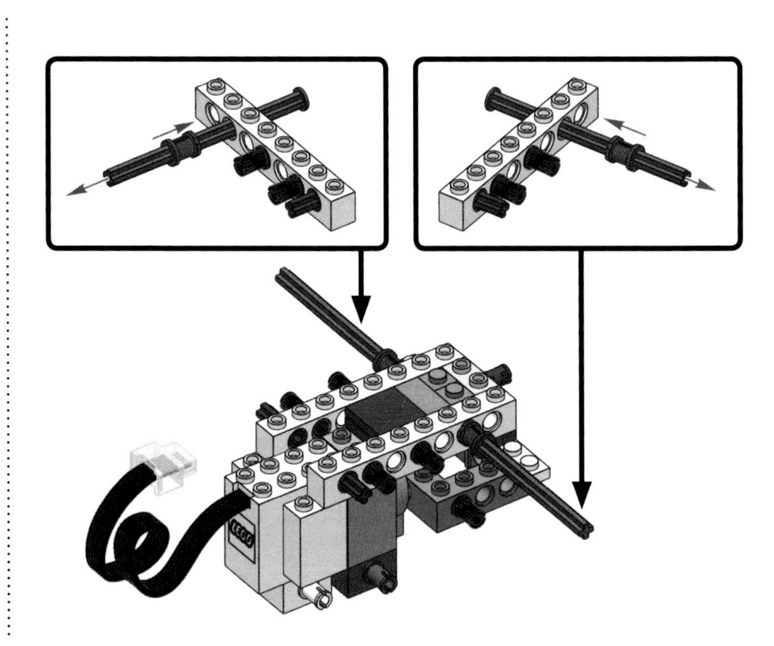

34

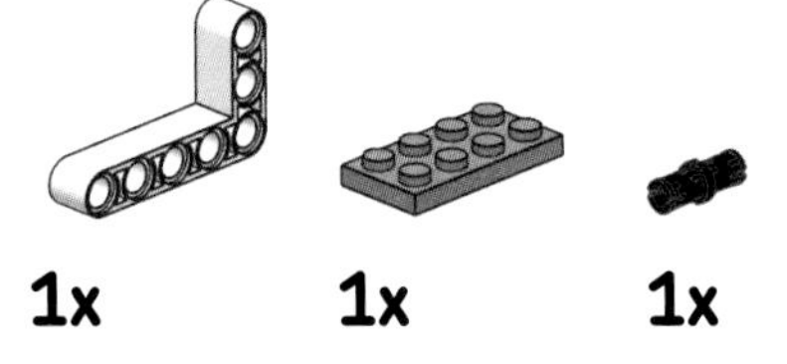

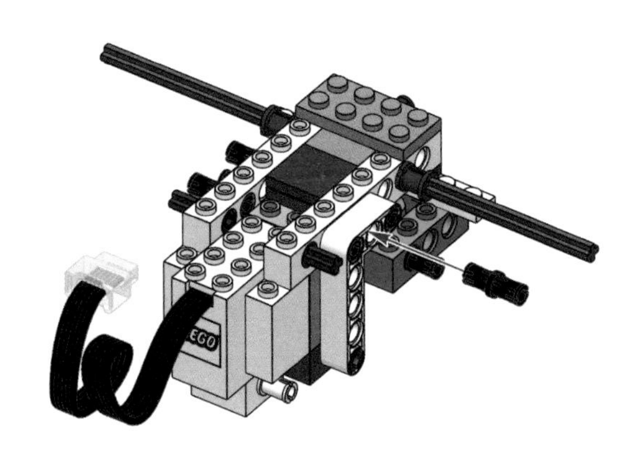

35

1x 1x

The 3x5 angular beams lock the motor and the Technic frame together so that they won't separate when you pull the torso away to change the batteries.

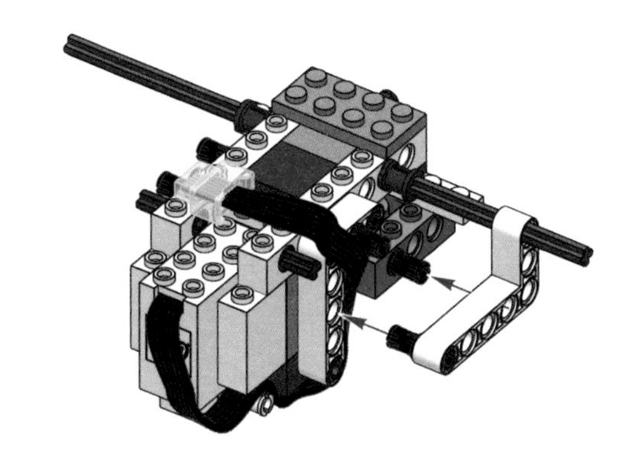

36

1x

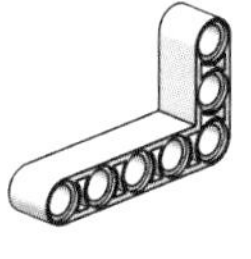

2x

3x

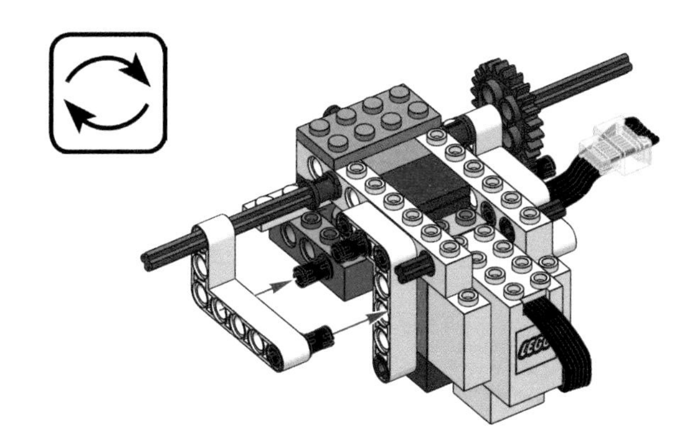

37

4

1x

1x

1x

1x

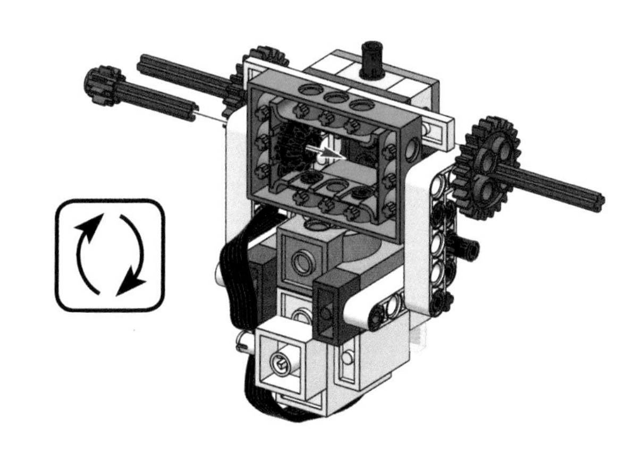

38

4

1x

1x

1x

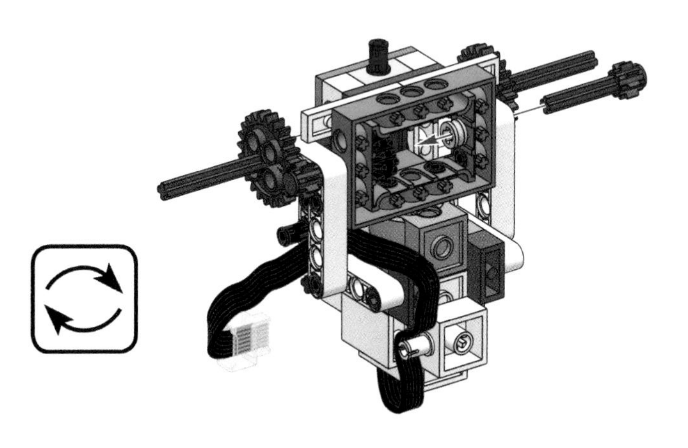

39

1x

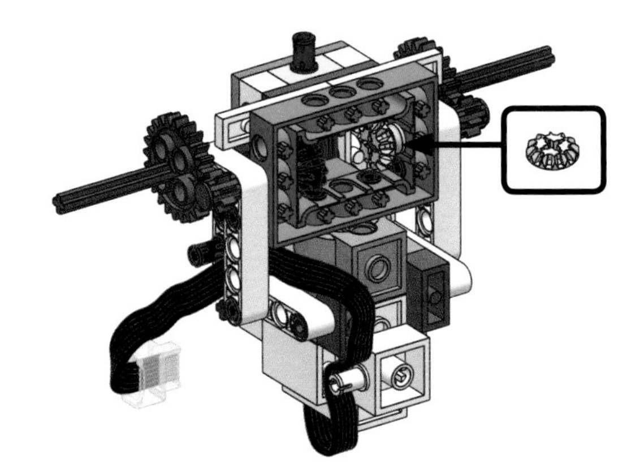

40

1x

1x

1x

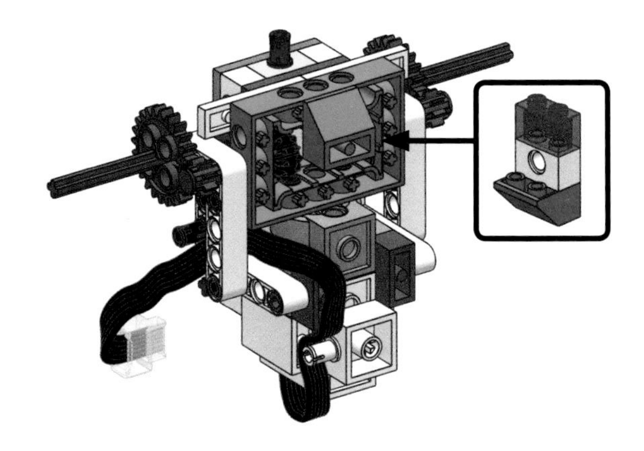

41

2x

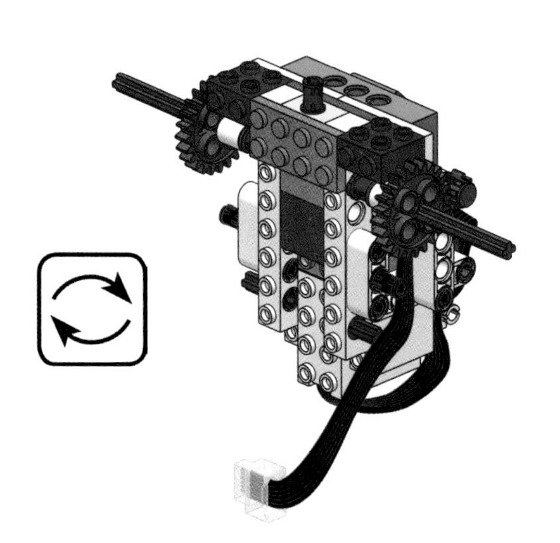

42

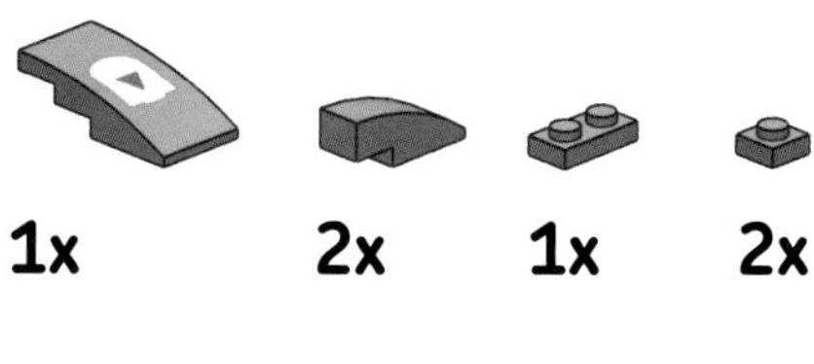
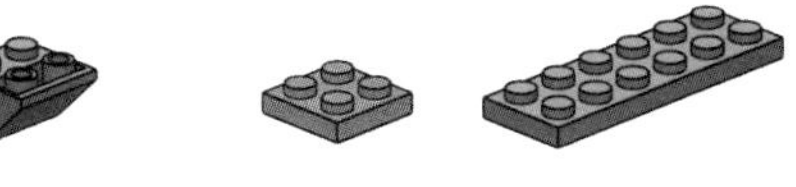
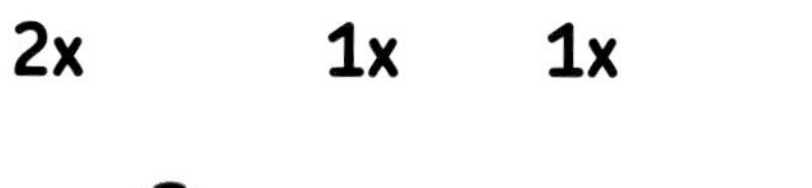
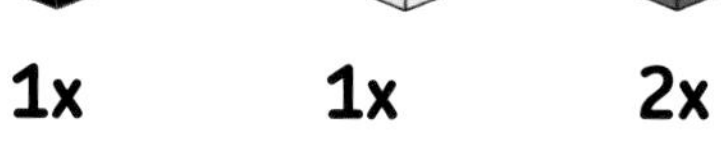

1x 2x 1x 2x

2x 1x 1x

1x 1x 2x

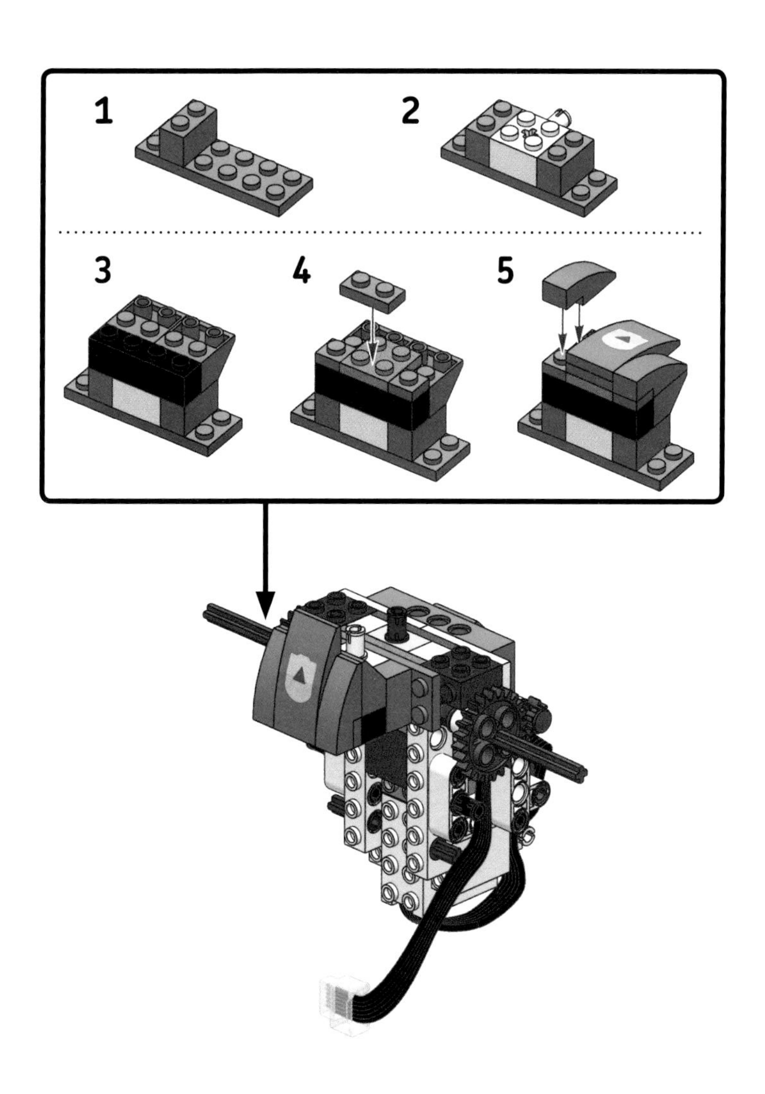

43

1x

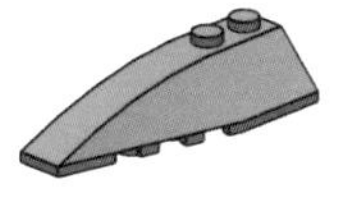

1x

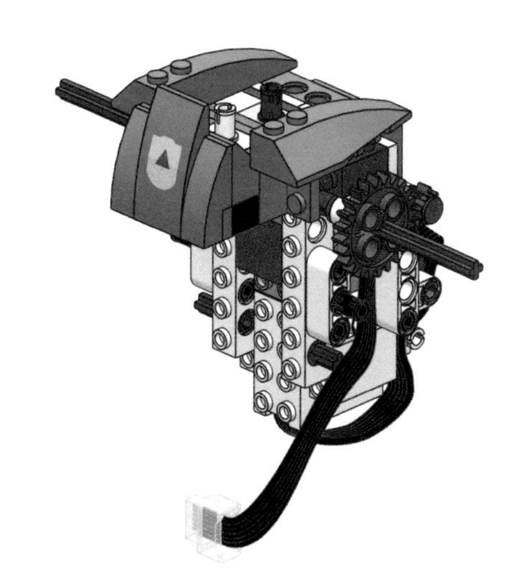

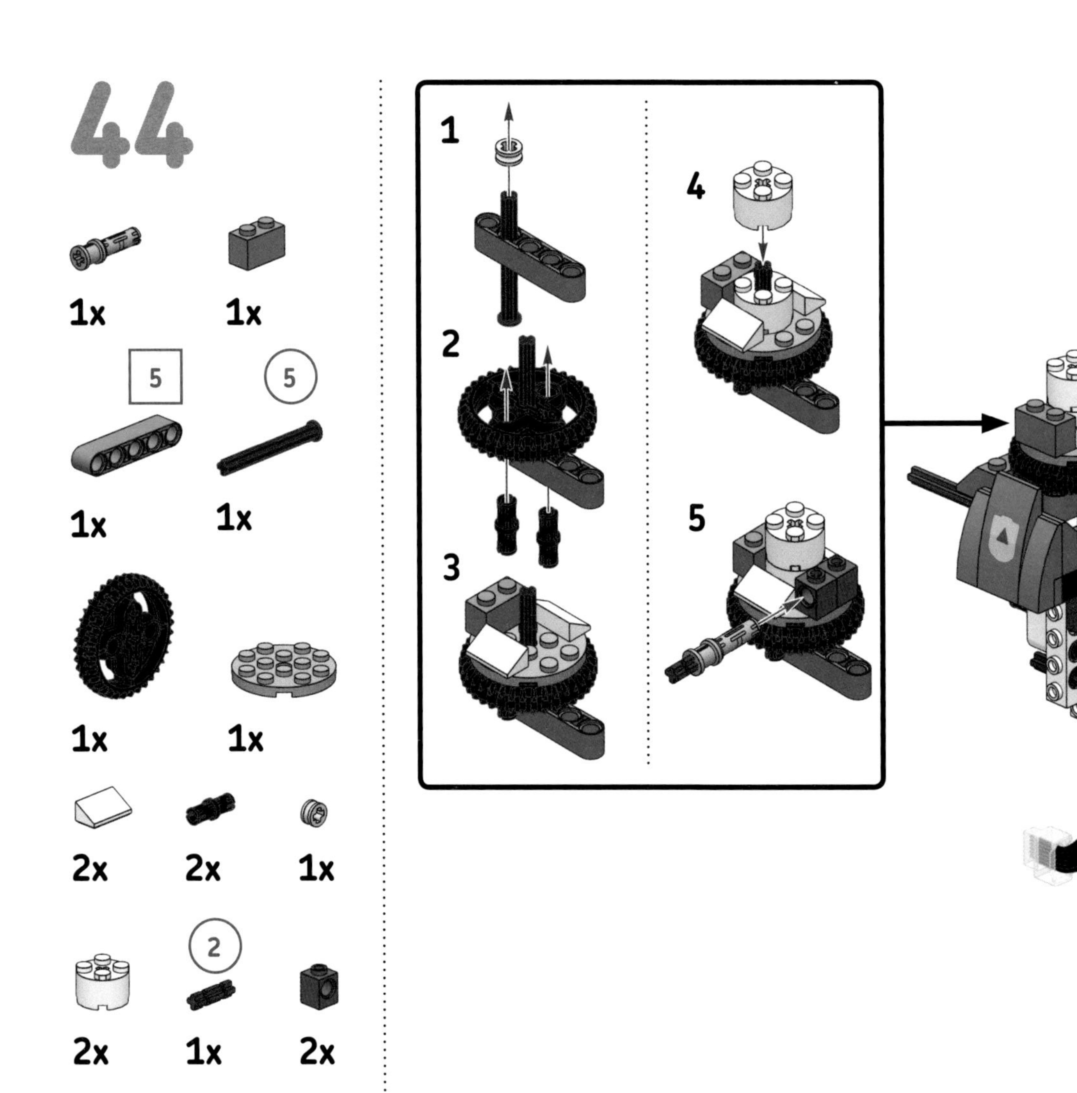

We use a complex gear train in the torso to make the head and arms move together. The gear ratio from the motor shaft to the head and to each arm is the same: 12/20 × 36/12 = 1.8 for the head, and 12/20 × 24/8 = 1.8 for the arms.

When adding the 20z bevel gear, be sure that the axles of the neck and arms are oriented as shown in **FIGURE 16-1**. (You can tweak the position later by sliding out the 24z gears.)

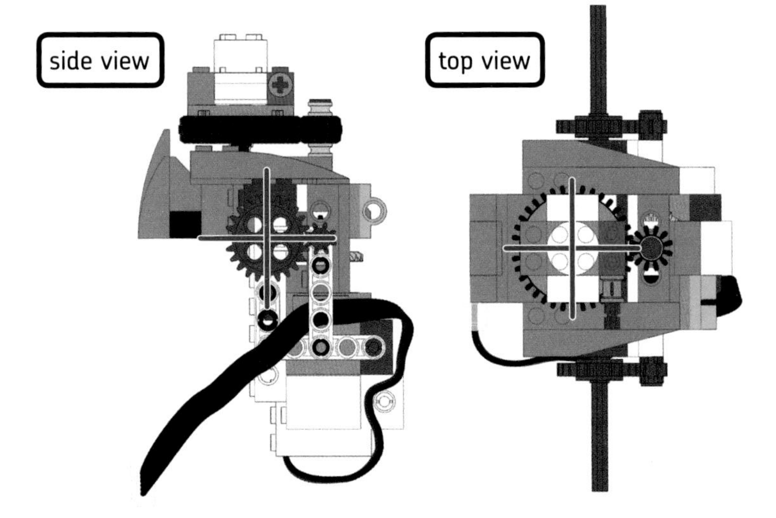

FIGURE 16-1 When adding the 20z bevel gear, align the axles of the neck and arms.

45

1x

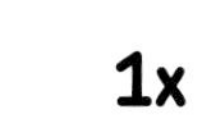

1x

2x

1x

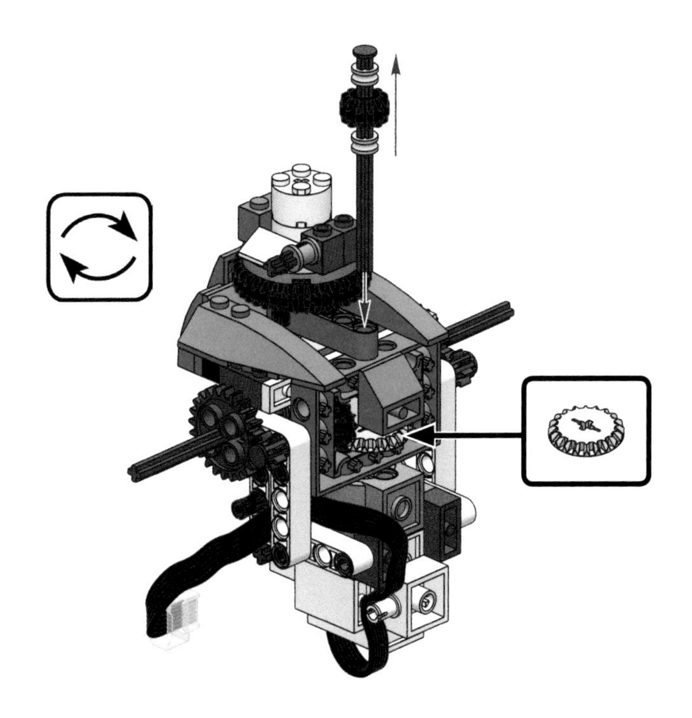

46

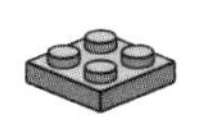
1x

1x

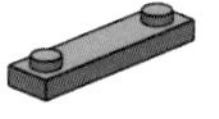
1x

1x

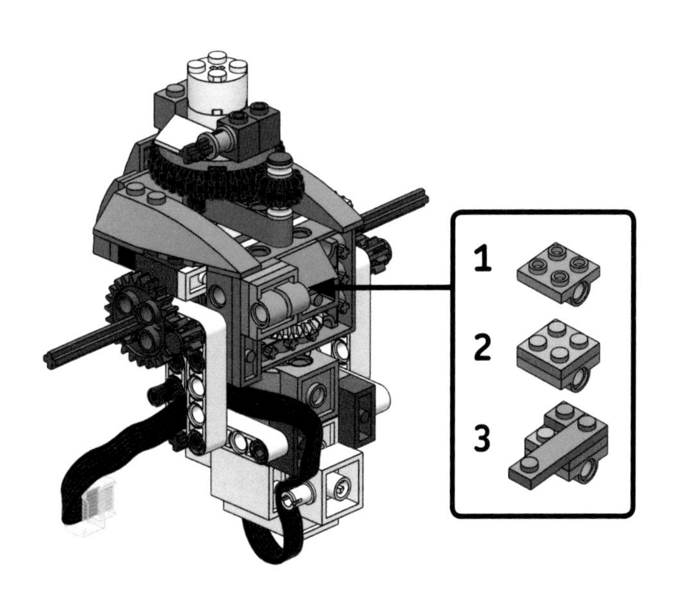

47

1x

1x

1x

1x

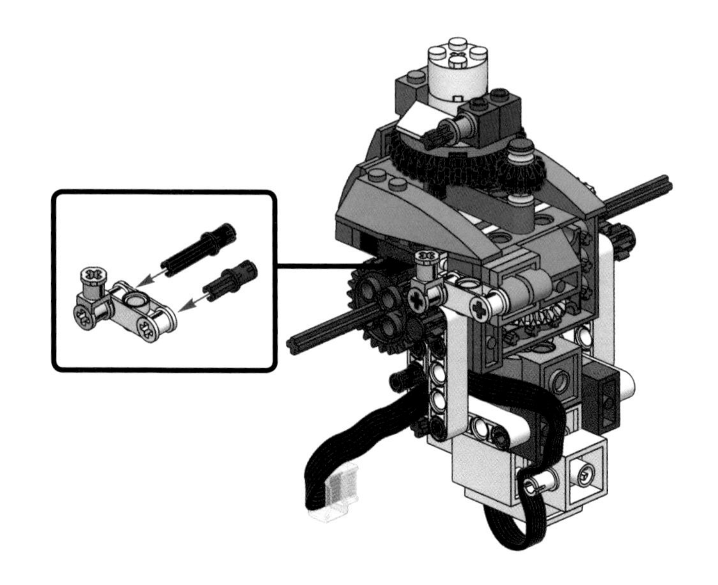

48

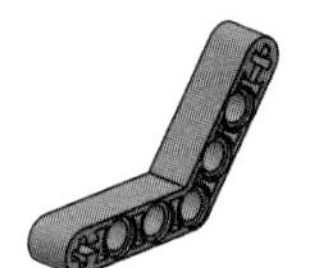

2x

2x

2x

4x

1x

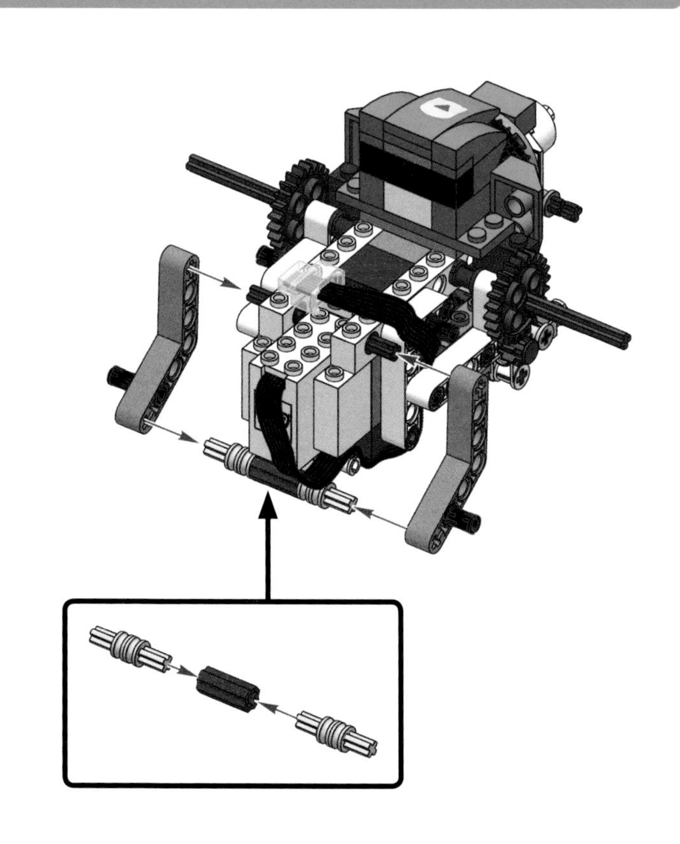

49

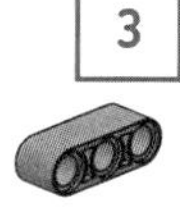

2x 2x

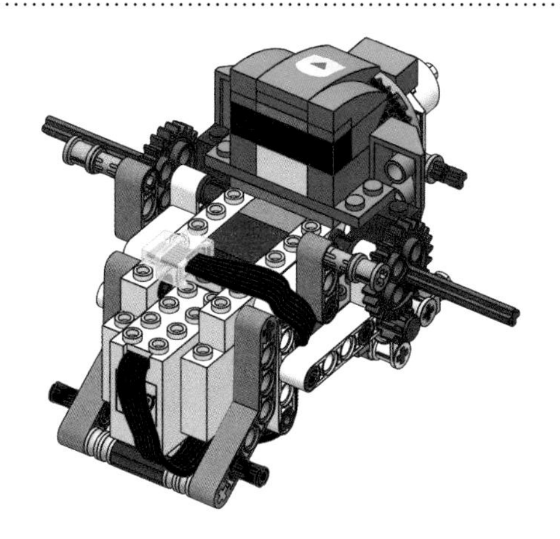

50

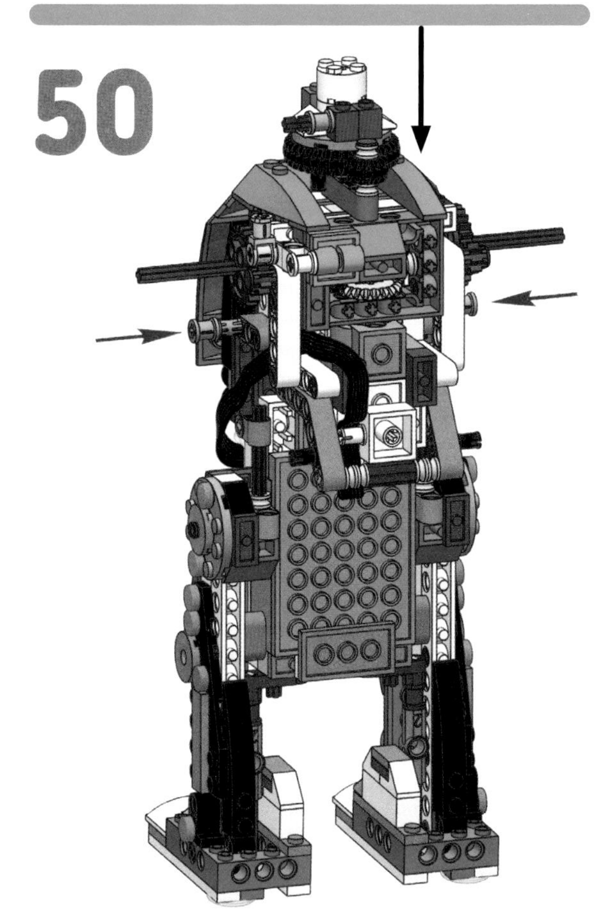

The 3M pegs with bushings attach the torso to the lower part of the body. They are easy to pull away when you need to change the batteries.

51

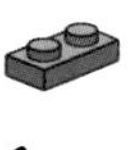

1x

1x

The head features many examples of the SNOT technique, producing results that would otherwise be impossible to achieve at this scale if we were simply stacking bricks and plates.

52

3x

Sensor cable omitted for space reasons.

53

1x 1x

54

 1x  2x

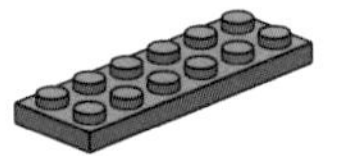 1x 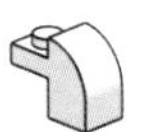 2x  1x

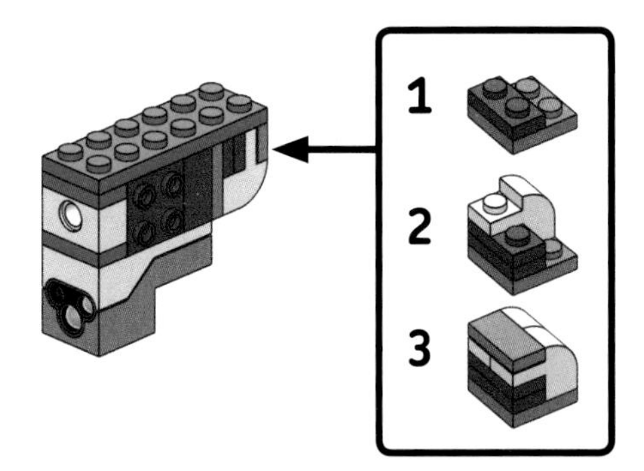

55

 1x  1x

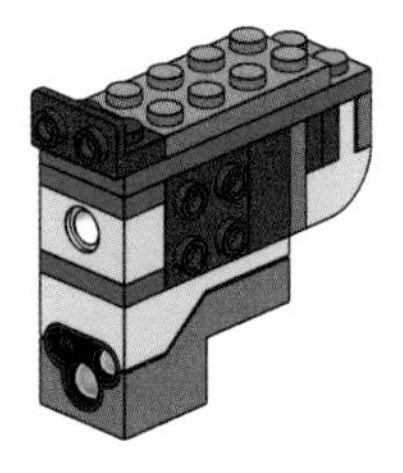

56

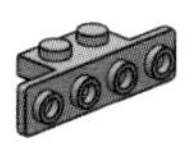 2x 1x

57

 2x 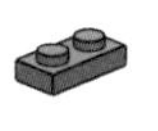 1x

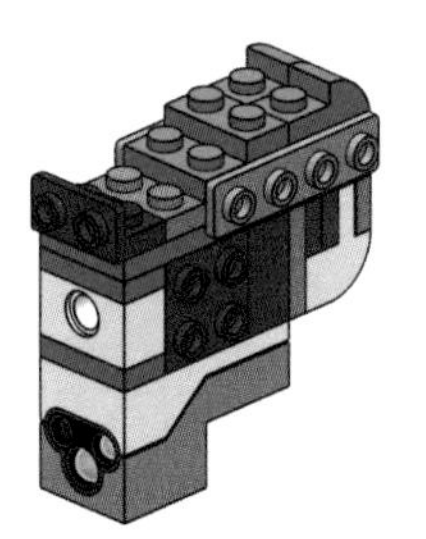

58

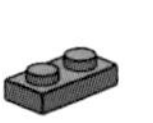 1x  1x

 1x  1x

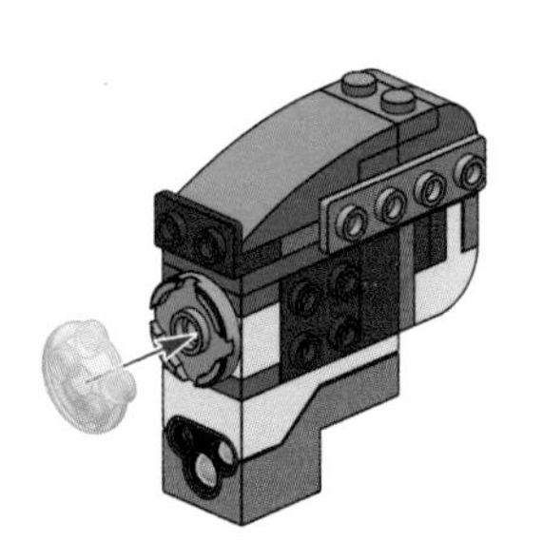

59

1x 1x 1x

1x 1x 1x

1x 1x

1x 2x 1x

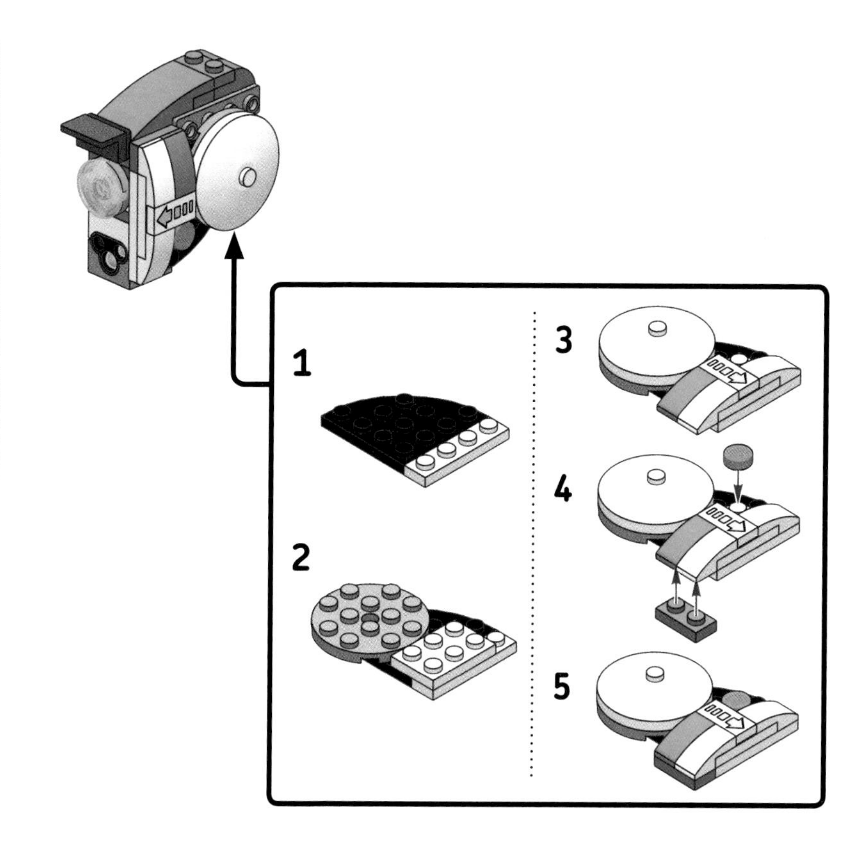

60

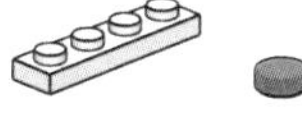

1x 1x 1x

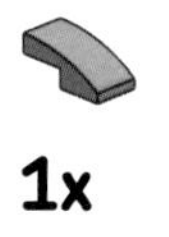

1x 1x 1x

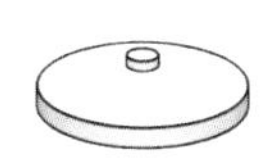

1x 1x

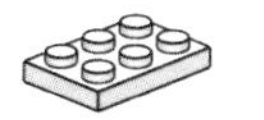
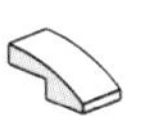
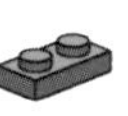
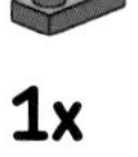

1x 2x 1x

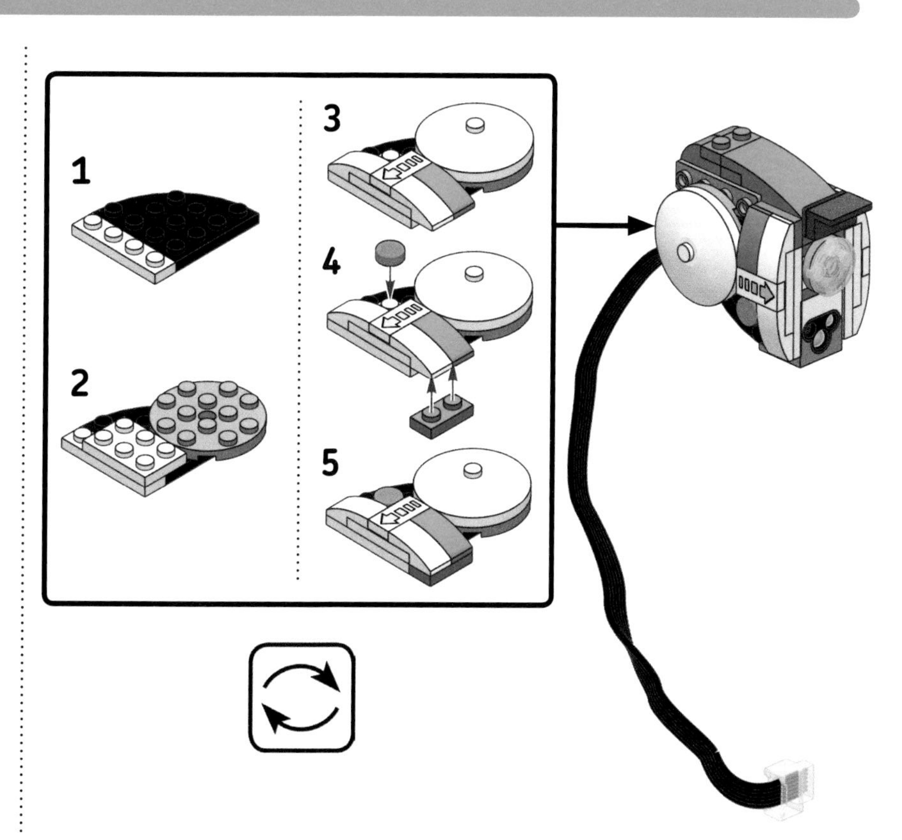

61

1x 1x

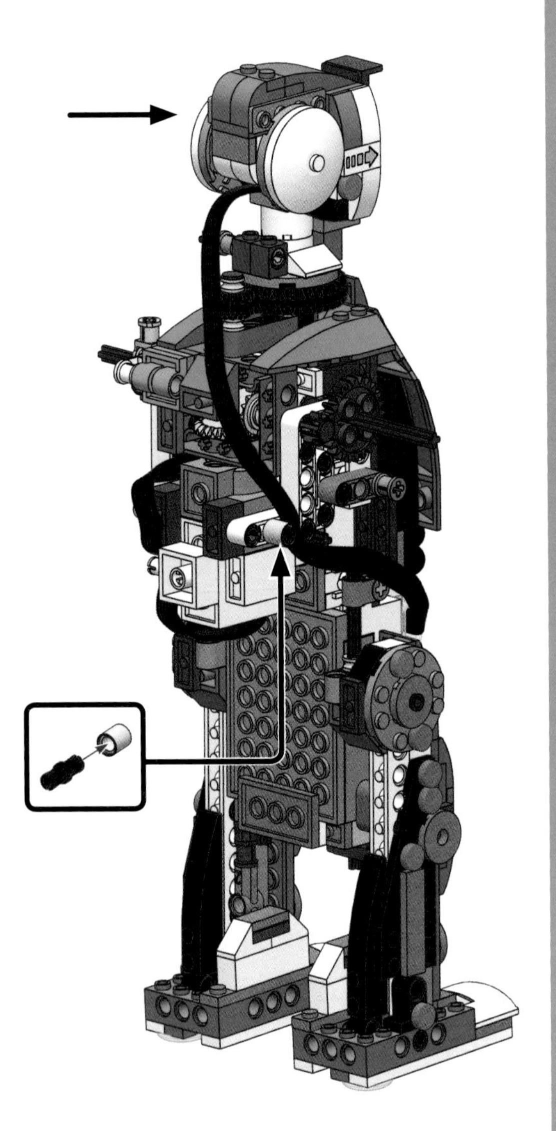

62

2x

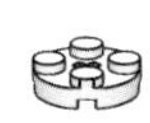

4x

2x

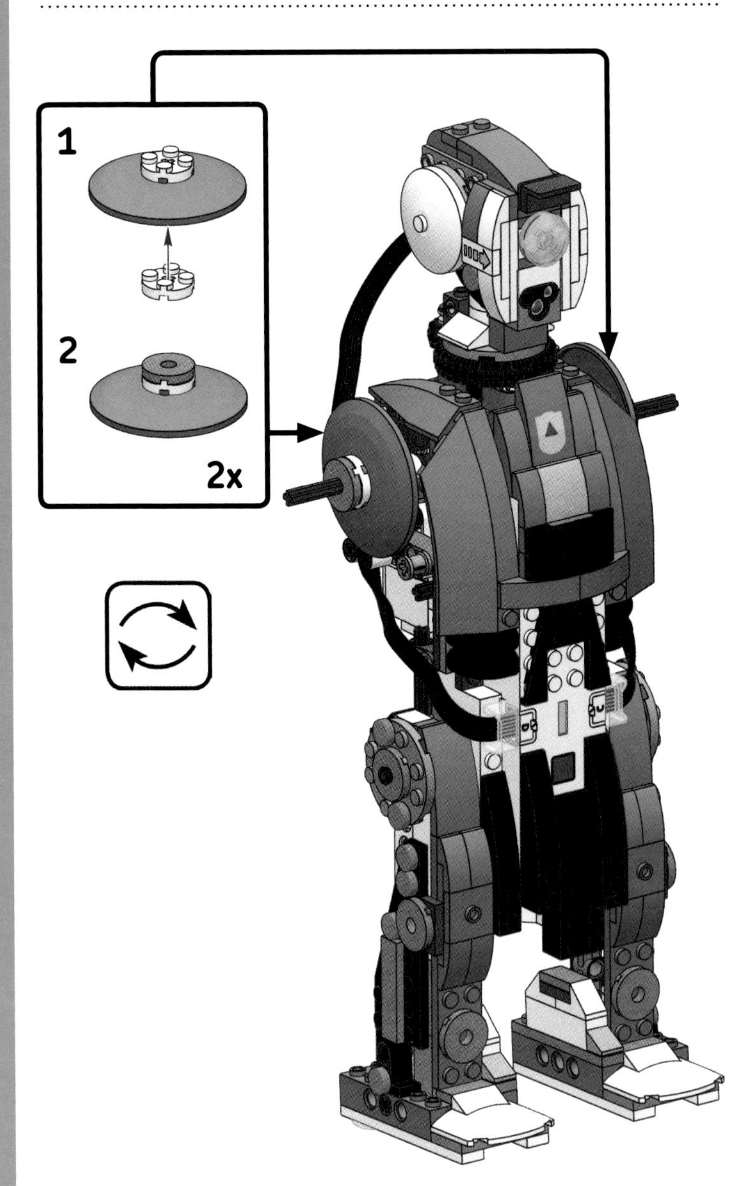

63

2x

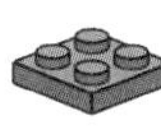

2x

2x

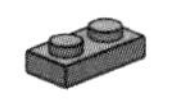

4x

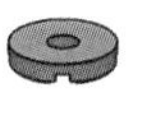

2x

2x

2x

2x

4x

4x

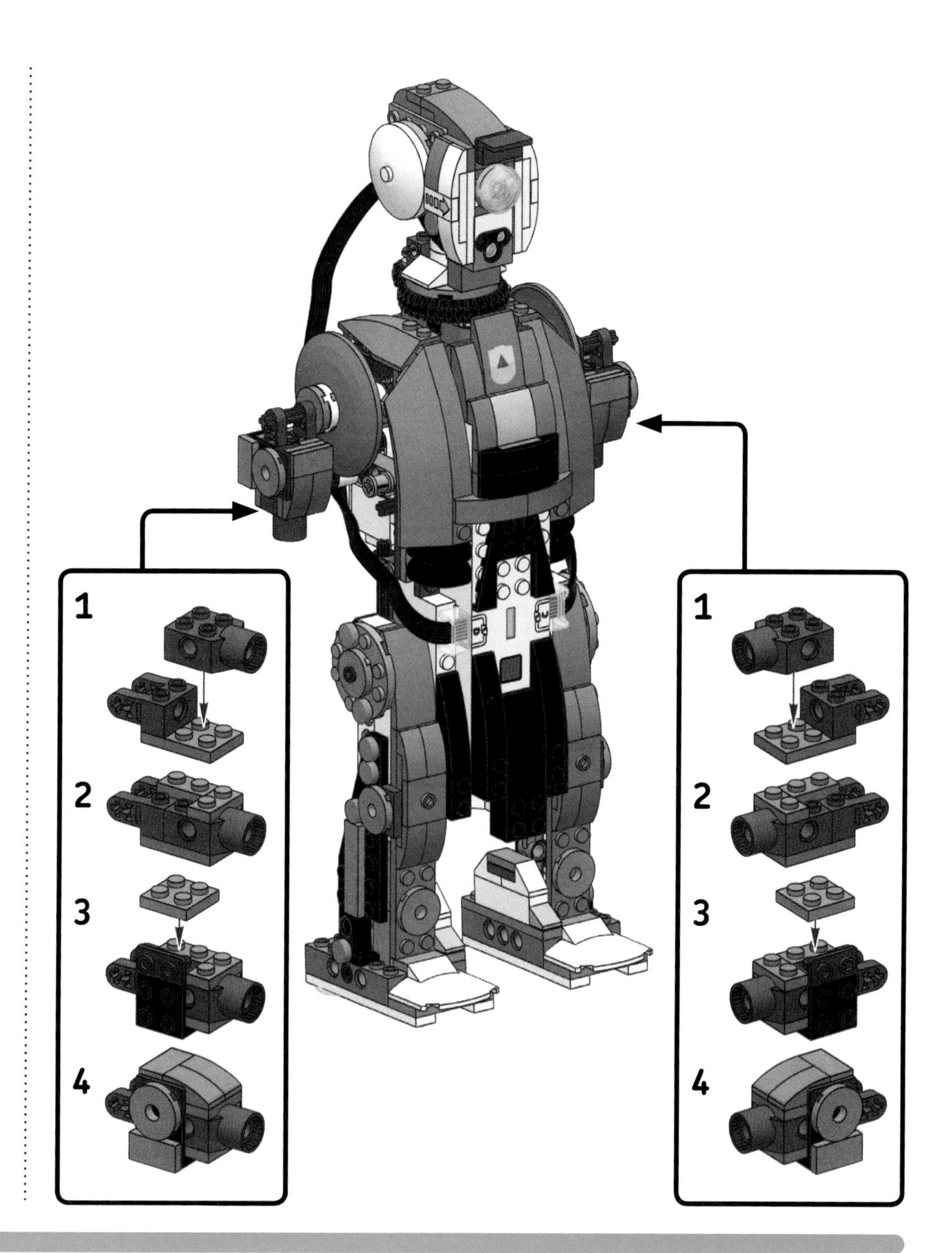

64

2x

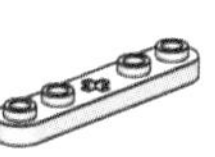
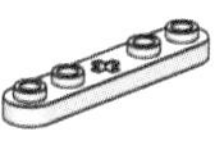

4x

2x

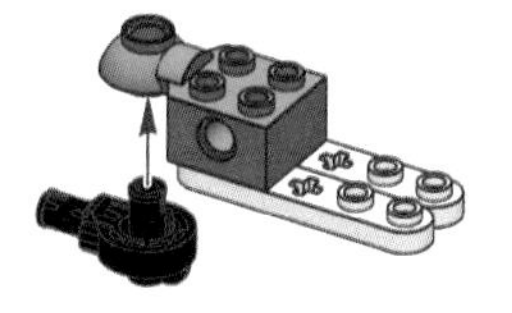

Build two copies of the forearm assembly.

65

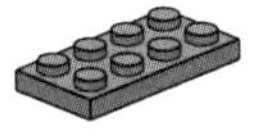

2x 2x 4x

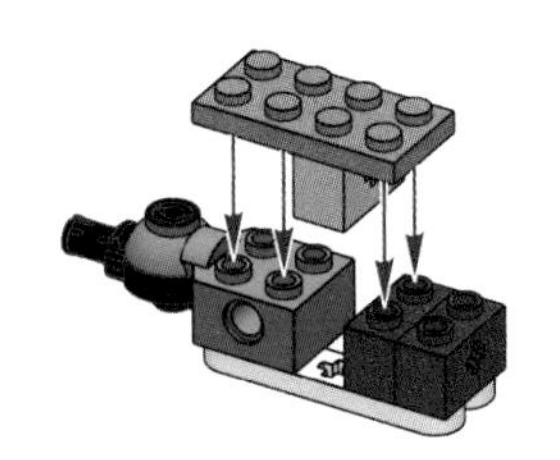

66

2x 2x 2x 2x

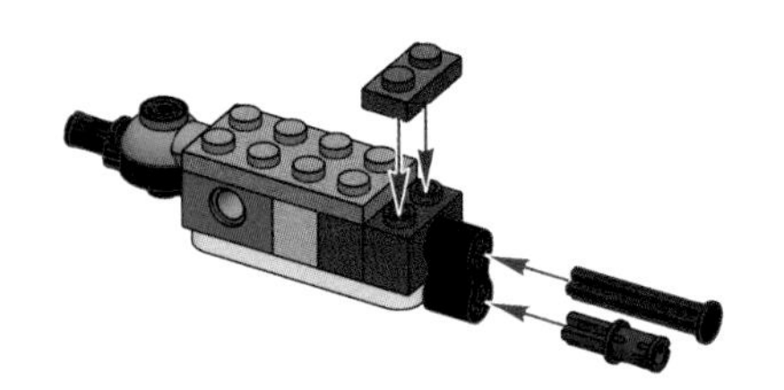

67

4x 2x

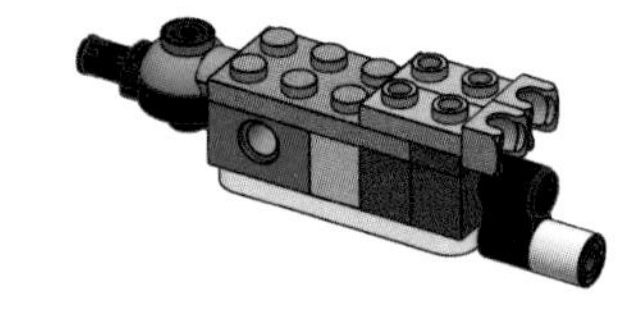

68

4x 2x 2x 4x

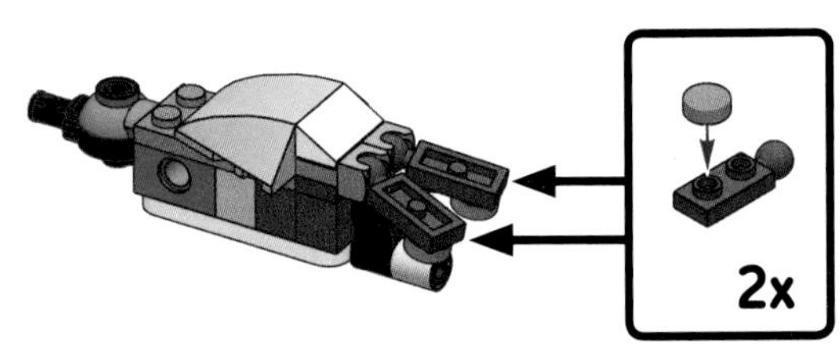

Each hand has two articulated fingers and a flexible thumb, allowing the robot to hold light, thin objects.

69

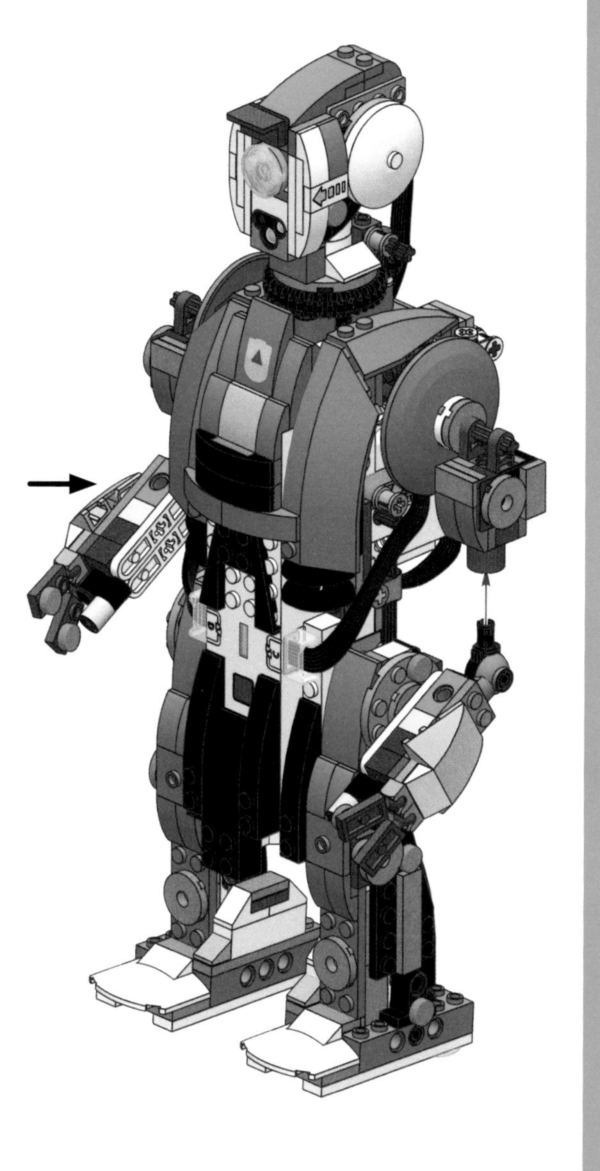

70

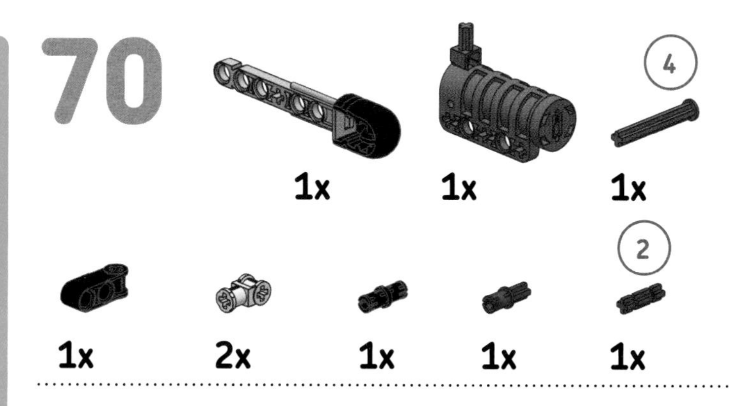

(No need to add the cannon to the robot if you don't want to!)

changing the batteries

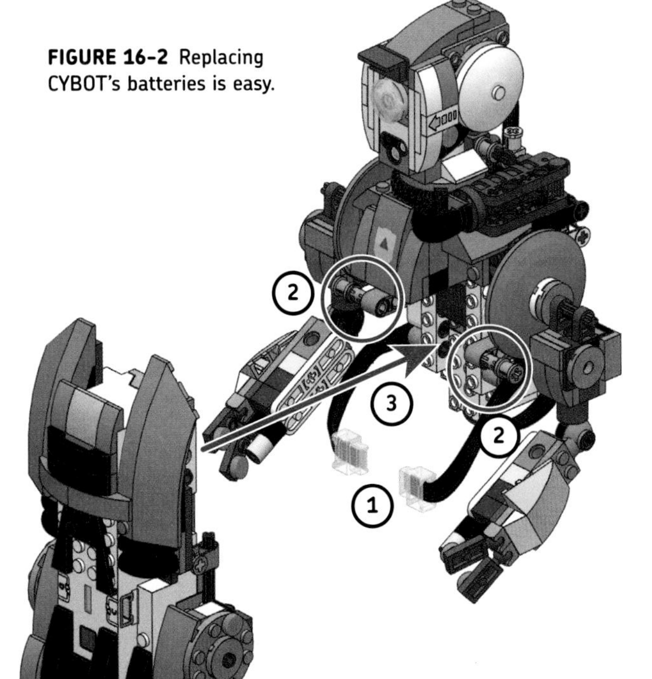

FIGURE 16-2 Replacing CYBOT's batteries is easy.

I designed the robot to make replacing the batteries quick and easy (see **FIGURE 16-2**). To remove the battery box:

1: Detach the cables.

2: Pull the grey 3M pegs out one LEGO unit by grabbing them at the bushing.

3: Grab the torso from the white 3x5 angular beams and pull it away from the LEGO BOOST Move Hub. It should come away in one piece.

Now change the batteries as usual by removing the screw and taking out the battery box. Once you've inserted a fresh set of batteries, reverse the steps above, making sure that the cables don't hinder the arm and leg movement.

what you've learned

Now that you've built CYBOT and learned how to replace the batteries, you're ready to program it. In Chapter 17, you'll learn how to program CYBOT to walk, talk, shoot, and even follow voice commands.

17

programming CYBOT

In this chapter, you will learn how to program the humanoid robot CYBOT. We'll make composite blocks to reset the robot's arms and legs and realign the legs each time the robot stops so that it can walk, turn, and shoot. You can reuse this collection of c-blocks to make your own original programs for CYBOT.

After that, we'll write a program to make CYBOT explore its surroundings, another program to control CYBOT remotely, and learn how to control CYBOT using your voice!

making the composite blocks

Before we build our programs, we have to prepare all the composite blocks for CYBOT. First, in the Creative Canvas menu, create a new project and name it **CYBOT**. Then create the following composite blocks.

Reset c-block

When you turn the Move Hub on, the position of the motor shafts is unknown. For the robot to work properly, the head, arms, and legs should be moved to the zero position, and all the motor rotation sensors set to 0. The sequence inside the **Reset** c-block shown in **FIGURE 17-1** takes care of that.

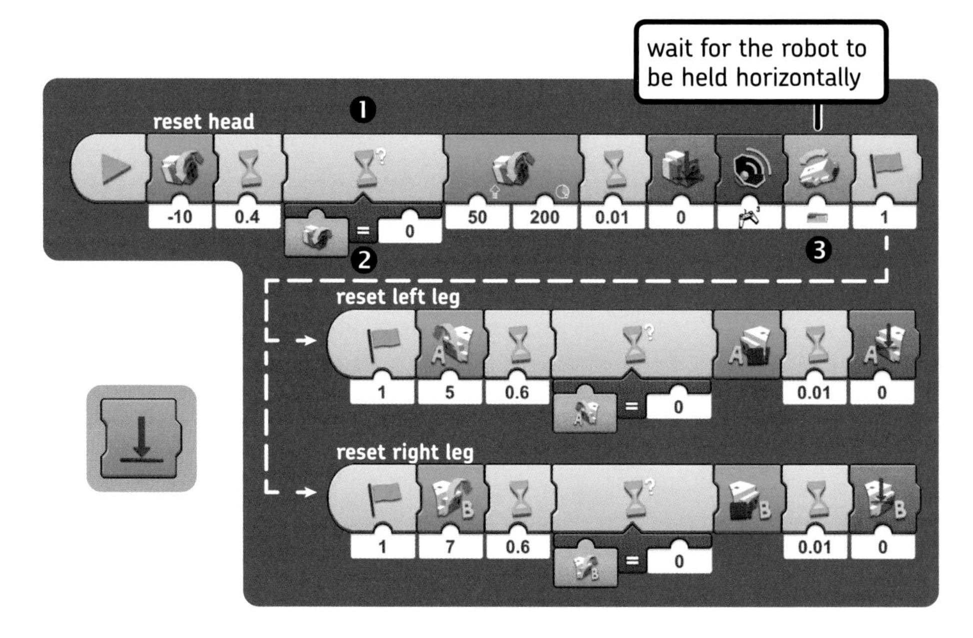

FIGURE 17-1 The Reset composite block's inner sequence and final appearance

In its main sequence, the **Reset** c-block resets the robot's head and arms, which are linked together by a gear train. The external motor runs until the pins attached to the 36-tooth gear at the base of the neck hit the blue 5M beam causing the motor to stall.

The motor stall, in turn, is detected by the **Wait for True** block ❶ in conjunction with a **Compare Equal** block ❷ that checks whether the motor's current speed is 0. Once this happens, the motor is rotated back to align the head with the robot's midline and move the arms down.

Once the head is centered, a sound (Game Sound 3) is played to tell you it's time to place the robot horizontally, so you rotate it to a horizontal position. The **Wait for Hub Orientation** block ❸ waits for you to do this. Once the robot is horizontal, two sequences are triggered to run in parallel and both legs' motors start moving slowly until their movement is blocked by a handle, which you should manually lower to reset the robot (as described in the next section). Once this happens, the motors are stopped, the rotation sensor of each motor is set to 0, and the **Reset** c-block ends when both sequences finish.

resetting CYBOT

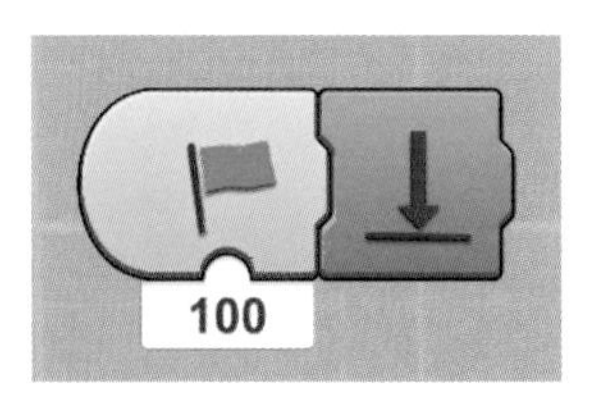

FIGURE 17-2 Place this short sequence in your program to perform the manual reset procedure.

To walk properly, CYBOT needs its legs to be in a known starting position. Since the cams that drive the legs can spin freely, CYBOT needs your help to reset its legs every time the Move Hub is turned on. To accomplish this, we'll use the short sequence shown in **FIGURE 17-2**.

The **Reset** c-block should be executed manually only once when you turn the Move Hub on. For this reason, the **Reset** c-block is attached to a **Start on Flag** block, not to a **Start Sequence** block. This way, the sequence does not automatically start every time you tap the green Play button.

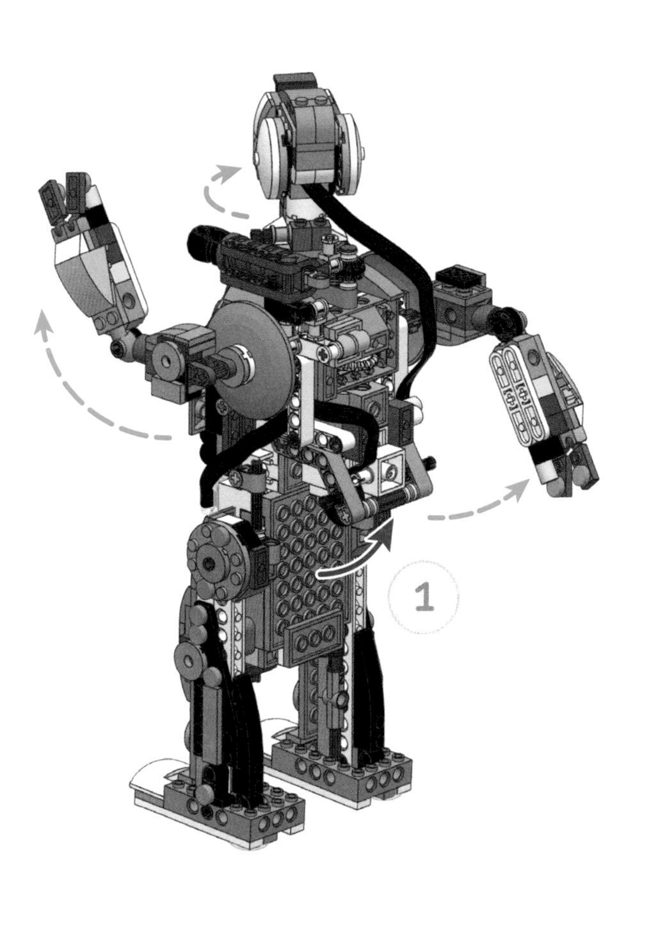

Here is the step-by-step procedure to reset CYBOT.

1: With CYBOT standing on its feet, raise the orange handlebar on its back and then start the reset sequence by tapping the **Start on Flag** block shown in **FIGURE 17-2**. The head should turn as far as it can and then rotate back to the center. The arms should move along with the head and rotate down at the end of this sequence.

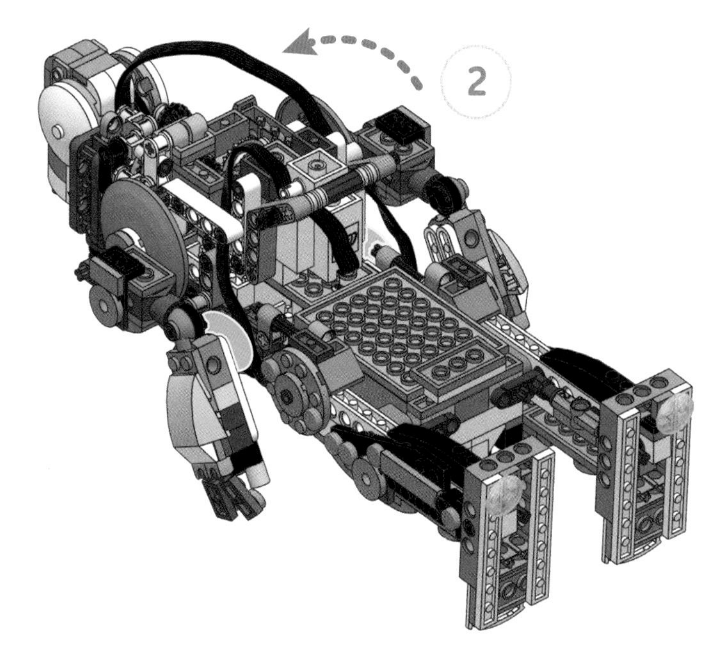

2: When the sound is played, gently grab CYBOT by the parts that look like its ribs, pick it up, and hold it horizontally so you can see its back.

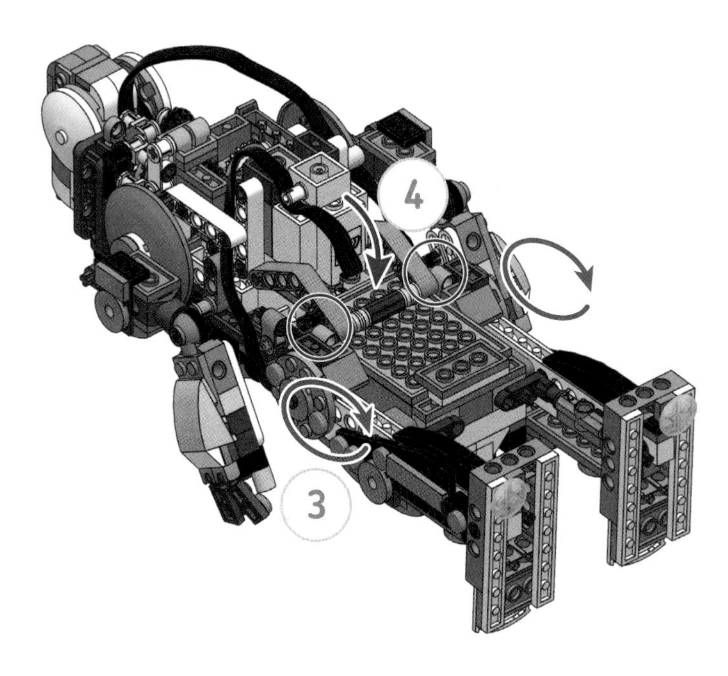

3: The legs should start moving at slightly different speeds. Be ready to bring the handlebar down against the robot's back when both legs are in their downmost position.

4: Once the bar is down, the grey blocks attached to the legs should hit against the handlebar pins and stop. That's the zero position for the legs. Raise the handlebar again to let CYBOT walk freely. Now, place CYBOT on its feet, and it should be stable, with both feet on the ground. The body should be perfectly straight, not leaning backward or forward.

If one of the legs does not move until the grey block hits the black pin, repeat the reset procedure from the beginning, making sure that nothing is slowing down the leg movement. (The reset procedure might fail repeatedly if the batteries are low.)

MoveHead c-block

The **MoveHead** c-block, shown in **FIGURE 17-3**, rotates the scanner head relative to the zero position.

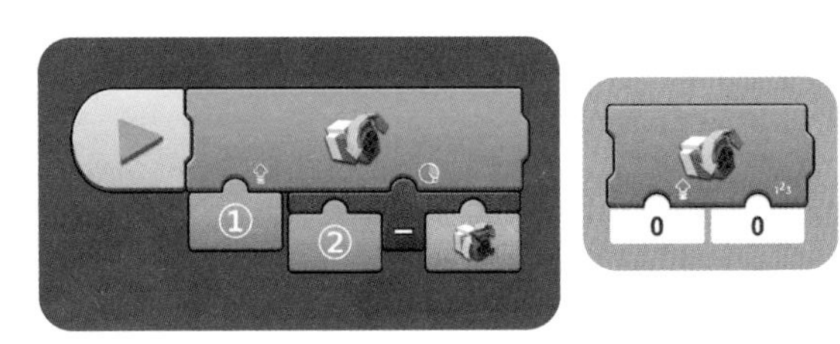

FIGURE 17-3 The MoveHead composite block's inner sequence and final appearance

The motor should rotate by an amount equal to the angle that you want the head to move minus the angle reported by the rotation sensor. This ensures the motor rotates at an angle relative to the zero position instead of its last position.

Realign c-block

Use the **Realign** c-block (**FIGURE 17-4**) to bring the arms and legs back to their zero position. Running this block is faster than repeating the semiautomatic reset procedure, and the block can be used at the beginning of every sequence to realign the limbs. (Note that if the Move Hub turns off, you'll need to perform the reset procedure again.)

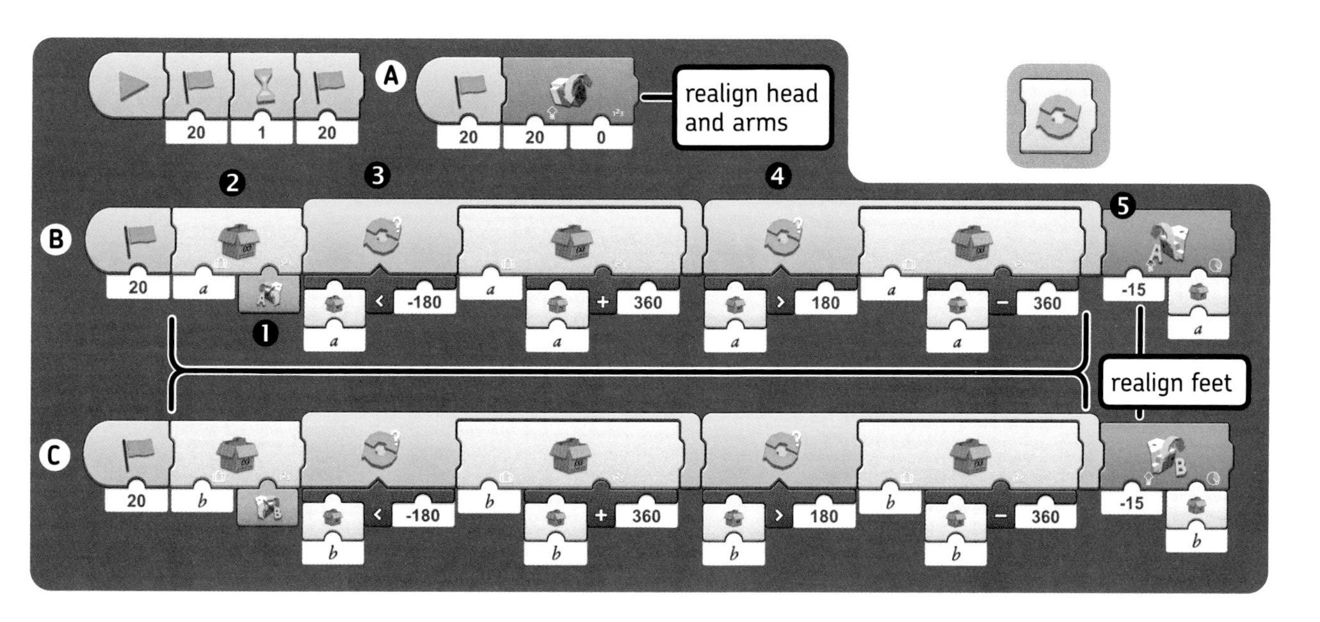

FIGURE 17-4 The Realign composite block's sequence

The **Realign** c-block starts three parallel sequences. One sequence (**A**) calls the **MoveHead** block to realign the head and arms to their zero positions (the second input of the **MoveHead** block sets the angle to 0).

The bottom two parallel sequences (**B**) and (**C**) realign the feet so that both fully touch the ground. You might think that it would be straightforward to do this, but it's actually a bit trickier than simply aligning the external motor that moves the head and the arms. The challenge is that the legs' motors can turn more than one full rotation, as they make one full rotation for each step. For example, after three steps, the motors have gone through three complete 360 degree rotations so the motor angle is 3 × 360 = 1,080 degrees, but the cranks that drive the legs are in fact at 0 degrees. To bring the motor shaft back to the zero position, the motor has to rotate backward only by a number of degrees that exceeds a full 360 degree rotation (see **FIGURE 17-5**). For example, if the angle reported by the sensor is 450 degrees, the motor should rotate backward by only 90 degrees to get back to the zero position.

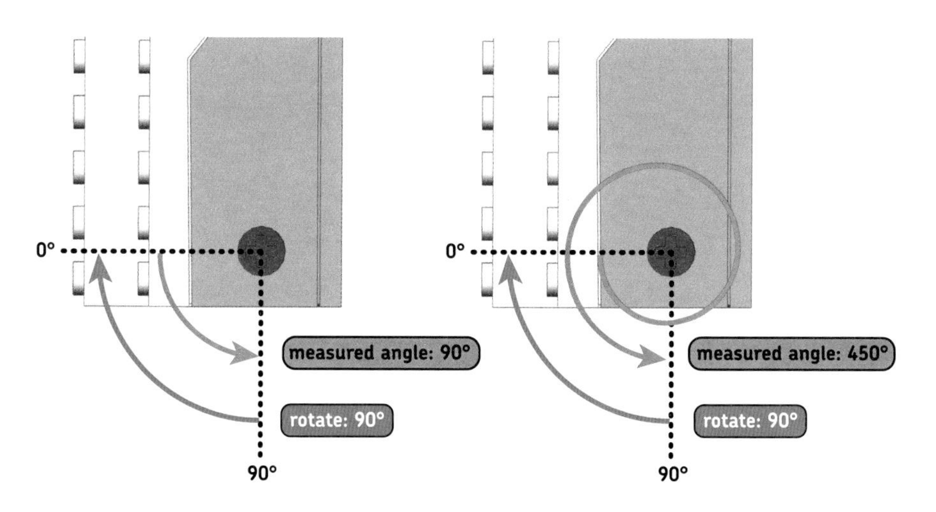

FIGURE 17-5 The Realign composite block brings all motors to the zero position. If a motor has turned more than one full rotation, it simply has to be rotated back by the value of its current angle in degrees, discounted by a whole number of rotations. In this case, the motor would need to be rotated back by 90 degrees: 450 − 360 = 90 degrees.

To calculate the number of degrees to rotate the motor, we subtract 360 degrees (the number of degrees in one rotation) from the measured angle as many times as necessary until the resulting value is between –180 and 180 degrees. If the starting angle is negative, we add 360 degrees until the value is within this same range. We use the resulting value as the Degrees input of the **Motor Run for Angle** block ❺, with the Speed input set to a negative value.

This entire procedure is coded in parallel sequences (**B**) and (**C**) in the **Realign** c-block shown in **FIGURE 17-4**. The value of the angle read by the **Motor A Angle Reporter** block ❶ is stored in a variable (using the **Write Variable** block ❷) that is then discounted by whole rotations (360 degrees) by updating the variable value either inside the first **Loop While True** block ❸, if the value is exceeding half a turn (180 degrees) and negative, or the second **Loop While True** block ❹, if the value is exceeding half a turn and positive. The top sequence (**B**) controls Motor A (the left leg) and the bottom sequence (**C**) controls Motor B (the right leg).

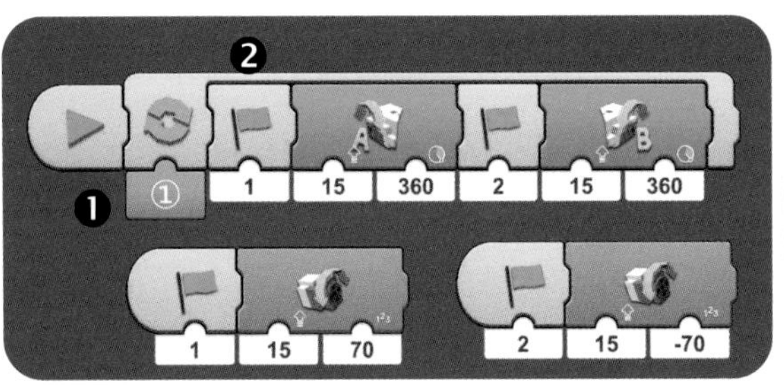

FIGURE 17-6 The Forward composite block

Forward c-block

The **Forward** c-block (**FIGURE 17-6**) makes CYBOT step forward by rotating the leg motors one whole rotation, one leg at a time. The arms move in sync with each step to simulate the way a human walks.

To control the number of steps that CYBOT will take, the **Numeric Input 1** ❶ of the **Forward** c-block lets you choose how many steps CYBOT should take by controlling the number of times the **Loop for Count** block ❷ repeats.

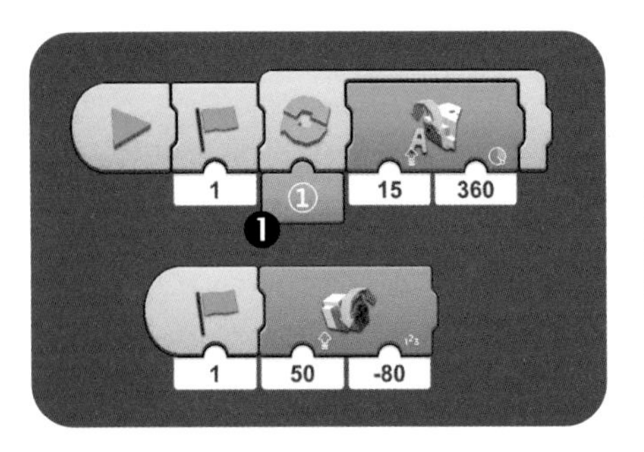

FIGURE 17-7 The TurnRight composite block

TurnRight c-block

The **TurnRight** c-block, shown in **FIGURE 17-7**, makes CYBOT turn right by stepping forward repeatedly with the left leg only. The block's input ❶ sets the number of steps to take. For each step, the robot turns 15 degrees clockwise. It takes six steps to make a right-angle turn (90 degrees).

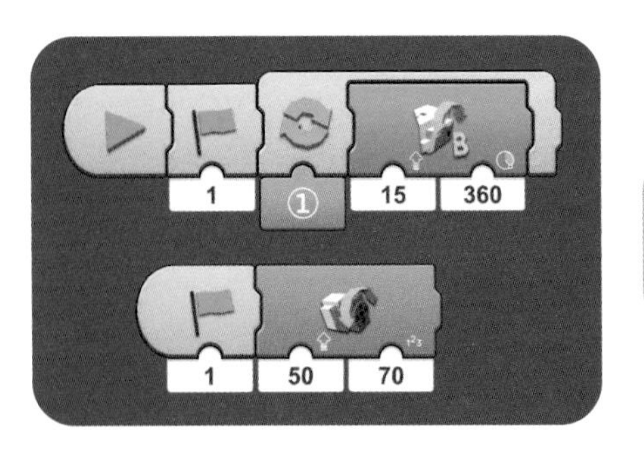

FIGURE 17-8 The TurnLeft composite block

TurnLeft c-block

The **TurnLeft** c-block, shown in **FIGURE 17-8**, is very similar to the **TurnRight** c-block. It makes CYBOT turn left by stepping forward repeatedly using the right leg only. For each step, the robot turns by about 15 degrees counterclockwise, and again, it takes six steps to make a right-angle turn.

SpinRight c-block

The **SpinRight** c-block, shown in **FIGURE 17-9**, makes CYBOT spin in place to its right by stepping forward repeatedly with the left leg and backward with the right leg. The **Numeric Input 1** block ❶ tells it how many steps to take. For each step, the robot turns by almost 30 degrees clockwise, so it takes three steps to make a right-angle turn.

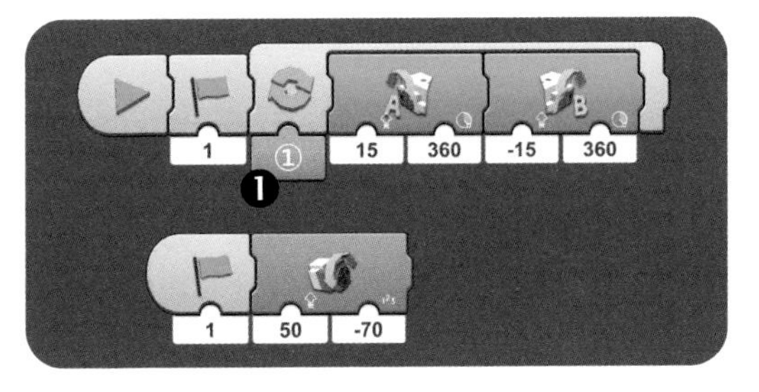

FIGURE 17-9 The SpinRight composite block's inner sequence

SpinLeft c-block

The **SpinLeft** c-block, shown in **FIGURE 17-10**, is much like the **SpinRight** c-block. It makes CYBOT spin in place to its left by stepping forward repeatedly with the right leg and backward with the left leg. For each step, the robot turns 30 degrees counterclockwise. It takes three steps to make a right-angle turn.

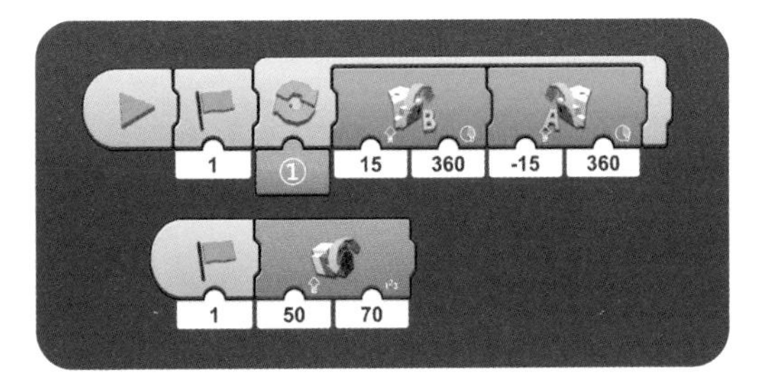

FIGURE 17-10 The SpinLeft composite block's inner sequence

Shoot c-block

The **Shoot** c-block, shown in **FIGURE 17-11**, activates the shoulder-mounted cannon trigger by rotating the head to the left. As the dart is fired, a shooting sound (Punch and Shoot Sound Effects Number 7) is played with the Distortion filter set to 50. The filter is cleared afterward in case you want to play other sounds without distortion.

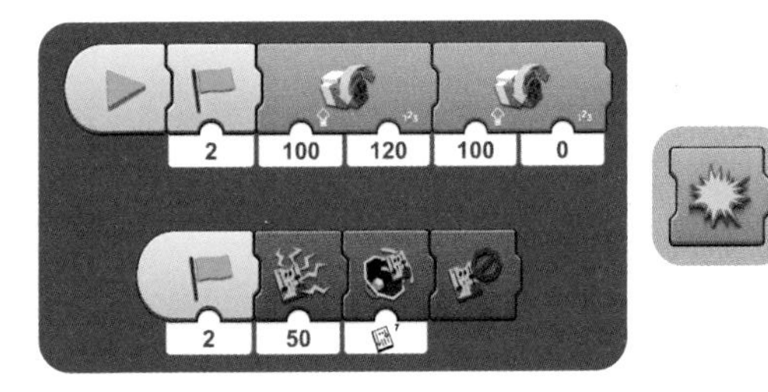

FIGURE 17-11 The Shoot composite block's inner sequence

experiment 17-1

Using the c-blocks above, create a program to make CYBOT go on patrol, walking a square path. Hint: review the descriptions of the **TurnRight** and **SpinRight** c-blocks to recall how many degrees the robot turns for each step.

experiment 17-2

What should you change in the solution to experiment 17-1 to make the robot travel back and forth on a line, as though it is a sentry in front of a building?

Explore program

In this section, we'll program CYBOT to explore its surroundings. The *Explore* program works in much the same way as the *Go to Free Area* program described in "navigating around clutter" on page 118. CYBOT walks forward until it sees an obstacle, looks around, and then decides to turn in the direction where it sees the fewest obstacles. Here's the pseudocode that describes this operation:

```
Realign all moving parts
Infinite loop begins
   Loop While (distance is greater than 8)
      Move forward by 1 step
   End While Loop
   Play alarm sound
   Turn head to the right
   Store the distance read by the sensor in variable A
   Turn head to the left
   Store the distance read by the sensor in variable B
   Rotate head back to look straight
   If (distance stored in A is greater than distance stored in B),
      then Spin right for 2 steps
   Else
      Spin left for 2 steps
   End If
Go back the start of the infinite loop
```

FIGURE 17-12 shows the completed *Explore* program. The sound played in the parallel sequence is number 19 of Audience Noises and Alarms (?). The labels on the program should help you make sense of it.

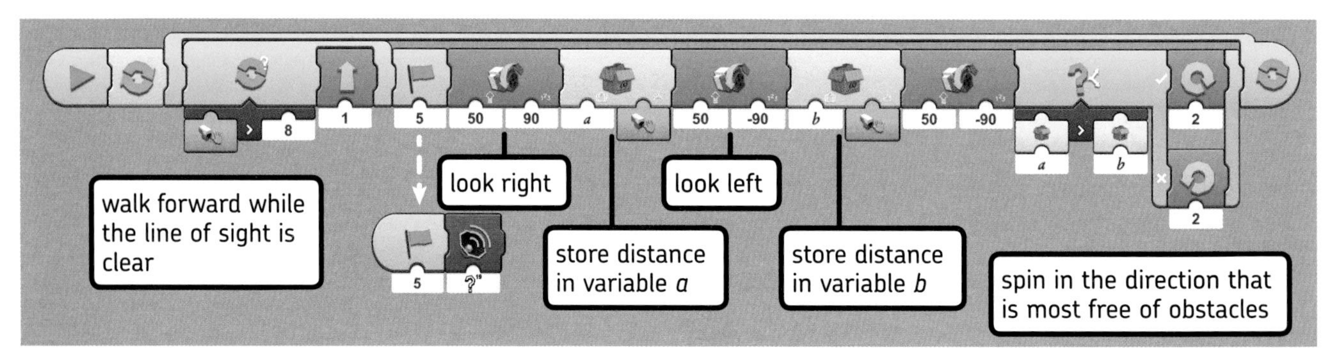

FIGURE 17-12 The *Explore* program

Remote Control program

With the *Remote Control* program shown in **FIGURE 17-13**, you can control CYBOT using the LEGO BOOST remote-control interface. Use the joystick to make the robot walk forward and turn, and press the button to shoot. After shooting, the program ends.

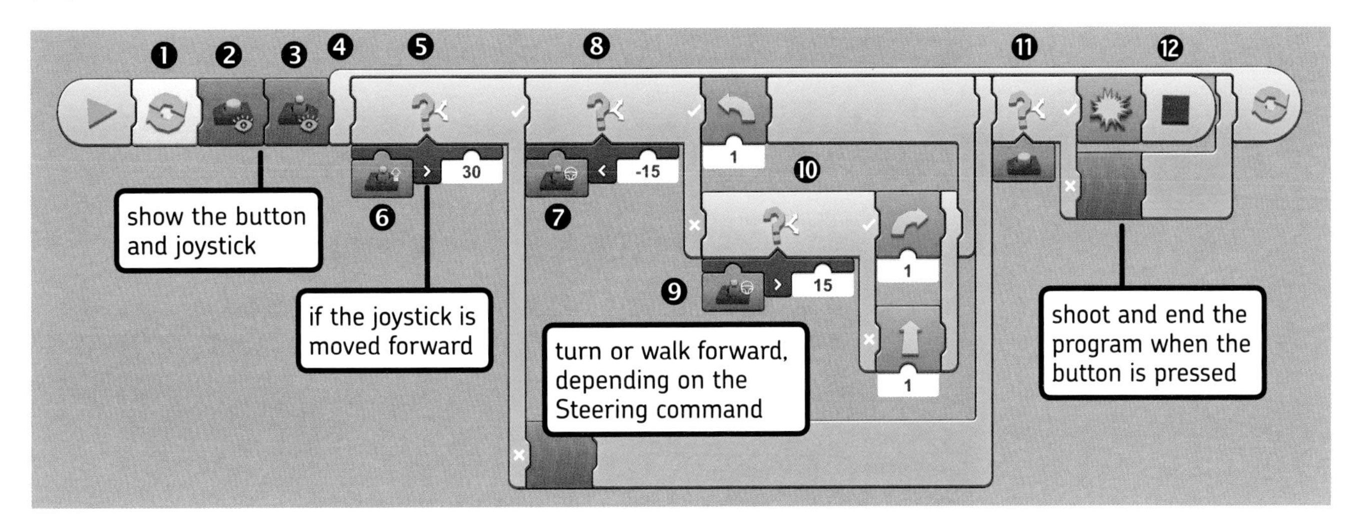

FIGURE 17-13 The *Remote Control* program

As you can see in **FIGURE 17-13**, the program begins by realigning the arms and legs with the **Realign** c-block ❶. (Remember that you have to perform the semiautomatic reset procedure if the Move Hub has just been turned on.) The remote-control interface is created by showing the button and the joystick. There are two **Switch** blocks inside the **Infinite Loop** block ❹. The first **Switch** block ❺ checks whether the value returned by the **Joystick Speed Reporter** block ❻ is greater than 30. This makes the robot walk if you push the joystick forward.

If the joystick is moved away from the center, the robot will walk according to the value reported by the **Joystick Steering Reporter** blocks ❼ and ❾. To determine in which direction you've pushed the joystick, we use two **Switch** blocks ❽ and ❿, one nested within the other. If the Steering value is less than -15 (the joystick is moved to the left), CYBOT will turn one step to the left. Otherwise, the second check is performed by the second **Switch** block ❿ that will turn CYBOT one step to the right if the Steering value is greater than 15. If both conditions are false, the joystick was pushed straight ahead or nearly so, and CYBOT will walk forward. (We use the values -15 and 15 to define the range of movement for the joystick that will make CYBOT walk straight, even if the joystick is not perfectly straight.)

The last **Switch** block ⓫ makes the robot shoot if the button is pressed. Once the robot has shot its cannon, the program is stopped by the **Stop All Sequences** block ⓬.

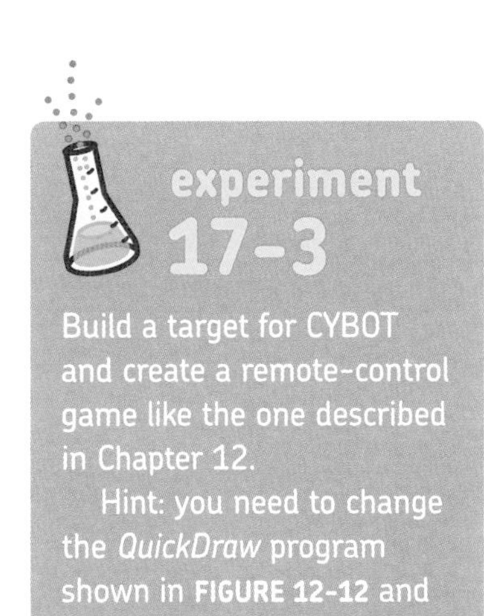

experiment 17-3

Build a target for CYBOT and create a remote-control game like the one described in Chapter 12.

Hint: you need to change the *QuickDraw* program shown in **FIGURE 12-12** and recreate the **Countdown** c-block in **FIGURE 12-9**.

voice control

Although the LEGO BOOST app can't recognize words, we can make a really cool program that makes it look as if CYBOT is responding to your specific voice commands (it really only responds to the number of words spoken). If you're a good actor, you can amaze your friends by pretending that CYBOT understands what you're telling it to do.

counting words

CYBOT distinguishes commands based on the numbers of words spoken. The trick here is to articulate the words clearly and leave silent spaces between them so the program can detect each word as a distinct sound and count the words properly.

Here's how it works. When your device microphone detects the first word, a timer is started. Each time the next word is heard, the word counter is increased, and the timer is reset. If you don't say any more words, then after some silence, the timer value exceeds a time-out value, and the program executes a command according to the number of words previously counted. The robot will take three steps, but you can stop it at any time by saying "Stop!" (Any sound will do, so you could clap your hands or yell "Ice cream!")

TABLE 17-1 summarizes the vocal commands you can give the robot. The vocal commands can be given in any language, as long as the number of words is the same. For example, to make CYBOT walk forward, you can say "Forward!" or "*Cammina!*" or "*Adelante!*" or "*Gehen!*" Try to speak slowly because, if the sounds are too short, the app might fail to count them as words—especially when running on a slow device.

TABLE 17-1 vocal commands

ACTION	EXAMPLE COMMAND	NUMBER OF WORDS
walk forward	go walk	1
turn right	turn right walk right	2
turn left	now turn left please turn left	3
shoot	now shoot it down! look—a LEGO knockoff is approaching!	more than 3

Command c-block

Before you can create a program to control CYBOT with your voice, you'll need to make the **Command** c-block shown in **FIGURE 17-14**. This c-block has two numeric inputs, the first specifies which command to execute (the value comes from the variable that holds the word count), and the second determines the number of steps the robot should take. Logic Input block 3 on the c-block specifies whether the execution of the command can be interrupted by a sound like "Stop!"

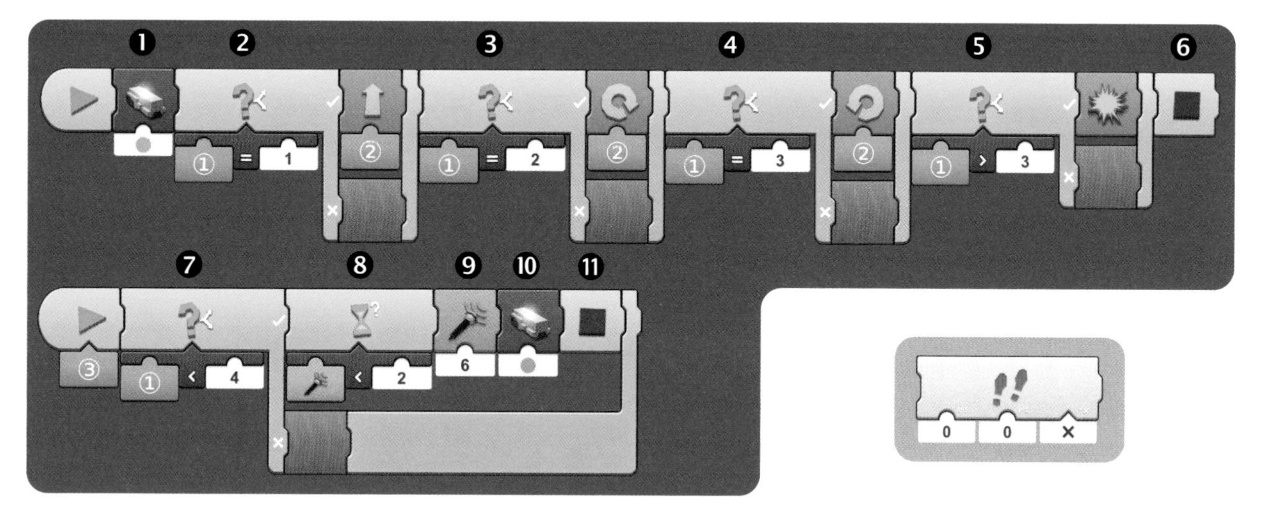

FIGURE 17-14 The Command composite block

In the main sequence of this c-block, the **Set Hub LED Color** block ❶ input is green, telling us that the command is being executed. A series of **Switch** blocks (❷, ❸, ❹, and ❺) tell CYBOT to walk according to the number of words detected, as listed in **TABLE 17-1**. For example, the **Switch** block ❷ executes the **Walk Straight** c-block only if the value of Numeric Input 1 is equal to 1.

Inside each **Switch** blocks' top sequence (executed when the condition is true), there's a c-block to make CYBOT walk. Each of these inner c-blocks' input is set by the value of the Numeric Input 2. The last **Switch** block ❺ executes the **Shoot** c-block if the value of Numeric Input block 1 is above 3. Once the robot finishes walking, the **Stop All Other Sequences** block ❻ interrupts the parallel sequence and the program.

The parallel sequence is started only if Logic Input block 3 is true. Set this input to true to be able to stop CYBOT at any time by saying "Stop!"

The **Switch** block ❼ attached to the **Start on True** block checks whether the Numeric Input block 1 (number of words) is less than 4. This condition lets you stop only the walking actions, not the shooting action (see **TABLE 17-1**). In fact, the **Shoot** c-block produces a loud sound that might be detected by the **Wait for True** block in this parallel sequence, stopping the **Shoot** c-block's execution too soon.

Inside the **Switch** block ❼, the **Wait for True** block ❽ waits for the sound level to fall (after the last word of the spoken command), and then a **Wait for Sound Level** block ❾ waits for a loud sound (you saying "Stop!"). When that happens, the **Set Hub LED Color** block ❿ sets the color of the Move Hub's light to blue and the **Stop All Other Sequences** block ⓫ interrupts the main sequence, and the robot stops.

NOTE:

*To make multiple choices, the **Switch** blocks could be nested within one another. In FIGURE 17-14, the **Switch** blocks are placed one after another because only one of the conditions involved can be true at a time.*

the code

FIGURE 17-15 shows the *Voice Control* program.

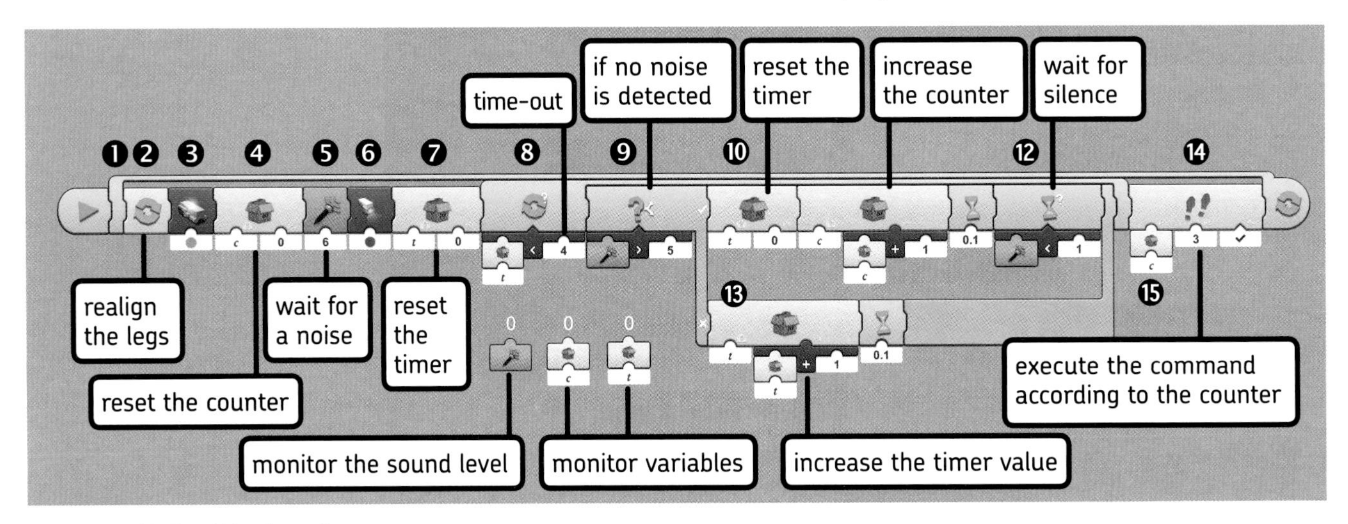

FIGURE 17-15 The *Voice Control* program

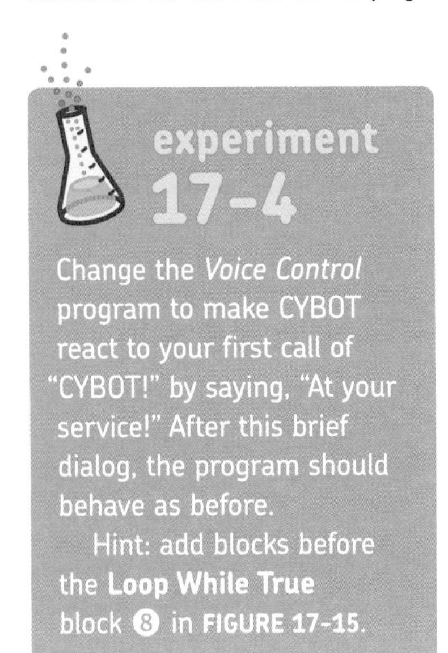

experiment 17-4

Change the *Voice Control* program to make CYBOT react to your first call of "CYBOT!" by saying, "At your service!" After this brief dialog, the program should behave as before.

Hint: add blocks before the **Loop While True** block ❽ in **FIGURE 17-15**.

As you can see, the program is run forever by an **Infinite Loop** block ❶. Working our way through the loop, we see that the legs are realigned ❷, the Move Hub light is turned blue ❸, and the variable *c*, which functions as the *word counter*, is reset to 0 ❹. A **Wait for Sound Level** block ❺ pauses the program until a sound greater than 5 is detected (presumably, the first word of the command). The Move Hub light then turns red ❻ to indicate the robot is listening, and the variable *t*, our *timer*, is reset to 0 ❼.

The operation described in the section "counting words" on page 234 is coded inside a **Loop While True** block ❽ that runs while the value of the variable *t* is less than 4. This is the *time-out*, and it should be modified according to your device's processing speed. On the tablet used to test the program while writing this book, a value of 4 made the robot wait for a silence longer than 1 second. If you are using a faster device, you might have to set this time-out value to 6 or 7.

Inside the **Loop While True** block ❽, a **Switch** block ❾ checks whether the sound level is above 5. When a sound is detected, the true case of the **Switch** block is executed: the timer variable *t* is reset to 0 ❿, the word counter *c* is increased ⓫, and the program waits for the sound level to fall again between words ⓬. (Tweak these sound levels according to the sensitivity of your device's microphone.)

If the sound level is 5 or below, the timer variable *t* is increased ⓭ every 0.1 seconds in the false case of the **Switch** block ❾. The actual length of this pause depends on the speed of the device running the LEGO BOOST app.

Once the timer has finished, the **Command** c-block ⓮ (described above) makes the robot move according to the number of words detected, as retrieved from the variable *c* ⓯.

experiment 17-5

Try changing the value of the Numeric Input block 2 of the **Command** c-block to make CYBOT spin by half a turn when asked to turn.

experiment 17-6

Make a program to control CYBOT by placing colored tiles in front of its sensor. Hint: See Chapter 7 to review how to do this.

what you've learned

In this chapter, you taught CYBOT to walk, turn, look around, and shoot. You also taught CYBOT to patrol, explore, and even respond to vocal commands. You used c-blocks extensively in this chapter, building a rich library of c-blocks that will allow you to make your own custom programs for CYBOT.

experiment answer key

Here are the answers for the experiments throughout the book. If a chapter is not listed, it means that there were no experiments in it. If an experiment is not listed, it means there is no single right answer, and it was meant for you to explore the possibilities on your own!

chapter 2

experiment 2-1

MARIO drives backward.

chapter 3

experiment 3-1

The Steering input value must be negative.

experiment 3-2

Time = 2

experiment 3-3

Speed = 20, Steering = –100, Time = 0.5

chapter 5

experiment 5-1

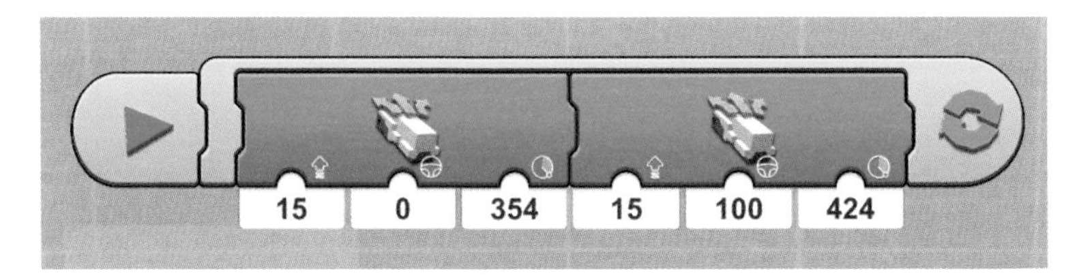

experiment 5-2

In general, when the robot has to travel on a closed path, its heading at the end will be the same as when it started. This means that the robot will turn 360 degrees in total. Since a triangle has three sides, to travel a triangular path, the robot should turn by 360 / 3 = 120 degrees. The Degrees parameter must be set to 120 × 120 / 51 = 282 degrees. The **Loop** block should repeat the sequence three times.

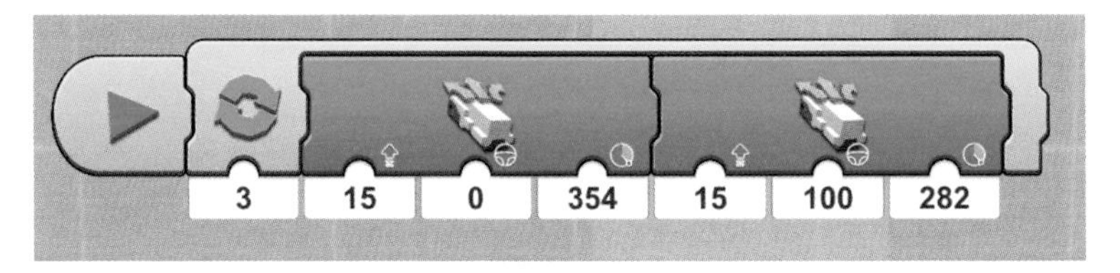

experiment 5-3

As before, when the robot has to travel on a closed path, it will turn 360 degrees in total. Since a hexagon has six sides, to travel a hexagonal (six-sided) path, the robot should turn by 360 / 6 = 60 degrees. That means that the Degrees input must be set to 120 × 60 / 51 = 141 degrees. The **Loop for Count** block should repeat the sequence six times.

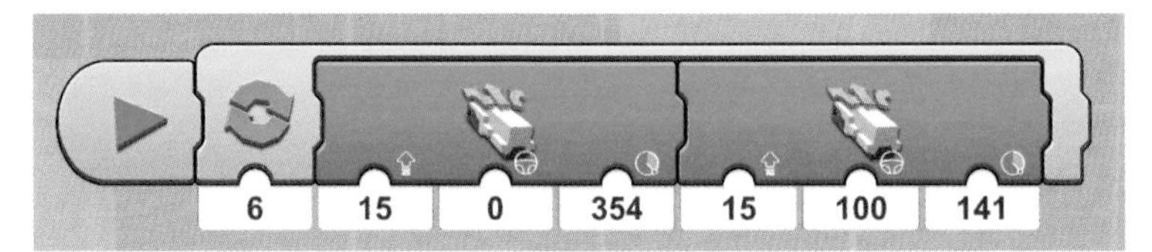

chapter 6

experiment 6-2

A possible solution is the following one.

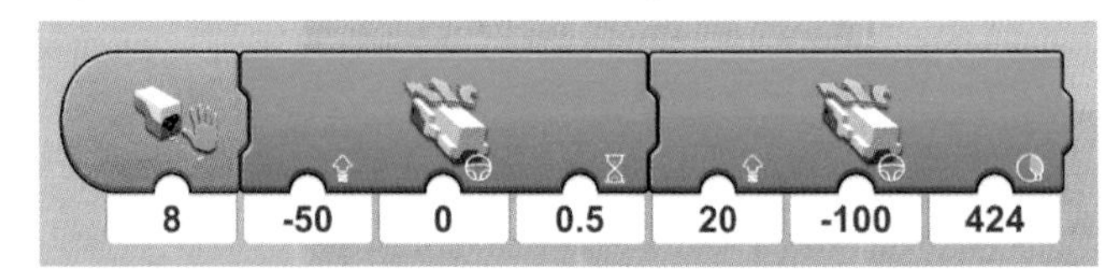

chapter 7

experiment 7-2

Yellow, yellow

experiment 7-3

Fire: Yellow, yellow, yellow, green, yellow.
Blue area: Yellow, yellow, yellow, yellow, yellow.

chapter 8

experiment 8-2

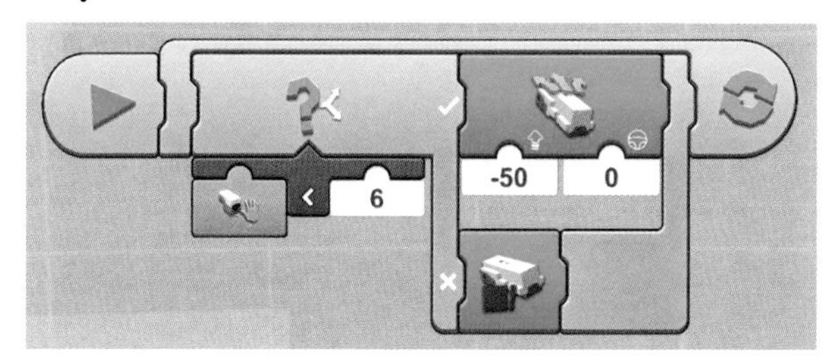

experiment 8-3

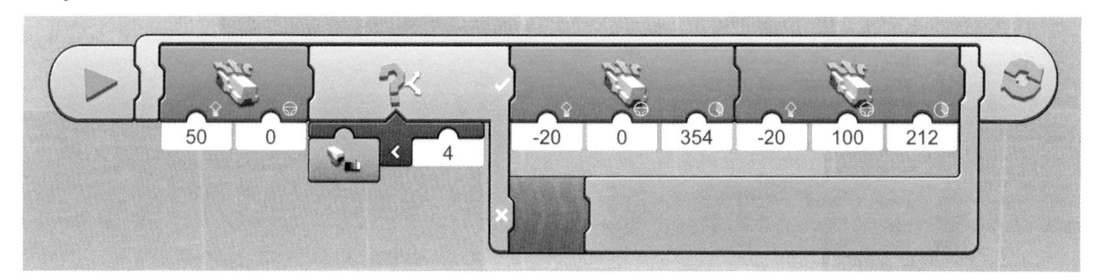

experiment 8-4

This program:

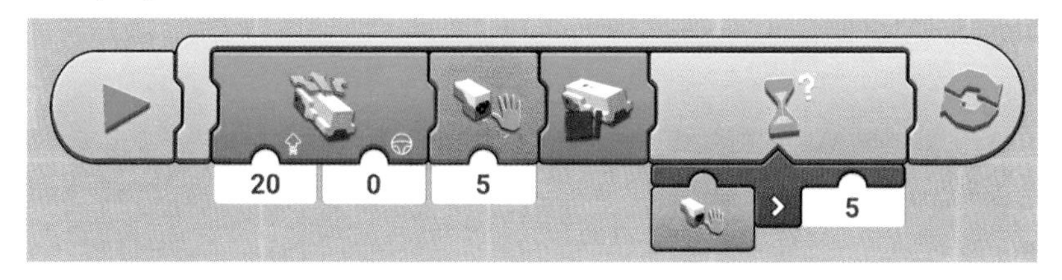

works the same as this one:

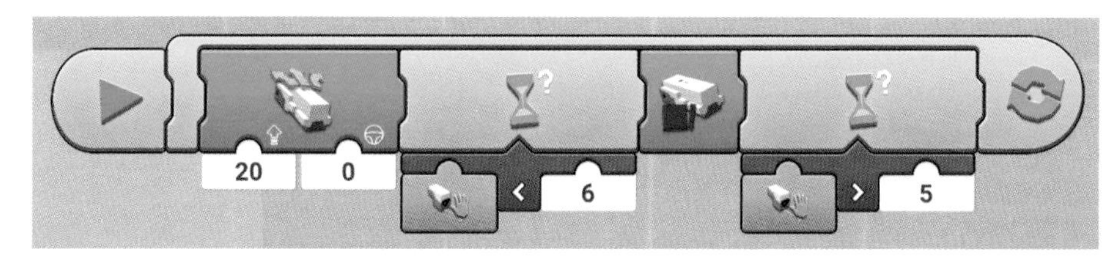

experiment 8-5

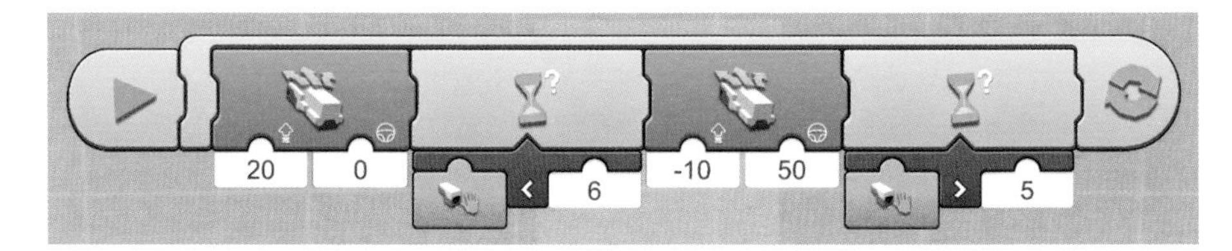

experiment 8-6

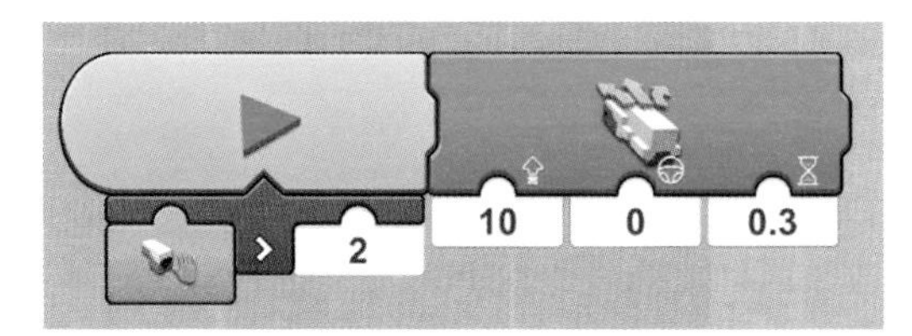

experiment 8-7

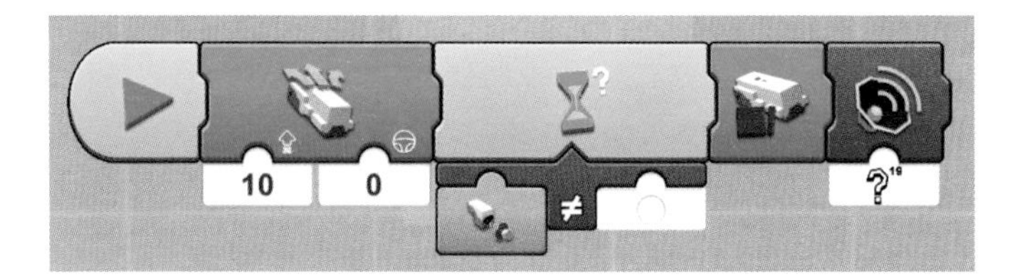

experiment 8-8

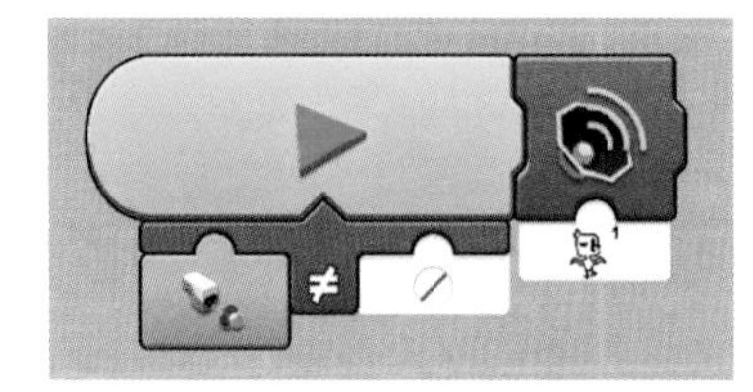

experiment 8-9

experiment 8-10

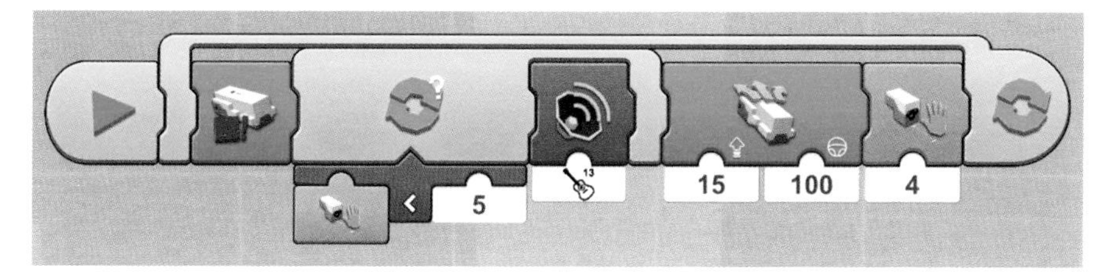

chapter 9

experiment 9-2

To make the robot follow the wall on its left, alter the proportional controller sequence, and change the number K to –10 in the second input of the **Multiply Operator** block. In the escape sequence, change the sign of the Steering input of each **Drivebase Move Steering for Angle** block.

experiment 9-4

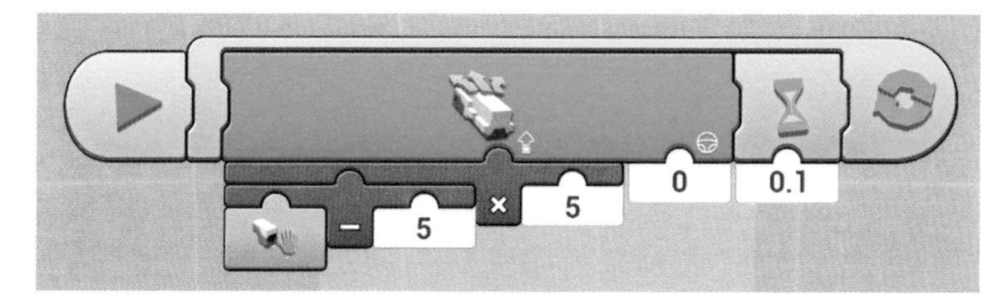

Note that the robot won't stop completely when it's at the correct distance but it will move back and forth a bit. This is due to the delay in communication (see "problems with communication delay" on page 71 in Chapter 8). Removing the 0.1-second pause won't help.

chapter 10

experiment 10-1

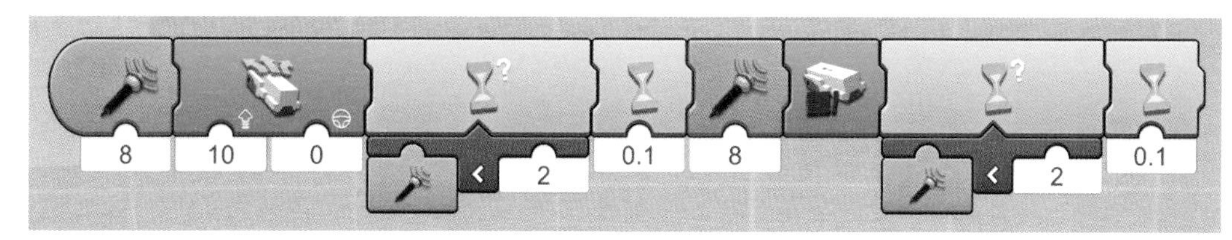

experiment 10-2

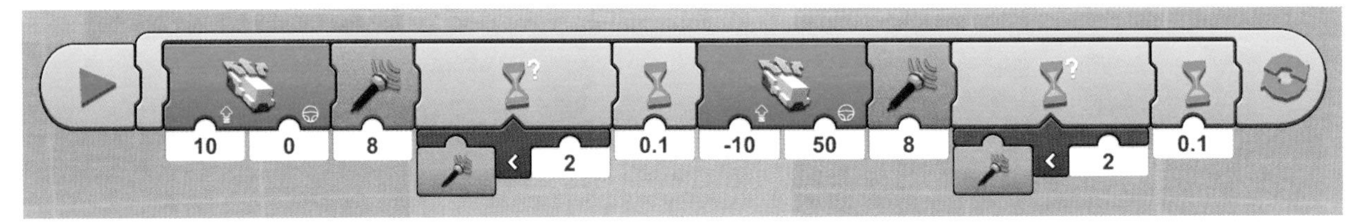

To be sure to detect each sound separately, each **Wait for Sound Level** block must be followed by a **Wait for True** block that waits until the sound level goes below a low number (in this example program, the number is 2).

experiment 10-3

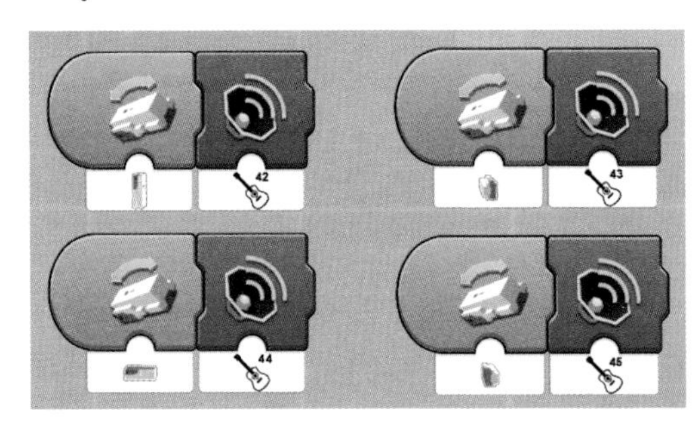

experiment 10-4

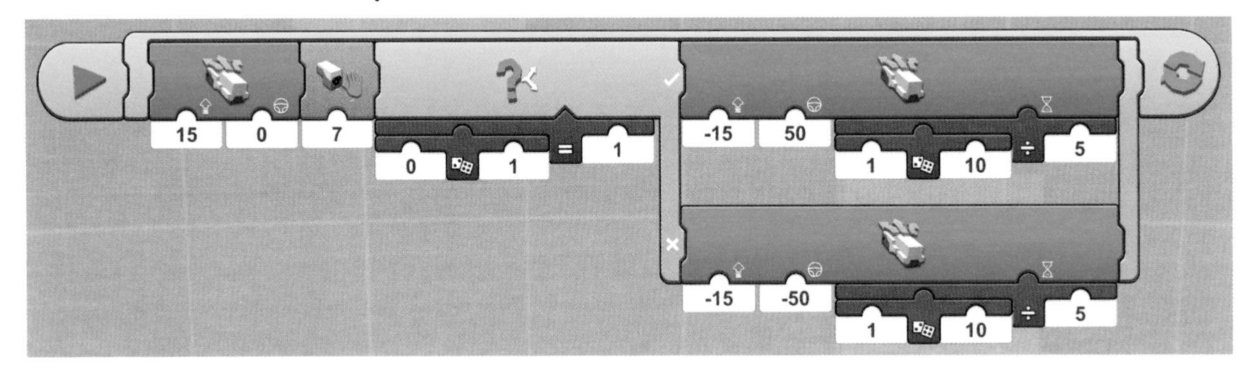

experiment 10-5

Change the two inputs of the Random block attached to the Sound block.

chapter 11

experiment 11-1

You should input the exact values you want the head to rotate to, without having to consider the current head position: 45, −90, 0.

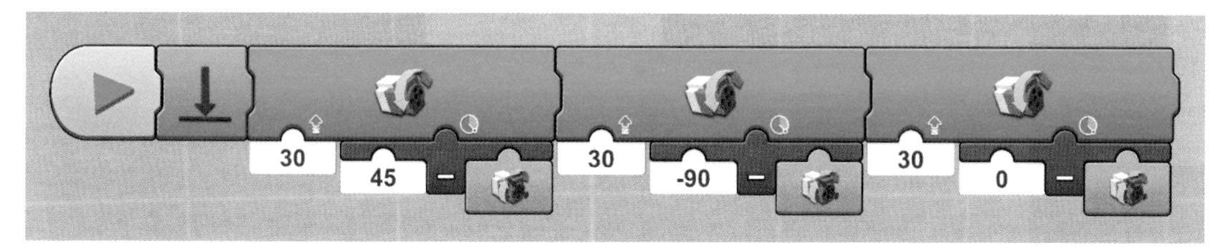

experiment 11-2

60, −60, 0

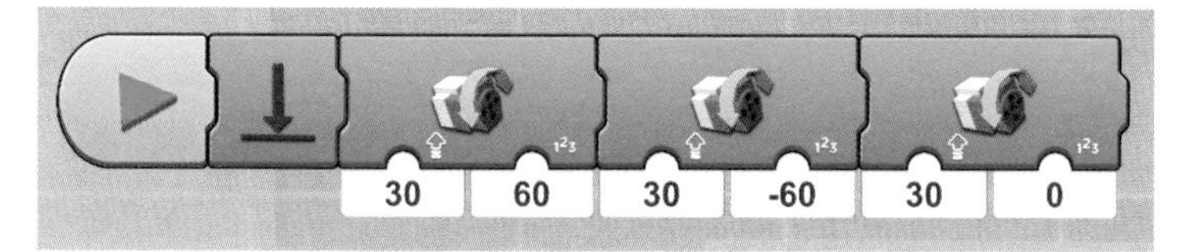

experiment 11-3

chapter 12

experiment 12-1

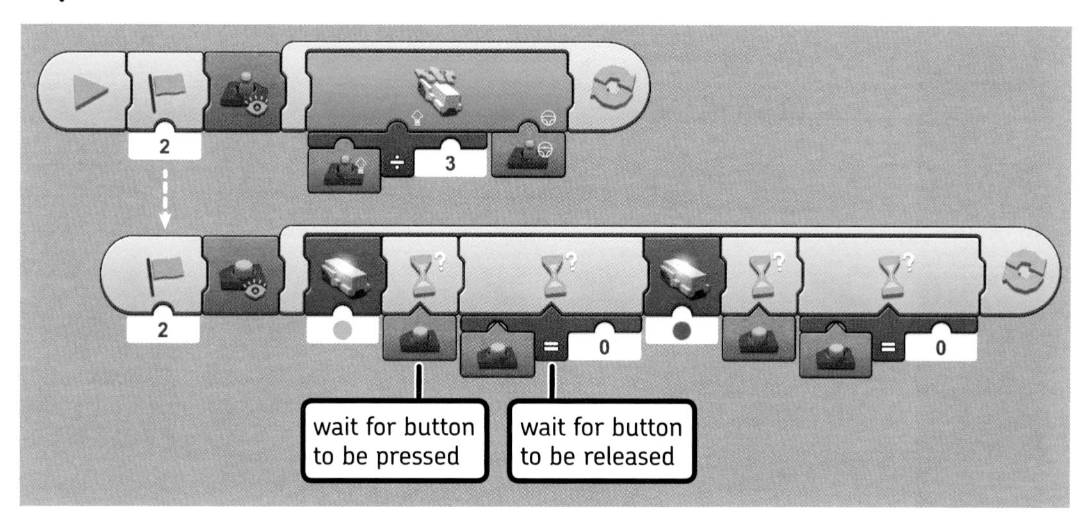

experiment 12-2

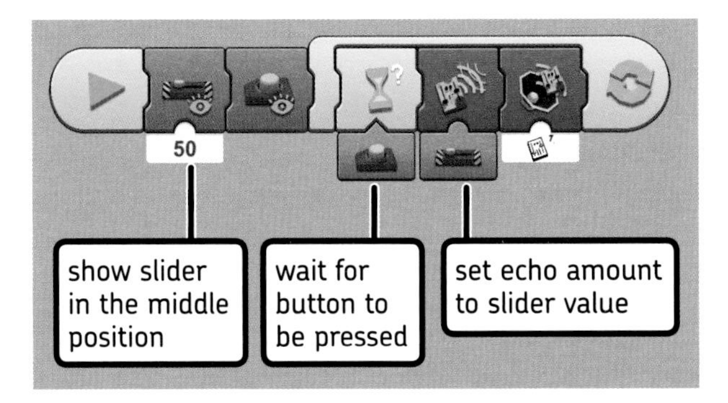

experiment 12-3

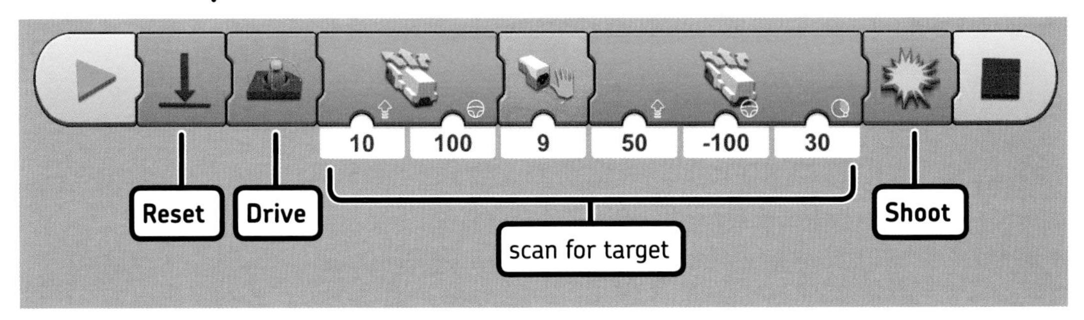

experiment 12-4

This is the program for MARIO's firefighting game. Below the program, you can see the new **DriveUntilColor** c-block.

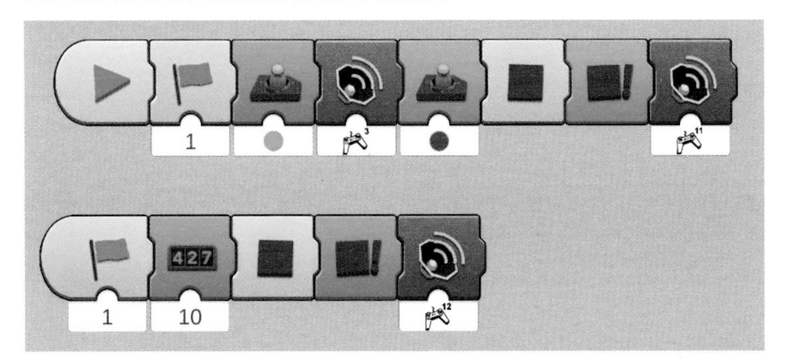

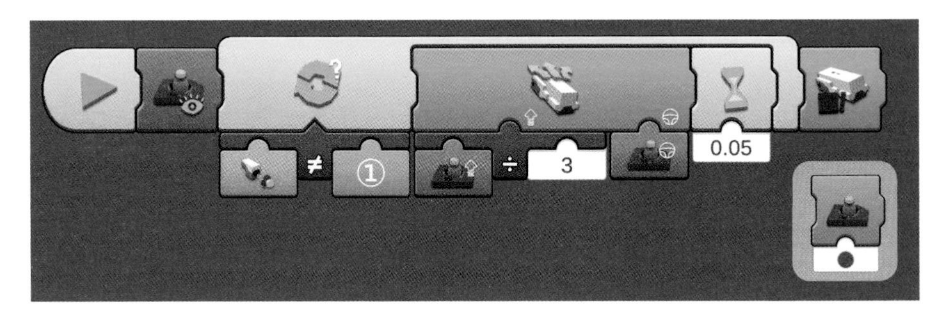

chapter 15

experiment 15-1

Add a **Sound** block in the **Switch** block before the **Set Hub LED Color** block, with the sound effect set to Animal Sound 1 ( ).

experiment 15-2

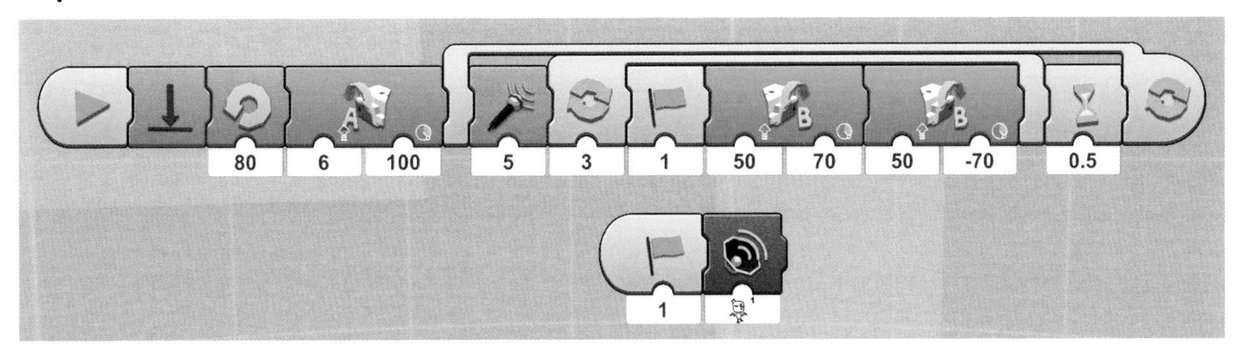

experiment 15-3

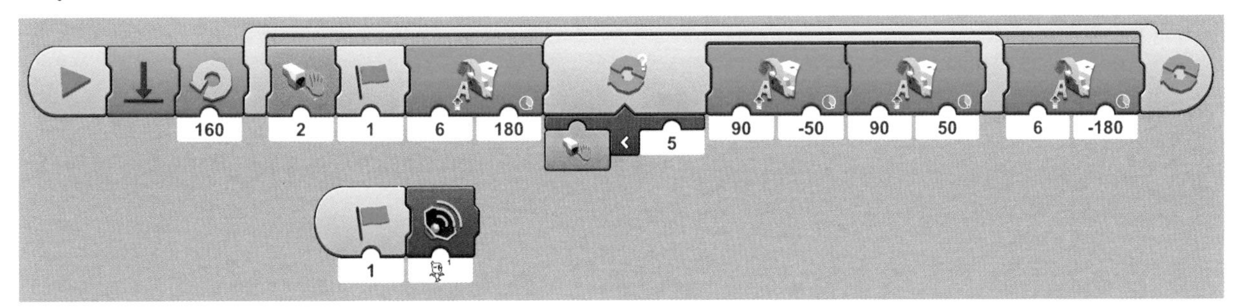

chapter 17

experiment 17-1

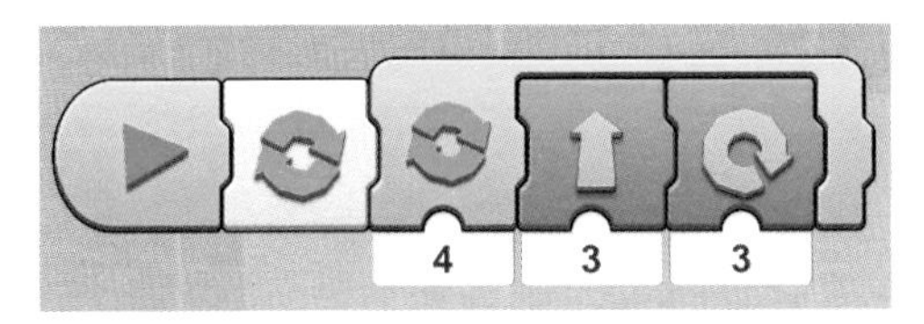

experiment 17-2

In the solution above, replace the **Loop for Count** with an **Infinite Loop** block and change the **SpinRight** c-block input to 6.

experiment 17-5

Change the value of Input 2 from 3 to 6.

index

D

E

F

G

H

I

J

L

M

N

O

P

U

V

W

Y

Z